RASTAFARI

Rastafari

The Evolution of a People and Their Identity

Charles Price

NEW YORK UNIVERSITY PRESS
New York

NEW YORK UNIVERSITY PRESS
New York
www.nyupress.org

Please contact the Library of Congress for Cataloging-in-Publication data.

ISBN: 9781479807154 (hardback)
ISBN: 9781479888122 (paperback)
ISBN: 9781479871599 (library eBook)
ISBN: 9781479825974 (consumer eBook)

New York University Press books are printed on acid-free paper, and their binding materials are chosen for strength and durability. We strive to use environmentally responsible suppliers and materials to the greatest extent possible in publishing our books.

Manufactured in the United States of America

10 9 8 7 6 5 4 3 2 1

Also available as an ebook

CONTENTS

ABBREVIATIONS

AWIWL Afro-West Indian Welfare League

ANPM African Nationalist Pioneer Movement

ARC African Reform Church

BMPP Black Man's Political Party

BSUE Brotherhood Solidarity of United Ethiopians

CID Criminal Investigation Division

CSO Colonial Secretary Office

EABIC Ethiopian Africa Black International Congress

ESS Ethiopian Salvation Society

EWF Ethiopian World Federation

FAC First Africa Corp

JLP Jamaican Labor Party

KJV King James Version (of the Bible); also known as the "Authorized Version"

KSACL Kingston–St. Andrew Civic League

LSIC Local Standing Intelligence Committee

MRA Moral Re-Armament Movement

MtA Mission to Africa

PFM People's Freedom Movement

PNP People's Nationalist Party

PPP People's Political Party

RF Rastafari Federation

RMA Rastafari Movement Association

RMC Rastafari Millennium Council

UCWI University College of the West Indies

UFO unidentified flying object

UNIA Universal Negro Improvement Association

YBF Youth Black Faith

Introduction

For it [is] a new name, precious name, new name, Ras Tafari. . . .
For when I call him Rastafari watch how weak heart tremble,

For it is a new name Jah got, and it [is] terrible among men;
heathen don't like Jah name.
—Rastafari chant (hymn)

Ras Tafari Makonnen, the Ethiopian nobleman and claimant on the biblical King Solomon's lineage, became King of Ethiopia in 1928. King Ras Tafari became the crowned Emperor of Ethiopia in November 1930, assuming the royal title Emperor Haile Selassie I (might of the Holy Trinity). Emperor Selassie would continue to be known as Ras Tafari by the people—Rastafari—who bear his name and hold him to be the Messiah referenced in the King James Bible's book of Revelations. By emphasizing the Ethiopian noble title of Ras, meaning "head," the Rastafari recognize Ras Tafari and Emperor Selassie, the same personage, as the divine head of humankind.

"New Name," like many a favored hymn, celebrates how the Rastafari imagined themselves in the face of their adversaries. Declaiming the Messiah, this chant celebrated his new name. It also disclosed the negative reactions to the Rastafari's revelation. Again and again, the Rastafari denounced the rejection and persecution they suffered because they claimed that King Ras Tafari, Emperor of Ethiopia, was the Anointed One, successor to Jesus Christ. The new Messiah's name roused fear in the hearts of nonbelievers, and this fear manifested in wrath unleashed on the Rastafari. Nonbelievers did not want to hear about the new Messiah, a Black and African one at that. But what was so compelling about King Ras Tafari that his identity became their identity? And why did other Jamaicans so vehemently reject the Rastafari, to the point that they sought to stamp out both them *and* their beliefs?

"'Ras Tafari' Disciple Found Guilty of Sedition," shrieked the head-line in the March 16, 1934, edition of Jamaica's leading newspaper, the *Daily Gleaner*. Seven years later, another prominent newspaper, the *Jamaica Times*, trumpeted, "Victims Tell of Ras Tafarians' Reign of Terror in St. Catherine."[1] Thirteen years after that, a *Daily Gleaner* story banner reported, "Police Raid [the commune] Pinnacle Again."[2] From 1933 onward, the number of stories published in the *Daily Gleaner* and other newspapers about the Rastafari grew steadily. This Jamaican obsession with the Rastafari dragged into the open fundamental beliefs and identity concerns that *all* segments of Jamaican society had about race, inequality, miseducation, class privilege, and colonial governance. In developing an identity and community, the Rastafari bruised the body politic and opened wounds, exposing sores of social conflict. Their pursuit of repatriation, self-knowledge, and a cooperative spirit, though fundamentally beneficent, registered with most Jamaicans as malevolent. The Rastafari were villains.

The March 16 story was the third of four stories that reported on the five-day trial of founding Rastafari evangelists Leonard Howell and Robert Hinds. Howell and Hinds appeared before the court for sedition. Charged with preaching allegiance to King Ras Tafari, Howell, Hinds, and a handful of other eccentric men and women committed themselves to birthing a community that would inaugurate a new millennium. Their trial received national news coverage through the *Daily Gleaner* as well as another national paper, the *Jamaica Times*. During their March 1934 courtroom contest, the two fledgling Rastafari evangelists explained the cardinal tenets of their new faith while critiquing and offering an alternative to Jamaica's established institutions. The *Daily Gleaner* trial reports ridiculed the nascent Rastafari and, unwittingly, introduced them and their beliefs to the nation. The newspaper gave them attention that they perhaps could never have attained on their own. The trial was intended to defang the Rastafari, and given any new group's survival chances, the Rastafari had low odds of enduring. Yet eventually they flourished, though continually embattled because of their detractors. The efforts of non-Rastafari—elites in particular—to ascribe villainous and pariah qualities to the Rastafari shaped their experience and developing communal identity, particularly as their gatherings were sometimes viciously disrupted by vigilante bands or constables. Indeed,

Howell and his followers built the rural commune Pinnacle both to evade persecutors and to create a new society removed from the profane world.

Race, religion, and a history steeped in almost unceasing contention fashioned the Rastafari's collective identity. The Rastafari worshiped an African Emperor, inspiring their fellow Jamaicans to treat them and their beliefs as absurdities. Yet despite their negative reputation, they grew from a few persecuted adherents into a self-perpetuating people who by the 1980s numbered in the tens of thousands. They grew from a handful of people into a diverse community, developing an identity that altered Jamaican's understandings of race, nationality, and Christianity.

The Rastafari created a new vision of the Christian God—an African Emperor who is Christ returned or some variation thereof—and they set out to preach and live this new vision. Their effort met resistance at nearly every turn. Yet they found interested people willing to sacrifice their well-being to affirm and live the new vision. The outcome? The ethnogenesis—origin and development—of a new people, faith, and identity, part of an unfolding saga. Three factors knit together this decades-long story of Rastafari ethnogenesis and collective identity formation: (1) Rastafari persistence in the face of relentless punishment, (2) varied vectors disseminating information—positive and negative—about them, and (3) the interventions of outsiders (nonmembers).

Stirring the Historical Imagination: The Making of a People and Collective Identity

This book chronicles the development of the first through fourth generations of Rastafari, the period between the 1930s and early 2000s, focusing on their collective identity formation in Jamaica, along with limited attention to their global presence. The Rastafari emerged out of a specific cultural and political context, and the forces that were marshaled against them and the forces that increased their popularity must be examined in order to better understand their development. As members jointly resisted those hostile forces and developed cultural practices that resonated with Jamaicans, they developed their collective identity in particular ways. The relentless effort to delegitimize Rastafari beliefs constituted a dialectical identity dialogue that nourished Rastafari ethnogenesis: the Rastafari created narratives to counter the detractors while the detractors continue to disparage.

It is worth making explicit how British colonialism itself facilitated the international influences and the conflict that fed into Rastafari ethnogenesis. At varying times, Britain claimed colonies or territories in South and Central America, the Caribbean, Africa, and Asia. Elites and nonelites moved between the colonies, sometimes with consequential effects. Happenings in Central America or Africa could induce repercussions in Jamaica. Lessons that the British learned about Ethiopianism and native revolts in Central Africa, for example, informed colonial thinking in Jamaica. Many of the colonized resented the British colonizers. Therefore, the British were keen to demolish uprisings or other native challenges to their authority. Two proven British strategies for managing the colonies were to pit native elites against other natives and to use naked oppression, suppression, and repression. The move toward decolonization raised new issues for Jamaica and the Rastafari, in particular the impact manifest in anticolonial and independence movements at home and abroad and the spread of communist, Marxist, socialist, and Black consciousness ideas into the colony.

Our narrative journey begins in the 1890s, when Jamaica's roiling waters gave birth to disparate groups and movements, though few that endured long enough to spawn a second generation. The Rastafari, however, have persisted for several generations, through to the present. While scholarly depictions of their origins and development have tended to fix on a single dimension—Revival religion, achieving accommodation with mainstream Jamaica, social movement resistance, or cultural revitalization—this book shows how Rastafari collective identity developed over decades through contention and exchanges between Jamaican Rastafari and non-Rastafari. It illuminates how collective identifications are molded through the activities and experiences of members, through dialogue with nonmembers, through self and other recognition, and through contentious encounters.

In an earlier publication, *Becoming Rasta*, I focused on why and how individuals became Rastafari. The book focused on the early converts to the Rastafari tradition, asking why Jamaicans became Rastafari despite rampant discrimination and situating their identity transformation within a social and historical framework.[3] The current volume develops in historical detail the nonlinear processes, interactions, and events that explain the Rastafari's evolution into a durable identity and collectivity, a people who conceive of themselves as a living and coherent entity. *Becoming Rasta* explained how individuals identified themselves as Rastafari, while this book shifts from the individual to the collective level to describe and explain how Rastafari identity evolved.

This book conjures the "historical imagination" by integrating the "small acts" of history with the bigger ideas they signify.[4] For instance, it is in the details of Howell's and Hinds's March 1934 trial that the clashing and competing views of history, politics, and scripture assumed meaning. In the courtroom exchanges between Howell and Hinds, who deemed King Ras Tafari divine, and the chief justice, who saw him as the leader of an insignificant African polity, we learn about the symbolic import of race and the power of international hierarchies.

As we will see, Rastafari ethnogenesis occurs within a context in which they are cast as villains. The historical treatment will show why this is the case (e.g., promotion of a new and Black God, threat to the established order, Black consciousness). This theme is persistent until the later years of Rastafari ethnogenesis, and the book reflects this. During the later years, new challenges arise.

My voice shifts over the course of the book as I move from distant to recent aspects of Rastafari ethnogenesis. The later chapters raise normative issues specific to Jamaica's postcolonial period and to neoliberal capitalism, such as cultural appropriation. As the Rastafari star rose steadily (if unpredictably) from the 1950s into the 1980s, it acquired recognition and value that outsiders spun to their advantage. Thus, we can ask, for example, how has growth and popularity shaped Rastafari ethnogenesis?

Explaining the Growth and Development of a People and Their Identity

Ethnogenesis and collective identity frame this book's central analytic concerns. Simply put, ethnogenesis is the study of the evolution of a people over time; collective identity formation addresses how such a people acquire and maintain distinctiveness within a field populated with other collectivities. An essential feature of ethnogenesis is collective identity formation itself. Becoming and being require identification, and groups create collective identification through activities and exchanges involving both members and nonmembers. An ethnogenesis and collective identity approach develops a new angle for interpreting the Rastafari and, by extension, other people.

An ethnogenesis approach compels us to recognize that groups like the Rastafari do not endure solely because their members' conviction is virtuous, their ideas are appealing, or recruiting new members comes easy. Rather, it highlights the unpredictable interactions among events; cultural resources; identity building; technologies like print, visual, and audio media; and direct and indirect intervention by nonmembers that mesh into a durable collectivity. Identifying the links between the distant and recent past, assessing the cultural resources transmitted across generations and populations, and describing the molding of institutions, interventions, and happenstance reveal the traction of Rastafari ethnogenesis.

Vectors

Rastafari ethnogenesis developed under conditions of oppression, suppression, and repression—not uncommon to the colonized people of the world—but with less direct recruitment than one might expect of a group whose numbers continue to grow and whose ethos continues to spread.

During the 1930s, Leonard Howell, Robert Hinds, Joseph Hibbert, and Altamont Reid (and others unknown) would stand on a ramshackle platform, lecturing about the new Black Messiah and about the struggles of Black Jamaicans. They were street-preaching vectors. Some listeners were smitten by the information, embracing and internalizing it, evolving into a living embodiment of the knowledge, becoming Rastafari. I have met many of them. The speakers transmitted content and power that urged their listeners to reconsider their beliefs and transform their self-concept. The first generation of Rastafari are no longer among the living. Rasta Ivey and Brother Dee, both born during the early 1900s, come to mind.[5] When the first generation of Rastafari, like Rasta Ivey and Brother Dee, first heard the Rastafari street preachers, they embraced the idea of Emperor Selassie as the returned Messiah. Many of the first- and second-generation Rastafari called the Emperor

"King Ras Tafari," "King Rasta," or "The King." (These terms refer to the same person, the Black Messiah.) Rasta Ivey was intrigued by the notion of a Black Messiah and sought to learn as much as she could from the several people preaching about King Ras Tafari.[6] Brother Dee drew on his admiration for the race man, activist, and Black philosopher and entrepreneur Marcus Garvey to interpret the notion of a Black Messiah. In his view, Garvey presaged the coming of the Messiah as well as the deliverance of Black people. And Rasta Ivey and Brother Dee, like the street preachers they so admired, in turn professed Rastafari to all who would listen and to many who preferred not. They suffered the consequences for doing so.

The term "vector," used in the context of ethnogenesis, is different from its usage in biology, math, or physics. For example, my application is not focused on measurement of magnitude or transmission of a pathogen—though I draw on the metaphors associated with those uses. I use "vector" here to emphasize movement or transmission of information or cultural resources for ethnogenesis, from one person to another, from one place to another, through a medium conditioned by its surrounding environment.

One way that a community of believers grows is through the dissemination of its ideology and identity through vectors. Believers do not have to do all the spreading themselves; dissemination occurs through members beyond the community. Vectors important to Rastafari ethnogenesis disseminated Rastafari beliefs, practices, and experiences to people who might not otherwise know about them or not recognize becoming Rastafari as a possibility.

Rastafari vectors, cultural in nature, included street preachers, magazines and newspapers, displacement and relocation, Rastafari chants (especially with drumming), scholarship, reggae music, art, domestic or international travel, advertisements, and today the internet. Vectors are malleable and conventional cultural media, not intrinsic or deterministic properties of persons or things.

The range of a vector varies according to the medium itself. For example, a story published in a national newspaper or a popular recording has greater reach than the Rastafari soapbox orator or the itinerant Rastafari proselytizer does. Vectors shift as times change. While street orators and proselytizers persisted, new media such as records and international travel created opportunities to reach new audiences. A range of vectors operating at multiple scales carried, amplified, or distorted Rastafari ideology.

Design, Method, Data

This book offers a multivariate historical anthropology that utilizes interviews with elder Rastafari, field notes, archival data (news stories, government memos, letters, etc.), primary and secondary publications, and cultural products such as hymns, musical recordings, tracts, and websites. Information drawn from newspapers provides a preponderance of the data. Nevertheless, I do not want to minimize the role of other data. I conducted field research over several years—1996, 1998, 2000–2002, 2007—which provided many formal and informal interviews and many opportunities for participant observation. It is an invaluable experience to take part in and observe what one studies.

News Media and Archival Documents

There is much to learn about the Rastafari (and Jamaica) through an analysis of archived documents, especially newspapers. The sociologist Anita Waters's *Race, Class, and Political Symbols* is an underappreciated account of how public opinion shaped Rastafari identity and how Rastafari used the *Daily Gleaner* to promote their perspectives about who they are.[7] The sociologist Frank Jan van Dijk's *Jahmaica* draws on news stories and colonial records to provide a detailed (though uncritical) history of the Rastafari between 1930 and 1990.[8] The journalist Hélène Lee's *First Rasta* relies on news stories and colonial documents to narrate a biographical sketch of Leonard Howell.[9] The historian Diana Paton used news stories to construct her account of Obeah in Jamaica, as well as accounts of Jamaicans practicing medicine without a license.[10] *Prophets of Rebellion*, the historian Michael Adas's comparative study of prophet-inspired upheavals against European colonialism, draws heavily on secondary sources and government documents yet is aware of the bias attendant to these sources.[11] This book builds on those approaches.

Except for a wealth of content published in the *Daily Gleaner* and later in *The Star*, pre-1970s information on the Rastafari is scarce. Jamaican newspapers, an underutilized resource, serve a vital role in my analysis. The serial coverage of the Rastafari in the *Daily Gleaner* and *The Star*, for example, made them an active part of Rastafari collective identity formation. "Everybody read in the 'Gleaner' of the treatment of black people in Cuba," the Rastafari Altamonte Reid lamented in a public speech in 1938.[12] Reid used the *Daily Gleaner* to learn about the condition of Black people within and beyond Jamaica and to disseminate his messages. Colonial authorities themselves used the *Daily Gleaner* to inform their pronouncements about the Rastafari: "I read in this morning's Gleaner that they [Rastafari] attempted to establish a village on some waste ground belonging to the K.S.A.C. [Kingston–St. Andrew Civic League] but have been ejected. I do not think that there is any likelihood of the movement gaining many adherents in Kingston."[13] Ras Brenton, a second-generation Rastafari, told me how he and other Rastafari would "sit [together] and reason 'pon the news," paying attention to how the stories "scandalize[d] we."

The anthropologist Peter Hervik used news stories to explain the emergence and development of Neonationalism in Denmark.[14] He points out how newspapers are cultural products shaped by historical, institutional, and social moments and that they provide a story angle of cues and tropes that are informed by the values and motives of news producers, though this is not necessarily obvious to news consumers. The audience of a paper is likely, however, to be familiar with the political and moral discourse employed by its producers. For example, a newspaper may be considered liberal, conservative, or radical. Regardless, reader engagement with the news producer's texts is an "ongoing negotiation" between the producers and consumers of news.[15]

I treat the news stories as both actor and content. The news can be a proxy for action. The *Daily Gleaner*, for example, published pieces on founding Rastafari Howell and Hinds with the express purpose of influencing how readers perceived them. The historian Benedict Anderson, in his book *Imagined Communities: Reflections on the Origin and Spread of Nationalism* (1983), shows the power of print media to shape people's conception of collective identity in ways affirmative and reprehensible. I draw on more than nine hundred news stories, with roughly three-fourths of them focused primarily on the Rastafari. The other quarter addresses international events such as the Italo-Ethiopian War (1935–37), the Mau Mau Rebellion in Kenya (1950s), the Cuban Revolution of 1959, and local Jamaican affairs involving conflict, politics, arts, and music. Most of the news stories and documents that I reviewed did not make it into the final version of this book. They were chopped out, left on the cutting-room floor, as it were, casualties of revisions and copyediting. Nevertheless, the corpus of material that I reviewed informs my account.

The Daily Gleaner, Jamaica Times, *and* The Star *Newspapers: Context, Editorial Motivations, and Ethos*

The original name of what became the *Daily Gleaner* was *The Gleaner and Weekly Compendium of News*, first published on September 13, 1834, by Joshua and Jacob deCordova. From the start, the paper favored the moral perspective of the elites, and a scant three months later, it announced its new title, *The Gleaner: A Weekly Family Newspaper Devoted to Literature, Morality, the Arts and Science and Amusements. The Gleaner's* standpoint reflected the island's business and colonial elites; it retained a conservative and steadfast tenor through the 1900s, publishing six days a week until September 10, 1939, when a Sunday edition was added. In the notes, I cite the news articles with the newspaper title, month, date, year, and where available, the page number.[16] Many of the *Daily Gleaner* editorial columns were written by the editor in chief, although before the 1960s, writers rarely identified themselves on brief stories.

The *Daily Gleaner* was never the only newspaper in Jamaica, but for considerable stretches, it was the primary paper and has been the longest running daily in Jamaica. Its target audience during the period of examination was the nation and its international diaspora. Though there were competing papers, rarely did they ever have the *Daily Gleaner's* broad coverage and readership. Among the most recognized were *Jamaica Times, The Star, Jamaica Observer, Jamaica Advocate, Public Opinion, Black Man,* and *Plain Talk.* I draw on these papers when available, especially the *Jamaica Times* and *The Star.* Nearly all *Daily Gleaner* papers have been digitized and are available through subscription. That is not so for the others (copies of *Public Opinion* are now accessible in digital format).

Critics and devotees alike read the *Daily Gleaner,* though it mostly spoke to devotees. The Jamaican socialist and journalist Wilfred

Domingo complained that the paper "tabooed topics such as criticism of capitalism or the needs and rights of working-class people in Jamaica."[17] Another complaint that critics lodged was its Anglophile bias: "*The Gleaner* seems to have become so British that it won't print a word said of the British unless it is in praise of them. . . . We should not be compelled to be British."[18]

Chief editor from 1904 to 1943, Herbert de Lisser led the *Daily Gleaner*. His editorship covered the first decade of the Rastafari. De Lisser's ideology, attitude, and biases informed the stances that the *Daily Gleaner* took toward race-conscious leaders and their supporters. For de Lisser, these folks personified the flaws of Black people.

De Lisser was a complex and ambitious man with insecurities about his racial and class identity. He was born into to a Jewish-Black family. His father was a newspaper man, working for a local newspaper in Trelawney Parish. Although de Lisser could be characterized as "Brown" (interracial), he strove to make his status and identity White. He married into a well-off White family, emphasized his Jewish last name, and endeavored to stay connected to "Englishmen."[19]

The *Daily Gleaner*, under de Lisser's guidance, became the voice of Jamaican public opinion, which meant that it was the opinion of the upper classes. As a self-appointed spokesperson, he communicated his views on Jamaican society and public affairs through editorial and satire columns and his serial novels. His views were profoundly shaped by the nineteenth-century Englishman James Anthony Froude, a historian, novelist, and social commentator. Froude subscribed to the pseudoscientific race thinking of his time. He believed in the inherent superiority of Whites, the British in particular, and in the inherent inferiority of Blacks. For example, Froude wrote of Black people in his *The English in the West Indies*, "Morals in the technical sense they have none, but they cannot be said to sin, because they have no knowledge of law, and therefore they can commit no breach of the law. They are naked and not ashamed."[20] For de Lisser, Black Jamaicans were gullible, prone to immediate gratification, happy-go-lucky, and lacking in creative ability.

The Library of Congress and similar institutions list the run dates of the *Jamaica Times* as 1900–1963, although it existed before 1900. Thomas MacDermot served as the editor of *Jamaica Times* between 1900 and 1920 (de Lisser briefly served as editor of the *Jamaica Times* before

MacDermot). MacDermot, a poet, nationalist, and advocate of the British empire, has been described as of Irish and African ancestry, born into Jamaica's middle class.[21] The *Jamaica Times* boasted the largest circulation of any West Indian weekly. Published on Saturdays, it expressed a literary, conservative, and family-oriented tone geared toward the middle and upper classes. It sometimes covered the Rastafari—primarily when Rastafari stirrings rattled elite sensibilities—but not nearly as prolifically as the *Daily Gleaner*. Unlike the *Daily Gleaner*, the *Jamaica Times* had little to say about King Ras Tafari and his coronation until after it transpired; it did give regular attention to the Italo-Ethiopian War and Emperor Selassie. Much of the attention to the Rastafari during their early years stemmed from the "Pepper Pot" column writer, "Ginger," who, for example, mocked Leonard Howell's religio-racial tract *Promise Key*, saying, "[It is the] greatest farrago of blasphemous nonsense it was ever my lot to wade through. . . . I can well understand the race prejudice and bitter hatred which is now so clearly manifested in certain of the lower strata of our society here."[22]

A third major news source of information about the Rastafari is *The Star*. A subsidiary of the Gleaner Company, *The Star* was first published in 1951 and is still in publication. Although it has evolved, it has always had a tabloid flavor. *The Star* was tailored to the toiling and untutored class and thus served audiences different from the *Daily Gleaner* and *Jamaica Times*, although people may have read any of the three papers if warranted, say, to get different perspectives on a story of interest. *The Star*, like its prim relative, the *Daily Gleaner*, covered the Rastafari on a regular basis from the mid-1950s on, favoring a sensational slant.

I have drawn very little on one of Jamaica's recent newspapers, the *Jamaica Observer*, originating in 1993. In general, my use of post-mid-1970s news sources declines sharply given the wide range of other sources of information such as scholarship, Rastafari publications, and social media as a source of news and popular communication.

Who orchestrated campaigns to discredit the Rastafari during their first few decades, and who enforced policies that prohibited their ability to associate? Jamaican elites: the governor, the inspector general, the attorney general, the leadership of the *Daily Gleaner*, leading clergy of the mainstream denominations, the chief of the Supreme Court, large business and landowners in central and eastern Jamaica, and even some of Marcus Garvey's UNIA leadership. Within less than a year of Howell and Hinds's effort to build a following, organizing in St. Thomas Parish, the planter John Ross had mobilized segments of the nonelite citizenry against the Rastafari. Labeling theory tells us that some people have more power than others to ascribe degrading "labels" and make them stick.[23] Elites played an important role in the first four decades of Rastafari ethnogenesis. They included people who could propose, implement, and enforce policies or campaigns against grassroots religio-racial leadership; later, some among their ranks also initiated tolerance of the Rastafari. Elites contributed mightily to defining the Rastafari, while the Rastafari mightily contested their labels and policies.

Undoubtedly, elites are not a monolithic category, and Jamaica's class structure and the conceptions of its elites shifted between the 1930s and 2000s. The political scientist Obika Gray has described Jamaican elites as inclusive of "colonial rulers" and "native leaders."[24] Elites are the politically, economically, and socially influential members of the upper and middle classes, but I also include in the category elite "opinion shapers" such as the uppermost leadership of schoolteachers, clergy, labor and voluntary associations, and the arts.[25] Until the 1960s, Whites and Browns were dominant among elites, with increasing numbers of Blacks joining their ranks from the 1950s onward.

Critical Concerns in Using News Sources

The Black literature scholar Michael Hoenisch has argued that we have to read the press "against the grain."[26] He counsels that the "traces of the Rastafari movement are preserved to a large extent in the language of the rulers. In the pages of the conservative *Daily Gleaner* the middle-class reading public was offered strategies for rearranging in their consciousness the threat, which the black lower classes began to exert. . . . Leonard Howell was cast in a central role of this process."[27] His counsel I have tried to follow consistently. I acknowledge the subjectivity surrounding news stories and their creation and my interpretation of them. I did not have access to the "total population" of news stories; therefore, I drew on available Rastafari-relevant content.[28]

It is reasonable to cast a critical eye on research that draws substantially on news stories; but I use a range of other data as well, and the payoff of drawing on news stories offsets their limitations. The social movement scholar Jennifer Earl and colleagues demonstrate that "newspaper data also facilitate both comparative and historical research. . . . In addition to these numerous advantages, there is often no other alternative available for researchers interested in work beyond case studies of particular movements."[29] Earl and colleagues tell how newspaper data contributed to the "development of major theories" in the field of social movement studies.[30] One of the hindrances to constructing a narrative of Rastafari ethnogenesis is the lack of data beyond news stories and a limited corpus of archived documents. Rastafari such as Howell, Hinds, Reid, Claudius Henry, and others left few or no records of their work. This obstacle persisted into the 2000s. In 1998, the second-generation Rastafari Ras Sam Brown, a well-known Rastafari figure in Jamaica, showed me a book-length manuscript he wrote, but I have no idea what happened to it after his passing. Ras Sydney DaSilva, a well-known organizer of the Rastafari Centralization Organization, had over the years amassed a trove of documents about the Rastafari. With dissolution of the Rastafari Centralization Organization and the passing of Ras DaSilva, I have been unable to determine what happened to the organization's records. Yet, with the growth of the internet and social media, Rastafari experience is better and widely documented, and sometimes valuable documents or other information from the past are made available through these media.

Another advantage of news stories is that they provide shifting points of view on the Rastafari and encourage a reassessment of existing scholarship by providing fresh material and new connections. For example, through the news stories and other data, I can elaborate on the Jamaican fascination with Emperor Selassie, the concatenation of foreign and native religio-racial ideas and actors, the suppression of Rastafari activities, the pre-1960s repatriation activities, the political machinations involving the Rastafari, and the countless ways in which Rastafari defied and adapted to the challenges posed by Jamaica's elite and otherwise.

Also, in many cases, news reports either corroborate scholarship or archived documents or offer unexamined information that can be substantiated by scholarship or documents. For example, I discovered a series of news stories about weapons smuggled from New York into Jamaica in 1960 by ship, packed in a refrigerator, to arm guerilla fighters in Jamaica. The stories seemed exaggerated given the plot and the stumblebum characters involved. Nevertheless, I found corroboration for the stories in government documents and recent scholarship.[31] The implicated refrigerator, an artifact of an uprising, was auctioned off.[32] Such stories facilitate the historical imagination, finding and connecting small acts with larger concerns.

Nonnewspaper Archival Documents

Archived documents are a fourth major source of data for this book. The archived documents that I draw on have varied origins and motivations. A substantial number of the records were generated within Jamaica's colonial government and the post-1938 government: colonial secretaries, attorneys general, secretaries of home affairs, commissioners of police, clerks of parochial boards, and the island medical officers. Other documents owe to civic, business, and religious elites: society leaders, business owners, and preachers, concerned in various ways that the Rastafari were a threat to Jamaican society. Then there are the occasional records from the foot soldiers themselves: low-level police officers such as constables and corporals (who, arguably, command status by virtue of being a part of the law enforcement apparatus, although unable to shape policies or priorities, but certainly capable of enacting whim). And there are the Rastafari who complain about their mistreatment at the hands of authorities and who sometimes defend their faith, identity, and rights in letters to authorities and in submissions to newspapers.

The Colonial Service was the administrative arm that oversaw Britain's colonies. By late 1933, the colonial government saw fit to direct the Constabulary to surveil Rastafari leaders and their public meetings. Their strategy relied on direct observation, use of informants, and longhand note taking. Drawing primarily on the Jamaica National Archives, I utilize a range of documents, including some that were deposited with the Colonial Secretary Office (Jamaica) (CSO) between April 1934 and the mid-1950s. The documents—minutes, confidential memos, handwritten and typed letters and notes, telegraphs, and other documents—detail the political and social perambulations of the Rastafari and their opponents. The archival record is spotty, and news stories and other data are useful in filling these gaps. The National Library at Kew, London, provided copies of Jamaican government documents pertaining to national intelligence and security, 1960–62. Other records were collected from internet-based sites and are cited accordingly. Like the news stories, the archived documents—interesting though some are—must be read carefully and critically.

Outline of the Book

Given space limitations, I lean toward providing less detail about the Rastafari that has been substantially covered in other books and more detail on lesser-known episodes. In some cases, I offer a fresh take on established episodes, such as the trial of Howell and Hinds.

Chapter 1 employs a dual format—an introduction to the Rastafari, combined with a discussion of theoretical concerns relevant to ethnogenesis and collective identity formation—to set the stage for subsequent chapters. I intend the book to satisfy any curious reader. The theoretical discussion will meet the needs of specialists while introducing nonspecialists to a framework for interpreting the sociohistorical and normative account that follows. Chapter 2 identifies people, events, and ideas that formed the cultural matrix out of which the Rastafari emerged. We see how Black Jamaicans' interests in healing and racial redemption provoked the colonial authorities and other elites to crack down on religio-racial leaders, how British colonialism connected Africa and Jamaica, and how the *Daily Gleaner* created a narrative about King Ras Tafari that fed into the messages of Ethiopianism. Chapter 3 addresses the first eighteen months of the Rastafari, beginning with the return of Leonard Howell to Jamaica in 1932. It describes the connection between Howell and the first Rastafari and Black Israelites, Annie and David Harvey. Chapter 4 offers a detailed analysis of the trial of Howell and Hinds, showing that it provided a platform for disseminating an inchoate Rastafari doctrine that informed Rastafari collective identity.

The authorities' tenacious effort to weed out the Rastafari inspired in them a sense of persecution and specialness. The invasion of Ethiopia by Italy in 1935 and the development of the Pinnacle community became significant to Rastafari ethnogenesis. Chapter 5 takes up these concerns and more. Chapter 6 shows how Rastafari identity became sullied through its conflation with criminality. A second generation of Rastafari developed, facilitating cultural innovation and Rastafari diversity. The Rastafari concern with relocation to Africa creeps into public consciousness, while international visitors and events continue to exert influence on Rastafari ethnogenesis. Chapter 7 digs into the intensifying fear of the Rastafari. The Reverend Claudius Henry, for example, strode onto the Rastafari stage during the late 1950s, generating turmoil in Jamaica, drawing explicit attention to the international influence of Black nationalism, Marxism, and revolutionary politics on the Rastafari. Yet, another trend was emergent: public attitudes—elite and popular— began to shift. The results were mixed and contradictory, as we shall see. Chapter 8 focuses on the Rastafari and the political machinations that involved several missions to Africa, Jamaican security forces, Cold War politics, and the violence attendant to what became known as the Coral Gardens Incident.

The visit of Emperor Selassie to Jamaica and the Walter Rodney Rebellion created new opportunities for the Rastafari, contributing to a shift in Jamaican attitudes toward race and class. The status of the Rastafari was further elevated by their contributions to Jamaican art and music. Yet the expanding influence of the Rastafari has caused them to grapple with organizing to protect their collective heritage and interests. Chapter 9 examines new influences shaping Rastafari ethnogenesis— including popularity and rapid growth—and the normative concerns the challenges raise. Chapter 10 continues the analysis of normative concerns attendant to Rastafari ethnogenesis in a postcolonial Jamaica regulated by neoliberal capitalism. Among the major concerns are adjustments the Rastafari made in reaction to the disappearance of Emperor Selassie, the waning of the influence of existing vectors, the commodification and appropriation of Rastafari identity, and shifting gender dynamics among the Rastafari.

* * *

The Rastafari, who still struggle, in Jamaica at least, continue to sanctify the "New Name" and its icon, Emperor Haile Selassie. The sanctification takes many forms, as it always has, though the contours are etched in ways that are more formal than in the past. There are many Houses and

Mansions, many versions of Rastafari, some with their own rules and guidelines. Nevertheless, as we shall see, from the 1950s on, they regularly pursued efforts to unify. The elastic diversity among groups that have survived multiple generations and become swept into the maelstrom of accelerating change, like the Rastafari, is nothing unusual.

1

Explaining Rastafari Ethnogenesis

A Framework

Let me arrange the stage before we get to the theory.

Ethnogenesis is an emergent phenomenon. People, ideas, events, and objects interact in complex ways in which the interacting elements produce something greater than the elements, thus defying deterministic prediction. Nevertheless, we can qualitatively construct, describe, and explain ethnogenesis. Detail and history are vital to an ethnogenesis narrative. Indeed, detail and history may overshadow explanation, unless one exerts the effort to make theory explicit. The theory, even if faint, ought to help the reader make sense of the history and detail.

So, how do we explain the origins and evolution of a complex phenomenon like the Rastafari people? We begin with establishing the initial conditions that made the Rastafari possible. "Initial conditions" describe the state of key points in a system at an established time. They involve a field of actors, relationships, and institutions, which are already historical. Initial conditions are based in identifiable antecedents that make possible a given set of outcomes. While initial conditions do not determine historical outcomes, they constrain and spur change.[1] By specifying initial conditions, we can better explain the emergence and development of groups.

Initial conditions are not clean or bounded starting points; they are temporal and permeable frames that span a period vital to the emergence or transformation of a people and their identity. Initial conditions include the relevant time frame that precedes the people studied *and* the time frame after their emergence that is vital to their persistence. The relevant span of time before and after emergence will depend on each investigation and investigator's judgment.

The initial conditions for the Rastafari in Jamaica ensued roughly between 1910 and 1932, spanning the last two decades of the life of the

Jamaican anticolonial gadfly and Christian Revival minister Reverend Alexander Bedward and the first few years after the coronation of King Ras Tafari of Ethiopia as Emperor in 1930. Bedward, girded by thousands of followers, espoused provocative pro-Black and anticolonial rhetoric toward the end of the 1800s through 1921. Revival, a form of Afro-Christianity indigenous to Jamaica and practiced mostly by Black Jamaicans, emphasizes communication with spirits, stern moral conduct, and healing. Revival practitioners see themselves as called by God to counteract evil and repair bodies and souls. Revival leaders like Bedward saw White oppression as both evil and necessitating the use of one's abilities to heal the oppressed. The Rastafari were concerned with evil, moral conduct, and healing the Black body and community. However, they would abandon concern with spirits by the second generation, while developing a racial critique of evil, immoral conduct, and healing the Black body. The coronation of King Ras Tafari as Emperor in 1930 perturbed the "system" in Jamaica by inducing a range of people to busy themselves in constructing narratives about the new Emperor according to their existing concerns regarding Black theology. Stories about Ethiopia and King Ras Tafari and Emperor Selassie published in Jamaican print media during 1930 and after sparked discussion and historical analysis. These conversations were twofold, encompassing both coverage of his coronation and who he really was. Such interest in the Ethiopian King-become-Emperor begs for a cursory introduction to Ethiopianism and its contributions to the emergence of Rastafari identity and ideology.

Backdrop to Rastafari Ethnogenesis and Collective Identity

Ethiopianism is a religio-racial ideology (i.e., both religious and racial) that describes an extensive lineage of recurrent ideas about race, social justice, biblical history, and biblical prophecy that became central to the origin and development of Rastafari identity. A brief examination of Ethiopianism will give context to why the Rastafari—in particular— have exalted Black identity and have identified themselves as Israelites, as chosen people, as awaiting a Black Messiah, as moral superiors, and as Ethiopians, even though they were not born in Abyssinia.

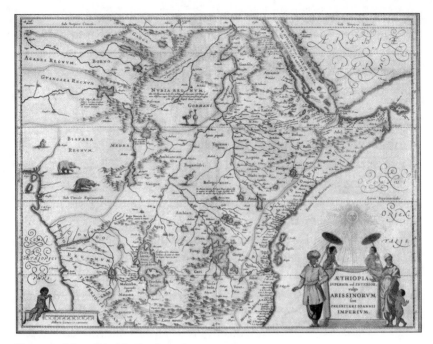

Figure 1.1. Map of Aethiopia, circa 1640.

Ethiopianism

When the King James Bible was published in 1611, much of the continent that today we call "Africa" was known to Europeans as "Aethiopia," land of dark-skinned people (figure 1.1). During the eighteenth and nineteenth centuries, people in the United States, the Caribbean, and England commonly used "Ethiopian" to refer to both enslaved and free people of African descent. As a categorical identifier, it gradually slid into disuse by the mid-1800s, superseded by a range of terms, including ugly epithets. However, African and African-descended people continued to use "Ethiopian" as an identification through World War II in their arts, drama, politics, and religious matters.[2]

Ethiopianists believe that African-descended people are a special people, their chosen status tied to Europeans' forced relocation of Africans to the New World and their experience of enslavement. Confronted with life in a new land, adapting to a regime of enslavement, and socialized into Christianity, Africans and their descendants gradually shifted from a multiplicity of African languages and identities toward a Pan-Black identity. "Pan-Black" does not mean that they shared the same understanding of Blackness, moral or otherwise. Nevertheless, experiences of forced relocation, bondage, and systemic discrimination became durable schemas that facilitated the creation of race-laden ideas of community, solidarity, and the shared fate of Black people.

MORAL BLACKNESS AS CULTURAL RESOURCE

"Moral Blackness" describes conceptions of Black racial identity in which equity, social justice, and spirituality are collective notions that define Blackness, a cultural and existential state and process of being marked as or embracing being Black. With Ethiopianism, moral concerns were coupled with beliefs about divine ordination attuned to Black people's degraded condition, as exemplified in Jamaica by the Rastafari but also by many of their predecessors, as we shall see. Based in grievances real and imagined, moral Blackness inspired both social movements' and individuals' critiques of racial oppression.

Ethiopianism was from the start millenarian and messianic. It anticipated a divine intervention that would pry Black people from the vice grip of oppression and release them into a glorious pasture of prosperity and entitlement. The Rastafari did not invent this deliverance, though they further developed it. They drafted a new script for the Ethiopianist stage. The Rastafari version claims that the spiritual kinship of Black people courses through the blood lines of the biblical Israelite kings David and Solomon and the Queen of Sheba (in the Ethiopianist narrative, the queen, Makeda, is Ethiopian). They assert that Africa was the ancestral and spiritual home of Black people—their Promised Land—and that they should repatriate to Africa. They argue that forced relocation, enslavement, and the regimes of White supremacy that succeeded slavery, such as colonialism, were abominable and sinful acts that will cause Whites to suffer God's wrath. Colonialism, for the Rastafari, is a continuation of slavery under a different yoke, and they insistently denounce it. In classic messianic and millenarian fashion, the Rastafari expected Godly redemption, which was dependent on their fidelity. The crowning of King Ras Tafari as Emperor in 1930 signaled the "Ras Tafari's" redemption because it was they who correctly interpreted the signs and who would demonstrate fidelity under severe persecution.

Ethiopianism provided cultural resources for creating a collective identity, a means to achieve an identification that positively defines oneself and one's people as possessing the power to counteract White supremacy. "White supremacy" here means that Europeans understood themselves—as White people—as exceptional to all other racial categories. Ethiopianism offered a salient religio-racial narrative that was coherent, historically grounded, and future oriented and encouraged a sense of solidarity and mutual fate. It was sufficiently broad to allow multiple interpretations, sidestepping the exhaustion that can come with a restricted set of meanings. Yet critics have derided Ethiopianism as unsophisticated wishful thinking mired in teleology, African American exceptionalism, and erroneous beliefs about Africa.[3] Such a critique, however, neglects exactly what a religio-racial ideology like Ethiopianism does: paint the world and people in broad but meaningful strokes. Empirical fidelity was not the concern of Ethiopianists, nor is it a common preoccupation of ideology.

EARLY ETHIOPIANISM

By the 1770s, African-descended people were defining themselves as Ethiopian (i.e., Black). At the same time, a specific Black theology began to take shape. For example, David Margrett (a.k.a. David Margate) and John Marrant, two free African Christian missionaries, compared Black people's experience to that of the Israelites of the ancient Near East. Both men were recruited to minister to the enslaved and free Africans of the thirteen colonies by the English Methodist philanthropist Selina Hastings. She was interested in promoting Methodism, though her two ministers had a take on Christianity different from that of the Methodists. Hastings sent Margrett to Charleston, South Carolina, in 1774. He announced himself to Black colonial audiences as a "second Moses" who had come to lead Black people out of bondage, just as the "children of Israel were delivered out of the hands of Pharo [sic] . . . and God will deliver his own people from slavery."[4]

John Marrant preached mainly in Nova Scotia and Massachusetts and created a theological framework for his ideas through his sermons tracing to the mid-1770s. Marrant dubbed Black people a "chosen" and "peculiar people," God's people.[5] In the budding Ethiopianist narrative, the ancient Israelites' failure to be faithful to their God caused their conquest and subsequent captivity in foreign lands, which roused in them a yearning to dwell in the land that God promised as reward for their fidelity. Ethiopianism designates the people of the African Diaspora as latter-day Israelites.

By 1790, Ethiopianism was an international presence in the British colonies. For example, George Liele, born into enslavement in the Virginia colony during the early 1750s, became an unstinting Baptist missionary active in the Georgia and South Carolina colonies. The theologian David Shannon Sr. observed, "By teaching other enslaved persons, Liele discovered his love for other enslaved people on the same plantation where he resided. His engagement with the oppressed enslaved people is also an example of liberation theology."[6] With an emphasis on the liberation of oppressed Black people, Ethiopianist-inspired social movements prefigured liberation theology. In 1775, Liele became the first ordained Black minister in what would soon become the United States of America. Liele and Marrant were among the first White-sanctioned Black preachers in the United States. Liele formed the first Black congregations, first in 1773 in Silver Bluff, South Carolina, and then in 1783 in Savannah, Georgia (officially established in 1788).[7] He sided with the Tories during the American Revolution and gained his freedom, and upon the Tory loss to the colonists, he and his family fled the United States to Jamaica with a group of Tories. In Jamaica, Liele became an effective vector of Ethiopianism, where he established the first Black Baptist church.

ETHIOPIANISM IN BRITISH CENTRAL AFRICA

Ethiopianism developed into numerous transnational strands in the United States and Africa that had a significant but underappreciated impact on Jamaica. It smoldered during the late 1800s into the early 1900s. Around the beginning of World War I, it reignited in the United States, the Caribbean, and Africa, fueled by war-related angst and a surge in Black social movements (e.g., the Universal Negro Improvement Association [UNIA], the New Negro movement, and the Watchtower Movement).

In Africa, John Chilembwe, an ethnic Yao African born in 1871 in the territory originally called Nyasaland (later named British Central Africa, then Malawi), concluded that European colonialism was too repressive.

He would have to destroy it by waging a spiritually inspired war against colonialism and European settlers. Studying theology at Virginia Theological Seminary, Chilembwe was introduced to notions of Ethiopianism by the school's faculty and its president during the late 1890s. He learned about the Black liberation efforts of the enslaved Black preacher Nat Turner and the White militant abolitionist John Brown. The experience and learning had a profound effect on his thinking, and he used it to build a like-minded community in Africa upon his return in 1900. Chilembwe launched his rebellion in 1915; it met a swift and brutal end at the hands of the British. Nevertheless, the rebellion became a lesson for the British in how Ethiopianism challenged their authority by engendering Black resistance.

The British strategies for addressing native resistance in British Central Africa (and India) did not always result in new laws but certainly shaped the attitudes of colonialists toward the Black populations they governed. While Chilembwe's Ethiopianist consciousness stirred him to conclude that violent rebellion was the only tool that might cause the British to release their grip on Central Africa, the impact of his disastrous rebellion rippled across the Atlantic to Jamaica. The British Commission on the Chilembwe "Native Rising" in Nyasaland that convened to inquire into the causes of the rebellion concluded that it was the result of a combination of Ethiopianism, race literature from the United States (e.g., the UNIA newspaper the *Negro World*), emigrant Africans like Chilembwe returning home, and local factors like the spread of Ethiopianist-inspired African independent churches. The British deemed Ethiopianism a subversive ideology.

ETHIOPIANISM IN JAMAICA, 1910–32

During the later years of the Reverend Alexander Bedward, he branded himself as a Black savior and promoted among his followers a belief in the looming redemption of Black people living in colonial Jamaica. Through his ideas and charisma, Bedward led a band of intrepid loyalists who on more than one occasion clashed with the Constabulary. We know that one of the loyalists was Robert Hinds, who later worked with Leonard Howell in developing and propagating the Rastafari doctrine.

The connection between Bedward and the Rastafari involves the Bedwardites, who were drawn to the message of a Black savior. Some of these

Bedwardites populated the first generation of Rastafari. Moreover, beginning with Bedward, we see a pattern in how the colonial authorities managed charismatic, religio-racial leaders. They were surveilled, sometimes by constables, sometimes by citizen informants. With their speeches and movements recorded, they were often arrested on insubstantial grounds, minor offenses, or trumped-up charges. Finally, their cases made the mainstream newspapers, usually the *Daily Gleaner* and, later, *The Star*. Authorities and their elite Jamaican allies used this strategy to grind down and break the enemies of the colonial polity. The courts judged Bedward a lunatic, and he eventually died a broken man in 1930.

Jamaica's colonial authorities thus had considerable practice undermining Black religio-racial leadership by the time the Rastafari emerged, though, as the Rastafari confirmed, their strategy proved less effective than they hoped. Colonial suppression of Bedward and the Bedwardites began well after Bedward had gained a large following, not at the beginning of his journey, as with the Rastafari. For the Rastafari, oppression, suppression, and repression had the paradoxical effect of spawning solidarity, resistance, and resilience.

Beyond Bedward, several strands of moral Blackness, including newly introduced forms, circulated through Jamaica between the 1910s and the crowning of King Ras Tafari as Emperor in 1930. These ideas and their purveyors in various ways contributed cultural resources and foot soldiers to the nascent Rastafari. In addition to the ideas of Marcus Garvey, the Ethiopianist-inspired founder and leader of the UNIA movement who urged Black pride and economic and political empowerment, the Black American Reverend James Morris Webb, the Anguillan minister Robert Athlyi Rogers, and the Black American Reverend Fitz Pettersburgh represent other strands of Ethiopianist thought in Jamaica during the 1920s and 1930s. Webb presented his theory of a Black Messiah in his tract *A Black Man Will Be the Coming Universal King Proven by Biblical History*.[8] Rogers's conception of Africans and African-descended people as chosen people who would be led out of oppression by "saviors" like Marcus Garvey or himself was introduced in his tract *The Holy Piby*.[9] Pettersburgh's Ethiopianist tract *The Royal Parchment Scroll of Black Supremacy* argued for the moral superiority of Black people given their endurance of oppression and their status as chosen people.[10] These people and ideas constituted Black theologies that could be crafted into a collective identification.

The Ethiopianist-inspired notions flowing through Jamaica drew both ire and interest. Some of the indignation was played out in the pages of the *Daily Gleaner* and the *Jamaica Times*. Both newspapers and the elites for whom they spoke were consistent in their condemnation and ridicule of moral Blackness and its purveyors. The editorial column of the *Gleaner* fumed, "We have received two publications of the new Ethiopian religion to which we have alluded more than once recently. These books or pamphlets are complementary to the *Holy Piby*, the Bible of the Garveyites, which is to replace the *Holy Bible*. . . . [It is] indistinguishable from nonsense, and the whole concoction is so putrid that we wonder what class of people could ever take such rubbish seriously."[11] The writer mocked Ethiopianism and the people who consumed such literature, believing that *The Holy Piby* "widely circulated amongst a section of the population of Jamaica."[12] Soaked in ethnocentric conceit, the writer proceeded to share the content of *The Holy Piby* with his audience. Many Black Jamaicans among that "section of the population" found interest in the content of *The Holy Piby* and its two "companions," in part because of the newspapers' editorializing and in part a result of the content circulating through Jamaica by vectors in the form of street preachers and tracts.

Another thread contributing to the fabric that would become Rastafari were the race-conscious Jamaican Revival healers Annie and David Harvey. At some point in 1925, the Harveys, who had previously spent time in Panama and Cuba, traveled to Ethiopia. In 1930, they returned to Jamaica carrying firsthand knowledge of Ethiopia and its ruler, King Ras Tafari.[13]

The Harveys knew that the King was interested in recruiting skilled people of the African Diaspora to migrate to Ethiopia. Annie, a confident and charismatic woman, upon her return to Jamaica, set about developing a following attuned to her healing and spiritual abilities. She advertised her curative talent and her identity ("Israelite") in the *Daily Gleaner* between 1930 and 1931. By invoking "Israelite," Annie signaled her subscription to a view of African people's connection to ancient Israel and ancient Judah—that she was a member of a chosen people.

By combining "Israelite" and "Healer," Annie announced that she was a race-conscious healer. One of Annie's newspaper advertisements read,

> The Israelites Healer,
> curing all disease of the body and eyes.
> Also chronic indigestion, consumption, and asthma[14]

The historian Robert Hill and others believe that Leonard Howell, one of the founding Rastafari, sought out Annie Harvey when he returned to Jamaica in 1932.[15] It is likely that in Jamaica, Harvey told stories of her experience in Ethiopia, the colony of Black Diaspora settlers in Ethiopia, and the Ethiopian government's call for more Black settlers. Many of the early Rastafari wanted to join the migration to Ethiopia, though their desires were portrayed by elites as ludicrous fantasies.

Annie Harvey was a famous and revered religio-racial leader and organizer in her own right. She was repeatedly in the news for performing Obeah and for practicing medicine without a license. Obeah is a repertoire of practices that trace to Jamaica's earliest enslaved Africans of the post-Spaniard era. The Jamaican establishment associated Obeah with trouble. During enslavement, the island's elites, especially the planters, connected Obeah with violence and danger because it encouraged enslaved people to do things that they would not do, such as challenge White authority, if they did not believe they had the protection of Obeah. Obeah practitioners were known for their ability to command uncontested loyalty from their followers, thus undermining White control over Black Jamaicans. They used their art in ways that people believed harmful or dangerous, though it involved curing maladies and was used in ways both positive and nefarious. However, an esteemed Revival leader might claim the ability to counteract Obeah. Annie Harvey was one such Revival leader.

Colonial authorities repeatedly arrested the Harveys for their spiritual activities. In a hearing for one of the arrests, a reporter wrote that the Harveys were charged with breaching the Obeah Act (1898) and the Medical Law (1908) because they were "associated with holding certain meetings at nights and are referred to as 'Israelites.'"[16]

Authorities used the Obeah Act and Medical Law to control practitioners of Obeah and the healing arts. The Obeah Act gave the colonial government a legal means to punish people who engaged in what was essentially a complex of religious, magical, and healing practices developed to address uncertainty, misfortune, illness, and well-being. Legislators and medical professionals urged for the Medical Law to restrict the practice of medicine to licensed professionals. It was a useful way to curtail the island's flourishing balm yard (healing) industry while also promoting professional standards (which was the publicly stated goal). The unstated goal was to suppress Jamaica's religio-racial communities and their practices that contested colonial control and elites' sensibilities.

Like Bedward, Annie Harvey had a following that she was trying to grow but that colonial authorities sought to eliminate. By continuing to heal people and by defying colonial Jamaica's laws, she became an aggravating splinter in the hands of the Colonial Service and the Constabulary but was eventually forced by frequent arrests and fines to abandon her work in Jamaica.

Chilembwe, Bedward, Garvey, Webb, Rogers, Pettersburgh, and the Harveys, among others, were part of the sundry streams of people and notions of moral Blackness flowing through several continents yet generating impact in Jamaica between the 1910s and 1930, all of them contributing to the pool of cultural content from which Rastafari identity emerged. They epitomized the "Black International," which, according to the sociologists Michael West and William Martin, describes the international network of people and struggles pursuing Black liberation and a quest for "universal emancipation."[17]

A Disintegrating British Colonialism and a British Fear of Moral Blackness

Britain experienced growing difficulty in managing its colonies after World War I, partly due to a realignment of nation-states, the financial strain from the war, and the development of homegrown nationalism and anticolonialism in the colonies.

The colonial government in Jamaica became suspicious of any activity that might upset the colonial order. It turned its attention, beginning in the 1890s, to eradicating influential religio-racial leaders. By the mid-1920s, promoters of Black nationalism were added to the list of threats. In 1930, for example, Jamaican elites concluded that Marcus Garvey's People's Political Party (PPP), Jamaica's first political party, was perilous to the status quo because it called for independence from Britain and majority rule (implying an independent government by the Black majority). A *Daily Gleaner* writer described PPP candidate speeches as "noxious doctrines," introduced to an "ignorant minority, . . . a criminal minority; and it is always possible that these might at any moment, being intoxicated by foolish doctrines, break out of control and suffer the consequences."[18] The writer's assessment is noteworthy because it expresses a general attitude held by elites about the Black majority and, later, toward all manner of Rastafari activity.

Ethnogenesis and Collective Identity Formation: A Framework

Imagine traveling back to March 1934, when both founding Rastafari evangelists, Leonard Howell and Robert Hinds, were defending themselves in a Jamaican court for preaching allegiance to King Ras Tafari instead of King George V of England. Although Howell and Hinds were preaching to audiences of several hundred by the end of 1933, they had been at it for about a year and at best had a tiny base committed to the new faith and identity of Rastafari. The chief justice found Howell and Hinds guilty of sedition and ordered them to serve prison terms. We could have reasonably concluded that this was the end of the road for the Rastafari. Twenty-seven years later, however, the colonial government that sought to stamp out the Rastafari sponsored an expedition to several African nations to determine the feasibility of repatriating the Rastafari and other Jamaicans to Africa. Forty years after Howell's and Hinds's sentence, the Rastafari had spread beyond Jamaica and gained global recognition. Hinds had died, and Howell was living in semiseclusion. How did the race-conscious Rastafari coalesce into a collectivity that gained traction and substantial presence in a modernizing nation where Blackness was disparaged and Whiteness and Britishness privileged? This book answers this question.

The Idea of Ethnogenesis

As we have seen, ethnogenesis is the process of collective emergence and development and the study of that process. It focuses on the factors that define a collectivity such as a social movement, religious community, ethnic group, or racial category. It is not a theory but a conceptual framework that has been proven to be durable and productive. Since the 1970s, scholars have published a wide range and considerable volume of studies of ethnogenesis.

Ethnogenesis has two major dimensions. The process can involve the development of an entirely new collectivity, ab initio, like the Rastafari, or it can involve the reorganization and redefinition of an existing collective identity, which also applies to the Rastafari. Whether to emphasize one or the other manifestation of ethnogenesis, or both, depends on the focus of inquiry. Whether focused on a new or a transformed collectivity, ethnogenesis encourages the analysis of connections between the present and past and searches out multiple roots and sources of collectivities. The anthropologist John Moore points out that this "rhizotic" conception of ethnogenesis (evoking a subterranean system of multiple roots invisible to the eye, able to produce new shoots even if part of the root system is disrupted) focuses on the development of cultural qualities that people express and that mark them as distinct, emphasizing the "extent to which each human language, culture, or population is considered to be derived from or rooted in several different antecedent groups."[19] History is indispensable to the explanation of ethnogenesis. So, too, is theory. Rather than rely solely on historical description, I present a framework for Rastafari ethnogenesis that culminates in five propositions. The framework—the propositions in particular—established here should prepare us to "see" ethnogenesis in operation in the narrative that follows.

A primary strength of the ethnogenesis approach is the attention that it brings to the interaction of social change, power, and culture that are embodied in people's identity. Collective identity formation is a fundamental dimension of ethnogenesis because a collectivity recognizes (identifies) itself and is recognized (identified) by others. It helps to explain how a collective identity came to be what it is.[20] Recent discussions of ethnogenesis have begun to address the role of identity in the process, but obliquely. For example, the historians James Sidbury and Jorge Cañizares-Esguerra examine multidimensional identity transformations involved in the ethnogenesis of Atlantic Basin peoples without specifying the identity processes at work.[21] Scholars have yet to link explicitly collective identity formation and ethnogenesis and present propositions about some of the fundamental processes at work. I take a step toward filling this gap by explaining and describing what ethnogenesis and collective identity formation look like among the Rastafari.

In less than fifty years, the Rastafari shifted from a tiny number experiencing pitiless oppression to tens of thousands in Jamaica to a global presence in the neighborhood of a million adherents.[22] The sociologist Rodney Stark tackled a similar problem in his book *The Rise of Christianity* (1996), showing how Christianity grew from a tiny Jewish sect into an official and, later, a world religion. Stark emphasized the role of intimate influences like relatives and friends in religious conversion. I do not dispute Stark's explanation regarding Christians, but I give substantial attention to the influence of nonmembers in Rastafari ethnogenesis. Rastafari efforts at recruiting were indirect and limited, occurring within a field of competing identity options such as those offered by other religious groups or voluntary associations like the UNIA. In this regard, the Rastafari's growth as a collectivity depended ultimately on each Rastafari acting as his or her own guardian against the enticements of competitive religious, political, racial, or other collectivities. Ultimately, the Rastafari proved adaptable, resilient, and appealing, adjusting to politico-economic shifts and other changes. While I call the Rastafari a people, and many Jamaican Rastafari use the term "Rasta people," I should be clear that "people" as used in this book assumes that "a people" are a diverse and dynamic entity, not a static thing.

What gave the Rastafari traction? "Traction" is a metaphor for what a new collectivity must do: gain a position that facilitates development and persistence. Collectivities face obstacles to surviving beyond their first generation. They must be able to enlist new members or retain the offspring of current adherents and survive in an environment in which members are tempted by other groups or interests. Cultural selection, cultural transmission, and cultural evolution theorists might argue (differently) that Rastafari ideas and practices are transmitted recurrently because they can solve problems.[23] Their theories offer an intuitively appealing explanation for a collectivity like the Rastafari: Over the course of several centuries, Jamaicans entrenched a system of racial organization and classification. Moreover, African-descended people in Jamaica developed millenarian, messianic, healing, and prophetic traditions. Therefore, the Rastafari were amenable to cultural selection and survival once they emerged; they embodied the characteristics— racialism, millenarianism, messianism, prophetic traditions, healing traditions—likely to survive and replicate in Jamaica's environment. But how would the selectionists, transmissionists, or evolutionists explain the emergence and development of the Rastafari themselves? Well, they might argue that the first Rastafari were the cultural equivalent of a mutation—memes that went rogue—that sank roots and successfully replicated.

Cultural selection, cultural transmission, cultural evolution, and ethnogenesis are different frameworks suitable for explaining how collectivities and other cultural forms develop, persist, and spread. Cultural selection, transmission, and evolution continue in resurrected form the intransigent problem of quantifying and slicing complex behavior into parcels and numerical expressions deprived of the rich and nuanced context, history, situations, and meanings that explain a given trait in the first place. An ethnogenesis approach offers an alternative. However, I should say a bit about other alternatives.

Cultural Selection, Cultural Transmission, and Cultural Evolution: Nonethnogenesis Models of the Emergence, Durability, and Spread of Cultural Forms

Theorists of cultural selection, cultural transmission, and cultural evolution explain durable "collective behavior-patterns" by focusing on how individuals transmit and internalize information within a population and across generations.[24] They ask, What enhances the opportunity for information complexes like cultural traditions or collective identity to persist over time? How do individuals transmit beliefs and values to support group distinctions? And how do information complexes compete? It is these questions and more that a qualitative ethnogenesis- and collective-identity-focused approach can answer, without the baggage of evoking Darwinian selection or fitness, without fathoming the human mind's evolutionary predispositions, without dependence on the individual as the central unit of analysis, and without abstracting cultural beliefs and practices through quantitative modeling. By focusing on historical influences, power asymmetries, and the circulation of ideas among populations, we can accomplish in detail what cultural selection, cultural transmission, and cultural evolution theorists seek to explain.

Cultural selection theory explains historical phenomena like collective identities in terms of Darwinian evolution in a way that draws on notions of variation, selection, and retention of cultural forms that stops short of applying biological claims of evolution to cultural forms.[25] Cultural components, or memes, are treated as if they were gene-like in that they face selection and replication pressure: they mutate, flow, and are more compatible with some environments than others. Ideas and behaviors are the stand-in for genes.[26] In this view, the Rastafari might be selected for survival because their belief system is consonant with—has "intrinsic attraction" or "cultural appeal" to—sectors of Black Jamaicans concerned with racial and theological issues; Jamaica's environment is conducive to Rastafari.[27]

Cultural transmission theory shares similarity with the selectionists in its treatment of information or knowledge (culture) as heritable and gene-like in behavior (but not genetic) and in its preference for formal theoretical models.[28] Transmissionists seek to explain how culture (similarities in behavior) is spread by individual learning. While not much concerned with the origins of practices and beliefs, transmissionists would explain how specific aspects of Rastafari identity and knowledge, such as the divinity of Emperor Selassie or particular rituals, are disseminated across Jamaica and across generations.

Cultural evolutionists draw on abstract populational modeling approaches toward culture, identifying the exogenous (environmental) and endogenous (internal) factors that explain how behavior (culture) spreads and changes within and across populations over time and across space.[29] Cultural evolution is evolutionary not because of its emphasis on replication or selection in culture but because it concentrates on building models of cultural stasis and cultural change grounded in the interactions of individuals.[30] The focus here, for example, would be on how singular Rastafari create complex patterns of behavior and thinking and how such behavior and thinking persists, spreads, and changes. Cultural evolution theorists would be interested in identifying the individual, psychological, and behavioral activities that explain how a handful of adherents persist and increase their numbers in the face of suppression and oppression (e.g., endogenous and exogeneous change).

Cultural selection, cultural transmission, and cultural evolution theorists disembody a cultural "unit" by tearing it out of its context to identify cause-and-effect relationships. They isolate variables in a well-known scientific strategy and, conscious of this imperfection, see it as necessary to understanding the aggregation of individual human behaviors. They contravene, however, a fundamental claim of contemporary sociocultural anthropology: context, history, power asymmetries, and the other multiple influences that bear on a cultural unit make interpretation possible. Isolate the unit and we lose sight of the synergies that animate it. Some cultural selection, cultural transmission, and cultural evolution analysts recognize that context details are important to explanation and that contextual detail is lost through abstract modeling but accept the loss in favor of models deemed more powerful and accurate than qualitative detail.[31] In such formalized accounts of knowledge, identity transmission, and cultural change, the human is reduced to its brain and the paths that information moves among socially linked brains.[32] However, human brains are impelled by social interaction; the identities and influences of the actors matter to those involved. We need to know who is involved and the nature of the interaction. These theorists have layered a new veneer over the classic problems posed by quantitative models of sociocultural analysis. By translating sociocultural behavior into numbers and variables such as a "transmission coefficient" or by stressing only those traits that can be measured or observed, they move their explanations further away from the phenomena they seek to explain.[33] The sociologist Walter Runciman, a selectionist himself, aptly summarized a weakness of selection theory: "In any but the smallest and simplest societies, the sequence of events through which mutant or recombinant practices come to alter the mode of the distribution of power is likely to be too complex, . . . [too] extraordinarily difficult to unravel."[34]

An ethnogenesis approach is appropriate for a broad and detailed sociohistorical understanding of collective identity formation and group evolution. The ethnogenesis approach sidesteps the demonstration of selection, transmission, or evolution in favor of constructing a comprehensive narrative of how ideas and behaviors emerge, take root, endure, and change and how they are shaped by multiple ingroup and outgroup influences. This book adopts this approach. Rather than argue that ethnogenesis is a superior approach, I emphasize ethnogenesis's strength: it explains human activity in the context of history, power, institutional patterns, and human agency.

Ethnogenesis Processes

A prophet's message cannot gain traction solely on its content or a prophet's charisma. The message must engage, persuade, and attract, but it will ultimately depend on the formation of a community and identity and all that that entails: marshaling cultural resources; developing networks; establishing difference and similarity; pursuing agency; engaging in dialogue with members and nonmembers; and developing common interests, purposes, and a sense of communion.

Scholars have developed an extensive literature on ethnogenesis since the 1970s. I conducted an internet search for the term "ethnogenesis" three days in a row using the same computer in the same location to ascertain the consistency of the results. A search of Google Scholar returned roughly 33,000 results, while a search of Google delivered roughly 650,000 results (July 2021). Scholars of ethnogenesis provide revealing accounts of how new collectivities form, how they persist and change over time, and how existing groups become redefined entities. Like the Rastafari, groups that we think of as having long natural histories, Indian or Chinese ethnic minorities, for example, have manifested identities that shifted over time.

The anthropologist William Sturtevant, among the earliest developers of the ethnogenesis approach, reconstructs how people of the Creek Confederacy in North America became Seminole Indians and, later, the contemporary Miccosukee Indians.[35] The archaeologist Patricia Galloway shows how the historic Choctaw people of Mississippi and Alabama began as an amalgam of prehistoric prairie and Mobile Delta indigenous groups that moved into the Mississippi region during the latter part of the 1600s. Over time, these different groups developed trading relationships, intermarried, and banded together to create a powerful collectivity able to defend its interests. European recognition of the people as Choctaw and as a collectivity fed into the Choctaw's own growing sense of themselves as a distinct people.[36] The anthropologists Brian Haley and Larry Wilcoxon analyze kin lineages and historical documents to explain the ethnogenesis of the "neo-Chumash" Indians (Chumash are not Indian in the sense of descent from contact-era Indian communities). The neo-Chumash began as immigrants from the northwestern Mexico frontier who between the 1500s and late 1990s shifted through a range of identifications, from "Gente de razón" to "Californio" to "White Spanish," before coming to identify themselves and to be identified as Chumash.[37] Similarly, the archaeologist Alison Bell explains how over time a diverse grouping of Europeans in the seventeenth-century Chesapeake region of Virginia crafted an encompassing category, White, that permitted them a sense of sameness while cleaving clear demarcation between them and the Africans and Native Americans among them.[38] The anthropologist Dru Gladney shows how the contemporary Uighur people of Eastern and Central Asia over the course of centuries "lost" their name (but not their identity) while transitioning from steppe nomads to a federation of tribes to traders and then to a national minority that officially "regained" the name Uighur during the mid-1930s, when a Soviet administrator making official designations discovered and revived the name.[39] Historical and contemporary peoples have tangled and complicated histories that are expressed at least partially though their identities. An ethnogenesis approach provides a way to untangle intricate histories and identities.

Groups' origins and evolution are complex. A collectivity might emerge in different places at different times under different conditions. However, with persistent research and appropriate evidence, one can explain such complex ethnogenesis. For example, the Métis of Canada and the United States trace their origins to French, English, or Scottish colonists and Native Americans like the Cree or Chippewa. They formed at different points during the 1800s, developing across Saskatchewan, Alberta, Manitoba, and Ontario, Canada, and the Great Lakes region of the United States. The Métis self-identify and are identified by non-Métis as embodying mixed White and Native American ancestry but are nevertheless recognized as indigenous people by Canada's government. The Métis remained mostly obscure until the 1960s, when they began to organize for recognition. The Métis represent a case of a scattered grouping of people with similar backgrounds and experience—fur trading, hunting, mixed ancestry, linguistic distinctiveness, dispossession, and discriminated against—seeking to create a coherent collective identity.[40]

Archaeologists have made substantial recent contributions to explaining ethnogenesis.[41] For example, some of them are drawing on theories of ethnicity to explain collective identifications of the prehistorical and historical past. "Ethnicity" describes the characteristics of an "ethnos" (i.e., ethnic group), such as an assumed shared common ancestry, shared experience, and shared cultural beliefs and practices taken to be emblematic of a collective, such as cosmology, dress, speech, or music. An ethnos's claims about itself need not be based in verifiable evidence. People make up their origins and lineage all the time. The challenge is to distinguish fact from fantasy. Fantasy is important, though, because it may have cultural significance, telling something that the collectivity believes important. Archaeologists are drawing attention to ethnicity concepts such as instrumentality. Instrumentality involves how collectivities use their identity, say, for political purposes such as gaining official recognition or for ritual purposes that reinforce a sense of being a collective. Archaeologists challenge the predominant sociocultural anthropological focus on the emic or self-perspective of collectivities to explicitly incorporate an etic or outsider and analytic perspective. What do outsiders like colonizers or anthropologists think about a given collectivity in relation to any emic evidence? Archaeologists like Mark Hudson promote an etic perspective in tandem with an emic perspective because there are prehistorical and historical collectivities whose emic perspective is inaccessible because of a lack of evidence or because existing accounts of outsiders like colonizers or missionaries may misrepresent the people they write about.[42]

Nevertheless, these scholars and others who have resuscitated ethnicity and cleverly integrated it with ethnogenesis risk reducing the discourse to ethnic groups.[43] Absent intellectual vigilance, analysts might slide down into a muddy pool of unresolved ethnicity squabbles of old: Who is ethnic and who is not? Are Sephardic and Ashkenazi Jews a separate or the same Jewish ethnicity? Or what about Native American peoples such as the Paiute, Eastern Shoshone, or Western Cherokee? Are they ethnic groups, or would designating them "ethnic" clash with their Indigenous status? Perhaps all fit some conception of ethnicity. Such conundrums delimit our focus on the dynamics of group formation, which is the crux of an ethnogenetic analysis: how a given group forms and evolves over time. My approach is about group formation, whether ethnic, religious, racial, political, community, or some other collectivity. The Rastafari of Jamaica are instructive in that, like living Venn diagrams, they embody multiple intersecting categories of faith, race, and ethnicity.

Ethnic or not, Christianity is an instructive example of ethnogenesis. Like Christians, the Rastafari trace their origins to a core group of charismatic leadership, and they suffered persecution from adversaries bent on liquidating them. Christians emerged as a localized handful of people committed to the charismatic figure Jesus Christ and—notwithstanding persecution and fragmentation—evolved into a global, diverse collectivity. The Rastafari began with the evangelism of several charismatic men concerned with Black identity, suffered persecution from adversaries, and evolved into a diverse and global collectivity and identity. An important difference between the two, though, is that evangelists and missionaries aggressively recruited people to become Christians (using their message and, sometimes, by force), while Rastafari growth has occurred without a methodical practice of recruitment. True, individuals are at the heart of Rastafari ethnogenesis, but the decisions of individuals to become Rastafari are insufficient to understand how the Rastafari became a durable collectivity. What the sprawling literature of ethnogenesis lacks is a framework that specifies the key processes at work across different cases at different times in different places.

Collective Identity Formation and Ethnogenesis

Interest in collective identity has increased for nearly two decades because it facilitates asking and answering new questions about how collectivities form and evolve. Focusing on social movements, for example, the sociologists Francesca Polletta and James Jasper see collective identity as a way to explain how and why collectivities emerge when they do, why people participate in them, and how collective actors make the choices that they do.[44] By addressing such questions, the roles of power, politics, culture, environment, temporality, and subjectivity become relevant, enlarging the scope of the analytic frame.

Collective identity formation is an essential part of ethnogenesis. We can treat identity formation and ethnogenesis as mutually associated without totally conflating them. My emphasis is on both "formation" and "process," the actions through which people generate and employ a collective identity. "Identification" describes the "activation" of collective identity—how people use the categories that constitute a collective identity.[45] Through collective identity, people create a sense of belonging, a basis for solidarity, a basis for action, grounded in a sense of real and imagined relationships with political ramifications. Yet members may disagree over how to frame their collective identity; one result of such a dispute is variation in key categorical frameworks that members draw on. For example, Christian denominations are legion. They may recognize the Father, the Son, the Holy Ghost, and sacred scripture but differ significantly over ideology and practice, thus drafting boundaries and crafting narratives that distinguish their own frames from those of other Christians. Interpretations of categorical frameworks change over time; thus, collective identity is dynamic and malleable, though members may portray their identity as ancient or unchanging, as do some Rastafari. Members do not exert sole control over their collective identification: nonmembers can influence it through their involvement with identifications (and people) they do not claim as their own. In fundamental ways, ethnogenesis involves social and cognitive processes of group formation and group behavior consonant with development of collective identity.

A collective identity is social in how its existence and meanings derive from members and nonmembers. Collective identity is different from personal or individual identity. Though ultimately embodied by individuals, collective identity is shared with others. It is both an achieved and ascribed identity, both subjective and objective. It is achieved and subjective in the sense that agency is involved in how individuals develop their relation to and understanding of a collective identity; some measure of self-definition as a member must be involved. A collective identity is ascribed and objective in how nonmembers mark members with their own symbols and labels and in how members mark each other. Persons may be phenotypically dark in complexion, have tightly coiled hair, and speak a distinctive dialect; however, this does not inherently make them African, Black Jamaican, or something else, unless they themselves see it that way. At the same time, members and nonmembers may treat someone with such characteristics as if they were African or a Black Jamaican or something else, even though the person might vehemently reject the categorization. Even when members disagree with nonmember labels, their identity may be rendered more salient by the act of misrecognition: "By defining me as something that I am not, you have made me more aware of my own identity and what I should think about it." The tension between achievement and ascription is a fundamental aspect of collective identity formation. Rastafari ethnogenesis has been a dialectical exchange between and among the efforts of Rastafari and non-Rastafari to define what constitutes Rastafari.

Collective identity formation involves the generation and internalization of sameness and difference. Sameness encompasses how members recognize and evaluate each other according to perceived commitment to and competence in group beliefs, practices, and experiences. However, we should not understand sameness as uniformity. Difference comprises the ways in which members distinguish themselves from nonmembers or from members who reframe identity-relevant categories. Indeed, members of a collectivity may clash over the "right" interpretation or practice of a frame, as theories of collective identity suggest.

My conception of ethnogenetic collective identity formation emphasizes four interrelated factors: (1) evaluation and recognition of the self and other; (2) attachment, interdependence, solidarity, and belonging; (3) meaning, ideology, and narrative; and (4) contention.[46]

(1) Evaluation concerns how members and nonmembers positively and negatively assess a given collective identification. It involves self- and other recognition, achieved and ascribed identities, and the drawing of (shifting and permeable) boundaries within and across identity frames. Members have varied degrees of emotional connection to a collective identity, have varied understandings of and reactions to how others treat them, and have varied understandings of how their personal fate is intertwined with that of the collectivity. (2) Nonetheless, the notions of attachment, interdependence, solidarity, belonging, and involvement remind us of the bonding features of collective identity. Bonding can be facilitated and enhanced by members' participation in activities that cast the identity into relief, such as rituals or collectivity-relevant practices: living in proximity, participating in particular occupations, or sharing experience of oppression, suppression, or repression.[47] (3) A collectivity's identity is based in meaning—people define, explain, and value who they are and what they believe in, in ways that are evocative to them.

Members' beliefs about themselves constitute an ideology. They create narratives to tell their history, experience, and relation to other collectivities to express their values. At least some beliefs about themselves and others are "identity scripts." The script analogy borrows from stage direction and actor lines to underscore how identities are connected to audiences and understandings.[48] For example, Rastafari-identity scripts provide clues as to what is expected of a Rastafari: Rastas are peace-loving; Rastas are dangerous; Rastas are vegetarians; Rastas smoke cannabis (ganja); and countless other claims. An identity script need not be accurate; it can also be misapplied: not all Rastafari smoke cannabis. Therefore, one might question the identity of a Rastafari who does not smoke cannabis. One may embrace parts of an identity script—Emperor Selassie is the returned Messiah—while neglecting (or rejecting) other parts such as physical repatriation to Ethiopia. The ability to revise and improvise an identity script is a source of creativity, dynamism, and conflict. (4) We should consider whether rivalry, competition, or conflict with other collectivities affects members' experiences and understandings of their collective identity. Contention can facilitate oppositional consciousness (though it does not have to be the cause of it), in which a sense of "we-ness" or solidarity is heightened because of conflict with other groups or institutions.[49] Between the 1930s and 1970s, contention played a central role in Rastafari ethnogenesis in Jamaica.

Any new group like the Rastafari seeks to legitimize its own discourse and delegitimize competing discourses (e.g., other Jamaican religions). Relevant here is the identity work whereby people invent boundaries between "us" (the Rastafari) and "them" (the non-Rastafari). The Rastafari defined who they were while distinguishing themselves from other faiths and other Jamaicans. During Leonard Howell's trial for sedition, he sat for questioning. His testimony was thusly summarized: "After 1934 every Church must be closed down, for the spirit of God did not exist in the churches, as it was ONLY LIP WORSHIP. The clergymen were not telling them the truth, and a great shame would come over them."[50] Howell issued a challenge. He denounced the churches and charged their clergy with miseducation, insinuating that the Rastafari were different from the Christian denominations, that they were a superior alternative. Outsiders reinforced difference, especially through demonization and persecution. Yet the Rastafari were not deterred from becoming because of defamation or abuse. Rastafari efforts to validate their own discourse and invalidate competing discourses spawned animosity, contention, and violent reprisal from non-Rastafari. In a letter to the "Officer Administering the Government," the Jamaican Francilla McNish told how she and a female companion were assaulted by a district constable because they were known to entertain the Rastafari message.[51]

On the basis of the preceding analysis, I propose five general propositions about ethnogenesis that consider collective identity formation.

Fundamental Processes of Ethnogenesis

Ethnogenesis entails collective identity formation, though what this looks like should be spelled out in each case. Five factors are common to ethnogenesis: (1) power asymmetry; (2) nonlinearity; (3) engines of growth; (4) nonmember effects; and (5) and mobilization of cultural or ecological resources.

Factors that catalyze ethnogenesis—that generate the conditions for new and reconfigured peoples and identifications—include oppression, inequity, colonization, migration, dislocation, conquest, social movements, ecological factors, or some combination thereof. These factors are implied in the first proposition—power asymmetry—because groups are not equal in the power that they can wield over others and because such factors contribute to power disparities. Power asymmetries, however, infuse other aspects of ethnogenesis, like nonmember effects, engines of growth, or mobilization of resources. We must determine the role of power in a group's ethnogenesis—such as its ability to exercise agency in its own interests. For example, Jamaican elites could use the resources and power of government against the Rastafari, and news media organizations could widely broadcast negative images of the Rastafari. It was not that the Rastafari were powerless; rather, the ways in which different groups exercised power is vital to explaining their development.

Proposition 2: the nonlinearity of ethnogenesis. One cannot predict a group's developmental trajectory, though one might confidently offer ideas about the short-term direction of development. Our inability to predict group development with certainty is simple: emergence means that unpredictability always lurks as a spoiler to any claim to predict what might happen in the world of human interaction. In a February

1937 Colonial Secretary Office (CSO) memo, an unidentified citizen wrote to Jamaica's colonial governor, Edward Denham, noting that the Kingston–St. Andrew Civic League had complained about "the vile of the Rastafari doctrine." The citizen went on to tell Denham that the good citizens of Kingston had little to concern themselves with because of the "sound common sense of the great majority of the inhabitants. . . . [The] doctrines of the Ras Tafarists will not appeal to more than a very small number of feeble-minded persons."[52] Howell and Hinds had completed their prison terms by 1937, and both had gone underground, along with their followers. The CSO expected the Rastafari's demise anytime. It soon had a surprise. In retrospect, we can see that the Rastafari were incubating, reconstituting. They would reappear in a few years in significant numbers. The Rastafari had been "disrupted" by their antagonists but not destroyed. Soon it would be they who would perturb the colonial polity. We must pay attention to how disruption and other surprises shape members and outsiders. We must consider that there are multiple causes of ethnogenesis, interacting in complex ways, that there are multiple paths of development, and that development evolves across multiple locations.

Proposition 3: engines of growth. We must identify the factors that facilitate or inhibit the development and durability of a collectivity. How is a collective identity diffused so that others can claim or rebuff it? Engines of growth involve a collectivity developing new sources of adherents, new networks, or new alliances, incorporating new or re-purposed technologies, voluntary or forced migration, or the effects of persecution, conflict, or other power asymmetries. For the Rastafari, I use the notion of "vector" to identify and describe the factors contributing to the growth and spread of the Rastafari. The Rastafari commune Pinnacle, for example, is both an engine of growth and a vector. Occupied in considerable numbers from approximately late 1939 until the mid-1950s, Pinnacle rested in rural St. Catherine's Parish atop a lofty and craggy hill. Reflecting on the first iteration of Pinnacle (it was twice stormed by major police raids), a writer explained, "Years ago he [Howell] had summoned them [Rastafari] from all parts of the island. . . . He had told them that Pinnacle was to be their kingdom. They obeyed him and selling all their belongings flocked in from the different parishes and lived a community life, on the principle of 'one for all and all for one,' pooling their earnings and their food, often eating at the same communal board."[53] Pinnacle became a Rastafari stronghold and an engine of growth for the Rastafari because it spurred adherent growth and offered stability (the industriousness and mystique of the community attracted people). Engines of growth shift over time. By the 1970s, Pinnacle was a dimming memory, and reggae music had become an engine of growth because it grew the ranks of the Rastafari by disseminating their beliefs. Reggae's popularity declined by the 2000s, however, along with its influence in attracting new members. Along with engines of growth are factors that work against group persistence, such as the countless efforts to eradicate the Rastafari, as we will see.

Proposition 4: the involvement of nonmembers or outsiders in ethnogenesis. Groups do not evolve in isolation. We must identify what and how outside institutions, groups, roles, ideas, and individuals influence how members interpret their experience and identity. For example, outsiders may ascribe pejorative characteristics to members. In a *Daily Gleaner* story, an observer recounted how Jamaican men in St. Thomas Parish "believed that if they allowed their beards to grow—this they were actually told by their leaders—they would use them to part the waters through which they would march to Abyssinia! . . . Their chins became bearded, so much so that a few persons of higher intelligence incurred the risk of prosecution for assault, when they held some of the deluded creatures and scraped the hair from their faces."[54] From his media platform, the writer provided people with ideas about how to treat and characterize the Rastafari. Jamaicans of higher intelligence should discipline those of lower intelligence, like the Rastafari, forcibly if necessary.

Members internalize, reject, or revise negative identity scripts. In the canonical language book *Jamaica Talk*, the linguist Frederic Cassidy reports that "Congo" describes a person who "is the butt of his fellows" and that "Bongo" is a derogatory term for African, Black, or an "article of poor quality."[55] The Rastafari men were dubbed "Congos" and "Bongos"—clowns, people of low worth and intelligence—in the sight of their fellow Jamaicans. They internalized the labels, revised them, and rejected the stigma. They turned "Bongo" and "Congo" into titles of honor. The point is that nonmembers *and* members shape ethnogenesis and collective identity formation.

Proposition 5: mobilization of cultural or ecological resources. Members use cultural or ecological resources to establish identity in the many ways described earlier, for example, to distinguish themselves and to produce "sameness" and as "material" for creating narratives about themselves. Proposition 5 entails (a) members generating ideologies and origin narratives that "naturalize" or "essentialize" their identity and beliefs; (b) members creating activities such as rituals and celebrations to nurture and communicate their identity and beliefs; and subpropositions a and b are directly relevant to (c) identity scripts. Identity scripts articulate sameness and difference, are elements of group narratives, and assist in the identity work entailed in rituals and community activities. During Howell's and Hinds's sedition trial in March 1934, Assistant Attorney General Radcliffe asked Hinds, "Did you tell them [his audiences] Ras Tafari was their king"? Hinds replied, "Yes sir. I told them he was Jesus Christ, Son of God, King of Kings."[56] Although the Rastafari doctrine was still inchoate, they would draw on Old and New Testament scripture, Ethiopianism, Ethiopianist tracts, and other cultural resources to cast themselves as anointed people in their complex identity script, which connected ancient Israel and Africa to contemporary Jamaica and contemporary Africa. Members create and revise stories about their origins, history, and identity that brand themselves distinctive and different from nonmembers. Therefore, we must identify the cultural resources marshaled in the construction of collective identity and historical narratives. Lastly, (d) ecological resources may shape a collectivity's identity. For example, the fortune of many Indigenous people of North America's plains briefly rested on the buffalo and the horse. A disruption to their ecological resources—a decline in buffalo herds—affected their survival, persistence, and collective identity. The Rastafari developed the concept of Ital living, which rejected industrial production and exalted notions of living and eating in harmony with nature. An extreme standpoint in 1950s Jamaica, Ital living became appealing during the 1980s and beyond to an international world whose citizens increasingly cited the benefits of living and eating in harmony with the physical environment.

The five ethnogenesis propositions inform my analysis but should also draw the reader's attention to the complex assortment of interactions and activities involved in Rastafari ethnogenesis. For example, there is the power asymmetry between the colonial government and the

Rastafari; there are the Rastafari innovations utilizing local and foreign cultural resources; there are the different vectors at work, such as the Pinnacle commune that aided the incubation and growth of the Rastafari; there are outsider influences such as police brutality and media depictions of the Rastafari in the press; and there is the unpredictability attendant to the nonlinear nature of Rastafari ethnogenesis itself, for instance, how they teetered between the spreading allure they presented to growing numbers of Jamaicans and their persisting status as pariahs. These five propositions, independently and in combination, address general but significant elements of ethnogenesis that explain Rastafari collective identity and experience.

* * *

We can better understand a group's identity by specifying the cultural matrix of their origins and by charting how they evolve over time, attentive to the interaction of power, cultural resources, nonmembers, and the often unpredictable results of these dynamic interactions. Let us now turn to examine in detail the initial conditions that gave rise to the Rastafari.

2

Initial Conditions

*Converging Streams of Moral Black Consciousness
in Jamaica and Elites' Fear of Black Supremacy*

"Blessed be the King of Israel," chanted Ethiopian bishops, priests, princes, "high dignitaries," and others during a tour of the grand Cathedral of St. George in Addis Ababa. It was November 1930, during the final ceremony of King Ras Tafari's coronation, and they were led by the newly crowned Emperor Haile Selassie I and Empress Menen.[1] During the late 1990s, I noticed that an elder Rastafari woman, Prophetess Esther, had painted the words "King of Israel" in several places on the walls of her temple and compound. Throughout Jamaica, particularly in Kingston, a keen observer can find "King of Israel" scrawled graffiti-like on any medium that will convey the message. The King of Israel, for these Jamaicans, is Emperor Haile Selassie. Rasta Ivey, a first-generation Rastafari woman, almost ninety years old when I met her in 1998, told me that "[Robert] Hinds speak of King Melchizedec and King of Israel; him say Black people is [modern-day] Israelites and Melchizedec is their king."[2] The inscrutable Melchizedec is an Old Testament figure, both a king and a high priest described as "without father, without mother, without descent, having neither beginning of days, nor end of life; but made like unto the Son of God."[3] He heralds Christ, serving as the base of a lineage that includes King David, Christ, and Emperor Selassie as successor to Christ.

The designation "King of Israel" seats the Emperor among exalted biblical company, including the other "good" kings of the United Kingdom of Israel and Judah, in particular Kings David and Solomon. The book of Isaiah (11:1) proclaims that "there shall come forth a rod out of the stem of Jesse, and a Branch shall grow out of his roots." Jesse was the father of King David, and Jesus Christ was the branch. However, Christ was not the final fruit born of the Branch of David; indeed, the line of David can be imagined as persisting indeterminably into the future. Christ, according to biblical scripture, promised humankind that after his crucifixion he would return to rule and redeem humankind in a new and equitable dispensation. People have interpreted this ancient narrative in innumerable ways, with race being a significant trope in some versions.[4] The Rastafari are exemplars in this regard. The Rastafari of the early 1930s maintained that the crowning of King Ras Tafari as Emperor signaled the fruiting of the branch once again, the inauguration of a new dispensation for the world and people of African descent, in particular.

Thus, we have a script soaked with anciency, an account that people of the present draw on to define and present themselves to themselves and to the world. Parts of the script are age-old; however, the people, the Rastafari, were born in the twentieth century. *Fundamentally, a new group must acquire an identity.* There is, however, always a backdrop—history—to collective identity formation, and like an elaborately painted canvas to set a stage, we focus on the actors in the foreground but not at the expense of the backdrop. It is crucial to interpreting what the actors do and say.

The stories that follow detail the initial conditions of Rastafari ethnogenesis between the 1890s and early 1930s. Jamaica was fertile ground for Black resistance and millenarian movements long before the Rastafari. Factors and people converged, however, in ways that made possible an identity and people called Rastafari. Issues of imperial control, elite fears, and Black political agency were intertwined with race, religion, resistance, and moral concerns. Even the people who would become key actors in the emergence of the Rastafari could not entirely fathom their role and impact, only their own desires and goals. Ostensibly discrete events and actors—people and happenings in Jamaica, Central Africa, Central America, the United States, and Ethiopia—generated something greater than its many parts. Many small things added to something far greater, but there was no logic for determining how things would "add up."

Bedward the Healer, the Prophet, and the Savior of Black Jamaicans

Alexander Bedward became a part of a long line of critics of Jamaican colonialism and White supremacy. Bedward merged Revival religion with appeals to the grievances and desires of Black Jamaicans and with public displays of resistance. His concerns about and methods of mobilizing rank-and-file Black Jamaicans along the lines of Black resistance would be echoed in the Rastafari movement.

Bedward catalyzed a movement that cohered around spiritual and physical healing, prophetic revelation, and a racial critique of colonialism in Jamaica. The critique was blunt: White supremacy had run its course, and it was time for Black people to rule. Through the examination of Bedward's case, we can gain a sense of an emergent pattern of elite reaction to Black religio-racial leaders. Bedward became a triple threat to elites: he competed for religious attention, he competed with the healing power of doctors, and he mobilized Black Jamaicans. He and his followers brought religio-racial collective action to the attention of elites, and in response, elites developed strategies of surveillance, arrest, and public ridicule to contain, if not destroy, such efforts. These strategies in turn influenced attitudes toward the Rastafari. Policies such as the Obeah Act (1898) and Medical Law (1908), discussed in chapter 1, were formed while Bedward was active to suppress Black grassroots religious activities, and the Seditious Meetings Act (1836), intended to curtail the religious activities of Black Jamaicans, was repurposed to police the speech of religio-racial leaders.

We also gain perspective on the vectors through which Bedward's script traveled: public sermons, news reports, and word of mouth. Cultural continuity and cultural matrix (or environment) are relevant here to collective identity formation because dominant tropes among the Bedwardites, such as a Black Christ, deliverance, and a religio-racial critique of colonialism, were continued (though differently) by the Rastafari, as were direct connections between Bedwardites and the Rastafari. Bedward's man Robert Hinds became one of the first Rastafari evangelists, while other Bedwardites, like Rasta Ivey, one of the few first-generation Rastafari women we have an account of, became Rastafari.

Bedward was a reluctant warrior who probably would have been totally content to focus on his ministry. His message became successful, drawing followers and attention, and both got him into trouble. Had Bedward been less successful in his art and mission, he might have been no more than a blip on this historical radar. Between 1892 and 1895, constables, news reporters, physicians, medical officials, businessmen, ministers, and others attended Bedward's sermons and healing ceremonies to prove that he was engaged in illicit, unethical, and uncivilized practices.

While we have much to learn about Bedward's history and his influence on his fellow Jamaicans, we know a bit about his life trajectory.[5] Born in St. Andrew's Parish, Jamaica, in 1859, he left for Colon, Panama, in 1883, hoping the climate would cure an unknown illness that tortured him.[6] In 1885, Bedward had visions that he interpreted as calling him to return to Jamaica and become a healer, which was what he did.

In October 1891, Bedward formally began his ministration with the Jamaica Native Baptist Church.[7] During his early years, Bedward was described as standing about "five feet ten in height and miserably thin and emaciated. His step, however, was full of vigor and he seemed to be possessed of a good deal of strength, . . . being perhaps 35 years of age. His eyes were perhaps the most characteristic of his features. They were small and very blood shot, scarcely a particle of white showing."[8] In December 1891, Bedward saw in a vision that the water in the Mona River of upper St. Andrew Parish had healing power. One of Bedward's detractors reported later that an "ignorant black man [Bedward] living somewhere in the Long Mountain announced . . . that he had been chosen from amongst the rest of [the] people to perform certain miracles. . . . In his dream he was told that there was a river near August Town . . . which would heal and cure diseases and sickness of every description. He was instructed how the water was to be administered—without money and without price."[9] The detractor told how "the news of this alleged miraculous recovery was assiduously spread by Bedward and a few of his following with the result that he soon found himself at the head of a large gathering. . . . He selected Wednesday for his appearance and demonstration. . . . It has become quite an institution."[10] Effective and charismatic healers can draw large followings.

The Bedward "Craze": Crescendo to Sedition

By the beginning of 1895, Bedward had become such a threat to Jamaica's colonial status quo that elites determined to liquidate him by charging him with sedition.

By mid-1893, thousands of people were showing up for Bedward's Wednesday healing assembly. On one Wednesday in early September 1893, observers estimated that approximately twelve thousand people were present.[11] A group of Whites, acquaintances and employees of the *Daily Gleaner*, attended one of Bedward's river "dipping" ceremonies. They reported that at the river, Black Jamaicans "were packed like sardines in a tin on either bank for at least a hundred yards on either side of the road. . . . For nearly a quarter of a mile one could see men, perfectly nude, bathing in the water, and on the left were women in the same condition."[12] In contemporary terms, Bedward had gone viral.

Bedward had to be cut down to size. He had too many followers, and people were switching their religious allegiance to him. At a Wednesday river "dipping" ceremony, some clergy showed up and pleaded with the disrobing and already-nude supplicants to forswear Bedward's authority. A woman preparing to imbibe the Mona waters told the naysaying clergy that she "would rather follow Bedward than the ministers, that Bedward was God's servant and more powerful than they."[13] The campaign to liquidate Bedward attacked his reputation and mental faculty. Bedward allegedly told a Dr. Bronstorph that he was a "man sent from God, that God had appeared to him in a dream, and that he possessed miraculous powers."[14] Bronstorph examined Bedward and concluded that he was "insane—dangerously so—and suffering from religious monomania" and recommended that he be sent immediately to the lunatic asylum.[15] Such a conclusion was not unusual for the time: "Mental health problems were also attributed to obeah and more generally to popular religion. The Jamaican Lunatic Asylum's annual reports always listed 'religious excitement' as a cause of insanity."[16] Such reports by the *Daily Gleaner* about Bedward were a glimpse of what became an informal strategy: pathologize and ridicule Black religio-racial leaders to discredit them.

"We Must Oppress the White Wall": The Seditious Speech

On January 16, 1895, Bedward delivered a sermon to a crowd of roughly a thousand. The speech became the grounds for his arrest and prosecution for sedition. John Lanigan, a *Daily Gleaner* subeditor, and police inspector William Calder attended the sermon, along with other constables.

Lanigan claimed that he recorded Bedward's speech in shorthand, while Calder said that he scribbled notes on his shirtsleeve cuff, which he claimed he later rewrote and used for his official police report.[17] Inspector Calder's actions exemplified the shoddy evidence gathering that would also plague Howell, Hinds, and other early Rastafari.

On January 21, at 2:30 a.m., thirty policemen, five inspectors, and three "mounted orderlies" jammed into two "wagonettes" and swooped down on the abode of an unsuspecting Alexander Bedward to arrest him.[18] I quote at length the arrest warrant read to Bedward to make the point that the 1895 speech has been commonly presented in scholarship as if it were the actual speech rather than the *Daily Gleaner*'s rendition of what Bedward said and meant. The indictment described Bedward as a "wicked, malicious, seditious and evil disposed person" who was "contriving and intending the peace of Our Lady the Queen and of this island to disquiet and disturb, . . . to incite and to move to hatred and dislike . . . [of] the Queen and of the Government . . . [and to incite] insurrections, riots, tumults and breach of the Peace." The indictment alleged that Bedward said (with the *Daily Gleaner*'s translation in brackets),

> We [meaning hereby the black subjects of our said Lady the Queen in this island] are the true people; the white men [meaning hereby the subjects of the Queen . . . other than the black subjects aforesaid] are hypocrites, robbers, and thieves. They [meaning thereby the white men aforesaid] are all liars. . . . Hell will be your [meaning thereby the liege subjects] portion if you do not rise up and crush the white men. The time is coming, I tell you the time coming. There is a white wall and a black wall, [meaning thereby that there were black and also white subjects of our said Lady the Queen] and the white wall has been closing round the black wall; but now the black wall has become bigger than the white wall and they must knock the white wall down. The white wall has oppressed us [meaning thereby the said Alexander Bedward, himself and the other black subjects] for years; now we must oppress the white wall. . . . Let them remember the Morant War [meaning thereby an insurrection which arose nearly 30 years ago at Morant Bay (Jamaica)].[19]

To the extent that the speech accurately represented Bedward's attitude and concerns, it spoke to the grievance-laden leitmotifs of the religio-racial and anticolonial discourses circulating through Jamaica, leitmotifs that the Rastafari would adapt to their own purposes. Such ideas and words could be used to stir emotions and mobilize people into a community. Some elites were genuinely fearful that Bedward could incite his followers to insurrection. Philip Stern, Bedward's lawyer, warned that a trial might stir up Bedward's followers and turn him into a "martyr."[20]

Two Black constables present at the speech heard something different from what was published in the *Daily Gleaner* and what was presented in the court. The different interpretations underscore the ways in which race informed Jamaican's thinking. Whites emphasized blasphemy and insurrection; Blacks emphasized slavery and freedom. Sergeant Nelson, a Black officer, held that this is what he heard: "The Pharisees and Sadducees are here. . . . Every minister and every doctor is a thief and a liar. When the Governor try to do something for the people, the ministers go in the Council and tell the Governor 'no.' Your [European] forefathers came from over yonder, and put pothooks and hand cuffs . . . on my grandfather's and grandmother's necks. Thanks to God we take them off now. . . . I am the rock and I will trample you. There is a white wall and a black wall, and the black wall will have to fall on the white wall and crush them."[21] Bedward's targets, said Nelson, were ministers and physicians, primarily because they had come to his meetings and disparaged him.[22] They were the Pharisees and Sadducees, while Bedward was the Christ who rebuked them. Inspector James, a Black member of the St. Andrew Constabulary, said that he had attended many of Bedward's meetings and never heard him utter seditious language. The conflicting testimony of the constables failed to strengthen Bedward's case.

"You Don't Know How the Black People Are Treated": Liquidating Bedward, Part 1

A *Daily Gleaner* representative visited Bedward in August Town after the arrest to interview him. Bedward told the interviewer (whom he assumed to be from the United States), "You do not understand the people here."[23] Using the color of the back of his hand to emphasize race, Bedward continued,

The people of my own colour are not so bad. It is the white and the co-loured [Brown people]. They have tried to kill me but they can't do it. I tell you that the day of reckoning is coming for them. . . . The people who come from other places believe in me and know that I am the servant of Jesus. The white people are the oppressors. This is a black man's country and the black man must rule it. . . . You don't know how the black people are treated.[24]

Bedward identified Whites and Browns as oppressors, along with some of his own "color." The Rastafari too would condemn Whites and their Brown and Black allies.

Chief Justice Sir Henry Hancock presided over the trial of Bedward, who, dressed in a white suit, sat stoically throughout his trial. Justice Hancock defined sedition as a "malicious endeavor by word or deed or writing to promote public disorder or to induce riot, rebellion, or civil war and these words must be spoken with the intent to produce the consequences . . . necessary to constitute sedition."[25] We have here a definition of sedition that was worked out and used to silence grass-roots dissent. The jury foreman, Mr. Archibald Munro, read aloud to the court, "We are satisfied that the accused did make use of the sedi-tious language with which he is charged; but he is acquitted on the ground of insanity."[26] Bedward was ordered to the lunatic asylum for an undetermined period and released a month or so later. Bedward had been shut down, for a while at least. The record of what Bedward did after release from the asylum is sparse. He did, however, reconstruct his ministry.

"I Must Take Out the Children": Liquidating Bedward, Part 2

Twenty-five years later, Bedward again became the focus of the elites. In this iteration, Bedward was not so much the healer of bodies and souls. He now promoted a millenarian and messianic message and referred to himself as the Son of God, commanded by his father to redeem his oppressed Black children. He had a core unit of loyalists who embraced his identity claims and who were unafraid of clashing with the police. One of the loyalists was Robert Hinds, who twelve years later would serve as Rastafari Leonard Howell's lieutenant.

Bedward claimed in December 1920 that he would soar to heaven on the thirty-first of the month. Once more, thousands of people converged on August Town, seeking out the prophet Bedward. He said that after his ascension, he would return to gather a select group of his followers and that the world would end. Bedward's apocalyptic proclamation gave pause to his detractors because he again reminded them of his ability to inspire the Black rank and file: "the deluded people who believed this [Bedward's] story sold at a sacrifice all their belongings and betook themselves to August Town, handing over all their worldly possessions in the shape of money or whatever they had that could easily be converted into money, to this so called 'Prophet.'"[27] Jamaicans have on numerous occasions demonstrated their readiness to leave Jamaica, long before the Rastafari came along. Supernatural departure was one way; physical relocation another, as we shall see with the Rastafari.

On the day of the proposed ascension, "There was a chair prepared, and covered with white cloth," which Bedward "put on top of a platform in his church. From that chair he was to have ascended. The day came, however, but he did not go up."[28] Rasta Ivey, a first-generation Rastafari who was also a Bedwardite, vociferously disagreed with this account of Bedward's promise to venture into the heavens.[29] She believed that by flight into the heavens, Bedward meant that he would take an airplane trip, but he did not let on that this was his plan. Perhaps Bedward sought to astonish both his adherents and detractors by using the then-new technology of flight, the first Black man to fly in an airplane in Jamaica. One of the first flights in Jamaica dated to December 1911; more than one thousand people showed up to witness the historic event. Commercial flight was still a decade away when Bedward made his claim in 1921.

Many people believed that Bedward's flight stunt was a flop and that, as a result, he sought to redeem himself by one-upping himself: He would lead a protest march eleven kilometers from August Town to Kingston to deliver his "children" from oppression and impending calamity. On the night of April 26, 1921, Sergeant Williams traveled with Inspector Wright to August Town. Bedward was apparently preparing to march to Kingston the next day. He claimed that the Lord had commanded him, the Son of the Lord, to deliver his people in Kingston. Inspector Wright said that he asked Bedward to forgo leading the procession the next day. His reply was fired in stridence and determination: "I must go, I must obey my father. Do you know who I am? I am the Lord Jesus Christ. Must I obey you and disobey the command of my father? The only way I do not take out the children you must cut off my neck or kill me now."[30] On April 27, 1921, Bedward and a band of hundreds of his followers tramped along Parochial Road heading toward Kingston. He was stopped by Sergeant Williams and arrested.

In this second iteration of confrontation, Bedward was not reluctant; he came off as a righteous warrior. He was perhaps seeking to fulfill his idea of the Black wall closing in the White wall, that is, catalyzing Black dominion. He imagined that he was a Black savior who had "returned to free his people."[31] With this context, we can see that the idea of Emperor Selassie as a Black Messiah was not at all far-fetched given a cultural matrix where those who claimed to be mortal Messiahs are a regular occurrence.

Bedward was not alone in his belief that he was the Son of God. Robert Hinds, of Linstead, Jamaica, and four other men were held for medical observation because they told the judge that "Bedward is Jesus Christ."[32] Dr. Edwards noted that "every one of them firmly believe that Bedward is Jesus Christ." The judge confronted Hinds and company, mockingly: "I cannot understand how you get such extraordinary ideas into your head. . . . I may tell you at once that Bedward your leader, is going to the Asylum: and when that person whom you believe is Jesus Christ is locked up you will realize how foolish your belief."[33] The judge believed that locking up Bedward would cause his adherents to recognize their error. However, Hinds did not abandon his idea of a Black Messiah. He would on more than one occasion be admonished by a judge for his conviction in a Black Messiah. One admonishment was meted out by a former attorney general that served in Nyasaland, Central Africa.

Ethiopianist Movements in Nyasaland and Jamaica: John Chilembwe and the Chief Justice Lyall-Grant Connection

During the 1880s, Ethiopianism developed in areas of Central and Southern Africa. African American ministers visiting Central and Southern Africa, Africans who had visited the United States, and publications such as the African Methodist Episcopal (AME) Church's *Review* and the *Missionary Review of the World* were vectors that circulated Ethiopianism in Africa.

Robert Lyall-Grant, once a colonial administrator in Kenya, would play an influential role in the early phase of Rastafari ethnogenesis. During Lyall-Grant's time working in Africa, he learned how anti-White rebellions of indigenous Africans in Kenya and Nyasaland were linked with the ideas of Ethiopianism and incipient Black nationalism. Lyall-Grant chaired the commission that published the "Nyasaland Native Rising Commission Report," a study of the causes of the John Chilembwe rebellion.[34] Lyall-Grant later relocated to Jamaica, bringing with him his views of Ethiopianism as a threat to colonial security. In Jamaica, he served as a chief justice and in 1934 presided over the trial of Leonard Howell and Robert Hinds. Lyall-Grant was not the only connection between Jamaica and Nyasaland. Other British colonial administrators also moved between the two colonies. These travelers influenced the attitude and policies of Jamaican elites and government officials toward religio-racial communities like the Rastafari. As we will see, the suppositions of the commission's report are like some of the Jamaican government's policy responses toward the Rastafari. Let us survey the Chilembwe tale. In both Nyasaland and Jamaica, Ethiopianism was used in resistance against White supremacy.

Turbulence in Nyasaland

The British founded Nyasaland Protectorate in 1907 as a step toward protecting its appropriated territory from other European land grabbers. In 1913, a famine swept through Central Africa. The famine intensified the tumult that Central Africans had experienced during the decade or so that preceded the famine. Interethnic African rivalries, British and German land grabbing, British taxation, religious activism, and chiliastic social movements were key factors grinding against each other during a phase of turbulent rapid change. The taxes levied by the British on African households forced men to shift from subsistence production to migrate in search of paid labor or to participate in cash cropping. There were millenarian expectations among Central Africans of a looming Armageddon and an impending new order favoring Blacks, expected to commence around 1914, as claimed, for instance, by the Watch Tower movement.[35] Like in Jamaica, the period between the 1890s and 1930s in Nyasaland was a maelstrom of racial, religious, apocalyptic, protonationalist, and anticolonial sentiments.

Africa for the Africans: Ethiopianism and Insurrection

The English Baptist missionary Joseph Booth arrived in Nyasaland from England in February 1892. Booth was committed to Christianizing Africans and helping them set up commercial enterprises. He befriended John Chilembwe, an ethnic Yao African, who was a young boy at the time. As Chilembwe matured, the two men developed respect for each other. Booth's genuine sympathy and humility toward indigenous Africans impressed Chilembwe.

Booth, a White man, believed that indigenous Africans should rule Africa, that "black and white should work side by side," and that Europeans should cede control over African livelihoods.[36] Booth articulated his view at length in his book *Africa for the Africans* (the phrase usually attributed to Marcus Garvey).[37] Booth's racial justice politics made him a threat to Britain's Nyasaland colonial government. Colonial authorities threatened to arrest Booth for sedition because of his boisterous criticism of British government and missionary policies.

In 1897, Booth took Chilembwe with him to the United States, where Chilembwe remained until 1900. Chilembwe studied at Virginia Theological Seminary and College, in Lynchburg, Virginia.[38] His network of Black ministers and educators immersed him in racial politics, while his visit coincided with a spike in violence against Black Americans. Chilembwe learned about Ethiopianism, the radical abolitionist John Brown, other abolitionists, and issues of racial injustice in the United States and the African Diaspora.

Chilembwe plaited together Booth's teaching and his experience in the United States to create an Ethiopianist anticolonial discourse. After he returned to Nyasaland, Chilembwe became a preacher who was interested in expelling Europeans from the African continent (Nyasaland in particular) and in creating a theocratic indigenous African state. He became obsessed with the Old Testament, especially the stories of Jewish resilience in the grip of Egyptian and Philistine tyranny. He embraced a racial interpretation of scripture that he preached to his congregants.

Between January 15 and 23, 1915, Chilembwe and a small number of African coconspirators contrived a violent attack on British colonialism, which they executed on the twenty-third. Perhaps as many as nine hundred Africans altogether were involved in the attack; they were motivated to join Chilembwe because they too were fed up with British policies of taxation, obligatory labor, and land confiscation. The Germans knew about Chilembwe's plot but kept quiet because the British were their enemies. Chilembwe's assault would favor German interests if it disrupted Britain's ability to manage its colonial settlements in East and Central Africa.

Chilembwe's ethics demanded that his rebels not harm White women or children and that they engage in no looting during the rising.[39] The British response to the rebellion, on the other hand, would demonstrate no such moral concern for the lives of African women and children because they reasoned that the more extreme the violence that they inflicted, the greater the deterrent effect against potential African conspirators. Chilembwe and his rebels determined to focus on European "men of war," who embodied colonialism and the destructive change that it had wrought on Central Africa. The rebels also singled out Roman Catholics for destruction because they believed that Britain was binding "together all the churches of Babylon that they may pray for their chief, the Pope."[40] The notion of a modern Babylon as wicked oppressor preceded the Rastafari.

Chilembwe's insurgents lopped off the head of the estate manager William Livingstone as he lay in bed minding his infant while his wife took a bath. The rebels abducted the infant and mother but did not harm them. The rebels killed several Whites and Africans. They fixed Livingstone's head atop a pole in a manner that, in a merciless way, seemed staged to give it an unrivaled view of the sermon that Chilembwe delivered to his adherents after the massacre.

Repercussions of Chilembwe's Uprising in Nyasaland and Jamaica

George Smith, the governor of Nyasaland during the Chilembwe rebellion, commissioned a panel, the Nyasaland Native Rising Commission, to inquire into and explain the rebellion. Lyall-Grant chaired the commission. A primary factor, the commission concluded, was the influence of emigrant natives who brought "false ideas" and literature from abroad into Nyasaland: "A few emigrant natives had come into touch with Ethiopianist ideas and shared Chilembwe's aims. The rising may be said to have been an ebullition of the form of Ethiopianism which has as its watchword 'Africa for the Africans'; and aims at securing for the native sole political control."[41]

The commissioners feared Ethiopianism because they believed that it promoted Black nationalism and anticolonialism, which, at the time, was certainly one of the uses applied by Black people of Africa and the Diaspora.[42] The commission noted that "American negro publications" brought into Nyasaland by Chilembwe had influenced growing numbers of Africans to identify themselves as Black Africans, who had a rich history and who should determine their own future. For example, George Mwase, an African interviewed by the commission about the rising, had received the Universal Negro Improvement Association's *Negro World*.[43] The commission recommended prohibiting "inflammatory religious literatures" and "any literature inculcating Ethiopianism or other dangerous political doctrine" from entering Nyasaland.[44] This essentially was a ban on Black redemption literature, much of which at the time originated in the United States. Jamaican authorities would implement similar measures beginning in the late 1930s.

The cultural infrastructure for an Ethiopianist collective identification in Jamaica was further elaborated and strengthened during the 1920s. Among the new actors was a Black Jamaican, Marcus Garvey. Born in 1887, in St. Ann's Parish, Jamaica, Garvey became a printer's apprentice and active in Jamaica's printer's union during the early 1900s. Garvey visited Central America, England, and the United States, learning about the condition of Black people during his travels. Beginning with his founding of the UNIA in Jamaica 1914, Garvey and the organization became added nourishment for the myriad forms of moral Blackness circulating through the Caribbean, North and Central America, and Africa, providing an inspirational ideology of Black uplift as well as a structure for organizing members. The UNIA became a massive vector that spread Garvey's Black nationalism through its chapters in dozens of countries and through two newspapers with global reach, the *Negro World* and the *Black Man*. Garvey's Black nationalism emphasized Black pride, self-reliance, political and economic empowerment, and collective action. Although secular, the Garvey movement nurtured a racial spirituality fed by Ethiopianism. Garvey made the case for seeing God through Black eyes.

Between 1916 and 1927, the UNIA registered millions of members and undertook daring ventures like the international Black Star shipping line and its international Black Cross Nurses to provide health care and education to Black people, becoming perhaps the largest Black movement in history. The movement excited White fears of Black insurrection wherever UNIA chapters or Garvey newspapers were present. Fear or hatred of Garvey combined with mismanagement of UNIA business affairs to land Garvey in jail on fraud charges in 1923. While locked up in a notorious jail in New York City, Garvey contemplated his own motivation to create the UNIA when he asked himself, "Where is the black man's Government? Where is his King and his kingdom? Where is his President, his country, and his ambassador, his army, his navy, his men of big affairs? I could not find them." He concluded, "I will help to make them."[45] This ideal of Black self-direction and self-organization sparked countless Black minds to organize and defend their interests, in the process raising Garvey to prophet standing among many UNIA members and nonmembers alike.

Stirring White Fears and Black Fancies in Jamaica: Black God, Black Supremacy, and the Hamatic Church

Reverend James Morris Webb, born in the late 1870s in Tennessee, became both an accomplished proselytizer of a racial conception of biblical history and a prominent Garveyite. Reverend Webb promoted his message of a Black God and King linked to Israel and Zion through public lectures and sermons, news advertisements, UNIA media, and self-published tracts (figure 2.1). Webb imagined a hopeful future for a miseducated and oppressed Black people once the Black King revealed himself: "This [coming] black king's Capitol will be at Jerusalem. He shall roar out of Zion and utter His voice from Jerusalem and He will be the hope of his people in that day all nations will desire Him, regardless of Him being a Negro king. . . . The black race will have the greatest hope for Him; because the black race is more oppressed, more segregated,

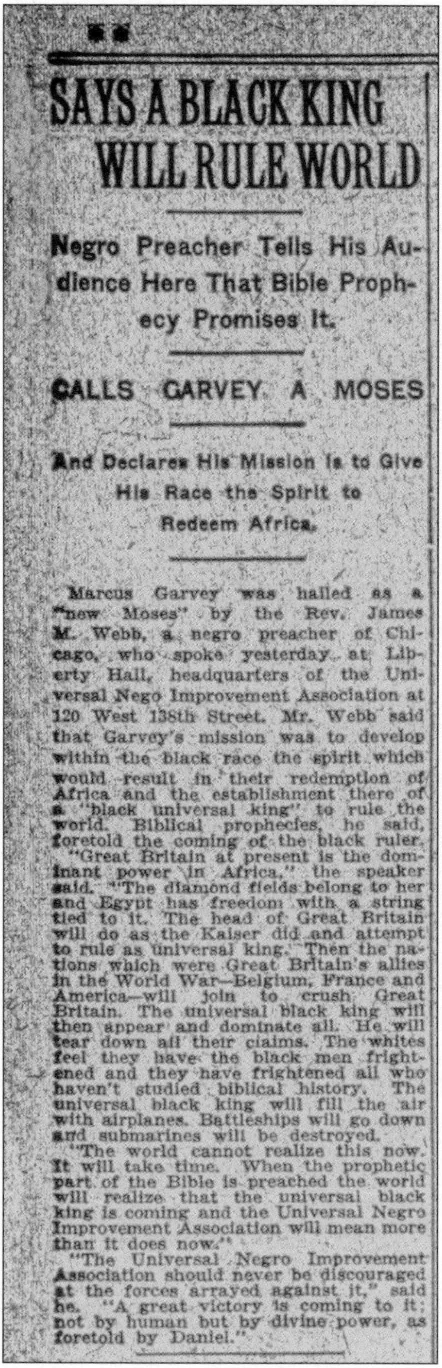

Figure 2.1. Reverend James Webb's notion of a "'black universal king' to rule the world," reported in the *New York Times*, September 15, 1924.

SAYS A BLACK KING WILL RULE WORLD

Negro Preacher Tells His Audience Here That Bible Prophecy Promises It.

CALLS GARVEY A MOSES

And Declares His Mission Is to Give His Race the Spirit to Redeem Africa.

Marcus Garvey was hailed as a "new Moses" by the Rev. James M. Webb, a negro preacher of Chicago, who spoke yesterday at Liberty Hall, headquarters of the Universal Nego Improvement Association at 120 West 138th Street. Mr. Webb said that Garvey's mission was to develop within the black race the spirit which would result in their redemption of Africa and the establishment there of a "black universal king" to rule the world. Biblical prophecies, he said, foretold the coming of the black ruler.

"Great Britain at present is the dominant power in Africa," the speaker said. "The diamond fields belong to her and Egypt has freedom with a string tied to it. The head of Great Britain will do as the Kaiser did and attempt to rule as universal king. Then the nations which were Great Britain's allies in the World War—Belgium, France and America—will join to crush Great Britain. The universal black king will then appear and dominate all. He will tear down all their claims. The whites feel they have the black men frightened and they have frightened all who haven't studied biblical history. The universal black king will fill the air with airplanes. Battleships will go down and submarines will be destroyed.

"The world cannot realize this now. It will take time. When the prophetic part of the Bible is preached the world will realize that the universal black king is coming and the Universal Negro Improvement Association will mean more than it does now."

"The Universal Negro Improvement Association should never be discouraged at the forces arrayed against it," said he. "A great victory is coming to it; not by human but by divine power, as foretold by Daniel."

more discriminated against on account of their Hamitic blood."[46] While it is unlikely that Webb visited Jamaica, we find ideas like his flowing through Jamaica around the same time. Webb was a Garveyite with access to the UNIA's most powerful vectors: Liberty Hall in New York City and the *Negro World*.[47] Webb sold pictures of a "Negro" King Solomon and a "Colored" Queen of Sheba, spreading awareness of these figures among various Black communities.[48]

Robert Athlyi Rogers and Fitz Balantine Pettersburgh were two Ethiopianist-oriented thinkers and proselytizers who during the 1920s influenced Black Jamaican thinking about race and redemption. Rogers authored *The Holy Piby*, while Pettersburgh authored *The Royal Parchment Scroll of Black Supremacy*. *The Holy Piby* was, in Rogers's words, a "book founded by the Holy Spirit to deliver the gospel commanded by the Almighty God for the full salvation of Ethiopia's posterities."[49] The introduction to Pettersburgh's booklet begins by saying, "My dear inhabitants of this world, we are the foundation stones of the resurrection of the Kingdom of Ethiopia."[50] Both booklets paint God Black, critique White supremacy, castigate what they view as slack behavior by some Blacks (e.g., fornication, Obeah), and claim Ethiopia as the physical and spiritual home of African descendants. The ideas of Webb, Rogers, and Pettersburgh were stitched into Rastafari ideology and identity.

Rogers, an Anguillan, initiated an effort to establish his presence and views in Jamaica through founding a church there. Also known as "Athlyi," Rogers formed the Afro Athlican Constructive Gaathly, or the Afro Athlican Constructive Church, in New Jersey in 1918 (see figure 2.2). During 1922, Rogers and Marcus Garvey established a relationship that grew out of a UNIA meeting in Newark that they both addressed. The pair agreed that Rogers's spiritual agenda was a complement to Garvey's political and economic agenda.[51] How and why Rogers set up a mission in Jamaica is uncertain. Both the journalist Hélène Lee and the historian Robert Hill, however, note that the first pastor of Rogers's church, Grace Garrison, arrived in Jamaica from Panama (according to a *Daily Gleaner* passenger list, Garrison was in Jamaica in 1920 and left for Panama the same year).[52] Of note is that many of these people knew of each other even if they did not collaborate. Pettersburgh and Rogers, for example, knew of each other and of Garvey and Grace Garrison. Rogers set about

Figure 2.2. Robert Athlyi Rogers, 1927.
(*New York Daily News*, 11/16/1927)

spreading his ministry beyond its New Jersey base. One of his international satellites was established in Smith Village, Kingston.[53] The church was known in Jamaica by several names, African Baptist Church and Hamatic Church among them (the latter was the one commonly used). The Hamatic Church was the "first in the island as a principal branch of the House of Athlyi," and it was first pastored by the Reverend Grace Garrison, also known as the "Comet."[54] Reverend Garrison was reputed to have "received the Holy Ghost at the age of fifteen.[55] The cornerstone for the church was laid in December 1925, and it was scheduled to open in March 1926.[56]

The *Gleaner* discovered the "new Ethiopian religion" and its tract, Rogers's *Holy Piby*, and linked both to the Hamatic Church and the UNIA.[57] One motivation for the new religion, the editorialist argued, was money: the Hamatic Church's goal was to fleece Black Jamaicans to fill its own coffers. Elites commonly charged the Rastafari leadership with swindling their own brethren and sistren. Another concern of the editorialist was the connection between the Hamatic Church and Rogers's operation in Kimberly, South Africa. The South African Joseph Masogha established a House of Athlyi mission in 1924, in Kimberly, South Africa. The Hamatic Church became a lurking peril in Jamaica (and South Africa). One of the threatening ideas of the new religion was Black supremacy.

The idea of Black supremacy was not about superiority in the sense of White supremacy. Both discourses fashioned their respective race as superior, but for different reasons. White supremacy was based in beliefs about the biological and cultural superiority of Europeans and their descendants. Black supremacy attributed Black superiority to moral uprightness (e.g., not being engaged in the enslavement or colonization of other people), a glorious but erased African past, and God's will. Black people had suffered and endured brutality, and their reward would be to reign over the kingdom of God and "man." Elite Jamaicans interpreted Black supremacy as a farce and a fantasy of domination.

We must situate the emergent of Rastafari within this context of White and British paranoia and the increasing Black Jamaican interest in Black religio-racial discourse.

The Rise of Ras Tafari in Ethiopia: A Brief Sketch

The rise of King Ras Tafari in Ethiopia served as the foundation for Rastafari ethnogenesis in Jamaica, and Jamaican newspapers played an influential role, especially the *Daily Gleaner*. King Ras Tafari was covered in the *Daily Gleaner*, the *Jamaica Times*, *Plain Talk*, and other Jamaican news organs, as well as in internationally distributed periodicals such as *Time* magazine and *National Geographic*. The stories about the King are tales—cultural resources—that became integral to the development of both a historical narrative and an identity script that infused Rastafari collective identity. The story of King Ras Tafari was told in detail *and* with hyperbole in the *Daily Gleaner*. Consumers of the *Daily Gleaner* were exposed to such tales as those shared in this section, though in far more detail and variety. I am unsure about how well the audience—especially the proto-Rastafari—distinguished among historical fact, fantasy, and ethnocentric caricature. Nevertheless, it seems that many people embraced all, especially the history and fantasy.

According to the Acts of the Apostles, Christianity in Ethiopia traces back to the first century, Common Era (Acts 8:26–39), although some scholars contest the accuracy of the account.[58] Archbishop Yesehaq of the Ethiopian Orthodox Church in the Western Hemisphere claims that the church is over fifteen hundred years old, existing before there were churches in some parts of western Europe.[59] The Ethiopian Orthodox Church traces its lineage to both the Hebrews of the Old Testament and Jesus Christ (Iyasus Kristos) of the New Testament.

The *Kebra Negast*, an Ethiopian religious and literary epic, tells the story of the connections among ancient Ethiopia, ancient Israel, and modern Ethiopia. It chronicles the story of Queen Makeda of Sheba's visit to the kingdom of Judah to meet the mighty King Solomon. According to the story, the Queen wanted to consult with Solomon about what makes a great leader. During her stay in Judah, she bore Solomon a son, Menelek I. Solomon confirmed Menelek's paternity by giving him a royal ring. Sheba returned to her territory, then considered a part of southern Ethiopia (now known as Somalia) during the early biblical period. Menelek I became the symbol of the union between King Solomon and the Queen of Sheba and the root source of the royal Ethiopian lineage to which King Ras Tafari and others laid claim. King Ras Tafari was born Lij Tafari Makonnen, on July 23, 1892, in Harar, a city in the eastern province of Harege, Ethiopia ("Lij" is a title reserved for royal males who are not yet adults).

In 1896, Ethiopia went to war against the invading Italians. Led by Emperor Menelek II, the Ethiopians defeated the Italians at the Battle of Adwa (forty years later, the Italians would again invade Ethiopia). The Ethiopian victory at the Battle of Adwa was celebrated by Black people in the United States and Jamaica: an African nation had defeated a colonizing European nation.

In 1907, Emperor Menelek II suffered a debilitating stroke, sparking royal intrigue. After considerable deliberation, Emperor Menelek II chose his grandson, a young Lij Iyasu, to succeed him. Lij Iyasu ruled with the aid of a mentor, Taytu Betel, Emperor Menelek II's wife. Betel was a shrewd political player who herself wanted the throne, desirous of becoming the ruler of Ethiopia.

Lij Iyasu turned out to be an untrustworthy leader who undermined himself and aided the ambitions of Ras Tafari Makonnen. Ethiopia's Council of Ministers, under pressure from the Ethiopian Coptic Church, removed Iyasu from the throne in 1916 and named Emperor Menelek II's daughter Zewditu to the throne, with her cousin Ras Tafari Makonnen acting as her trustee. Empress Zewditu, entitled the "Queen of Kings," ruled from 1916 through 1930. During this period, though, Ras Tafari Makonnen was the de facto ruler. Due to political conspiracy that led to a failed effort to undo Ras Tafari Makonnen's authority, Empress Zewditu had to solidify it by making him *Negus*, or King, in 1928. By this time, King Ras Tafari, Zewditu's cousin, was on his path to becoming Emperor, possessing a vision for modernizing Ethiopia. King Ras Tafari sought to eradicate slavery, democratize citizen participation in government, and develop schools that produced progressive-minded Ethiopians.[60] It was King Ras Tafari who fought to get the then-backwater Ethiopia into the League of Nations in 1924.

By 1930, King Ras Tafari was becoming the man, image, and story that led Whites and Blacks alike to give him top ranking among non-European world leaders. The *Daily Gleaner* marveled at how King Ras Tafari was the "black man who has mastered the white man's magic."[61] The media fixation on Ras Tafari and Ethiopia during 1930 was motivated by both historical and contemporary reasons. Historically, there was Ethiopia's ancient Christian and biblical heritage and the fact that the little African territory had never been colonized by Europeans. The contemporary concerns reminded people of the historical reasons. Ras Tafari's rise to power made for a great story: perseverance, intrigue, surprise, an epic journey.

Collective Identity Requires Stories: The "Black Napoleon" Captures the Imagination of Jamaicans

Fashioning a collective identity demands cultural resources—existing or minted for current purposes—that members can spin into meaningful scripts to define themselves and others. News media like the *Daily Gleaner* dwelled on the ancient connection of Ethiopia to Jerusalem and treated King Ras Tafari as the embodiment of that connection. The King, described by some as the "Black Napoleon," did more than captivate Jamaicans; he captured their hearts and imagination.[62]

The Jamaican press, the British press, and British royalty all contributed to the anointment of King Ras Tafari as a preternatural monarch. The press bestowed him with magical abilities, which he used to triumph in near-impossible situations. His ascendance to Emperor was described as "more astounding than any African adventure novel."[63] The press created stock characters: the gallant Prince (Ras Tafari Makonnen); the cunning and ruthless Queen of Kings, Empress Zewditu, a man eater of the caliber of Cleopatra; her blundering husband, Ras Gugsa; and her evil stepmother, Empress Taytu. In doing so, the Jamaican press contributed to mythologizing the King, who strolled unscathed from the settling dust of deadly royal Ethiopian intrigue to gather the scattered shards of the royal family and Ethiopia and usher them into a new era: "Out of the chaos emerging [was] the directing genius—Ras Tafari. An Old Testament battle story completed with twentieth century machines."[64] Ras Tafari was installed as the "unchallenged King of Ethiopia." The sudden death of Empress Zewditu in April 1930 cleared the way for King Ras Tafari to assume the seat of Emperor, as if divine intervention had it predestined. With the story spun this way—stock characters, high drama, intrigue, and the brilliance of King Ras Tafari's strategy—in retrospect, it is unsurprising that the King's rise to Emperor fueled the imaginations of Jamaicans and little wonder that some considered the Black Napoleon greater than a mortal human. The tales and truths were translated into Rastafari lore and identity. The first-generation Rastafari woman Rasta Ivey would say to me things like, "King Rasta always win" and "No one can trick King Rasta." Rasta Ivey's maxims about the King's supernatural abilities were also statements about the exceptional abilities that she possessed by virtue of being one of King Ras Tafari's adherents. She recognized herself as indomitable, as shrewd, and as a fighter.

Europeans, Africans, and people of the African Diaspora followed local news reports on the King's coronation. The British press signaled in advance the participation of British royalty in the coronation. The *Daily Gleaner* announced that the Duke of Gloucester would attend King Ras

Tafari's coronation.[65] Such announcements stirred anticipation: Black Jamaicans knew that the coronation was in the works, and they debated what it meant.

Despite paying tribute to the history of Ethiopia and the Emperor's lineage, British elites saw Ethiopia as an antiquated and underdeveloped polity unprepared for the twentieth century, and they saw the King as a diminutive (figuratively and literally) African leader. How could they grasp the Rastafari's reverence for Ethiopia given that even their better views of Ethiopia were conflicted?

There were Black Jamaicans, on the other hand, who interpreted Ethiopia and King Ras Tafari through an entirely different frame. They saw England sending the King's son to pay tribute to King Ras Tafari. They saw a tiny African polity with an indomitable will that had made its imprint on biblical history and was about to do something similar in the present. They saw African Black royalty awash in lavishness that rivaled the opulence of European royalty. These Jamaicans were enthralled by King Ras Tafari and the stories spun around him. For at least some of these enthralled Jamaicans, the coronation indicated that a shift in the world order was at hand, the imminence of a new dispensation of immense magnitude. Some Black Jamaicans understood the tales—both the embroidered and unembellished—literally, through biblical and Ethiopianist lenses. It is no wonder that the early Rastafari believed that no feat was beyond the ability of the Emperor to achieve, such as sending ships to retrieve them from Jamaica and ferry them to Ethiopia.

On October 28, 1930, Reuters's West Indian Press Service reported that the Duke of Gloucester, representing "His Majesty the King," had arrived in Addis Ababa for King Ras Tafari's coronation.[66] The Duke brought exquisite presents for the monarch. As the coronation drew near, momentousness and gaiety were omnipresent. There were swarming crowds of Ethiopians, predominantly rank-and-file folk, many of them arrayed in white linen-like fabric loosely wrapped around their bodies and heads; many of the men carried spears and shields; groupings of Ethiopian nobles showed off their aristocratic finery; pith-helmeted Europeans milled around coronation-related ceremonies and toured Addis Abba's monuments. The impending coronation caught the attention of elite and commoner alike, in Ethiopia and in Jamaica.

At the age of thirty-eight, on November 2, 1930, King Tafari Makonnen was crowned Emperor of Ethiopia, at St. Georges Cathedral, Addis Ababa. He assumed the name Haile Selassie I (power of the Trinity). The day after the coronation, the *Daily Gleaner* reported that the "coronation gives Ras Tafari, who claims descent from King Solomon and the Queen of Sheba, the titles of Emperor, Lord of Lords, King of Kings of Ethiopia, Conquering Lion of the Tribe of Judah, the Elect of God, and the Light of the World. Simultaneously."[67] During the same ceremony, the Emperor's wife, Menen Asfaw, was crowned Empress Menen (one could interpret this as a gesture toward raising the status of women in Ethiopia). The coronation lasted ten days and was attended by representatives of seventy-two nations.[68] The attendance of the Duke of Gloucester received special attention in the *Daily Gleaner*. This was partially because Jamaica was a British colony at the time and therefore emphasized things British. During the coronation, the Duke formally presented a gold scepter to the Emperor and an ivory-hilted sword to the Empress, both of whom were dressed in brilliant royal Ethiopian regalia, seated on golden thrones, under a canopy announcing the "Crown of Judah."[69] The Duke wished him a "long and prosperous reign."[70]

These images of and information about King Rastafari inspired the first Rastafari evangelists and exemplified a fundamental ethnogenesis process: people inscribe and revise extant cultural resources in ways that enable the generation of a collective identity.

On November 2, 1932, the *Daily Gleaner* announced that Jamaica's new chief justice, Robert Lyall-Grant, was aboard Elder and Fyffe's steamer *Patuca*, on his way to Kingston from England.[71] Several Jamaican colonial officials accompanied him. It is likely that during their week of travel across the Atlantic, their conversation turned to questions of race and of public safety in Jamaica. It is also reasonable to assume that Lyall-Grant talked about his experience in Nyasaland with his government colleagues.

Almost two weeks later, the *Daily Gleaner* enthusiastically welcomed Robert Lyall-Grant to Jamaica. Chief Justice Lyall-Grant "took his seat for the first time yesterday [November 14, 1932, during] . . . the opening of the Autumn Session of the Appellate Division of the Supreme Court."[72] His service in other parts of the empire was acknowledged, in particular, his work in Nyasaland and in Kenya, where he served as attorney general.

Fatefully, Leonard Howell would be landing in Jamaica just four days after Lyall-Grant's appearance on the bench. Individuals can be essential to ethnogenesis during different phases of the process, as both Lyall-Grant and Howell will demonstrate. Their roles would be antagonistic—the guardian of the White and elite status quo and the charismatic and visionary Black prophet—but, paradoxically, complementary in that by each seeking advantage for their interest, a collective Rastafari identity was forged in a crucible of contention that would itself inform the Rastafari's understanding of themselves and non-Rastafari understandings of the Rastafari.

* * *

Jamaica's history and cultural resources, mingled with foreigners, foreign ideas, and its own citizens tramping between home and abroad, provided a fertile ecosystem for the emergence of novel experiments. Jamaica's Ethiopianism, anticolonialism, and race relations, for example, blended with foreign understandings of Ethiopianism, anticolonialism, and race relations. In this teeming environment, new and diverse groups formed—Bedwardites, Black Israelites, the Hamatic Church, the UNIA—but they lacked durability (for different reasons). Their numbers and impact waned before a second generation could establish itself in Jamaica's cultural substrate. Although the Garveyites persisted for decades, their numbers and influence continued to decline. The Rastafari, however, germinating from the same soil, experienced a different outcome despite facing similar odds and challenges. We will see how and why.

3

Vectors, Collisions, Contention

Collective Identity Formation, 1930–34

> And how shall they believe in him of whom they have not
> heard? And how shall they hear without a preacher? And
> how shall they preach, except they be sent? . . . So then faith
> *cometh* by hearing. . . . But Esaias [Isaiah] is very bold, and
> saith, I was found of them that sought me not; I was made
> manifest unto them that asked not after me.
> —Romans 10:14–20 (KJV)

Paul, in Romans 10, asked how Israelites could become Christians if
they did not know of Christ and his message. The situation of the early
Rastafari evokes Paul's puzzle: How can a new collectivity grow if only
a handful of people are aware of its embryonic message and identity?
Paul pointed out the need for emissaries to broadcast Christ's message
in Rome, Jerusalem, and Spain, and he became that messenger. Christ's
message consisted of content suitable for generating an identity, a community, and even a people. If embraced wholeheartedly, the message
showed a way to salvation and, thus, redemption. Perhaps the early
Rastafari evangelists like Leonard Howell and Robert Hinds were aware
of the paradox that Paul explored in Romans 10 and were inspired by
it. Christianity, after all, grew out of the activity of a small number of
messengers and believers, received both warm and hostile reception,
and gradually gained a global presence.[1] Christ developed an effective
collective identity message around ideas of sacrifice, commitment, righteousness, and redemption. And so too did the Rastafari evangelists.

The activities, events, and exchanges examined in chapter 2 tell us
about the beginnings of Rastafari ethnogenesis. Howell, Hinds, and
other early Rastafari evangelists had visions of a new identity, faith, and
world, and each was compelled to share his slightly different vision.

They might have been deeply convinced of the rightness of their beliefs, but at the outset, all of them were merely sowing seeds in wind. They could not know for sure the extent to which their message would appeal to or repulse people, let alone whether it would sink roots and grow. Nonetheless, after November 1932, Jamaicans began to collide both with information about the Rastafari and literally with the bodies of the Rastafari themselves, causing forceful and sometimes violent contact. People encountered the Rastafari in the form of news reports, government memos, gossip, and living Rastafari. Collisions also occurred during the first years of the Rastafari because of staged and impromptu public meetings convened by the Rastafari and because individual or bands of Rastafari canvassers broadcast their message when they traveled about their business. As we shall see, some people were attracted to the Rastafari, others bent on opposing them.

A Saga Begins

On Monday, November 14, 1932, the *Daily Gleaner* published a concise announcement on page 2: "Sixola's Passengers." The notice, which was so easy to miss, was buried among blaring advertisements hawking "Useful Cars at Moderate Prices," "Apples," a "Pre-Xmas Sale," and underneath columns announcing "Births," "Deaths," "In Memoriam," "Personal," and so on. It declared that the SS *Sixola* had left New York and would dock in Jamaica in three days. Among the passengers listed was Leonard Howell, the "first Rasta," as the journalist Hélène Lee has called him.[2] He was returning to Jamaica broke and unknown on a ship whose history and international itinerary—New York, Panama, Costa Rica, Europe—paralleled his own. The SS *Sixola* was probably named for the Rio (river) Sixola and the town of the same name in Costa Rica's banana territory, near the border with Panama. The *Sixola* was a part of the United Fruit Company's "White Fleet," its steamship cargo and passenger service. During the *Sixola*'s career, in addition to fruit, it also hauled mail and people.

On Friday, November 18, 1932, the *Sixola* debarked twelve passengers. Howell had returned to Jamaica on November 17, 1932, around seven in the morning. Ten of the *Sixola*'s passengers were society folk—elites—mainly men of commerce and means and women vacationing and visiting. The United Fruit Company accountant Allan Archer and his wife had made a "short visit to the United States," while the US real estate dealer Charles Noyes and his wife were visiting Jamaica, perhaps seeking both business and pleasure. At least two of the passengers were not elites, and the nature of their return was noted: "Messrs. Leonard Howell and AIvin Lindo arrived in the Sixola, having been deported from America by the United States Emigration Department on the ground that they overstayed their time."[3] Howell had lived in New York City between 1924 and 1932 and, during the time, developed an interest in ideas about Black liberation and politics.[4]

Soon after King Ras Tafari assumed the throne as Emperor of Ethiopia, Howell proclaimed that he prophesized that King Ras Tafari was the Messiah returned. In March 1934, Mr. H. M. Radcliffe, assistant to the attorney general, asked Howell to elaborate on his claim about King Ras Tafari when Radcliffe cross-examined him during his trial for sedition:

RADCLIFFE: When did you first conceive the idea that Ras Tafari was the Messiah?
HOWELL: Through the prophecy.
RADCLIFFE: Is it a long time since you made the discovery?
HOWELL: Yes, since 1930.
RADCLIFFE: Up to then you didn't know of it? Was that the time when Ras Tafari was crowned?
HOWELL: Yes, Your Worship.[5]

Prophecy, in the Jamaican context of the time, described both visionary and supernatural abilities to reveal what is unknown to the ordinary person. If we take Howell seriously here, he had reasoned out the divinity of King Ras Tafari two years before returning to Jamaica and did so independently of Robert Hinds, Joseph Hibbert, Archibald Dunkley, and other Jamaicans in Jamaica. The idea of a soon-to-arrive Black savior had circulated in both New York and Jamaica during the 1920s, and Howell was probably keenly aware of it.[6] A well-known advocate of the idea of the Black Messiah as King was the Garveyite Reverend James Webb (see chapter 2). Webb, citing scripture, argued that "to prove this king will be a black man, (Negro or Colored) and a Universal King forever, Jacob on his dying bed prophesied that this coming King would be an offspring from his son Judah."[7] Webb had been promoting this line of thought since the early 1900s, arguing that Christ was a member of the tribe of Judah. Emperor Selassie also claimed the Judah lineage.

Howell was well acquainted with Marcus Garvey's Black nationalism. Ethiopianism was a potent presence in race-conscious Black communities in New York City, and Emperor Selassie was revered by African Americans and West Indians aware of international affairs and Black history and culture. In Harlem, New York, Howell was probably aware, for instance, of the parade on March 28, 1931, in which Garveyites, the Black Jewish sect, the Commandment Keepers, and other Black Nationalists proclaimed Emperor Selassie I to be the "King of All Negroes"; Marcus Garvey was anointed "second greatest man in the world."[8]

Even though we know much about the environment in which Howell moved, we cannot know *exactly* what he was thinking about a Black Messiah before arriving in Jamaica. We do know, though, that Howell was not the only Jamaican of the time preoccupied with the idea. King Ras Tafari had captivated Robert Hinds before November 1930; Hinds was already familiar with the idea of a Black Christ or savior before Howell arrived in Jamaica because of his experience with Alexander Bedward. Archibald Dunkley, an ardent Ethiopianist who worked for the United Fruit Company, in 1930 returned to Jamaica, where he soon founded the King of Kings Mission in Port Antonio before moving it to Kingston.[9] Dunkley claimed that Emperor Selassie was the "Black Christ returned in the flesh, in his Kingly character."[10] Joseph Hibbert returned to Jamaica from Costa Rica in 1931; he soon founded the Ethiopian Coptic Faith (see figure 3.1). These men, and others less known, were organizing around a permutation of the idea that King Ras Tafari, become Emperor Haile Selassie I, was divine—a Black Christ or God embodied in mortal flesh. Howell quickly made himself a prominent spokesperson for the message promoting King Ras Tafari as Messiah and Redeemer. Llewellin Walker, a Howell acolyte from the beginning, recalled hearing about Howell in November 1932: "I heard a fellow giving the announcement: says to tell all black inhabitants around the area . . . that an ambassador from Ethiopia landed in Jamaica to preach Rastafari doctrine. . . . That night we traveled out a mile and a half to Port Morant and I see a tall gentleman [Howell]. He had a suit on. . . . And he says that 'Black people, black people at this western hemisphere, arise for the light of the

Figure 3.1. Joseph Nathaniel Hibbert, photographed in Jonestown, Kingston, 1953, by the anthropologist George Eaton Simpson. Hibbert's garb and crown signal his leader status; note the drawing of Emperor Haile Selassie and Empress Menen Asfaw in the background. Aside from some well-known photographs of Leonard Howell, there are few images of the earliest Rastafari evangelists. (National Anthropological Archives, Smithsonian Institution)

Lord God of Israel is now risen upon you.'"[11] While Walker's recollection that Howell broadcast his presence and ideas soon after he arrived in Jamaica is plausible, we can safely say that by January 1933 Howell was preaching an inchoate identity script focused on King Ras Tafari as the Messiah returned to fulfill his role in redeeming Black people in Jamaica from their oppressive condition.

Once in Kingston, Howell made haste in talking to Jamaicans about the coronation and its meaning. He met with Hibbert, Dunkley, Hinds, and David and Annie Harvey, though we do not know how he found them or whether they found him. Dunkley recalled that soon after Howell arrived in Jamaica, he visited Annie Harvey and her Black Israelites in Kingston, where she kept a building on Paradise Street.[12] Dunkley believed that Howell acquired his famous photograph postcard of the "King of Kings of Ethiopia—A Descendant of King Solomon and the Queen of Sheba" from the Harveys (see figure 5.1). Howell said that he used the photograph of the Emperor to show the public what *their* Messiah looked like. Dunkley suggested that Howell may have briefly apprenticed to the Harveys, during which he "copied all of what they [the Israelites] were doing and launched out himself and formed a body of people, Back-to-Africa movement."[13]

Howell had stepped into a scene inhabited by people receptive to the Rastafari identity script he was hatching. In retrospect, we can see that the doctrine gained traction right away. Howell and other Rastafari proselytizers began the work of both generating *and* disseminating an ideology able to speak to the grievances and desires among Black Jamaicans. They began a process of constructing a cultural and historical narrative about their beliefs, a narrative that defined their identity. They did not conduct the work alone.

A Tangible Connection to Ethiopia: Annie and David Harvey, "Black Israelites," and Healers

Before returning to Jamaica from Ethiopia in 1930, the Harveys witnessed attempts of the African Diaspora, particularly Blacks residing in the United States, to settle in Ethiopia. Their activities after they returned to Jamaica are instructive of the many influences on Rastafari's origins, how Revivalism coexisted with Ethiopianism, how the laws and courts were used to regulate indigenous religions, and the challenges that Howell, Hinds, and other early Rastafari would face.

Black Israelites Settle in Ethiopia

In *Chosen People: The Rise of American Black Israelite Religions*, Jacob Dorman stresses that without Arnold Ford and other Black Israelites, "there would have been no Rastafarianism."[14] Dorman claims that the Rastafari are a permutation of Black Israelite religions. His observation is bold and entertainable but begging for further explanation to show why this is the case. Nonetheless, I will provide a bit more evidence that suggests linkages between a particular expression of Black Israelitism in Jamaica and the early Rastafari.

The Harveys met and married in Costa Rica in the early 1920s. In 1924 or 1925, they left Jamaica and traveled to Ethiopia, motivated by Annie's vision that urged them to perform missionary work there.[15] The Harveys were among a number of the African Diaspora—from the United States and the West Indies—who constituted a small outpost in Ethiopia. Arnold Ford was a key figure in this repatriation effort.

Ford, born in Barbados in 1876, was an erudite Black Nationalist, known particularly for his musical talents and his fluency in several languages. A devoted Garveyite, Ford composed the UNIA's "Universal Ethiopian Anthem," which we could call the theme song of Ethiopianist Black nationalism. He founded Beth B'Nai Abraham Synagogue for "Aethiopian Jews" in New York in 1924 and was one of several prominent Black Jews in the New York UNIA.

Ford arrived in Ethiopia in 1930, with some of his closest supporters. Ford posted alluring letters to his associates in the United States, pleading with them to come to Ethiopia, a land, he believed, of great possibility. Ford wanted to mobilize an exodus of African Americans to settle in Ethiopia: "Try and wake up interest in building homes here among Americans who want to come. Save your money and your people's money to come. . . . Do not turn back now. The thing is too big. God will bless us, love to all."[16] F. A. Cowan, a colleague of Ford's, exclaimed, "Aethiopia stretches out her hand for you, calling you to come."[17] Cowan spun myths about the condition of Ethiopia, bellowing that it was "rich beyond mention" and that "it is a veritable heaven."[18] Here we can find a source of the romanticization of Ethiopia by the early Rastafari. The nascent Rastafari were entertaining a jumble of claims about Ethiopia, some reasonably accurate, some utterly false. The Emperor was serious about inviting African Americans to Ethiopia, but the wealth beyond imagination was misleading. However, any invitation was under Ethiopia's terms. Ethiopian laws regulating the transfer of land to foreigners and their rigid racial and caste system stymied Ford and his followers. Around the time that Ford arrived in Ethiopia, the Harveys were probably preparing to return to Jamaica.

As we shall see, Jamaica's Chief Justice Lyall-Grant oversaw the Harveys' trial. The sedition trial of Leonard Howell and Robert Hinds occurred while the Harveys were also in court defending themselves because of the colonial authority's concerns about the nature of their collectivity-building efforts. Chief Justice Lyall-Grant sat on both cases. Was it coincidental that the Harveys and the fledgling Rastafari evangelists were in court at the same time?[19] Or that Chief Justice Lyall-Grant, lead investigator of the Chilembwe rebellion in Nyasaland, Central Africa, was performing similar work in Jamaica? I have not found evidence that the courts connected the cases of the Harveys with those of Howell and Hinds. Nevertheless, this is an area deserving further investigation. Did elites see the Harveys as a menace as they did the Rastafari? Yes. The court was determined to prosecute the Harveys, even though the activities that were the basis of the charges were difficult to prove and law enforcement sloppily handled their cases. Elites portrayed the Harveys, like Howell, as deceiving gullible people. A charismatic and inspired woman who embraced both race and spirit as the basis of identity and community, Annie's audaciousness probably magnified the aura of threat that elites perceived.

The Harveys contributed to developing a community around Ethiopia and Revival in Jamaica. They perhaps knew more about life in Ethiopia and about Emperor Selassie than anyone else in Jamaica. In Jamaica, Annie developed an associational base and an identity around the notion of the "Israelite healer." The Harveys disseminated their message through religious meetings, news advertisements, and we shall assume word of mouth, while the *Daily Gleaner* told the Jamaican nation about their prosecution (without the detail attendant to the reporting on Howell and Hinds). The work of Annie the healer and Revival leader gives us some insight into early Rastafari ethnogenesis.

It Pays and It Costs to Be a Healer

It is telling that the Harveys could travel on their own terms, while Ford and many of his followers could not raise the funds needed to support themselves in Ethiopia or to return to America (Ford himself planned never to return). One source of revenue for financing the Harveys' travel could have been Annie's healing work that she conducted in Jamaica. I focus on Annie rather than Annie *and* David because Annie was the leader and David the accomplice. Annie overshadowed her husband, David. Reports regularly mentioned the Harveys as a couple, but they never depict David as an active Black Israelite or Revival agent.

Whether the Harveys held the Emperor divine is uncertain, although the founding Rastafari evangelist Archibald Dunkley believed that they did: "if they [the Harveys] did not believe in Ras Tafari, I do not think they would bring that photograph of him and teach the people them of Africa."[20] We can assume, though, that the Harveys understood Emperor Selassie as the spiritual father of the people of the African Diaspora and that they understood themselves as Black Israelites and as Ethiopians (in the Ethiopianist sense). We can also assume that the Harveys gave Howell a sense that migrating to Ethiopia was feasible—here were two people who had made the journey there and back. And they perhaps fed Howell stories about Ethiopia both plausible and fantastic: that Black people were wanted and already settling there, that the Emperor and his Queen were awe-inspiring, and that it was a land of milk and honey.

Revival healers like Annie Harvey and Jamaica's medical and pharmacy professionals vied against each other. Alongside the accounts of Annie's trial on charges of practicing Obeah and practicing medicine without a license were advertisements evocative of Annie's own potions, with the difference being that chemists rather than healers hawked the concoctions. Examples of the advertisements include a "secret formula for gastric ulcers," "Dr. Morse's Indian Root Pills" (for "constipated housewives"), "Listerine antiseptic for dandruff" (a potion used today as mouthwash), and "Moones Emerald Oil," for "broken veins" and "old sores."[21]

Do Not Let Them Prosper: Disrupting the Harveys' Attempt to Build a Collectivity

As I noted earlier, many new groups never gain traction; for many reasons, they end up withering only to eventually vanish. It seems that Annie and David Harvey were seeking to create a new collectivity and identity in Jamaica but were repeatedly stymied by the colonial authorities. Their venture did not gain traction, though it seems Annie had the ability to make it manifest.

In August 1933, Annie and her husband, David, were appellants in a Kingston court contesting a charge of disorderly conduct lodged against them in the Portland Parish Petty Sessions Court. Law officers arrested Annie because of a meeting she convened in Portland, on Palm Sunday in 1933. The pretext for the arrest was that the meeting was so raucous that it would disturb nearby residents. The barrister and politician E. E. Campbell represented the Harveys, while H. M. Radcliffe represented the Crown. Radcliffe would prosecute Howell and Hinds in the coming year.

Campbell argued that all Annie and company were doing at the time in question was singing religious hymns.[22] Radcliffe countered that they spoke in an "unknown tongue" and made a racket in doing so.[23] Colonial authorities indiscriminately used "speaking in tongues" to encompass both Obeah and Revival inspiration, taking no care to distinguish between the two. Glossolalia, vigorous clamor, or even spirit possession was common behavior among the various nonconformist religious groups; however, the Obeah Act made common practice illegal. Campbell rebutted Radcliffe by pointing out that Annie and company were reading the book of Deuteronomy and that the police simply did not understand what they were saying.

Three important themes of Deuteronomy, though, were Moses warning the Israelites against occult practices, reminding them of the ignominy of their former bondage, and intimating the advent of a new prophet who would emerge from the wandering Israelites. Moses, speaking on behalf of God, condemned charmers, wizards, necromancers, witches, and "consulter[s] with familiar spirits."[24] A powerful Revival healer like Annie would see at least part of her responsibility to counteract such practices. In the same chapter, God says, "I will raise them up a Prophet from among their brethren, like unto thee, and will put my words in his mouth; and he shall speak unto them all that I shall command him."[25] Annie might have believed herself to be that new prophet, raised from the formerly enslaved Diaspora and hence wandering, Black Israelites. That God cast the prophet as male would have mattered little to a woman of Revival because women exercised charismatic leadership.

Campbell pointed out to the court that the activity in question was held on Palm Sunday, a day of religious celebration, and that the subjects were free to practice the religion of their choice. Nevertheless, the judge found Annie guilty. He ordered her to pay a fine.[26] The Harveys believed that the justices who found them guilty had the ulterior motive of silencing their brand of religious practice—an amalgam of the teachings of the Black Israelites and Revival.

It was unsurprising that the colonial authorities sought to dismantle Annie's operation given that Chief Justice Lyall-Grant could interpret her combination of race and religion with international travel as a threat in the making (Chilembwe had traveled internationally). From the scarce sources available, I cannot specify the content of Annie's thinking because she is not given voice in the reports, unlike Leonard Howell, Robert Hinds, and other Rastafari men who were quoted directly and at length in news stories and government reports. We can see, however, that Annie was gutsy, able in her organizing ability, and not overawed by men or the colonial order. These qualities alone would have marked Annie as a disruptive woman.

The Harveys' brushes with the law further entangled them in the judicial system. By mid-1933, they were being surveilled. On October 18, 1933, Detective Dawkins arrested the Harveys at their Portland Road address, this time for practicing Obeah and for practicing medicine without a license. Officers also arrested Myrtle Harvey and Ellen Bennett, of the same address. Constables charged Myrtle and Ellen with assailing Dawkins during the arrest. Myrtle and Ellen forcibly tried to prevent Dawkins from carrying out his mission at the Portland Road residence.

Once again, the Harveys were in court. His Honor Bertram Burrowes presided over their case. Burrowes had considerable experience trying

Obeah cases. He pointed out that the Harveys were (Black) "Israelites" known for "holding certain meetings at night."[27] The barrister, politician, and cofounder of Jamaica's National Club (Jamaica's first nationalist organization) H. A. L. Simpson represented the Harveys this time (they hired well-established lawyers). By charging Annie with violation of the Medical Law, elites had marked her as a dangerous quack who was providing medical advice and dispensing substances intended for healing purposes without a license. As the Harveys' entanglement in the courts deepened, Burrowes shifted his focus from Annie's Black "Israelism" to her alleged religious and healing activities. The emphasis shifted from race and religion to religion and magic. The switch suggested that the court recognized that it had to make the charges stick, and at the time, being a Black Israelite was insufficient ground for any serious punishment. Violation of the Medical Law and Obeah Act could be leveraged to deliver harsh punishment in the form of stiff fines or imprisonment.

Annie must have been an imposing persona. She showed up for her March 1, 1934, court hearing dressed in a helmet, a purple robe, and a white "cloth breastplate." A reporter noted that Annie had the "appearance of military authority."[28] Annie's garb doubtless conveyed her conviction in her own abilities, as well as signaling that she was a religious and racial warrior at war with the evil embodied in the law enforcement efforts to prevent her from manifesting her purpose.

After the Crown and Simpson presented their arguments, Burrowes found the Harveys guilty of practicing medicine without a license and for "working Obeah."[29] On the Obeah count, David got six months' hard labor, while Annie received three months' imprisonment. On the violation of the Medical Law, each received a fine of £10 or three months. Simpson appealed the verdict, and the couple were released on £25 bail.[30] The verdict came two weeks after the sentencing of Howell and Hinds on March 17, 1934.

What Campbell brought into relief during the trial was how the Harveys had influenced a vocal and evidently growing contingent of people who were absorbing their message about Ethiopia, Black Israelites, and Annie's healing power. The Obeah charge, in Campbell's view, was a distraction. Campbell concluded by asking that the court rescind the conviction. The court adjourned until the next day. And the record trails off there.

Initial Rastafari Organizing and Proselytizing, 1933–34: Sowing Identity Seeds in St. Thomas

The early Rastafari and their audiences were especially reliant on information delivered through face-to-face talk. Therefore, street meetings and impromptu assemblies were important vectors for disseminating information. The first generation of Rastafari who embraced the doctrine had to be wary of informers who might identify them as Rastafari acolytes. Rastafari advocates who talked publicly had to be concerned with any attention from people unsympathetic to their message. However, there was no way to guarantee a completely sympathetic audience. While there were people curious to hear the Rastafari doctrine, there were people who detested the doctrine and who readily informed elites and colonial authorities about meetings and the names of people who promoted the meetings. Some people, though, were so smitten by the Rastafari message that they openly professed their beliefs and bore the punishment. Rasta Ivey, the octogenarian, told me, "I stand with my God and King [Ras Tafari]. I will suffer what I must suffer because ah what I believe." Rasta Ivey was involved with the Bedwardites and knew Robert Hinds, whom she referred to as "our leader." Like Hinds, Rasta Ivey was a Rastafari evangelist in her own right, traveling between Kingston, Clarendon, and St. Thomas, selling her goods and promoting Rastafari. She struck me as being a militant advocate of the faith, which makes me wonder how many women like her were active during the time. As we shall see, women were active and visible at the outset.

Newspapers such as the *Daily Gleaner* and the *Jamaica Times* made Leonard Howell *the* face of the Rastafari and *the* source of the Rastafari doctrine. Howell became the big fish that the elites wanted to fry.

Howell began his evangelism in Kingston, soon after he returned to Jamaica. He recruited some former Bedwardites there, before moving on to St. Thomas. It is unclear why Howell left Kingston. The historian Robert Hill asserts that it was because Howell did not gain the attention there that he desired.[31] Kingston was already congested with religious competition, and law enforcement could also more easily control operations in Kingston. By January 1933, Howell had begun to concentrate his effort in St. Thomas, in the towns of Morant Bay and Port Morant and the districts of Pear Tree, Golden Grove, Trinityville, and Seaforth.

Many St. Thomas residents showed up to hear the message that Howell and other embryonic Rastafari had to tell about the new Black Messiah, impending Black redemption, and the end to White colonial rule.

Within five months of Howell's return to Jamaica, large audiences were gathering to hear his message. His message also attracted the attention of elites and colonial authorities. One ardent anti-Howell activist during the incipient years of the Rastafari was John Ross, a planter active in the politics and agricultural affairs of St. Thomas.[32] Ross would encourage other elites in Kingston and eastern Jamaica to join him in opposing Howell and the Rastafari. On April 18, 1933, Ross attended one of Howell's meetings in Trinityville, which, according to colonial records, attracted two to three hundred people.[33] The police officer Leonard Thomas reported a verbal clash between Ross and Howell, whose sermon that evening addressed religion, history, politics, and current events, connecting them to deep-seated desires and grievances of his audience. Howell told the assembled that the "Lion of Judah has broken the chain" that had subdued Blacks and that Black people were finally free. Howell's point: "You are Black. Why worship a White King when there is before you a Black African King whom scripture has foretold?"[34]

Ross and others like him were concerned that Howell's proclamation that Black redemption had commenced and that the oppressive White edifice was on the verge of collapse would stir their workers against them. They might decide to resist the heavy taxes and the grueling low-wage work for planters like Ross and instead wait on their Messiah. In an editorial reflecting on the early labors of Howell in St. Thomas, the writer bemoaned, "In the conception of some of his subjects, King Ras Tafari is referred to as the future ruler of the world. It is correct that some 1,000 persons actually gave up their provision fields to quit this land to which they belong to seek new fields in a distant country."[35] Although nonelites would soon treat the Rastafari as problematic, the elites set the tone of the discourse. The dilemma for elites at this point, though, was not simply the content of the Rastafari message (i.e., that it was "seditious"). The message itself would matter little if it simply went in one ear and out the other, if people heard it but failed to heed it. The problem, though, was that people were taking Howell seriously, even though at the time most knew little about King Ras Tafari or Ethiopia, even though the *Daily Gleaner* and other news organs provided such information. Howell and others filled an information gap. Elite and co-lonial authority designs to defeat Howell and the other Rastafari evange-lists were in effect a deliberate effort to suppress Rastafari, as the reggae music superstar Bob Marley sang, to stop it before it grows.

John Ricketts packed his grip and left Jamaica for Ethiopia on May 25, 1933. Howell was telling his audiences that King Ras Tafari would assist them when they arrived in Ethiopia. No one welcomed Ricketts upon his arrival in Ethiopia. Nevertheless, Howell's assertion was reasonable, if we recall that King Ras Tafari and his administrators were welcoming Black immigrants like Arnold Ford to Ethiopia. Ricketts was thrashed and robbed of his money while in Ethiopia and had to request the as-sistance of the British Crown, which he originally sought to escape, to return to Jamaica.[36] Editorialists held up Ricketts as the emblem of the impressionable Black bumpkin and proof of the nefarious influence of Howell and his message:

> It has been made to appear to the uninformed who have become devo-tees to the [Rastafari] cult that is being fostered in St. Thomas, and, it is understood, in lower St. Andrew, that gold can be gathered in Abyssinia as easily as stones can be gathered from the bed of any shallow stream in Jamaica. A Jamaican who became somewhat interested in the obviously far-fetched stories that were poured into his ears in St. Thomas, where he was domiciled, by Howell when he was preaching sedition in that area, thought he would journey to the "promised land" and investigate for himself. He did so, but has been repatriated to his native land a sadder but wiser man.[37]

Even though critics made Ricketts look the fool, by traveling to and returning from Ethiopia, he had showed that such a trip was feasible. The yearning of Black Jamaicans to resettle in Ethiopia would intensify rather than abate.

Toward the end of Howell's first year in Jamaica, he had broadcast his message across St. Thomas. The message was developing consistent themes and motifs, one being that King Ras Tafari was the Messiah spo-ken of in the book of Revelation and the other being migration to Africa (the term "repatriation" had not yet replaced "migration"). In an Octo-ber 1933 meeting in Port Morant, Howell told the crowd that King Ras

Tafari was working on their behalf and that in 1934 they would be taken by ship to Ethiopia. Scholars have treated these early claims about ships to Africa as millenarian fantasies or have claimed that the Rastafari were interested in symbolic rather than literal return to Africa. Howell, however, knew and knew of people who had been to Ethiopia.

Alongside planters like John Ross, clergy began to cry out against Howell in reaction to his criticism of preachers as connivers. By criticizing the churches, Howell was positioning his own message as a superior alternative. He was also addressing a property attendant to collective identity formation: a need to distinguish oneself within a field of competing identity discourses.

Disrupting the Early Rastafari Efforts to Build a Collectivity

By early 1934, both the Rastafari evangelists and colonial authorities were ratcheting up their game several notches. The tension between growth and suppression tightened; nevertheless, the Rastafari evangelists continued to preach and organize under an orchestrated crackdown. The Rastafari were at the first of several critical points of persistence. At this point, they were vulnerable to being stamped out. Thus, removing Howell and Hinds from the scene could have undone the nascent Rastafari. Nonetheless, they were rapidly gaining their footing.

Hundreds of people were turning out for Howell's meetings, and many more were hearing about the message. An opinion piece, "It is Not a Joke," published in late December 1933, signaled an increasingly grave attitude among elites who were in effect signaling their concern to the colonial authorities. The incredulous author wrote,

> A somewhat curious story has reached me from St. Thomas. . . . Recently about 400 men and women anxiously awaited the arrival of [Howell] their new found friend . . . to trek to a shipping port in the Island to embark for Ethiopia but he did not turn up. Some of them . . . purchased from the party photographs of the Abyssinian ruler who was crowned a few years ago amidst great pomp. . . . King Ras Tafari is referred to as the future ruler of the world. . . . My fervent hope is that by this time they have come to realise that they have been fooled. They are no better than the hundreds, if not a few thousand men and women who at

the command of Alexander Bedward sold their worldly goods, left their districts and journeyed to August Town some years ago, to follow their "prophet." . . . [Howell and Hinds say that] every other form of government is a snare, while the church is a delusion.[38]

Howell and Hinds were compared to Bedward, the charismatic Native Baptist and Revival leader who developed a collectivity around his religio-racial-inspired critique of Jamaica's colonial status quo (see chapter 2). The elites eviscerated Bedward and intended the same for Howell.

On December 10, 1933, Howell and Hinds participated in a now infamous joint meeting in Seaforth district. Until December 1933, there were only sporadic traces of Robert Hinds's presence, mainly in connection with Bedward. The December 10 meeting became the basis of an organized effort to vanquish Howell. An upper-level officer of the Constabulary had dispatched Constable Gayle and Corporal Brooks to Seaforth, to investigate Howell clandestinely. Authorities had considered charging Howell with treason but considered it as too difficult and hence risky to guarantee conviction. Therefore, by December 1933 or early in 1934, the attorney general must have made the decision to use the sedition charge and the December 10 speech to unseat Howell.

On December 10, Corporal Brooks, chief of the Seaforth police station, "accompanied by Constable Gayle, . . . went out to Seaforth around 7 p.m. He saw the accused, Howell, addressing a crowd of about 300 people of the labouring class. Both he and Gayle made notes."[39] The officers meandered around the meeting ground while waiting for the meeting to begin. Gayle and Brooks said that they hid behind some bushes to observe and record the meeting. Howell's and Hinds's speeches engaged the audience, their cheering for certain statements being evidence. Howell was getting more specific and detailed in his claims; the message was moving toward doctrine. For example, Howell was explaining that King Ras Tafari was not only the Black Messiah and Christ returned but also the "living Lord God of Ethiopia." The emphasis on living is notable because it conceived God as tangible and dwelling among his people, in contrast to the distant and remote God of the Christians.

Howell's themes become a basis for ousting him. The officers focused only on parts of the speech, those parts they believed constituted sedition, a grave offense that would probably result in imprisonment. It is relevant to briefly explore the December 10 and other meetings here, to get a sense of the emergent Rastafari identity script, exchanges between Rastafari and non-Rastafari, and the contours of a nascent collective identity.

December 10

At the December 10 meeting, Howell and Hinds sang a closing chant. "Led by Howell . . . the people sang a song of four verses, BIBLICAL IN CHARACTER, the 'psalm' terminated with a line which ran thus: 'Day by day I see what Leonard Howell is doing for my soul.'"[40] The chant offered thanks to Howell for his contribution to helping Black people better comprehend their own oppressed condition and their liberation. His self-focus in promoting his Rastafari message could be interpreted as inflated egotism. Overblown self-presentation in the form of charisma, though, has catalyzed the formation of countless new collectivities (especially religious and revitalization groups). Perhaps such personalities are vital to the early phases of development of a new collectivity hemmed in by the clutches of outsider oppressors.

After the hymn, "Howell paused in his speech to advertise for sale, at one shilling each, pictures of 'King Ras Tafari' of 'Ethiopia'" (figure 5.1).[41] During Howell's January 1934 examination for the charge of sedition, the arresting officer Inspector Isaac Brooks and Constable Gayle, testifying for the prosecution, recounted the evening, including the sale of King Ras Tafari photographs. Brooks said Gayle spoke with Howell and said that Howell

> offered copies of a [King Ras Tafari's] photograph to the gathering for 1/ each. Constable Gayle went to the accused and spoke to him, and the accused offered him one of the photographs and asked him for his name and age. . . . Accused said he wanted it to send to Africa and in six months time, Constable Gayle would receive a letter. Accused took back the photograph and said: "You shall be kicked soon." Accused continued his speech and ended by singing the National Anthem. He [Brooks] said Howell was not disorderly, but he spoke in a loud tone of voice.[42]

Howell claimed that the photos would serve as "passports . . . when the time came for the people to go back to Africa."[43] Howell would later explain that he distributed the pictures because he wanted people to know what their King looked like, which was reasonable: to show people unfamiliar with African royalty what King Ras Tafari looked like. Authorities, however, interpreted this as selling merchandise under false claims, insinuating that Howell was seeking personal gain and self-glorification (recall how healing and Obeah were similarly interpreted). It could have been the case, though, that Howell was raising money for transport to Ethiopia or to subsidize bail, or he may simply have been covering the cost of reproducing the images. Howell himself said that a major use of the money was to "Help a lot of poor people," which was plausible, as we shall see.[44]

During the December 10 meeting, Howell and Hinds exhorted Black Jamaicans to flee poverty, exploitation, and oppression by moving to Ethiopia and living under the governance of King Ras Tafari. They cast migration as a viable option for escaping persecution and poverty; at the time, they did not portray migration as an ideology of repatriation, a duty requiring Black people of the Diaspora to return to the land of their ancestors. The focus on migration is consistent with Ethiopian interest in attracting Black settlers. However, Howell's and Hinds's urgings for Black Jamaicans to leave did not provide the legal pretext for serious prosecution as much as their emphasis on praising King Ras Tafari while disparaging the United Kingdom's sovereign, King George. This was a kernel of the case that law enforcement would build against Howell.

Although the name King Ras Tafari was unfamiliar to most Jamaicans—Gayle said that December 10 was the first time that he had ever heard the name "Rasta Fari"—the Rastafari message articulated by Howell and Hinds was geared toward local audiences and their grievances, hopes, and imagination.[45] The emergent Rastafari script communicated a racial analysis of injustice and inequality that resonated with Black Jamaicans' beliefs about their heritage, identity, and rights and about supernatural intervention into the unjust system. Nevertheless, more trouble was brewing.

December 16

On December 16, Rastafari evangelists convened a meeting in Trinityville led by Robert Hinds and the cofounding Rastafari Joseph Hibbert

(Howell was absent).[46] John Ross the planter had prepared for Howell this time, which may be why Howell was not present. Ross had galvanized ministers, a justice of the peace, and a leader from the Jamaica Producers Association to stand with him and publicly confront Howell. Ross and other elites were charging Howell and the Rastafari evangelists with promoting atheism, rebellion, and bloodshed.[47] Again, law enforcement officers surveilled the meeting. The officers, for reasons unclear, tried to arrest Hinds and Hibbert. A scuffle ensued. The crowd intervened, defending Hinds in particular. Hibbert then waylaid the constables and freed Hinds. Hinds was deemed the "ringleader" of the meeting and the rumpus that it stirred: a "great crowd had gathered; Corporal Martin intervened and Hinds and company were not at all pleased over the Corporal's action and sought to eject him, and in doing so, they assaulted him injuring one of his fingers."[48] Of note, these early Rastafari were not averse to physically contesting police or their aggressive detractors. The Rastafari evangelists were simultaneously connecting with their audiences while their resistance communicated threat to elites and colonial authorities.

Police charged Hinds and eight others with disorderly conduct for the December 16 skirmish. The nine Rastafari detainees were portrayed as lawbreakers who initiated a skirmish with the police and who lacked "decency" (they used obscene language).[49] Perhaps because Howell was not involved, the magistrate delivered a feeble admonition apparently intended to frighten: he said that "should they [the detainees] continue to break the law, and were brought back before him, he was going to give them the full penalty of the law. . . . They should learn to behave and conduct themselves like decent and respectable citizens."[50] The nine were convicted; Hinds got thirty days' hard labor, the others a fine of forty shillings or thirty days.[51] Hinds was probably the first of the founding Rastafari evangelists to get a jail sentence for preaching the Rastafari message. The guilty verdict did not dampen his activism. Counsel, reporters, and scholars have made Howell the star of the Rastafari show, when in fact he was one among several shifting, leading actors in Rastafari ethnogenesis.

In contrast to the presiding judge, elites did not take the December 16 skirmish lightly. The anonymous author of "It is Not a Joke" urged, "It is time for the authorities to bring the activities of those who preach Ras

Tafari in Jamaica to an end."[52] Ross could have written the opinion him-self. Barely a year after Howell's return to Jamaica, a public announce-ment was calling for the containment of the Rastafari. The following evening (the seventeenth), Ross and a gang armed with cudgels and cutlasses prepared to ambush Howell. Again, Howell did not show up.[53] Perhaps he was aware of what awaited him. Nonetheless, such serendip-ity is the stuff of legends and rich material for fabricating myths. How-ell's ability to navigate traps and rebound from efforts to destroy him no doubt aided his reputation as special or chosen, a man possessing preternatural capability.

December 21, 1933, and January 1, 1934

Police arrested Howell again for using seditious language on December 21, in Port Morant. Detective Frederick Scott and Corporal Jacobs of Port Morant station attended the December 21 evening meeting, consist-ing of a large audience. The officers took notes on what they considered "important." They explained no obvious focus or method to the inves-tigations, other than that their observation concentrated on what they considered important.

We must wonder about the effect of the arrests and growing harass-ment on the nascent evangelists. By January 1934, they felt the sting of police surveillance, arrest, and the growing antagonism from elites and commoners, especially the emergence of organized vigilantes (stirred by elites such as planters, ministers, and commercial operators). Nev-ertheless, the evangelists continued to organize and agitate while under fire. The persecution itself had the unintended consequence of fortifying their conviction in their message, which was only beginning to be tested in late 1933 and early 1934. Oppression, suppression, and repression, real and imagined, are often attendant to ethnogenesis and are essential to the collective identity formation of the Rastafari. Persecution and con-flict can have the effect of urging people to bind together into some form of community.[54] They inform collective identification by serving as an image that people use to generate a sense of connection, interdepen-dence, boundary, and shared experience, crystallizing difference into a state of mind and being: We are singled out for what we believe. What we believe makes us different; therefore, we should pursue solidarity. We will enjoy redemption one day; therefore, we must have faith in what we believe. An emergent collective Rastafari identity is coming into focus.

* * *

If we could again transport ourselves to Kingston and eastern Jamaica in March 1934 and this time slip into the havens of the various cliques of elites, we might hear them talking about the impending end of Howell and, by implication, the Rastafari identity script. It is worth repeating that in early 1934, the focus was on getting rid of Howell. The consensus was, get rid of Howell before he gained too much influence and too many adherents, and the Rastafari problem would dissipate. This was not an irrational strategy. Imprisoning Bedward in an asylum, for example, crippled the development of the Bedwardites. An emergent collectivity can be disrupted by neutralizing its primary sources of growth and transmission. If the primary causes were an individual or a handful of individuals, elimination of them might curtail further development. If ethnogenesis, however, did not depend on the attainments of particular individuals, then we must consider a wider array of factors that facilitate persistence.

4

Rastafari on Trial, 1934

Expounding the Rastafari Doctrine

The Bible says we are not to obey an immoral Government.
Therefore, we are not bound to obey the Government of this
country [Jamaica], for it is immoral.
—Native Baptist preacher, May 1865

Thursday, March 15, 1934, was the third day of Leonard Howell and
Robert Hinds's sedition trial.[1] Under examination by H. M. Radcliffe,
assistant to the attorney general, Howell told a captivated courtroom
audience that the meetings he had convened in St. Thomas were "to tell
of Jehovah's Kingdom." He elaborated,

> I told them [the audiences] that at his [King Ras Tafari's] coronation . . .
> the King of England sent down his third son with great gifts. . . . Such
> wonderful and glorious gifts never had been given to other kings of the
> earth. . . . Representatives all over the world went to pay tribute to the
> greatest king. I told them that as Ethiopians, we were worshipping the god
> of idolatry—the king which Nebuchadnezzar set up in Babylon for the
> people to worship. . . . But there were three Jews who refused to worship
> the god which Nebuchadnezzar set up, and they said to Nebuchadnezzar:
> "We shall not worship that God you set up," . . . that the same God [Christ]
> had come back on earth to lead mankind in the path of righteousness. . . .
> He was 33 years and six months [old] when He was crucified. He must
> come back on earth and take HIS FULL POWER to reign. . . . I asked them
> as beloved Ethiopians to stamp their heart with the image of Ras Tafari,
> who said: "I am the beginning and the end."[2]

Howell fixed on and embellished the magnificent gifts England offered the new Emperor and Empress and how the world's principalities

and powers literally bowed before the Ethiopian monarchs. In King Ras Tafari, now Emperor Selassie, Howell saw the Christ returned, a message he would tell all who would listen. He was concerned that people did not understand what had happened November 2, 1930, and he used the trial to illustrate what he saw as the divine significance of the coronation of King Ras Tafari. Using Old Testament imagery and parables, Howell and Hinds cast themselves as Shadrach, Meshach, and Abednego, three Jews whom King Nebuchadnezzar had cast into a blazing furnace for failing to worship his idols. The three were unharmed by the inferno, displaying the power of their God to protect them and a warning not to praise false gods. Such parables were well-known to elite and nonelite Jamaicans alike. The allusions should be read within a history of Black Jamaicans using the Bible to resist government deemed immoral. Undoubtedly, the claims that Howell and Hinds made while testifying in court during the week of March 12, 1934, also piqued the curiosity of many other Jamaicans about King Ras Tafari and about Howell and Hinds. Jamaicans were introduced to a new set of beliefs via news reportage on the trial of Howell and Hinds.

The Court and the News: Two Major Vectors Expounding Rastafari Doctrine

During four consecutive days in court, Leonard Howell and Robert Hinds laid out the essence of their Rastafari beliefs. The legal proceedings provide a glimpse into some of the key tenets of an emergent Rastafari theology and identity and how the authorities used their control over the major institutions of Jamaican society to enforce their will and the interests of elites. While under oath, Howell and Hinds told what they believed, what they had grievances against, and theologically speaking, why it mattered: a new order was at hand, and it would be based in new understandings. They outlined major tropes—such as "Babylon"—that defined the systems of colonialism and White supremacy. Howell and Hinds said that Jamaica was a corrupt modern-day Babylon in collusion with the churches and that the entire arrangement existed by sucking away the vitality of Black Jamaicans. They submitted that there was an alternative to Babylon. The alternative involved embracing the new Messiah, relocating to Africa, and personifying love that is long, overflowing, virtuous, and eternal ("L.O.V.E.," as Howell called it).[3] Their tone and ideas were millenarian and messianic: the Messiah had returned in the form of an African King, inaugurating a new era in which the sons and daughters of enslaved Africans would assume their rightful position as God's chosen people. The trial functioned like a cauldron in which Howell's and Hinds's beliefs, boiled down, were easily broadcast throughout Jamaica in the pages of newspapers.

The trial of Howell and Hinds and the news coverage of it had two conflicting effects. It magnified the ability of government and media to demonize the Rastafari as deluded lunatics possessed by their fantasies about Ethiopia and a Black God. It also magnified the ability of Howell and Hinds to broadcast their message.

Early 1934: Building a Case against the Rastafari Evangelists

By the end of January 1934, the Jamaican constabulary had arrested many Rastafari activists in St. Thomas, some of them more than once. Howell and Hinds were prominent among the arrestees. Two other men who showed up on several occasions in the reports as arrestees were Theophilus Jackson and Osmond Shaw. Along with Howell and Hinds, Jackson and Shaw also were defendants charged with sedition. They and others were among a core group of people committed to the emergent Rastafari doctrine. While we know that Robert Hinds and Joseph Hibbert were active Rastafari evangelists, Jackson and Shaw were also probably preaching given that they too were charged with sedition (both Hibbert and Hinds would go on to independently develop the Rastafari doctrine).

It was ironic that the Morant Bay courthouse was the site of Howell's and Hinds's trial. In October 1865, the courthouse had been the target of Paul Bogle's band of race-conscious rebels who sparked the Morant Bay uprising. For Bogle and his comrades, the courthouse was a symbol of the system that oppressed them. Howell and Hinds, though, had become victims of the judicial system that Bogle challenged. Nevertheless, the two and their Rastafari collaborators represented a new generation of race-conscious rebels critical of colonial Jamaica and its inequities, and they were organizing in the same parish that gave birth to the Morant

Bay rebellion. In 1934, people—especially elites—were still sensitive about the Morant Bay rebellion. When Black Jamaicans spoke out loudly against the injustices they endured in the colonial regime, "we cannot have another Morant Bay" was often the reply from elites.

Sedition: A Means to Managing Dissent, Protest, and Charismatic Leadership

The March 1934 St. Thomas Circuit Court session promised to be a long one. Sir Robert Lyall-Grant, chief justice, was set to preside over the session, with assistant to the attorney general H. M. Radcliffe representing the Crown. Of the nine cases on the docket, three involved the founding Rastafari: Howell, Hinds, and Shaw.[4]

Great Britain was a colonial power that *had* to be concerned about threats to its supremacy in its many colonies. Therefore, we can read the colonial establishment's reaction to the incipient Rastafari in Jamaica within this wider field of international turmoil and internal dissent. We must also read the establishment's reaction within the context of Jamaica's history. We saw earlier how the colonial authorities created laws intended to give them the power to manage the situations in which race and religion collaborated to foment rebellion. The Seditious Meetings Act of 1836 threatened, "When any Justice, or Officer . . . shall receive information on oath, or have reasonable cause to suspect that any meeting or assembly is held for the purpose of stirring up or exciting any person or persons to commit any act of insurrection or insubordination, or to obtain otherwise than by lawful means any alteration or change in the constitution or government of this land as by law established . . . such Justice or Officer shall forthwith proceed to such meeting or assembly."[5] Fomenting rebellion, however, was broadly interpreted. As we saw with Bedward, a fiery speech could be defined as seditious, even when there was insufficient evidence to prove that the orator intended to act on the words or incite others to act on the words.

Opinions were mixed on how to handle the accused Rastafari. The debate occurring among the colonial administration's leadership was out of sync with what other elites were feeling. In Kingston, the attorney general and governor wanted to avoid legal action that might make a martyr of Howell. The leading Brown elites with political ambitions were concerned that the British colonial office might doubt their ability to govern themselves if they could not get rid of a handful of provocative evangelists (men such as Norman Manley and Alexander Bustamante were seeking to institute universal suffrage). Other elites—planters, clergy, business leaders—saw the Rastafari as a hazard to the status quo that required immediate liquidation. They reasoned that locking up Howell would disrupt the work of the Rastafari activists and disillusion his followers. Mounting pressure from business and religious elites and the recklessness of citizen vigilantes like John Ross attacking the Rastafari pushed the governor and attorney general to act. In the execution of the effort to suppress Howell and the early Rastafari, the *Daily Gleaner* saw a good story. What the Jamaican colonial government tried to avoid—publicizing Howell and the Rastafari—the *Daily Gleaner* and other newspapers did for them.

One reason that the colonial government could cautiously sift through its options was because it could draw on a repertoire of proven "legal" strategies for subduing religio-racial leadership. It used vagrancy, loitering, no public speech, and other ordinances to intimidate and imprison people perceived as hostile. The attorney general had the advantage of resources and the know-how to use the law to serve the government's purposes, irrespective of any concern with justice and fairness for defendants. At the same time, the trial and subsequent news coverage would also reveal how elite strategies of social control could backfire.

There were few legal options for getting rid of Howell. Given his ability to excite crowds, the prosecution opted to argue that Howell was a violent threat. Charging him with unlawful assembly or selling under false pretenses would be insufficient to jail him long enough to disrupt any following that he had developed. The colonial administration needed a charge that signaled that Howell was a serious threat. And the court had recent experience examining sedition cases. Radcliffe, for example, had successfully prosecuted a sedition charge against the politician, anti-immigrant activist, and "stump orator" Leonard Waison a few years earlier.[6]

The charge of sedition probably did not strike Howell, Hinds, and Rastafari adherents as a grave offense. With God Almighty and the

King James Bible the ultimate source of law for them, they offered a competing discourse. They were seeking to establish their views and legitimacy, and the Jamaican government, by hampering their mission, had become their adversary. This was revealed in their speeches and imagery: for example, Howell was documented as calling Queen Victoria the "Mother of Harlots and Abominations of the Earth." Howell was referring to the Babylon of the book of Revelations and therefore drawing on scriptural imagery to make a religious point: the Queen was associated with the evil kingdom that would be destroyed by the new Messiah. The early Rastafari people were not promoting political revolution, actual violence, or hatred when they lambasted the colonial government and the British monarchy. What evangelists like Howell and Hinds sought was to do was remind listeners that they lived in an oppressive system and that King Ras Tafari offered an enticing alternative.

What was at stake differed for each party. The prosecution had to draw a distinction between free and libelous speech for the jury. Radcliffe explained that Howell's preaching was libelous because even though a citizen could criticize government, he could not use language that stirred up "hatred between classes" or that aroused contempt for the government. Radcliff argued that Howell's sermons were "bosh and twaddle" that had an ill effect on people whose "intelligence was not high and who were ignorant."[7] Just as John Ricketts, the man who visited Ethiopia in 1933, was cast by elites as a gullible, unlettered Jamaican detrimentally influenced by Howell, so too were the people who dared to take the Rastafari doctrine seriously.

The law, speaking through the attorney general, his staff, and others, paid lip service to free speech and a right to criticize government, while saying that Howell could not preach beliefs that were critical of the colonial government and that aroused people's grievances. Radcliffe defined sedition as activity "calculated to disturb the peace of the community, to bring the sovereign into contempt, to bring the government and those administering it into hatred, to put class against class, and stir up discontent among the public."[8]

Radcliffe instructed the jury that if Howell meant to stir up ill, he should be found guilty. The authorities cleverly sought a means to frame talking against authority and its symbols as a threat to state security.

Rastafari on Trial: Lecturing to the People

Howell's and Hinds's trial for sedition began on March 13, 1934, and ended on the sixteenth. The case was highly anticipated and announced by the *Daily Gleaner* as the "cause celebre of the Assizes."[9] Each day the courtroom was "packed with anxious spectators," eager to see and hear Leonard Howell and Robert Hinds, to learn what the "Rastafarite" fuss was all about.[10] (The names and spelling of the names applied to the Rastafari shift over time, beginning with "Ras Tafarites" and including "Ras Tafarian" and later "Rastafarian" and "Rasta.")

In the opening report on the trial, Howell was portrayed as admirable, perhaps to invoke a sense of tragedy. A reporter described his "athlete figure" snappily dressed in black, with a beard similar to that "worn by the King of Abyssinia." Howell was a good specimen gone bad.

Howell and the "large number of men and women who accompanied him" sported "identifying insignias," rosettes brightly colored yellow, green, and black.[11] With the exception of the bearded men, the Rastafari looked no differently than other rank-and-file Jamaicans. The rosettes indicate that Rastafari were developing a repertoire of identity symbols; the rosettes and men's beards signaled their identity to other each, while also distinguishing them. By mid-1934, there was a committed, if small, coterie of "Rastafarites" building a community and identity under conditions of persecution. Without talking or gesturing, the rosettes and beards signaled identity and community.

Howell and Hinds were tried separately. Howell took the stand first. Howell showed glimpses of competence, which were downplayed in the trial coverage, while instances of erratic and strange behavior were highlighted. A staff reporter said as much: "Interest might have waned through the protracted nature of the trial, but up to the last, there was a good deal of mirth provoked by the fanatic utterances of a man, born in Jamaica, who from beginning to end propounded the doctrine that Ethiopia will rule the world."[12] The view of Howell and the Rastafari as utterly ridiculous, but menacing, set the tone for how people would perceive and talk about the Rastafari.

Although Howell had legal representation during the preliminary examinations, he represented himself at trial. Perhaps he felt confident that he could make a solid case for himself, or perhaps he could not afford an attorney. As his own attorney, Howell jousted vigorously with his court adversaries. His maneuvers were a hodgepodge and unconventional, confusing the court one moment and then amusing it at another. On some occasions, Howell displayed lawyerly judgment. He asked that jurors from Seaforth, Port Morant, and Morant Bay not sit on his trial because many were biased against him and in favor of elites and police. The court denied his request. He attacked the credibility of Constable Gayle and Corporal Brooks. In questioning the legitimacy of the court's application of the law, Howell satirized the judicial system and its officers in a way that resonated with the sensibility of many nonelite Jamaicans. Rank-and-file Black Jamaicans undoubtedly knew how capricious and careless the police could be. Howell, Hinds, the court, and the news reports were shaping people's attitudes—favorably and unfavorably—toward the Rastafari.

Howell tried to show that the crowd was well-behaved:

> "Did they act as if they were angry with the Government?" Howell asked.
>   Gayle replied, "Not at the time."
> HOWELL: "Everybody was perfectly orderly?"
> GAYLE: "At times."
> HOWELL: "At what times were they disorderly?"
> GAYLE: "They cheered" [for a statement that Howell made].
> HOWELL: "That is not disorderly."[13]

Howell was contesting the claim that he incited hatred among the crowd and that the crowd was unruly.

Howell's witnesses, his core member base, eagerly contested the prosecution. They found nothing treacherous about the speech because it spoke to issues of interest to them. Witnesses testified that they enjoyed Howell's "lecture" and that they heard nothing seditious.[14]

Three of Howell's witnesses on the second day of the trial were women. Rachael Patterson was Howell's first witness. She said that on December 10, she did not see Gayle and Brooks taking notes as they claimed. She also alleged that Brooks was tipsy. Albertha Laloo testified about a discussion she had with Constable Gayle about Howell. (Albertha was a Black woman married to an Indian man called "Laloo," who during the first years of the Rastafari was believed to be an influential adviser to Howell.)[15] According to Albertha, Gayle told her that his inspector had assigned him and Brooks to surveil Howell and that the best case that they could make against Howell was based on his December 10 speech in Seaforth, not other speeches such as those delivered at Port Morant. Apparently Laloo knew Gayle but felt enough attachment to Howell to give up the conversation with Gayle. Florence Jackson, a resident at Seaforth, testified to having been present at the December 10 meeting and listened to Howell's speech. She denied that Howell said anything seditious; she also asserted that she did not at any time see the officers taking notes.[16] Howell's witnesses challenged the Crown's claim of seditious speech, but for naught. The colonial government, detractors, and the Rastafari were talking past each other: what the government and detractors considered seditious was interpreted as interesting or harmless by the Rastafari and their sympathizers.

The prosecution was confident that it would convict Howell easily and barely prepared its witnesses for the trial. They recruited some of their key witnesses just days before their testimony.

Elite Strategies against the Rastafari

In the major news coverage of the trial, Howell is repeatedly ridiculed and any absurdity accentuated. Derision functioned as repression because it marginalized the Rastafari. On the first day of the trial, a *Daily Gleaner* reporter sprinkled the coverage of Howell's testimony with the parenthetical "laughter," "subdued snickering," and "outbursts of uncontrolled laughter," insinuating the silliness of Howell's testimony and the laugh value it provided the audience. Typical of the reporter's running commentary was this observation: "The prisoner then delved into the NEW TESTAMENT HISTORY for references to make present-day comparisons, with a rambling so-called religious story which ended with prognostications in connection with Armageddon."[17] Perhaps such "wit" helped sell papers. Disparaging Howell, Hinds, and the Rastafari became a methodical practice of news reportage, especially that of *Daily Gleaner's* editor in chief, Herbert de Lisser. The *Daily Gleaner* boasted that it brought down Alexander Bedward.[18] The editor must have believed he could do the same with the Rastafari.

For the colonial officials, there was more at stake in the sedition trial of Howell and Hinds than in handling a soapbox agitator like Leonard Waison. Sure, the court wanted to be convincing that it was unimpeachable in its decision to pursue a sedition conviction against Howell and Hinds. And the *Daily Gleaner* abetted the court and government in their endeavor. *Daily Gleaner* stories portrayed counsel as clever, apparently playing to the watchful eyes and ears of peer elites in law enforcement, colonial administration, politics, and commerce; the readers of the newspaper; and even Winston Churchill in England. Political elites wanted Churchill to believe that they were capable of self-governance. They wanted to show competence and ability in demolishing the Rastafari. The King's counsel sought to slay the Rastafari evangelists for their beliefs, right in front of their audiences. In reference to Howell's and Hind's alleged abuse of the King, Radcliffe asked the jury and audience, "What wrong has the King done us—a King whom we all respect?"[19] The elite tactic of ridiculing the Rastafari was forming and would develop into a persistent form of reactionary defamation that asserted the authority of the government (colonial and postcolonial) and the illegitimacy of the Rastafari. The prosecution depicted Howell, Hinds, and the Rastafari as people whose "caustic attitude toward the police" and whose "denouncement of Christianity knew no bounds."[20]

Early Rastafari Theology

The testimony of Howell and Hinds spoke to how the Rastafari were developing a unique identity and theology and how they were building a community of like-minded brothers and sisters. Howell and Hinds laid out the themes of the Rastafari doctrine throughout the trial: King Ras Tafari was the Messiah described in Revelations and other books of the Old and New Testament; the crowning of King Ras Tafari as Emperor of Ethiopia signaled impending Black redemption and the time for Black people to migrate to Africa; Black people had been colossally exploited by Whites for too long; church and political leaders were dishonest; and the courts and law enforcement were crooked.

On the stand, Howell and Hinds invoked aspirations of betterment, they elaborated on biblical lore, they raised grievances against the European settlers, and they painted a utopian conception of Africa as a

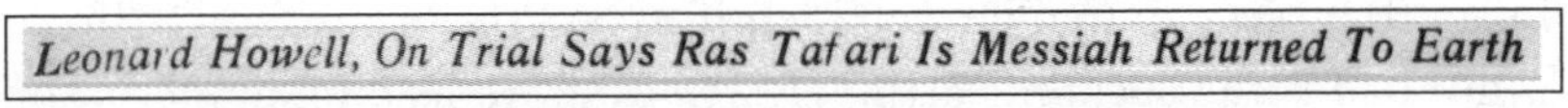

Leonard Howell, On Trial Says Ras Tafari Is Messiah Returned To Earth

Figure 4.1. Announcement of Leonard Howell's trial, *Daily Gleaner*, 1934. (Courtesy The Gleaner Co. [Media] Ltd.)

land of liberty, milk, and honey. They distilled Ethiopianism and early Black nationalism. These tropes appealed to many Jamaicans, the dispossessed in particular. In this sense, the relative-deprivation and cognitive-dissonance explanations offered during the 1970s and 1980s for the emergence of the Rastafari during the 1930s are understandable. Many of the early Rastafari were dissatisfied with poverty and exploitation and were interested in pursuing alternatives to their status, including migration to Africa. However, there was far more to the saga, as we shall see in subsequent chapters.

When on the courtroom floor, Howell preached minisermons. He told the court how a God of righteousness had returned to Earth to lead humankind: "as it was in the beginning, so will it be in the end," he said.[21] The first-generation Rastafari woman Rasta Ivey regularly told me the same: "As it was in the beginning, so shall it be in the end. What is new [now] was once old." The Rastafari hold a cyclical conception of time—the past repeats itself.[22] The idea here was that just as Jesus Christ inaugurated a new dispensation two millennia ago that would culminate in Judgment Day, King Ras Tafari was the Messiah returned to fulfill the works of Christ (see figure 4.1). Just as Christ was sent to prepare humankind for a new order, so too was King Rastafari. Howell was admonishing the court and the world that they were living in apocalyptic times.

The courtroom spectators would burst into laughter when Howell or Hinds said that King Ras Tafari was the Christ returned. It may have been nervous laughter, the kind that blurts out of one's mouth when one hears something uncomfortable. Audience members found preposterous the idea that the Messiah could be an African King.

Howell expounded to the court audience how Jesus Christ's lineage traced to King Solomon and his father, King David. This was no small point because it offered a Bible-based explanation for why King Ras Tafari was the Messiah. Jamaicans knew about Kings David and Solomon. Howell and other Rastafari evangelists connected the ancient biblical kings to Jesus Christ and the modern Ethiopian nobleman King Ras

Tafari. The Messiah that Howell identified was the "same God [Christ] [who] had come back on earth," Howell said, "to lead mankind in the path of righteousness" in an unjust and wicked society.[23] While some of the moral Blackness literature that influenced Jamaicans during the 1920s made a similar point, Howell's twist was to argue that the prophecy had been fulfilled. The wait was over.

Howell and Hinds made the coronation itself a fundamental basis of their Rastafari doctrine: it signaled a new dispensation. Howell pointed out that "the English Government accepted their king [Ras Tafari] because they sent diplomatical [sic] presentations and promised to serve Ras Tafari."[24] Note that Howell said "their king," indicating their allegiance to King Ras Tafari and implying that Britain (and other nations) were also in agreement on the religious significance of the coronation. With his depiction of White and non-White national leaders bowing to an African King, whose empire had eluded colonization, Howell was tapping into Black Jamaicans' admiration for King Ras Tafari and Ethiopia, while also suggesting an inversion in power relations. Europe, the colonizers, in particular, were bowing to Africa. King Ras Tafari's official titles attendant to his elevation to Emperor, such as "King of Kings," "Lord of Lords," and "Conquering Lion of the Tribe of Judah," were, said Howell, recognized by "all the persons of the earth." Even the cosmopolitan diplomat Addison Southard, who authored the 1931 *National Geographic* report on Ethiopia and King Ras Tafari's crowning, was "awed by the ritual, history, and spectacle of the coronation."[25] It followed, then, that the prosecutors were totally off-base in their prosecution; instead, the court was *persecuting* the Rastafari.

An Alternative Reading of Biblical Scripture

The historians Edward Blum and Paul Harvey argue that people define Christ to fit their needs.[26] Black Jamaicans worked in various ways with the idea of a phenotypically White Christ (as depicted in portraits and sculptures such as Michelangelo's *Risen Christ*). If Christ was White, it followed that the returning Christ would also be White, and therefore a White savior would redeem all.[27] The Ethiopianists explicitly racialized biblical narratives by substituting Whites and Whiteness with Blacks and Blackness. In the early formulations of Ethiopianism, Blacks were designated the chosen people who would enter a new Canaan. In some formulations, the Promised Land was in Ethiopia or another part of Africa.

The idea of a Black God and savior was a troubling idea for many Jamaicans, including Black Jamaicans. This irony—Black people reluctant to imagine God in their own image—attested to how Black Jamaicans had been socialized into a Eurocentric understanding. Howell rebuked the established religions and preachers as wrongheaded and self-absorbed. Every church should be shut down because, he said, their belief in God was misplaced. The clergy was misleading people—lying—by talking of a White God who inhabited an invisible realm.

Howell and other Rastafari evangelists offered a take on the King James Bible that brought issues of righteousness and social justice to the fore. During the trial, Howell and Hinds counseled the audience that their "Lord" King Ras Tafari had prepared a mansion for them but not in Jamaica, where they lived in huts, for which they had to pay taxes.[28] Howell had promised his December 10 audience that Ethiopia, a place better than their taxed huts in St. Thomas, awaited them. The parallel between the disdain that the Jews of Christ's era had for taxes collected by a colonizing Rome and the extraction of rent and taxes by well-off landowners and government from threadbare peasants in St. Thomas was not overlooked by the Rastafari preachers' audiences. Taxes were a big concern for the people of eastern Jamaica. For example, the Tax and Rate Payers Association of St. Thomas, formed a year later in 1935, had a millenarian and apocalyptic bent. Member Darrell Reid called out for Armageddon and a second coming of Christ to free Black Jamaicans from the grip of poverty, hunger, and "land parasites," which were squeezing them into destitution.[29] Early Rastafari evangelists and many residents of St. Thomas were receptive to ideas such as those promoted by Reid and sought to harness the widespread disaffection with government and landowners.

The emergent Rastafari were lacing together an ideology that utilized both historical and narrative truths. Historical truth subsists on documentable and documented occurrences, while narrative truth has its basis in the multiple and shifting but not necessarily verifiable meanings that people create.[30] Howell's and Hinds's testimony distanced the Rastafari from the conformist and nonconformist Christian denominations and thus demarcated their identity boundaries.

Howell delivered a prophetic analysis of Jamaican society and an argument for Rastafari doctrine. Drawing on the biblical books of Thessalonians and Revelations, Howell said, in reference to the members of his audiences, "I asked them as beloved Ethiopians to stomp in their hearts the image of Ras Tafari, who said: 'I am the beginning and the end.'"[31] Thessalonians 5:2 says that "the day of the Lord will come like a thief in the night," while Revelations 17:5 blares, "upon her forehead was a name written, 'MYSTERY, BABYLON THE GREAT, THE MOTHER OF HARLOTS AND ABOMINATIONS OF THE EARTH.'" Howell was pointing out that God had become manifest in plain sight. And "Babylon the great" was destined to fall now that the Messiah was on the scene. Babylon was conceived as a supernatural *and* a material political entity. It signified a cosmopolitan and advanced society, corroded with corruption, oppression, and depravity, and it signified supermundane powers (like governments) at odds with biblical provisos about godliness and God. Babylon was Jamaica; the police were Babylon's enforcers. Howell's mission was to tell all who would listen about the new era launched by the crowning of King Ras Tafari.

"L.O.V.E.," not animosity, was what Howell said he was promoting. Each letter signaled an element of caring affection that Black people as adherents of the doctrine of Rastafari should personify: "Long love, Overflowing love, Virtuous love, and Eternal love."[32] Embodying L.O.V.E. became an ideal integral to becoming and being Rastafari. L.O.V.E. provided an unadorned but profound ethical and moral code. The code stipulated that the Rastafari love generously and abundantly in an environment of scarcity, contention, exploitation; the code required being moral exemplars, setting a standard that in turn set the Rastafari as a distinct people and identity.

Christians emphasized how Christ loved without restrictions. From the point of view of the early Rastafari, few Christians practiced the love that Christ was known for. Separation from Babylon and practice of L.O.V.E. became bywords of the Rastafari, especially through the 1970s. Howell and other Rastafari evangelists were defining the contours of the emergent identity, here establishing a set of values and a stance of physical and social distance from other Jamaicans.

For Howell and Hinds, the instructions of the King James Bible superseded the laws of the colonial Jamaican government. Government was immoral (as noted in the chapter's epigraph). After all, like the ancient Jews who loathed Roman laws and occupation of Israel, Hinds and Howell saw the British and colonial Jamaican governments as colonizing occupiers and exploiters of their subjects. They were immoral *and* evil. Drawing on Revelations 12, Hinds compared the twelve stars in King Ras Tafari's crown to the woman who wore a crown of twelve stars on her head and who had to flee the dragon (Satan), which sought to slay her. The woman, protected by God and Earth, signified the elect of God—King Ras Tafari and his followers—whereas Britain and the Jamaican colonial government were the dragon. Hinds and Howell were teaching as well as preaching. Through their sermons, they developed and laid a substrate of symbol-laden information that could in turn be used as the basis for fashioning both collective and personal identifications. When Radcliffe questioned Hinds about his views of the Christ, Hinds told him, "If He [Christ] come in the spirit He could not wear a crown."[33] What Hinds meant was that Christian conceptions of Christ as an ethereal spirit meant that a Christ reborn as the new Messiah could not dwell among living people as he did in his previous incarnation. The emergent Rastafari view was that God lives among the people. Hinds's point was blunt: a spirit cannot wear a material crown, so it had to be a human—the Messiah manifest in flesh as a king to assume the throne of Kings David and Solomon. On the reincarnation of Christ, Hinds emphasized a material God, not an ethereal one.

The doctrine that Howell and Hinds expounded while on trial showed some uniformity, though it was only beginning to crystallize around a core cluster of beliefs, symbols, and practices, in the ways that characterize an established theology or collective identification. However, the theology harbored elements of other religions (e.g., spirit possession, healing rites, concern with Jesus). The Rastafari converts continued to cling to elements of their pre-Rastafari identity and theology, which is unsurprising given the prevalence of such practices, as we have seen. The rise of the "Dreadlocks" Rastafari in the late 1940s marked an identity shift in which converts began to disassociate themselves from the amalgamated practices of the first generation in favor of revising and revitalizing Rastafari identity in ways that further distinguished its distinction.[34]

Although the Rastafari doctrine would become stylized and essentialized as ethnogenesis continued, the hybridity of the emergent doctrine

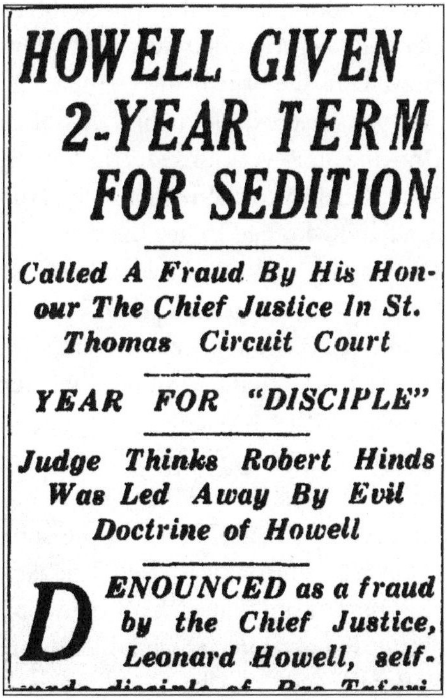

Figure 4.2. Announcement of the
sentencing of Leonard Howell and
Robert Hinds, *Daily Gleaner*, 1934.
(Courtesy The Gleaner Co.
[Media] Ltd.)

HOWELL GIVEN 2-YEAR TERM FOR SEDITION

Called A Fraud By His Honour The Chief Justice In St. Thomas Circuit Court

YEAR FOR "DISCIPLE"

Judge Thinks Robert Hinds Was Led Away By Evil Doctrine of Howell

DENOUNCED as a fraud by the Chief Justice, Leonard Howell, self-

might actually have contributed to it gaining traction. The first two generations of Rastafari were motivated by their interest in race, divinity, truth, and righteousness. They were skeptical of mainstream and White interpretations of the Bible, they wanted to better know history, and they were fixed on morality and justice. The Rastafari doctrine probably benefited from doctrinal diversity in its early years because the versions could speak to varied audiences whose members were ensconced in the already established religious discourses. For example, Ethiopianists and Black Nationalists were interested in the idea of a Black Messiah or God, and those who were close to Christianity were curious about the idea of Christ returned. The embryonic Rastafari doctrine was an amalgam of biblical lore, Ethiopianism, Black nationalism, Revival, Freemasonry, and Gnostic freewheeling. Each of these religious assemblages was partially utilized, combined in sometimes conflicting ways.

Howell and Hinds's claim for a God in the flesh whose arrival was signaled by a coronation, for example, contradicted many Christian ideas about the return of Christ. As the Rastafari theology developed, heaven was relocated to Earth, along with its counterpart, hell. Hell and heaven existed in the realm of the living. One did not have to die to gain entry to either. The Rastafari doctrine emphasized living; it urged people to create heaven on Earth and to stamp out hell on Earth.

Enter Robert Hinds

"I consider that you are a fraud," Chief Justice Lyall-Grant told Howell and the court on the final day of his trial, March 16, 1934 (see figure 4.2). Right after Howell's trial ended, Robert Hinds's began. Hinds's participation in propagating the Rastafari doctrine panned into focus.

Hinds's testimony was consistent with Howell's and Howell's witnesses. Hinds returned to a theme of Howell's defense, submitting that the police notes were inaccurate. During his testimony, Hinds further elaborated on the Rastafari doctrine. He expounded on the idea of King Ras Tafari as the Christ returned, how he reached the conclusion that Black people are Ethiopians, Jews, and Israelites. He also talked of Black Jamaicans' interest in migrating to Ethiopia.

Hinds was earnest, militant, and defiant, and this came through when time came for him to offer his own evidence. Why did the authorities not treat Hinds as a threat equal to Howell? Hinds was a charismatic and veteran proselytizer and a former devotee of Alexander Bedward with a record of jousting with police as a consequence of protest marches. He even told Radcliffe that he was a preacher before Howell's arrival and that he had marched with the Bedwardites from August Town to Halfway Tree in Kingston, where he was arrested on Hope Road. Howell may have had grandiose visions of himself as a prophet delivering the Rastafari gospel, but he must have recognized that the veteran Hinds could aid his mission. According to Constable Gayle, a fiery Hinds told the December 10 spectators that he would "get over to England and conquer the land" and that he would "tell King George that two kings cannot reign in the same land, and the Ethiopian king must rule."[35] One must wonder why Hinds was taken so lightly given his caustic condemnation, though it again suggests that Howell was seen as the real villain. The defiant Hinds crowed at the same meeting, "Anywhere I go with my angels flood come. I went to Kingston, flood come. And I went to

St. Elizabeth, and now St. Thomas. You better mind I don't call down my Angels and let flood come."[36] Here Hinds spoke as a prophet possessed of supernatural ability, flaunting his gift to command angels and nature to do his bidding. While Hinds's claims could be interpreted as ridiculous within the schema of the expert and rationalized knowledge characteristic of modern societies like Jamaica's colonial polity, it might be taken seriously by Jamaicans who believe that some people possess the abilities to heal and communicate with the supernatural. As we have seen, such people were both esteemed and feared among rank-and-file Black Jamaicans. The historian Anthony Bogues calls people like Hinds and Howell "redemptive prophets." Redemptive prophets are healers and diviners who seek to heal both people and communities. They disclose knowledge beyond the ken of ordinary folk, and they foretell the future. They condemn oppressive orders—in this case, colonialism and racial exploitation—and "call people to action."[37]

Hinds was unable to read well, but this did not hinder his intellectual or oratorical abilities. Given Hinds's detailed recall of both scripture and his December 10 speech, Radcliffe sarcastically said to him, "'You have a wonderful memory. How do you remember that?' Hinds replied, 'I got a reader to read for me' (laughter)." Radcliffe's interrogation of how Hinds concluded that King Ras Tafari was the Messiah suggests how Hinds and other founding Rastafari transformed themselves into Rastafari. Radcliffe continued his questioning along similar lines. He queried, "You say King Rastafari is Christ?" "Yes sir," Hinds replied. Radcliffe: "When was it you first heard that was so?" Hinds: "Not until L. P. Howell came, sir (laughter). But I read of the king of kings in the Bible." Hinds continued, saying that he had seen "photographs of Ras Tafari before Howell came there [because] . . . he saw a man from Cuba with one and he saw a magazine with pictures of the coronation."[38] Hinds had met someone from Cuba with a magazine that featured a story on King Ras Tafari, probably the *National Geographic* of 1931 or the November 3, 1930, cover story on Abyssinia published in *Time* magazine.

Radcliffe shifted his questioning from the rationale for King Ras Tafari's divinity to ethnicity and race: "Did Howell tell you that you are a Jew?" to which Hinds replied, "No sir. It was not Howell who tell us. . . . We found it in the Bible. The brethren who could write, search the Bible and use a dictionary and we find out that we are Ethiopians."

The idea of Black people defining themselves as Ethiopians was not new to Jamaica, but it was not common knowledge either. A man in the December 10 audience questioned the new Messiah's racial identity. He declared and challenged Hinds: "Jesus is a Jew. How you call him Black?" "Jews are Ethiopians," Hinds countered. "We are the Jews. We are called Israelites, otherwise Ethiopians."[39] A discussion of whether Jesus was White ensued. Hinds told the audience to read Jeremiah 8:20–22. The passage tells about a prophet who was persecuted for preaching of looming destruction and how he was gloomy because he believed that there was no redemption for Babylon: "For the hurt of the daughter of my people I am hurt, I am black."[40] It is likely that "black" in the biblical usage meant despairing, not a racial phenotype. Hinds, however, might have meant to imply both, that Jamaica was on the verge of destruction because of its sins and that Black Jamaicans had found pride in an identity that was stigmatized from its first days. An important aspect of what the Rastafari originators were doing was teaching by preaching, providing racialized lessons in history and scripture. They were projecting a new identity that designated them as pivotal to world history; although exploited and discriminated against, they now were real movers and shakers of history, ready to claim their rightful chosen people status.

The King's counsel assumed that they had shown everyone their cleverness and the ludicrousness of Howell, Hinds, and the Rastafari. Proof for them was in the "laugh value" generated by the statements of both defendants. For example, Radcliffe mockingly asked Hinds, "Were the people delighted at the idea of going over to Abyssinia?" Hinds replied, "'Yes sir. They said they would like to see the King' (laughter erupted in the courtroom)." Smiling at Hinds, Radcliffe retorted and elicited more laughter with what he probably thought was his rapier wit: "I myself would like to see the king."[41] The court, though, apparently did not catch on that Howell and Hinds were also seeking to discredit it. Radcliffe showing himself capable of polishing off two purportedly grandiloquent preachers might have led him to lose sight of the governor's initial concern that Howell and the Rastafari doctrine should not have an audience. Instead, the court, along with the *Gleaner* and other news organs, provided Howell and Hinds the opportunity to tell the nation about their Rastafari doctrine.

The Verdicts

With evidence and testimony complete, Chief Justice Lyall-Grant instructed the jury. He said that they should make a decision based on two questions: Did Howell actually say what he was indicted for saying? And was Howell's language on the evening in question (December 10) seditious? The chief justice qualified his instructions by adding that sedition was more serious than "political discussion" but not as serious as treason. The jury deliberated fifteen minutes and returned with a guilty verdict. Howell was momentarily stunned. Regaining composure, he asked for an appeal, which the chief justice denied. He then made what the reporter called a "verbose statement" to the jury when asked what he had to say to them. Howell was telling people what they needed and wanted to know: that the coronation signaled a new era. Continuing, Howell said that as a "brave hero," he would bear the consequences of the conviction and "come back much more gigantic than before."[42] These words were indeed prophetic whether Howell knew it or not. While the courtroom was split with laughter over Howell's prophecy, and with Radcliffe no doubt feeling confident that Howell was finished, it would be Howell, Hinds, and the Rastafari who would laugh longest.

Upon the chief justice's instructions, Hind's jurors deliberated for ten minutes and returned with a guilty verdict. He was pronounced guilty of sedition. Hinds bowed before the judge and gave him a salute. The second charge of sedition against both Howell and Hinds was dropped. Osmond Shaw's sedition case was postponed, though Radcliffe hinted that he might advise the attorney general to drop the case.[43]

The chief justice adjourned the court for fifteen minutes and then returned to sentence the pair of Rastafari evangelists. Speaking to Howell, the chief justice chastised him, "I consider you a fraud, that you pretend you have been to Ethiopia when you have never been near the place. . . . [Unfortunately] people take you for what you say you are." The chief justice considered Howell's "conduct to be dangerous to the people of the country." Howell was given a sentence of two years' imprisonment. Upon hearing this, Howell bowed, and said, "I thank you." The chief justice handed Hinds a twelve-month sentence. Hinds was charged with sedition, just like Howell. However, the chief justice concluded that Hinds was duped by Howell and thus gave him a lesser sentence: "You were led away by Howell, who is a fraud; who knows nothing about Ethiopia. I have spent a long time in Africa, and at one time was quite near to Ethiopia." The chief justice went on, lamenting, "Unfortunately, his evil doctrine got into your brain and you want to put it into others. I have seen the consequences of it in other countries, and the result has been serious rioting."[44] Chief Justice Lyall-Grant was probably referring to his experience in Nyasaland. Howell and Hinds were sent off to prison. Hinds's presence would become sporadic in the public record. Howell's career was just beginning.

* * *

The colonial authorities' strategy of discrediting and defusing the embryonic Rastafari by imprisoning two of its key propagators had limited effect. Without their recognizing it, the trial provided a platform for the Rastafari to profess their ideology, aided and amplified by the news coverage. The reporting shows how the early Rastafari had developed a coherent doctrine steeped in Ethiopianist and Christian content and imagery, and it shows the power asymmetries between the colonial government and Rastafari. Nevertheless, in Howell's and Hinds's sparring with the court officials, they showed wit and pluck that in hindsight is instructive of the character the Rastafari would develop. In time, it would become clear to authorities that removing Howell and Hinds from the scene was insufficient to halt Rastafari ethnogenesis.

5

Conflict and Retreat

Sinking Cultural Roots

The Beginnings of Rastafari Ethnogenesis

In July 1934, the *Daily Gleaner* ran an editorial column attacking Leonard Howell and Rastafari beliefs: "They believe the piffle that they are due to embark on August 4th for Abyssinia, to become subjects of King Ras-Tafari. A ship is to be sent here for them . . . for the country where there is more gold than stones at the bottom of a river. This is what scores of *deluded* people who have accepted the Ras-Tafari cult, have been told by mischievous individuals who are regarded by them as leaders, and have promised to guide them to the land of wealth and freedom."[1]

Howell and Hinds were in prison. Annie Harvey and Robert Athlyi Rogers were memories, if remembered at all. Garvey remained active after US authorities deported him to Jamaica in November 1927, when he completed his US federal prison sentence. His impact in Jamaica, however, was minuscule compared to the heady UNIA days of the late 1910s and early 1920s. Surely, the Rastafari were finished or withering on the vine, some self-assured elites reasoned. Law enforcement confidently predicted the Rastafari were on the verge of extinction. Far from decline, we know, in retrospect, they were still incubating.

In this chapter, I sketch the development of a Rastafari ethos and collective identity that formed during the period between Howell's and Hinds's imprisonment and the 1940s. We shall see the emergence of Rastafari disdain for law enforcement, the pope, and colonialism. We shall see the emergence of their sense of persecution; their growing exaltation of Emperor Selassie, Ethiopia, and Africa; and their use of cultural resources fundamental to crafting their collective identity. Interventions by outsiders, unanticipated events, and foreign influences—such as

Italy's invasion of Ethiopia and propaganda and tracts published outside Jamaica—were fundamental to Rastafari ethnogenesis.

Beware of the Bearded, Water-Cleaving Rastafari: Fanciful Identity Scripts

Some first-generation Rastafari have recalled that Leonard Howell declared August 1, 1934, "Exodus Day."[2] In the Old Testament, exodus described the departure of captive Israelites from bondage in Egypt. The notion of Rastafari leaving Jamaica was in play from the beginning.

According to rumors circulating though Kingston and St. Thomas, Rastafari of Seaforth and surrounding districts planned a march for August 1, 1934. The march would commence their migration, the culmination of which would be a walk across the sea to Ethiopia. The men would lead the way, walking in formation toward the sea. The male Rastafari were growing beards, one explanation for which was that the beard would allow them to carve their way unharmed through the high seas.[3] The writer exaggerated the Rastafari's story by giving serious attention to hyperbole. Given my conversations with first- and second-generation Rastafari about the role of ships in Rastafari thinking, it is likely the Rastafari talked of marching to Kingston to a ship landing. They also may have talked of walking through the ocean by cleaving a path with their beards. It is unlikely, however, that any Rastafari *actually* believed they could part the water; and I have discovered no reports of actual attempts to do so. The Rastafari *and* their detractors were weaving fantasy and hyperbole into identity scripts (see chapter 1). They spun fantastic stories in which they attributed to themselves supernatural and frightful powers—to part the seas like modern Moseses—while detractors spun stories that cast the Rastafari as nutty and illiterate peasants whom kleptomaniacs and self-anointed leaders misguided.

Actively stylizing their beliefs and identity, the Rastafari were self-fashioning, using the cultural resources at hand to create scripts that ran counter to prevailing notions of faith and race in Jamaica. Among Rastafari men, early on, the beard became an identity marker. The anthropologist and Rastafari scholar Barry Chevannes has argued that among Jamaicans, "hair cultivation . . . is paramount in the presentation of the self."[4] Black Jamaicans of the 1930s treated a man's beard as fearsome and thus antisocial. The Rastafari Filmore Alvaranga, a second-generation Rastafari who also traveled on the first official Jamaican mission to Ethiopia in 1961, recalled, "They held [down] men in this country and trim [haircut] and shave you for your beard. . . . If you go to get a work and have on your beard, them [employers] tell you must trim and come back. In those days [before the Rastafari], few people you see have on beards. . . . But not until Rastafari came into existence . . . [when Rastafari] man start to use beards, . . . they [Jamaicans] start to call you Rastafari."[5] To be clean-shaven was common among Black Jamaican men; it signified respectability. Although the Rastafari contributed to the gradual erosion of this norm, they had less immediate effect on the antisocial symbolism of the beard.

For the male Rastafari, the beard became a covenant with Emperor Selassie I and with being Rastafari. To wear a beard meant being identified as Rastafari, and to identify as Rastafari invited adverse consequences. The Emperor wore a beard, and Old Testament icons such as Moses, Samson, King David, and Ezekiel were bearded men. Forcibly shaving a man's beard during Old Testament times was a form of degradation, and perhaps the antagonists of the Rastafari recognized this. Identity fusion describes the process by which people make extreme sacrifices for a group with which they identify.[6]

Collective identity formation became shaped both by the reality of persecution and by creative imagination. Almost from the start, "bondage" became a fundamental idea informing Rastafari identity. They likened themselves as contemporary Israelites bound in colonial captivity but ready for exodus to their Promised Land. While beards and insignia physically distinguished the Rastafari, their metaphoric identification with ancient Israelites also differentiated them from other Jamaicans. The physical and metaphoric symbols made a basis for bonding under conditions of real and imagined oppression. They thrust bondage into high relief by juxtaposing it against the assumed liberty that would accompany migration. The notion of bondage evoked the memories of slavery, apprenticeship, and colonialism, as well as the realities of the enervating grip of poverty and exploitation, rolled up together in a form appropriate to early- to mid-twentieth-century Jamaica. The antithesis of bondage is liberation, liberation from oppression, liberation from

Jamaica, and liberation from miseducation (what decades later the Rastafari musician Bob Marley called "emancipation from mental slavery"). The Rastafari would continue to elaborate their notions of oppression and liberation as a part of distinguishing themselves (achievement), while outsiders crafted their own unflattering designations for the Rastafari (ascription).

Persecuting the "Deluded Creatures"

On August 4, 1934, a constable arrested Delrosa Francis, an alleged Rastafari woman from Seaforth district. Her written testimony and that of other Rastafari illuminate the evolving animosities and conflicts between Rastafari, ordinary Jamaicans, and the colonial police.[7]

"Rasta!" the district constable Robert Powers shouted at Francella McNish and Delrosa Francis, two women minding their business on the evening of Saturday, August 4.

McNish left her home that evening to patronize "Chang," a local business in Seaforth. Along the way, McNish met Francis. They were immersed in conversation when Powers's jeer interrupted their chit-chat. The women ignored Powell. Their snub, however, irritated the man, whom in addition to his disdain for the Rastafari, witnesses described as intoxicated. Powell hurled invective at the women. Another reputed Rastafari woman, Rachel Patterson, recounted how Powers "rushed inside the spirit-licensed-department and invited some young men to partake of some rum because he wanted them to assist him to play hell in Seaforth tonight with the Rasta-people."[8]

Francis said Powers threatened her: "he will arrest me because he was out for every dam [*sic*] Rasta-people in Seaforth." A heated verbal exchange ensued between Francis and Powers. Francis testified, "[Powers] held up a big stick, in his hand and said this is for every Rasta-people. These words were uttered at the top of his voice, which caught the attention of the young man whom I am along with."[9] James Findley, Francis's "paramour," heard the loud voices and walked toward the disturbance.[10] Finding his paramour the object of Powers's aggression, Findley urged Francis to sidestep the belligerent Powers and move on. Francis moved to Augustus Gordon's goldsmith shop. Powers followed, threatening to arrest Francis. She quipped, "You can't arrest me for I do nothing to be arrested."[11] Such unprofessional police conduct was common, as we have seen with the cases of Bedward, Howell, Hinds, and the Harveys.

Powers plied several men with drinks and then encouraged them to create a disturbance because he was the "King of Seaforth." Powers then "commanded them to make songs upon the people who [are] attached to the Rasta-Farie [Rastafari] religion."[12] Among the people ridiculed in verse were Mrs. Laloo, who testified on Howell's behalf during his sedition trial. She was also the female companion of one of Howell's colleagues, an Indian known as "Laloo."

Powers's son-in-law, Cyrus Grant, entered the fracas, assaulting Francis with a body slam and then lunging on top of her.[13] The disturbance "drew a vast crowd to witness the scene. . . . Many of the confused parties cried out that it was a state of mean advantage taken of Francis and that Powers himself had created the disturbance."[14] A man identified as Constable Taylor arrived, imposing order on the confusion but not justice. Taylor directed Powers to leave Francis alone and instructed Francis to follow him to the Seaforth police station, which she did. As they walked off, Grant struck Francis with a heavy stick, the blow grazing Taylor. It is unlikely that Grant's superiors punished his impudence.

Police charged eight people with disorderly conduct in relation to the melee.[15] The resident magistrate handed the case of the eight down to a local magistrate. The local magistrate summarily decreed punishment of thirty days' imprisonment in a Kingston or St. Catherine Parish prison or a fine of £40. The local magistrate did not allow the defendants to call witnesses. The defendants embarked on a letter-writing campaign to "His Excellency, The Officer, Administering the Government." The officials were not interested in meting out justice to the accused; the law provided no refuge for the Rastafari.[16] Such injustice would become a norm for the Rastafari's relationship to government.

None of the arrestees mentioned Rastafari or described themselves as Rastafari, though they referenced Powers's depiction of them as Rasta people. We know, though, that some of the people implicated in the indictment supported Leonard Howell—Patterson and Mrs. Lalloo, for example. Patterson noted how on her way home from the first scheduled hearing, Powers told her he "will have to persecute everyone that went to court with Delrosa Francis to give evidence for her."[17] The seven defendants rallied to support Francis, and this exacerbated their predicament. They were charged as accessories to the melee when they arrived at the local magistrate's office to provide testimony in support of McNish.

Nearly two weeks later, the acting colonial secretary wrote back to the accused that the court was independent and that there was nothing he could do.[18] The explanation was reasonable within the context of British colonial policy: the colonial secretary does not question matters adjudicated in a court of law. Yet the authorities were smug. An anonymous official scribbled at the bottom of a memo on the Rastafari, "If these people are dissatisfied with the J.P.'s [Justice of Peace's] findings, ... they have the right to appeal. They know this perfectly well and their only reason for not appealing is that they know or have been 'advised' that they have not got a hope in the appeal court."[19]

From the beginning, the Rastafari were oppressed, suppressed, and repressed. With the Rastafari, persecution stimulated ethnogenesis. There were also other factors feeding ethnogenesis, such as the continued presence of Emperor Selassie I and Ethiopia in the news. The Emperor and Ethiopia functioned for the Rastafari as real entities *and* as cultural resources, the living entities *and* their history occupying a central role in Rastafari identity and ideology.

Modern Incarnations of Rome and Babylon Assert Themselves: Cultural Resources, New and Old

Among the seminal texts important to the early development of Rastafari collective identity—the King James Bible, *The Holy Piby*, and *The Royal Parchment Scroll of Black Supremacy*, I add two more, *The Promised Key* and "Secret Society to Destroy Whites," both published in 1935, happening early in Rastafari ethnogenesis rather than before their emergence (like *The Holy Piby* or *The Royal Parchment Scroll*, both discussed earlier). These texts spoke directly to Rastafari experience and identity during the mid-1930s into the early 1940s, a period of restless religious, labor, and political groups, the Italo-Ethiopian War, and unnerved civic and business elites.

The Promised Key and "Secret Society to Destroy Whites": Vital Cultural Resources

Using the pen name G. G. Maragh, Leonard Howell published his own manifesto, *The Promised Key*. Exactly when, where, and how the tract was published is disputed, but it was probably published during 1935. *The Promised Key* continued the idea of Black supremacy or "Ethiopian dignity," lodging it as a new chronicle. The chronicle promoted Jamaica as the spiritual center of the world, integral to a new dispensation led by the "King of Kings": "His Majesty Ras Tafari is the head over all man for he is the Supreme God. . . . Forward to the King of Kings must be the cry of our social hope. . . . Forward to the King of Kings to learn His Laws and social order, so that virtue will eventually gain the victory over body and soul and the truth will drive away falsehood and fraud."[20]

Howell's manifesto called forth a new faith community anchored in the racial identity "Ethiopian." He set forth views that would become familiar tenets of Rastafari identity. Railing against churches, the Roman papacy, commerce, and politics as evil and ruinous, Howell contended that they fostered miseducation that that kept "people in ignorance."[21] The manifesto assigned infamy to Rome and equated the papacy with Satan. As Howell laid it out, the papacy had designs on ruling Ethiopia and Ethiopians (in the generic sense of Black people). However, such subjugation was not in the stars: "Dear inhabitants of the Western Hemisphere, the King of Kings' warriors can never be defeated, the Pope of Rome and his agents shall not prevail against the King of Kings. . . . You all must stand up, stand up, for the King of Kings. . . . From victory to victory King Alpha shall lead his army till every enemy is vanquished."[22] The theologian David Spencer views *The Promised Key* as a distillation of Howell's street preaching through 1935.[23]

The *Jamaica Times*'s columnist "Ginger" reviewed *The Promised Key* ("Ginger" is the pseudonym of the English architect and artist Byron Caws). Ginger reported verbatim some of *The Promised Key* to discredit Howell and make readers aware of the ideas and stamped the tract as diabolical.[24] Opinion shapers like Ginger set a tone in ascribing motives of hate and race prejudice to the early Rastafari, while the achievement aims of the Rastafari—Black solidarity or critiques of exploitation and miseducation, for example—were squelched. However, vying perceptions are not unusual where power asymmetries among groups means that marginalized people may struggle to position their self-presentation alongside those of outsiders. Power asymmetries may be enduring, but they also shift. Who represents the Rastafari and how will also change over time.

Around the same time as the publication of Howell's *Promised Key*, rumors of an international Black conspiracy and secret society—the Nya-Binghi—that focused on destroying Whites circulated through Austrian, Canadian, and Jamaican publications. On August 24, 1935, the Austrian newspaper *Neues Wiener Tagblatt* published "Die Verschwörung der Neger" (The Conspiracy of the Negro), authored by Federico Philos. Current consensus is that "Federico Philos" was a pseudonym for an unknown propagandist bent on creating justification for Italian aggression against Ethiopia. Philos's story was a hodgepodge of eugenics, millenarian anxieties, and fear of Black nationalism. His central conceit was the founding of a "secret federation of the black race," the Nya-Binghi, led by Emperor Selassie. Philos warned that the Nya-Binghi had surpassed the "Yellow Peril" (Japanese) as a danger to Whites; they constituted a "Black Peril." The Nya-Binghi's wellsprings were Egypt, Ethiopia, and Liberia, "self-administering" nations where "negroes can work on their plans, unchallenged by the control of whites." Nya-Binghi is "taken from the Abyssinian language," Philos wrote, and its English translation is "Death to the Whites."[25] This claim is unfounded, but its intent is clear: organized and united Black people are a menace to White people. Philos's tone was cautious but capable of sowing anxiety and terror in the imagination of White readers.

Philos combined truth and fantasy. He noted, for example, that Emperor Selassie sent emissaries to the United States, where Ethiopians met with African Americans. The emissaries, however, were not "tasked with organizing the negro peoples," as Philos claimed, but with organizing aid. Perhaps Philos knew that in July 1935, both the Provisional Committee and the Medical Committee for the Defense of Ethiopia had "sent several tons of medical supplies and a hospital unit to Ethiopia" and that the Ethiopian Tasfaye Zaphiro, of the Imperial Ethiopian Legation in London, was involved in the formation of United Aid for Ethiopia in the United States.[26] Philos cast the Emperor as a figure both international and godly, an observation consonant with the emergent Rastafari ideology.

The Austrian news story was republished in English under the title "The Black Peril" in a revised form in November 1935 by *Magazine Digest*, a Canadian popular literary periodical. The title "The Black Peril" portended evil. It made remarkable claims, such as this one in the opening paragraphs: "The Blacks are welded into an ominous secret league, most remarkable of which is that its existence is scarcely known. Nya-Binghi! The words mean 'Death to the Whites' or 'Death to the Europeans.' . . . It sprang to life in the Belgian Congo . . . [and] it has become a menace to Europe."[27]

Philos dragged into the open otherwise-obscure Native African anticolonial resistance movements in Central Africa. Of relevance to the Rastafari, one such movement, known as Nyabinghi, traces to the 1700s in what today is known as Tanzania and Rwanda. A precolonial faith complex, Nyabinghi focused on spirit possession and the leadership of female and male priests. Nyabinghi, a spirit, is personified in human form, commonly in women. The precolonial Nyabinghi movement leaders challenged injustice, especially cruel and oppressive leadership in the region. It evolved into an anticolonial movement during the late 1800s, when Muhumuza, a Rwandan queen, joined the Nyabinghi, becoming a personification of Nyabinghi. As a charismatic and fearless leader, Muhumuza attracted a considerable following by instigating attacks against the colonial Germans, Belgians, and British.

"The Black Peril" was republished again—this this time in the *Jamaica Times*—under the title "Secret Society to Destroy Whites."[28] The article was only slightly altered for publication in the *Jamaica Times* (both the *Magazine Digest* and *Jamaica Times* articles were tamer versions of the original). The subtitle shrieked, "Army of 20,000,000." A photograph of Emperor Selassie accompanied the story (figure 5.1). In Jamaica, the story became a cultural resource for the Rastafari. For example, the photograph of the Emperor became a revered image among the Rastafari. The article as cultural resource provided a rich trove. It suggested that the Rastafari were right to worship the Emperor; millions of people were doing as much. "Secret Society" affirmed the beliefs of emergent Rastafari: "Haile Selassie is regarded as a veritable Messiah, a saviour of the coloured people, the Emperor of the Negro Kingdom."[29] It painted a

Figure 5.1. Photograph of Ras Tafari, ca. 1917, comparable to the one captioned "Haile Selassie," published in the *Jamaica Times*, December 1935, under the title "Secret Society to Destroy Whites." (Bain News Service, Library of Congress)

picture of Pan-Africanism compatible with Black fantasies of the time, with the Emperor as ultimate leader. It hinted at the seething power of African-descended people, waiting to be unleashed when they banded together. And it suggested that colonialism and White supremacy were on their heels. Nonetheless, Philos's fear-mongering was obvious— oppressed Blacks the world over would subdue their oppressors: "A victory for Abyssinia in the war against Italy would set into motion the war of the entire negro race against the whites."[30] Philos hinted that Whites would probably lose such a war.

The origins of cultural resources do not determine their use. Once available to nonmembers, cultural resources can become a public good. The pre–World War II notion of an international Negro conspiracy, the "Black Peril," the global secret society of Blacks, may have sprung from racist and eugenic thinking of Whites, only to be reinterpreted in an affirmative way by some Black Jamaicans. Part of what made this reinterpretation possible was the ignorance on the part of both parties: Black Jamaicans neglected whether the Nya-Binghi narrative was White propaganda intended to stoke White anxiety, while White ideologues like Philos were unaware how their propaganda could be turned against them, further stoking their fears by deifying Emperor Selassie. We must look far and wide for the symbolic and narrative elements used to construct and maintain collective identification.

Both *Magazine Digest* and *Jamaica Times* ran Philos's story after the Italian invasion of Ethiopia. In the run-up to the invasion and afterward, African-descended people throughout the Diaspora rallied in support of the Emperor and Ethiopia.

Italy Invades Ethiopia

Indeed, the Rome Government, as it has today openly proclaimed, has never ceased to prepare for the conquest of Ethiopia.
—Emperor Haile Selassie I, "Appeal to the League of Nations," June 30, 1936

A serendipitous concatenation of activities and events reinforced Rastafari ethnogenesis. Fantasy found company in facts, and facts concurred with fantasy. Italy's invasion of Ethiopia bestowed legs on beliefs pronounced in texts like *The Promised Key* and "Secret Society." Italy began amassing equipment and soldiers in East Africa, in April 1935, in preparation for the invasion. The buildup occurred in plain sight. While Italy mobilized up-to-date weaponry, Ethiopia presented soldiers armed with spears and shields, horse-drawn supply carts, and a handful of feeble planes.

On October 3, 1935, the front page of the *Daily Gleaner* cried out, "Mussolini Strikes in East Africa! Italian Troops Invade Ethiopia and Prepare to Attack." The previous day, Italy had invaded Ethiopia, without a formal declaration of war. Italy wanted what much of Europe already had: African colonies. Italy had unsuccessfully tried to conquer Ethiopia almost four decades earlier. The vanquished Italian army, defeated by Emperor Menelek II's army at the Battle of Adwa in 1896, humiliated Italy's collective pride.

Italy advanced slowly against the Ethiopians, until late winter 1935. The Italians defeated the Emperor's Imperial Guard in late March 1936. Emperor Selassie left Ethiopia for Europe to organize resistance to the invasion. Mussolini annexed Ethiopia in May 1936, into a new territory called Italian East Africa that included Eritrea and Somaliland. He mocked the League of Nations and the Geneva Protocol of 1925 by slaughtering civilians, bombing Red Cross tents, and dispensing several hundred tons of mustard gas. Catholic Church bishops blessed the fascist Italian army's invasion, a matter that generated festering animosity among Rastafari people toward the Catholic Church.

By June 1936, the Emperor had gained an international bully pulpit, ironically, through the impotent League of Nations. He denounced the invasion and the League's timidity in a speech delivered to the League itself and the wider world:

> There is no precedent for a Head of State himself speaking in this assembly. But there is also no precedent for a people being victim of such injustice and being at present threatened by abandonment to its aggressor. Also, there has never before been an example of any Government proceeding to the systematic extermination of a nation by barbarous means, in violation of the most solemn promises made by the nations of the earth that there should not be used against innocent human beings

the terrible poison of harmful gases. It is to defend a people struggling for its age-old independence that the head of the Ethiopian Empire has come to Geneva to fulfil this supreme duty, after having himself fought at the head of his armies.[31]

The speech failed to galvanize League members to condemn Italy. What both the invasion and the speech roused, though, were the people of the Black Diaspora. In Jamaica, the United States, Trinidad, and countless other places, Black people sided with Ethiopia and offered their money and bodies to help Ethiopia regain its liberty. Black Jamaicans were prominent among the critics of Italy and the League and those willing to join in battle in support of Ethiopia.

Jamaica: Effects of the Italo-Ethiopian War and Emergence of the Ethiopian World Federation

One explanation for the heightened interest in the Emperor and Ethiopia was the coverage that both received in news media. During 1935, the *Jamaica Times*, for example, published many striking images of Emperor Selassie I, of Empress Menen, and of Ethiopian leaders and commoners, as well as publishing detailed political, historical, and firsthand accounts of visitors to Ethiopia, such as that of the Kingston businessman Monty Meek.[32]

Coverage of Emperor Selassie—whether overstated, accurate, or misleading—functioned as a cultural resource for the Rastafari: the Emperor's khaki uniform as a symbol of leadership and might; the Emperor "in the style of the Old Testament kings, on horseback, with his chief priest carrying the Ark of the Covenant close at hand" as evidence of divinity; and the Emperor who "calmly and resolutely mans machine gun as a bomb exploded near him" as proof of infinite courage and supernatural power.[33] The stories provided ideas for how the Rastafari as adherents of a new faith could style themselves as Ethiopians. They took such stories and wove them into their collective chronicle: indication of the leadership and divine power of Emperor Selassie. Such images served as placards of collective identity. Males and females wear these images to this day in forms such as necklaces and pins. The images signal "I am Rastafari" or "I sympathize with the Rastafari." I have seen

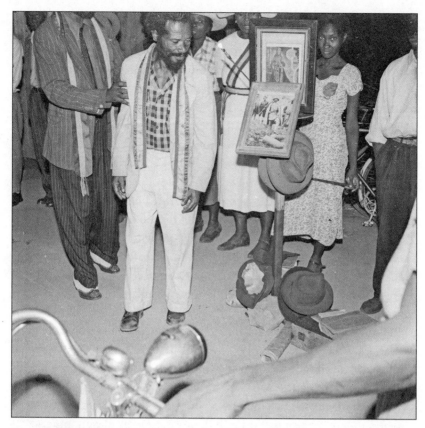

Figure 5.2. Rastafari street meeting, circa 1953, photographed by the anthropologist George Simpson. In the background stands a picture of Emperor Selassie with his foot perched on an unexploded bomb casing. Many Rastafari used the image as proof of Emperor Selassie's invincibility. (National Anthropological Archives, Smithsonian Institution)

Rastafari men adoring a photograph of Emperor Selassie I posing with his foot on an intact bombshell and heard many stories about the unexploded bomb being evidence of his divinity (figure 5.2). I learned that the story was traceable to a front-page *Jamaica Times* headline.[34] The press manufactured sensationalism, assisting in elevating the Emperor to the height of God.

As war between Italy and Ethiopia became likely, Black people across the Caribbean (and in the United States) wanted to join the Emperor's army: "The interest being taken in the West Indies in . . . an inevitable struggle between Italy and Abyssinia is remarkable. . . . A considerable number of coloured people . . . realize that Africa really matters to them. Five hundred Trinidadians demonstrated this a few days ago when they protested against Italy's planned invasion."[35] Crowds "assemble[d] daily" in Kingston's Victoria Park to discuss the impending invasion; "hundreds of people flocked to the U.N.I.A. office at Upper King Street and enlisted" upon hearing the news that a man from Canada was coming to Jamaica to recruit men to "defend Abyssinia."[36]

Black consciousness roared in the flurry of activity to protest the Italian invasion and to defend Ethiopia. Elites in some colonial nations were wary that heightened Black consciousness could inspire rebellion or even revolution. Philos expressed such fear in his propaganda about the Nya-Binghi: "Africans of one territory going to the assistance of Africans of another against Europeans would be a step of the greatest significance for it would prove clearly the existence of a national spirit of unity which must ultimately bring about the salvation of Africa from continuous exploitation."[37]

In the United States, groups formed the Menelek Club in 1936 to consolidate the "pro-Ethiopian organisations in New York."[38] The Menelek Club sent a delegation of African Americans to England to meet with the Emperor during the summer of 1936. Among the African American Ethiopian support organizations, the United Aid for Ethiopia was a leader in the fund-raising effort and in promoting racial camaraderie: "It is the hope of this organization [United Aid for Ethiopia] to develop to a high degree in Afro-Americans a keen sense of the ties which bind them to their blood-brothers in Ethiopia.[39] Those efforts to support Ethiopia impressed the Emperor, who sent his physician and confidant, Dr. Malaku Bayen, to meet with the people involved in the Ethiopian aid effort.

Bayen formally founded the Ethiopian World Federation (EWF) in New York City on August 25, 1937. The EWF grew rapidly, by 1940 attaining membership in the thousands in branches sprinkled across the United States.[40] The EWF charter emphasized Blackness, encouraging solidarity among Africans and the far-flung African Diaspora. The occasional writer on Ethiopianist concerns Levi Mantle announced his plan to open the first proposed EWF chapter at 22 Bond Street in Kingston, with the mission of cultivating "brotherly love" and developing a "keener national spirit."[41] Black Jamaicans showed interest in the EWF.

"Our inaugural meeting was held a few weeks ago," Mantle noted, "and already scores of persons have enrolled as members."[42] The historian and Rastafari scholar Giulia Bonacci recovered evidence that eight hundred people attended the opening.[43]

The Rastafari immediately sought participation in the EWF but were hardly welcomed with open arms. Bonacci shows how Jamaican EWF locals resisted Rastafari participation.[44] Rejection of race-conscious Rastafari from race-conscious organizations reinforced a notion that "Black man him own enemy," as the second-generation Rastafari Ras Brenton described what was essentially Black-on-Black animosity.[45] Second-generation elder Rastafari like Bongo J recalled attending UNIA meetings but having to remain outside.[46] One Rastafari reaction to exclusion from the EWF (and UNIA) was to form their own EWF-like organizations, such as the Brothers Solidarity United Ethiopia.

Persecution of the "Deluded Creatures": A Path to Identity Fusion

Howell was itinerant between 1933 and 1939, moving among Kingston, St. Thomas, and St. Catherine. After release from prison in 1936, he reestablished himself in St. Thomas in early 1937. There he set up a "yard" or base that he and his followers called "King's House." Howell planned an extended celebration of Ethiopian Christmas, beginning around January 7, 1937, in the Harbour Head section of St. Thomas.[47]

Word of the event traveled across St. Thomas and other parishes. By January 7, "Ras Tafarites" were streaming into the vicinity of King's House. At the Ethiopian Christmas celebration, they displayed symbols and expressed beliefs that became emblematic of Rastafari identity. A reporter told how a flag flew over King's House with an "artistic emblem of a Lion with a spear in his mouth, and beneath inscribed in bold letters, 'King of Kings and Lion of Judah.'" Some arrivals were adorned in the colors red, gold, and green, the shades of the Ethiopian flag. In unison they chanted the Ethiopian national anthem. The "'rejectors of his [Howell's] Cult' were called 'Babylon.'"[48]

The Rastafari were distinguishing themselves—culturally speaking—from non-Rastafari. Conditions for identity fusion were growing: the shared experience of dysphoria—violence and persecution—fused personal and collective identities. The anthropologist Harvey White-house and colleagues describe similar phenomena: "Driven by the conviction that group members share essence with oneself in ways that can transcend even the bonds of kinship, persons strongly fused to a group report willingness to engage in self-sacrifice. . . . One of the pathways to extreme pro-group action, whatever culturally distinctive forms it happens to take, is identity fusion."[49]

By January 9, the number of Rastafari pilgrims had ballooned to the point that police were noting their presence.[50] Local citizens harbored growing resentment against Howell. Nagging charges by elites that he was fleecing his followers gained credence, and residents of Harbour Head and nearby localities believed the Rastafari were tarnishing their reputation. Commoners were joining elites in treating them as undesirables.

A gang of locals took it upon themselves to rid their community of Howell and King's House. On the evening of the ninth, a mob of roughly one hundred locals attacked the celebration at King's House. Assaulting Rastafari with sticks, they wrecked King's House and set afire the beard of a Rastafari from Clarendon. One Rastafari, "held against the embankment of King's House with blows descending from all sides, begged for mercy, wailing, 'I am a cripple.'" Gang members retorted, "Cripples should remain at home, not follow Howell."[51] The mob sought out men with beards, which were taken to be markers of Rastafari identity. A *Daily Gleaner* reporter, a police inspector, and two constables observed the melee without lifting a finger. Indeed, a news reporter praised the assailants: "It was wonderful, the marvelous institution of the 'Vigilantes.'" The goons "broke in and ravaged the cult's headquarters, and sent the whole party of Ras Tafarites flying all over the district, beating some as they went."[52] The police inspector intervened when he feared someone might get killed. The reporter opined, "The citizens of Port Morant had rebelled against the machinations of a fanatic organization that had well-nigh over-run the parish."[53] Howell and his followers left St. Thomas under vigilante threat for their lives, though Howell vowed not to give in to their demands. In effect, Howell and his Rastafari adherents were chased out of St. Thomas.

Howell publicly contested the positive spin put on the destruction of his community: "I SEE TWO versions [his and critics] of what happened at Harbour Head last Saturday night [January 9]," he said, "between my people, the police and some civilians. . . . The Ministers in St. Thomas are behind the whole affair and are putting the police in front to do their dirty work."[54] Howell's account, at diametric odds with reporters and police, argued that the police instigated and turned a blind eye toward the melee: "A crowd gathered outside headquarters and by 9:30 were throwing stones at us in full swing. The Police Inspector and his men were in the yard while the stones were being thrown by the crowd but did not ask them to stop."[55] Howell defended his and his followers' right to live their faith in peace and blamed the police for aggravating their persecution: "The Police or the ministers of the civilians can't prevent me from going to my place. My people are there and they need me. We do not break any law. We conduct our meetings orderly. We disturb no one. Why should we be disturbed? We are all Jamaicans, and if Jamaica is a free and orderly country the Police should not be the ones to actually head people to create disturbances?"[56]

The Ethiopian Christmas celebration of 1937 signaled an emergent collective cultural formation consisting of many timid Rastafari. The timidity contrasted with the aggressiveness the Rastafari exhibited during some of their 1934 and 1935 gatherings, where they accosted police officers and others. Yet they had reason to be timid. They wanted to practice their faith and live their identity, but it was costly to do so. Rastafari timidity would soon be conjoined with bluster, unruliness, and resistance toward the people and institutions suppressing them. The melee, though, presented reason for Howell and his adherents to seek out seclusion greater than that of the hills and valleys of St. Thomas.

The Kingston–St. Andrew Civic League (KSACL), an association of middle- and upper-middle-class Jamaicans interested in the improvement of Kingston and St. Andrew Parish, worried that the Rastafari chased out of St. Thomas were reconstituting themselves in Kingston. The government believed that the Rastafari in St. Thomas had run out of fertile ground on which to cultivate new members. Given the crackdowns by police and vigilantes on the Rastafari and the "sound common sense" of citizens and their associations, officials reasoned that the "eccentric doctrines of the Ras Tafarists" were unlikely to appeal "to more than a very small number of feeble-minded persons."[57] Nevertheless, surveillance of the Rastafari began early in their existence and remained intense for several decades, as the anthropologist Deborah Thomas suggests in her analysis of exchanges among the KSACL, Governor Denham, and the Rastafari.[58]

Labeling theory tells us that some people have more power than others to ascribe labels and make them stick. Civic and business elites (like those of KSACL) conveyed an image of the Rastafari as a threat that bested all preceding racial threats. They compared the Rastafari to Soviet Communists; they depicted the Rastafari as godless anti-Christians; and they described the Rastafari as magnets that attracted people susceptible to any criticism of colonialism, Christianity, or race relations in Jamaica. While the KSACL's hyperbole is obvious to contemporary ears, it expressed a genuine self-interested concern that the Rastafari message was contagious and detrimental to middle-class mores. "We are afraid," KSACL declared, "that these highly inflammable doctrines . . . will do an incalculable amount of harm to the future progress and well-being of the different race[s] of people inhabiting this Island."[59]

KSACL stirred the Rastafari. They were following the reports. Several Rastafari responded formally. Altamont Reid, an Ethiopianist and self-proclaimed founder of the King of Kings Salvation, along with two other self-identified Rastafari, wrote to Governor Denham protesting KSACL's petition. They identified themselves as members of a "religious movement," "officers of the Ethiopian King of Kings Salvation," and as obedient British subjects.[60] That Reid and company called themselves obedient might be insincere obsequiousness, but it reminds us nonetheless that there was no single Rastafari script but multiple and competing scripts. Not all Rastafari held Howell's and Hinds's stance of rejecting all British trappings.

The tone of the officers' letter—respectful, sarcastic, unapologetic—also showed their awareness of their degraded status in the eyes of Jamaica's establishment: "we would not denounce by pity anyone who would look down on our 'Religious Movement.'" They zinged KSACL's condescension: "No human being can rise higher than his mental concept. . . . [Such beings are] not sufficiently evolved to grapple with the teachings which are too high for them." The Rastafari were too advanced for the leading lights of Kingston and St. Andrew to comprehend their vision of a redeeming Black Messiah. "God to any man is according to his concept," they wrote, justifying their faith as one among many

Jamaican faiths. They too invoked the Morant Bay Rebellion but clarified that for them it meant racial solidarity and not racial and class hatred.[61]

In less than four years, the Rastafari had evolved into a community of people willing to endure persecution and stigmatization to further their self- and collective identity. They enhanced their vital beliefs, made them durable by embedding them in symbols, rituals, and customs that conveyed personal and collective identification. Rastafari events, ongoing arrests of Rastafari people, large crowds, and news reportage all provided means for further developing and spreading ideas by and about the Rastafari.

"We Do Not Like What You Say": Altamont Reid Charged with Sedition

Britain's declaration of war against Germany in September 1939 amplified its concerns about maintaining the loyalty of its colonial citizenry. Authorities could use sedition laws to squelch any sign of dissension. "Under recent 'Sedition laws,'" an editorialist opined, "any magistrate can issue a warrant or the police can arrest without warrant or disperse any meeting if they decide that a speaker's utterances are likely to cause enmity between classes, or that a meeting is likely to lead to a breach of the peace."[62] The writer advised that the broad authority of the police encouraged abuse; they could disband any meeting by defining it as seditious. Vernacular expressions became a potential breach of the law. A street orator who used a metaphor such as "blood flowing" or "take an eye for an eye" did not ipso facto imply or urge physical violence. However, authorities could call such speech seditious if it were critical of government. The Rastafari faced a double bind because of their critical talk and because of their apocalyptic references to violence and destruction.

In December 1938, police arrested Altamont Reid for delivering a seditious speech. Born in Barbados to Jamaican parents, Reid moved to Jamaica as a boy, grew up in St. Catherine, and became Rastafari in 1933. Between 1933 and 1938, he worked as a gardener for an official of Jamaica's Public Service. Reid was described as a "33-year old ex-Public Service employee, North Parade [Park] orator, member of the Ras Tafari cult and self-styled President of the 'King of Kings Salvation Mission in Kingston.'"[63] The writer did not miss an opportunity to defame a Rastafari leader, and Reid was portrayed as a parasite: "Religious beliefs caused him [Reid] to leave his job, and after that he earned his livelihood by collections made at his meetings and from assistance from members of his association."[64] The gist: Rastafari leaders quit work so that they could live off the contributions of their fellows, many of whom were poor.

What got Reid into trouble? The attorney general charged that Reid "made certain dangerous utterances against government during a speech in a crowd of over three hundred people . . . [at] the Ward Theatre" on December 12, 1938.[65] Two officers said that they observed and recorded Reid's speech, one writing in longhand and the other in shorthand. Recorded portions of Reid's homily spoke to an evolving Rastafari critique of race, class, and politics and to elites' continuing effort to overthrow Rastafari leadership. A police inspector said that he found the crowd in a "disorderly state" because Reid and others had "inflamed" the audience.[66] A Sergeant Major said he warned Reid that his talk was "bordering on sedition."[67] I use several excerpts from Reid's speech to provide graphic examples of the language that he reportedly used and how officials interpreted it:

> No power in Europe can stop Hitler from killing. I am saying Jamaicans I have got a glance in the future and I see blood flowing. I say everyone one of us must make up our minds to get kill to free thousands. . . . Every black man must start practice to kill . . . so that when the time comes you will know how to kill.

> God says every white man neck must be cut off. Haile Selassie is going to send death to every white man in the world.

> Buy nothing from them [Chinese]. Support your own black man. . . . So I say it with power. . . . The Chinaman does not bank his money in Jamaica.

> The white man is thoroughly against the black man. Black men must make up their mind as everybody in the world is killing today. . . . We are expecting that the government of Jamaica should keep law and order, but how can this be done when starvation is among the people?

> Stealing started in Buckingham Palace. . . . Jamaicans, then "shall not steal." A lie. England stole Africa. The time has come when if Jamaicans don't strike government will wipe them off the scene of action.

The only salvation in the world today is in Africa. Africa for the Africans at home and abroad. We are going to march upon the Roman Catholic Church. . . . The last time they beat us up in St. Thomas, this time, let them try it.[68]

Reid's speech is a jumble of prophesies, claims, grievances, and innu-endoes. He prophesied that Hitler would overrun Europe; he suggested that Black Jamaicans must prepare to become soldiers (killers) in order to survive another world war; he called the British thieves. He criticized the poverty-stricken condition of Black Jamaicans and warned that vio-lence would beset Whites, Chinese, and Syrians (Whites were associated with colonization; the Chinese and Syrians were stigmatized as "alien traders"). He cautioned the Catholic Church and reminded his audience of Morant Bay; should another rebellion occur, Black people would be better positioned to win.

We must wonder about the officers' recording and interpretive abili-ties as well as their motives. Reid's speech, as reported, reads as a dis-cursive rant. It could be that the words were a tirade delivered by an unhinged man. Or it could have been a speech designed to resonate with ears attuned to Old Testament vengeance and people's dissatisfaction with the current political economy. The officers, using their discretion, probably emphasized what they took to be seditious language and omit-ted talk that provided context. Reid maintained the latter. For example, the transcriptions omitted his references to scripture. Reid argued that he was "framed up."[69] Nevertheless, his words buttress the examples of emergent Rastafari beliefs such as critiques of injustice, colonialism, and British hegemony alongside promotion of Black solidarity. Reid's talk was also the language of symbolic violence: graphic language intended to shock but not intended to cause physical harm.[70] In reference to blood flowing and neck chopping, Reid specified, for example, that the "killing he urged was that when the Italians came to grips with the British in the Mediterranean black-men would chop off their heads for what they had done to the Ethiopians."[71] Symbolic violence became a part of Rastafari discourse, a means to instill dread in the hearts of nonbelievers.

The jury refused to convict Reid. They did not agree unanimously that Reid committed sedition. The justice requested that Reid be tried again. During the second trial, Reid clarified how the police had misrepresented him. Reid explained that the assembly was not political and that it began with "chanting of psalms and the singing of hymns."[72] What was religious for Rastafari like Reid, Howell, and Hinds was racial and political for colonial officials and other elites. Reid said that he spoke in Amharic, an Ethiopian language, which the police did not understand; his talk was really about establishing the kingdom of Emperor Selassie on Earth. He stated that he preached this message to the 284 members of his King of Kings Salvation. Reid's account of what he said and meant was summed up this way: "[Reid] believed that the descendants of Africa should go back to Africa. He believed that the Government of Africa should be in the hands of Africans, including West Indians. . . . He felt those parts [of Africa] at present held by European powers would be restored to black men. . . . He had nothing against the white man or the Chinese, as God was of love and made no difference between colour, class and creed."[73] Like Howell, Reid defended himself, sometimes drawing boisterous laughter from the audience, for instance, with his claim that in the future all Jamaicans would be Rastafari.

The persistent justice won a conviction. Reid was convicted of sedition in the Circuit Court, in early May 1939, but it took three trials. Reid's talk did not qualify as free speech. What was decisive, the justice said, were Reid's motives, the audience, and the "effect" the speech had on them.[74] Reid was accused of "foment[ing] general discontent and disaffection" and of holding the government "in ridicule or contempt." The justice admonished Reid, "What you said that night was a lot of rubbish—serious rubbish—which might have led to trouble. I hope you regret it and will not do it again. You must go into imprisonment for four months."[75] In effect, the judge, using the sedition law, momentarily toppled another Rastafari leader, in this case depriving the King of King's mission of a key figure.

Retreat: The Ethiopian Salvation Society and the Pinnacle Community

On February 6, 1940, Governor A. F. Richards prohibited an announced meeting of Howell's newly formed Ethiopian Salvation Society that was to be held near Port Morant in St. Thomas. Governor Richards advertised the prohibition on the front page of the *Daily Gleaner*.[76] A concerted effort to stamp out the Rastafari was under way.

In 1939, Howell convened a two-day event described as the "Grand Review of Jubilee" at Marcus Garvey's Liberty Club in Kingston. The evening's activities included speeches, processional music, and a play, *The Prodigal's Return*. The biblical parable of the prodigal son is a story of love and redemption, two matters close to Howell's experience and mission. Howell had built a sizable following, despite setbacks with the law and with vigilantes. "Hundreds of members attended [the Grand Review] from St. Thomas, Portland, and other parishes," while more than five hundred were reported to have attended a similar event during late 1939.[77] The Grand Review celebrated the launch of the Ethiopian Salvation Society (ESS), which had been chartered under Jamaica's benevolent societies laws.

The acting attorney general certified the ESS's rules in February 1939. The ESS constitution described a mutual-aid society concerned with providing death, illness, and distress benefits that would support the financial well-being of its members.[78] Its mission was evocative of *Holy Piby* author Robert Athlyi Roger's "Living and Trading Scheme." Rogers's scheme was a plan for his flock, such as the Hamatic Church venture of the mid-1920s in Kingston (see chapter 2). The foundation of the plan was based in the requirements of collective investment, cooperation, and a communal spirit. The scheme sought to cultivate a mind-set conducive to Black solidarity and prosperity: "Teach the people love, by displaying the very actual deeds of love." It was also a vision of a cooperative and entrepreneurial venture for Rogers's flock. Members would pursue "unitedly working [together] to build up industries" and wipe out "idleness, poverty and want." The scheme proposed an "industrial branch" that would "include men and women of every craft," teaching them to "learn to make and sell such things . . . [that are of] of necessity in aiding human life."[79] Howell would pursue a similar path.

Pinnacle, Rastafari Compound, Act 1

The ESS had "relocated" to St. Catherine with Howell, a strategy to retreat from the hostilities of St. Thomas and to create a new community (in St. Thomas, Howell's King's House was also known as the Salvation

Society). "Retreat" should be understood in two senses of the word: withdraw and refuge: "Let us leave Babylon," literally, symbolically, and for some, both, and it also meant, "Let us create a refuge in the wilderness." The new location was named "Pinnacle."

Pinnacle was both an impressive and intimidating property. The views from Pinnacle were breathtaking. Toward the east, one could see Kingston and silhouettes of the Blue Mountain, and toward the south were the seawaters beyond the Hellshire Hills. It was intimidating because of its rocky, hilly, and brush-clogged terrain.

Voluntary associations can facilitate collective identity formation.[80] Such structures can provide a way for people to interact and to affirm their beliefs and values; provide a means to embody, preserve, and diffuse beliefs and practices; and, depending on the people involved, a way to mark boundaries among members and the wider worlds in which they operate. Pinnacle played an important role in this regard.

"Us and Them" is shorthand for the ways that people create and delineate collective identities. Humans have a propensity for organizing their "worlds" into categories, including themselves and others; they create ingroups or communities that generate distinctions that exclude others; they ascribe labels to themselves and to others. Interaction that involves conflict, power asymmetries, or inequities can accentuate the process of creating Us and Them.

Pinnacle became an important phase of Rastafari ethnogenesis because it functioned as an engine of growth and an incubator for the development of Rastafari cultural resources. It also became a cause of conflict between the Pinnacleites and outsiders. The Pinnacle compound facilitated the development of Rastafari, sometimes in paradoxical ways. For example, Pinnacle attracted Rastafari adherents, but it also attracted unwanted attention. By the end of 1940, various sources estimated that between seven hundred and one thousand people occupied Pinnacle. Entire families moved to Pinnacle. The influx of people facilitated numerical growth of the Rastafari, while outflow, such as the result of police raids, functioned as a vector that spread the emergent faith and identity.

By the end of 1940, the Pinnacle compound and Howell were gaining a reputation that would soon define a generation of Rastafari. The idea of the Rastafari as communal, self-reliant, and independent was surely a creation of and achievement of the Rastafari themselves—ideologically and actually—*and* also a creation and label of opinion shapers. For example, the writer David Carradine visited Pinnacle and interviewed Howell, describing the community as an industrious "socialist colony" consisting of "practical communists."[81] Politically speaking, the description was inaccurate; Howell was not following the doctrines of Marx, Lenin, or Trotsky (Howell was aware of Black leftist thought such as that of the Trinidadian Pan-Africanist George Padmore). What impressed Carradine as communist was the Pinnacleites' endeavor to build a self-reliant community where property and well-being were a collective good. Carradine expressed admiration for the effort. Howell explained that Pinnacle was not about religion or politics but economics; it was about making a living independent of Jamaica's colonial system. Outsiders had their own ideas about Pinnacle, irrespective of what Howell or other Pinnacleites said. For many outsiders, Pinnacle was either a religious or a political community rather than a Black community pursuing self-reliance.

Undermining Pinnacle

Late in 1940, the *Daily Gleaner* shoved "Camp Pinnacle" into public view, portraying it as a warren of pestilence and poverty, sensationalizing the "plight of Ras Tafarians at Camp Pinnacle."[82] Pinnacle the place and its inhabitants were presented as a threat—now a public health threat. Although Howell reportedly retained a doctor for Pinnacleites, a reporter claimed that "they had no medical service, and when a person was sick—and that was pretty often—they were either sent to a hospital or given herbs."[83] Eighteen alleged residents of Pinnacle were admitted to the Spanish Town Poor House. This led the medical officer of health to inquire into the living conditions at Pinnacle.

Because of the Pinnacleites admitted to the St. Catherine Poor House, the inspector of poor for St. Catherine collected statements from them for a report to "parochial authorities."[84] The report described Pinnacle as more than a mess; it was a living hell that threatened the stability of the surrounding areas. A listing of the Pinnacleites suggested that they came from across the island, hailing from the parishes of St. Thomas, Hanover, Manchester, Portland, St. Elisabeth, and Clarendon.

Pinnacle was depicted as a community of the dejected. A so-called Pinnacle refugee reportedly said, "I thought it was going to be a Paradise . . . but it was like hell to me." Contrary to Carradine's nuanced (but skeptical) account, this reporter emphasized that "wherever he looked he saw the same spectacle—men who had travelled from far off to find a Heaven on Earth, to find that it was all a mirage—that such a Paradise did not exist at Pinnacle."[85] Although the reporter was perhaps biased against Howell and interviewed the most disillusioned Pinnacleites, the stories provide a glimpse of Rastafari life during Pinnacle's early days from perspectives that are both sanguine and uncomplimentary.

The St. Catherine elected public servant E. McNeill read the *Sunday Gleaner* story about Pinnacle's unfortunates, and the following day, he visited a poor house in St. Catherine in Spanish Town.[86] He concluded that the Pinnacle story was "fairly accurate" and expressed concern with the alleged unreported deaths at Pinnacle.[87] He called for a "proper investigation" and resolved that the "state of affairs [at Pinnacle] should not be allowed to continue."[88] Nevertheless, the medical officer of health and the attorney general felt that both Pinnacle and the ESS (in effect, the same) would "gradually dwindle" in their numbers.[89] They would slide into irrelevance.

In a subsequent brief, the medical officer of health noted that the arrival of the dry season would facilitate the "disintegration of the 'Camp.'"[90] An assistant medical director took a stab at Howell's character by insinuating that malnourished and ragged Pinnacleites were "engaged on the construction of a substantial house for their leader."[91] The implication was that Howell was enriching himself on the backs of his flock. One official motivation for scrutinizing Pinnacle was to pin liability on Howell and the camp to obtain reimbursement for "monies expended from the Poor Funds of the Parish for the maintenance etc. of persons from Pinnacle."[92] The strategy afforded another opportunity to undermine Howell and his adherents.

By March 1941, there was a coordinated and unambiguous effort to destroy Howell and Pinnacle. For example, the assistant medical director was advised to request expensive renovations to Pinnacle (such as extra latrines), in the belief that if Howell did not comply, he could be forced to leave Pinnacle. Authorities also sought to identify ill "inmates," as they could be used to show Pinnacle to be a public health threat.[93]

A note to the colonial secretary argued that "steps should be taken to disperse the misguided people of this strange cult," and the existing laws could be used to achieve the goal.[94]

"Us and Them": Pinnacleites and Neighbors Clash

Pinnacle became fortress-like. Accusations of crookedness happening inside Pinnacle competed with rumors of crookedness outside the compound. Outsiders had to walk a winding path to meet an imposing gate and a gatekeeper. Gaining admittance could be challenging. Corporal R. Samuels and a couple of constables visited Pinnacle to execute warrants for an alleged gun man, James Nelson, whom police believed to reside at Pinnacle. Samuels was met by a "party of about 12 men [who] came to the gate all armed with sticks."[95] Samuels was rudely treated, for example, having his hat knocked off his head. Samuels apparently sparked Howell's anger, recalling that Howell had said to him that "no whiteman can come here again." Samuels himself acknowledged the reason for Howell's words: "I remember while in St. Thomas I accompanied Inspector Waters to Howell's camp and helped to smash it."[96] Howell had not forgotten what Samuels did; he reminded Samuels now who was in control of Pinnacle.

Howell's exercise of power against the government in the form of naked resistance was fleeting. Both elites and commoners undermined Howell and the Pinnacleites. Media reported that some of the "cultivators" surrounding Pinnacle were beset by a "period of fear," wary of being robbed or assaulted by Pinnacleites.[97] The Pinnacleites were accused of installing a "reign of terror" that issued outward from Pinnacle into the surrounding communities of St. Catherine.[98]

On the other hand, Pinnacleites told stories of being harassed or having their crops raided by local outsiders.[99] Pinnacleites seemed to feel justified in arming themselves and in physically punishing people who trespassed on Pinnacle grounds. Only occasionally did the Pinnacleite view gain exposure: the "Ras Tafari camp complain[s] that from time-to-time residents of the camp are way-laid and beaten by people of Sligoville and nearby districts."[100]

By the end of June 1941, authorities were ready to enter Pinnacle forcibly, the primary pretext being that of arresting James Nelson, who had missed his court appearance on a gun charge. Nelson asserted impudence, writing the sergeant major of the Spanish Town Police, "I was informed that police is out with a warrant for my arrest, wanted for fire arms, my reason why I would not turn up before now, is I was away making preparation with some Fire Arms. . . . I can be found at Pinnacle everyday or anyday, if you should insist, or anxious to intrude on my liberty."[101]

The police took Nelson's letter as an insult—he essentially boasted, "I have firearms; come and get me"—referring the matter to the attorney general.[102] The authorities concluded that the Pinnacleites were "preparing to declare war."[103] The situation compromised Pinnacle.

Government officials agreed that they should dismantle Pinnacle, though exactly how was unsettled. The goal of destroying Pinnacle was a state secret. What was important to officials like the solicitor general was that there be no appearance of an explicit effort to destroy Pinnacle. The reasoning was summarized this way by an official: "In no circumstances can there be any question of 'breaking up the camp.' The action of the police upon the premises should, primarily, be confined to the execution of the warrants, but any persons seeking to prevent such execution should, of course, be taken into custody and subsequently proceeded against."[104] The colonial secretary accepted the solicitor general's advice, though a high official disagreed: "Seems to me the height of folly to send unarmed police on such a job. . . . The Colonial Service is littered with experience bought with the lives of the police in following such advice. . . . If he [commissioner of police] prefers to take a force of unarmed men I have nothing to say, except to express surprise. At least the police in reserve should be fully armed."[105]

Several factors assisted the authorities' plot to stigmatize and destroy Pinnacle and the Rastafari. For one, Howell failed to screen those who moved into the camp. He admitted that occasionally "undesirables" found their way in or that a few residents misbehaved. A few Pinnacleites, for example, were charged with stealing coal from people living in the vicinity of Pinnacle. Two men and a woman who claimed that Pinnacleites pilfered their coal called on Howell at Pinnacle to air their grievances. Howell met them at the main Pinnacle entrance. He became enraged to know that the neighbors paid taxes to the government.[106] He ordered the three whipped. As a result, Howell had to defend himself against several counts of assault. Such attention bolstered the public image of Howell as a tyrant and of all Pinnacleites as troublemakers.

The First Raid of Pinnacle

On July 17, 1941, the commissioner of police wrote to the colonial secretary, "This matter has now been dealt with."[107] During the early morning of the July 14, 153 police officers (half of them armed) raided Pinnacle.[108] Along with executing outstanding warrants for Nelson and a warrant for Howell, police also claimed to seek redress for local residents who suffered injustice at the hands of Pinnacleites (crops stolen, floggings). Police confiscated quantities of cannabis and hand weapons called "supple jacks" and arrested seventy male Pinnacleites. Numerous Pinnacle dwellings were unoccupied at the time of the raid, and neither Nelson nor Howell was found during the search. Many of the Pinnacleites already had left to gather water, wood, food, and other necessities. Howell reportedly had a premonition that something bad was about to happen and left around three a.m., before the raid. The commissioner of police believed that barking dogs alerted Howell.[109]

The desired effect of the raid, dismantling Pinnacle, was only partially achieved. Some Pinnacleites left the camp, and locals issued a sigh of relief from the so-called terrorism of the Pinnacleites. Howell was caught by surprise at his home and arrested after struggling with a corporal. He was jailed in Spanish Town with sixty-seven of his followers. He was released on £100 bail. Twenty-eight of the sixty-seven received sentences of six months' hard labor for assault and larceny.[110] Resident Magistrate MacGregor convicted Howell on four charges of assault against four of the people who claimed that he had them whipped for trespassing on Pinnacle. Howell's attorney appealed the conviction. The sentence of two years' hard labor stood.

* * *

Drawing on a range of cultural resources, inspired by prophetic leadership, the Rastafari within the space of a few years of their emergence had forged a forcible collective identity that met up with both increasing interest and increasing enmity. Rastafari and outsiders had initiated a persistent pattern of development.

6

The Menace Becomes Dreadful

Rastafari Flex Their Muscle

Some say they want to leave Jamaica and go back to Africa.
Some talk about Ethiopia and others Liberia.
But no matter where, I do not care.
I know I must be there to get my share
of the riches and delicious dishes of Ethiopia.
—Lord Lebby and the Jamaican Calypsonians, "Etheopia" (*sic*)

Noel Williams, a Jamaican calypso and mento singer and hotel performer, is known by his stage name, Lord Lebby. In 1955, Lord Lebby recorded the song "Etheopia." The song tells much about the tenor of the times when the concerns of the Rastafari were filtering into the consciousness of other Jamaicans. "Etheopia" is a paean to voluntary migration, a dreamy story about what a sumptuous Ethiopia holds for those who migrate there, and Lebby suggests that he will be among them. Lebby was in tune with a broad social movement, the Back-to-Africa movement, which included the Rastafari.

Social movements exercise force and generate impact when they combine disruption, cultural influence, and organization.[1] The dynamics of Rastafari ethnogenesis shifted significantly between the 1940s and the 1960s. The Rastafari manifested demographic changes as a second generation of Rastafari materialized and as their relationship to outsiders grew more complex. As Rastafari ethnogenesis developed during this period, the Rastafari showed characteristics of a rising social movement—increasing in recognition, in force, in influence, and in numbers. Significant was the increasing number of Jamaicans swayed by notions about Africa, about migration to Liberia and Ethiopia, and about race.

The factors involved in local, ostensibly discrete events can interact in unpredictable ways to significantly alter a social field and the people who populate it. Rastafari ethnogenesis during the 1950s exemplifies this observation. The Rastafari themselves were diversifying their thought, practice, and social organization. They were beginning an ideological fission affected by new perspectives that the second generation of Rastafari brought to the collectivity, exemplified by youthful groups like Youth Black Faith and the I-Gelic House. The stigmatized status of the Rastafari continued apace, driven in part by events and people they had no control over, such as the criminal activity of outsiders or the violent responses of the police. Bad apples—not always their own—shaped public perception of Rastafari collective identity. International events, such as the Mau Mau Rebellion and Emperor Selassie's land grant resonated with Rastafari interests. These intersecting streams of events and responses raised new questions, such as, Where is home for the Rastafari? Toward the end of the 1950s, a qualitative shift developed in Rastafari ethnogenesis that elevated interest in repatriation and that magnified the negative image of the Rastafari. Let us proceed into a maelstrom of events that together facilitated and problematized Rastafari ethnogenesis.

The UNIA and Migration to Liberia

The Rastafari and Garveyites were Jamaica's vanguard promoting positive conceptions of Black identity. Their Black consciousness—not identical in expression—conjoined with a growing interest in Africa and in relocation to Africa that traces itself at least to the 1930s (or the mid-1800s, if we include the indentured West and Central African immigrants in Jamaica who wanted to return to Africa). The UNIA decision to relocate its US headquarters to Liberia offered another example that relocation to Africa was possible.

Marcus Garvey died on June 10, 1940, in London. James Stewart was elected to complete Garvey's term as president-general of the international UNIA headquarters, located in New York City. Stewart relocated the headquarters to Cleveland, Ohio, but had an even bigger move planned to relocate the UNIA to Liberia. Stewart, along with the president and the secretary of the Whitfield Division of the Kingston UNIA, announced that it was time to fulfill Garvey's plan by relocating the headquarters to Liberia, which happened in February 1949.[2] The

UNIA move to Liberia reminded Black Jamaicans that migration to Africa was feasible.

In September 1947, the Whitfield division of the UNIA petitioned the British secretary of state for the colonies, Creech Jones, to "see that those who desire to go back to Africa be given the opportunity to do so."[3] The petitioners claimed they wanted to leave Jamaica because the cost of living was too high and wages too low. They did not see the promise of a West Indian Federation or social programs as a solution. They wanted out.

A year later, the Pan-African Afro-West Indian Welfare League (AWIWL) petitioned the House of Representatives to support migration to Liberia. Representatives B. Coke (St. Elizabeth) and I. Barrant (St. Thomas) and the minister for education, J. McPherson, debated the petition, with the motion passing.[4] The AWIWL's intention was for the petition to reach the King of England via Jamaica's governor. The petition stressed the difficult living conditions that Black Jamaicans endured and requested that "steamships be made available to enable those who wished to proceed to Liberia at reasonable rates."[5] The AWIWL proposed a "rehabilitation scheme" that would address the needs of "indigent persons." The scheme spoke to authorities' criticism that most of the would-be migrants were poor and unlettered and that African nations wanted skilled migrants (this criticism persisted into the 1960s). House members argued for "full aid to these would-be immigrants" and "removal of all hindrances" to their travel.[6] Although it is unclear who directed the effort, shortly after the Liberia petition, sixteen Jamaicans were on their way, along with African Americans and others, to Liberia via Pan Am (the total number of migrants was projected to involve two hundred Jamaicans).[7]

Information on resettlement in Liberia during the late 1940s is scarce. During a visit to Haiti, an assistant secretary of state in Liberia, Momolu Dukuly, noted that "West Indians on the whole are doing very well in Liberia and the Liberian Government is doing everything to facilitate them under the Immigration Laws of the country."[8] The Liberian migration efforts were further indication that relocation to Africa was possible. A new generation of Rastafari would recast relocation to Africa as repatriation, a duty entwined with Jah's (God's) restoration of Africa to its rightful heirs, continental Africans and Africa-descended people of the Diaspora.

Growing Rastafari Diversity: Cultural Innovation, Ideological Fission

A fundamental innovation occurred among the Rastafari during the mid-1940s. A second generation was forming, many of whom were urban dwellers, and they took issue with some of the beliefs and practices of the founding generation. They sought to further distinguish Rastafari as a faith tradition distinctive from other Jamaican faith traditions. Many younger or "newer" Rastafari were contesting established Rastafari conventions with new ideas that, evocative of a multicellular organism, grew into new creations that assumed a life and energy of their own. Among the documented and emblematic instances of such innovation and fission are the Rastafari communities Youth Black Faith (YBF) and I-Gelic House.[9] They and Rastafari like them would eventuate as another significant shift within a complex ethnogenetic field. The new communities' critique of their elder Rastafari involved revising Rastafari identity. They initiated a process of collective "reidentification" or collective identity revision that involved alterations in attitudes and behaviors.[10]

Bongo Claudey, once a Christian Revivalist and one of the anthropologist John Homiak's research interlocutors, was among the founders of YBF. Claudey, recalling YBF's motivation for shifting its beliefs and practices, believed that the connection between Revival Christianity and the early Rastafari hindered the advancement of Rastafari's still budding faith and identity. The two had to go their separate way. He threw down the gauntlet, demanding a different way of being Rastafari. I quote him at length:

> De people dat were in de "gates" [residence] where I was at dat time were all people in de same "service"—de same "church" [faith community]. Well, one day I stand up and seh, "Look, all of dese things dat we are doing . . . we have something dat leave out. None of us right now is traveling [spiritually] as de "Fadda" [Father is Emperor Selassie] did. . . . We should travel his footsteps in spirit and in truth. . . . We should have our beard as he do and we should keep our head as he do. . . . [Before us] I-n-I [we] . . . see on de street [only] a couple of man who still wears a beard and a "head" in dat form [Afro-like]. Yet, at de same time, deh

doan [don't] have divinity. And really, no one even tried to find out what deh [they] was about. All de time, people stone them—[the] public is against dem very much. . . . So, I-n-I seh, *"To bear de name* [Rastafari], *we haffa* [must] *bear de shame"—so in dat way we could really carry de faith. Dat when I-n-I Hi-ce* [raise] *de "banner"* [the Dreadlocks]. But at de same time some of we were still using comb, ya know. . . . We start ta gather de "Children" [of Israel] and we "step" wid de name "Rastafari" as Ethiopians. . . . Dat time [circa 1947] we never use any akete drums [for music]. . . . De "Nyabinghi" [code] come and seh, "Each and every man is one—just one"—dat is de heights [principle] of de Nyabinghi. . . . I-n-I show dem reasoning of what de House of Boanerges [Sons of Thunder] really stand for—which is "a clean hands and a pure heart." . . . Nyabingi— death ta black and white "downpressor" [oppressor].[11]

Claudey and his brethren sought to remake Rastafari as Nyabinghi, as bearded, Afroed, and dreadlocked spiritual warriors who lived according to teachings of the "Father" and who embodied divinity, who embraced persecution, and who contested racial oppression. Note, though, that in the preceding quote, Claudey accentuates the patriarchal orientations of the Old Testament and Jamaican masculinity. A reorientation of gender relations toward male prominence and female subservience is embedded in the innovation and fission.

YBF set in motion novel cultural beliefs and practices: Nyabinghi became an essential "order" of Rastafari; untrimmed or uncombed hair became a fundamental marker of Rastafari identity; drums became central to ritual activity; a theory of the power of the sound of words informed communication; spiritual and natural living were glorified; and Blackness, Africa, and repatriation became lodestones to Rastafari ideology. The Nyabinghi Order would become hegemonic among Rastafari for decades.

Creating Dread: Rastafari Mysticism and Indigenous Music

In today's political parlance, I-Gelic House was to the left of the radical YBF. They were self-motivated to pursue their spiritual growth as far as possible and to distinguish themselves from outsiders through austere asceticism and shock theater. They intended to be *dread*—dreadful, dreaded, awesome.

Some of the reidentified Rastafari developed an ascetic disposition, another significant identity revision. The I-Gelic House ("I-Gelic" is a Rastafari take on "angelic") epitomized the shift. They challenged first- and second-generation Rastafari to move beyond Bible reading, outdoor preaching, and hymn singing, to develop themselves as uniquely enlightened and inspired beings. After being chased from downtown Kingston, the I-Gelics moved in two directions, one group making a base at Wareika Hill in East Kingston, the other residing at Back-O-Wall in West Kingston.[12] The Wareika Hill group created an ascetic lifestyle steeped in an ideal of "natural man" and "first man," a masculine being in sync with the physical and God-given world.[13] They viewed the human body as a holy and living temple. They rejected violence; they communed with nature; they lived communally; they gave up commercial goods such as shoes, utensils, and clothing; they stopped eating meat; they instituted a saltless, plant-based diet and avoided spices. They innovated the "I-tal" (natural) lifestyle that became synonymous with Rastafari.

I-Gelic House sought to get closer to nature rather than distance themselves from it. They lived like subsistence foragers, relying on what nature and the seasons offered instead of industrial subsistence. "I-tal," or natural, is what they dubbed their lifestyle. I-tal living meant avoiding bloodshed and, hence, the slaughter of animals and eating flesh. By living in communion with the natural world and human faculties, the I-Gelic House promoted the notion that the symbiosis bestowed them with the power to summon the natural elements—lightning, thunder, fire, earthquake—and to see and know what escapes the ken of ordinary people. They made themselves into mystics.

"Higes Knots" is the name I-Gelic House coined to describe their dress, appearance, and character. Styling themselves as prophets, they wore "crocus" material for garments, they doffed shoes and shirts, and they sometimes went naked. The linguist Frederic Cassidy explained that "hige" is a Jamaican patois term for "hag."[14] A hige is a hideous supernatural woman—old hag—who exists to agonize the living. Drawing on this cultural resource, the I-Gelic House crafted their image as masculine and fearsome (a hige can remove her skin). One of John Homiak's I-Gelic interlocutors, Brother Hyawhycuss, described how people reacted to them: "My group, the Higes Knots people, were despised—even some brethren [Rastafari] could not understand us. We were described as madmen. . . . We would trod and 'torment' the blin'ty [blind city] to let de enemy [Babylon] know dat Rasta would stand regardless. . . . De Righteous would never bow."[15] The I-Gelic House sought to sow anguish in the minds of their observers with their appearance and presence.[16] The I-Gelic House impact on Rastafari ethnogenesis became seminal, quickly. The stereotypical image of a "Rastafarian"—dreadlocked, male, righteous, living naturally, mystical, rhythmic, and critical of oppression—traces to the period between the mid-1940s and the mid- to late 1950s. I-Gelic House innovations met resistance among the Rastafari, including from YBF. One of YBF's major concerns was that I-Gelic innovations confirmed stereotypes of Rastafari as menaces and lunatics.[17]

First-generation Rastafari musical expression adapted the instruments and songs of other faith communities to their own purposes.[18] Shakers, rattles, drums, and songs were "borrowed" from Burru, Kumina, and Christian groups (Burru is described shortly). First-generation Rastafari sacred music was drawn from Kumina, an African-derived ancestor-oriented faith complex that emphasizes dancing and drumming as means to communicate with the living and the supernatural, and from Christian sources such as the "Sankey" hymnbook (hymns associated with the American gospel music composer and singer Ira Sankey). Sometime between the mid- and late 1940s, a distinguishable form of sacred Rastafari music developed—called Nyabinghi music. This music has been central to Rastafari identity and ideology.

Explanations for the origins of Rasta music are contested. Some scholars argue that the music of Revivalists or Kumina practitioners (or both) were sources of inspiration for Rasta music, which emphasized drumming to stimulate bodily movement and enhance supernatural communication.[19] However, the virtuoso Rasta music pioneer Count Ossie identified Burru as the primary inspiration for Rasta music. Burru describes a drumming ensemble, a distinctive form of drumming and dancing, and a community of practitioners. It emerged during the era of enslavement and is an adaptation of West African drumming practices.[20] By the 1930s, Burru drummers were established in West Kingston. Along the way, they became stigmatized as licentious criminals and idlers, burdened with a stigma similar to that borne by the Rastafari. The music scholar Verena Reckord maintains that Burru and Rasta met in Kingston and that by the late 1940s, pioneering Rastafari adopted and adapted the Burru repertoire for Rastafari needs.[21] The performance scholar Yoshiko Nagashima's oral history research supports this interpretation.[22]

Count Ossie, an originator of Rasta music, on different occasions told Reckord and Nagashima how he was trained by two Burru master drummers, Wato King and Brother Job.[23] Wato King made Count Ossie his first set of drums, which were Burru drums.[24] Based on the oral testimony of Count Ossie and others, Nyabinghi music existed by 1949 and remained confined to Rastafari communities until the late 1950s. More than a Rasta music pioneer, the drum virtuoso Ossie helped to popularize Rasta music by performing it in public venues.

Irrespective of origins, Rastafari music evolved around a three-drum ensemble: a large bass drum, a medium-size drum called the "funde," and a smaller syncopating drum called the "repeater" (or "peta"). The drum for the Rastafari corresponds to the sacred role of the biblical harp. Drumming was accompanied by hymns called "chants" (emphasizing community and unison) and by shakers and other instruments. Chants were both adapted from the Sankeys and created by Rastafari themselves.

Rasta music was an innovation, the creation of a novel indigenous musical tradition out of available cultural resources. I-Gelic House, however, did not see the musical innovation as extensive enough. They pushed further, in a "higher" direction. For one, I-Gelic House was dissatisfied with how their elder Rastafari clung to trappings of White hegemony, suppressing their inner inspiration: "Everyting dem [elders] bring up at 'binghi [Nyabinghi ceremony] come from the Church. Like . . . de same song book dem have in Church—wha yuh call Sankey. . . . [It] is a Christian interpretation dem give yuh. . . . Him [Rastafari] don't have nuttn of him own dat him create as an inspiration to de culture."[25] I-Gelic House emphasized life itself as a fundamental power of nature and thus rejected the practice of using drums made with the skin of dead animals.[26] Without drums, what was one to do? Answer: make the human voice itself an instrument. I-Gelic House created a new style of chanting based on repeating an "I/Ai" sound (ai, ai, ai, ai . . .) at undulating frequencies.[27] The I/Ai chant was sound rather than words, with literally no demarcated ending; it fluctuated according to the collective mood of the chanting community.

The name that the Wareika Hill militants gave themselves, I-Gelic House, and their lifestyle, I-tal, point to another of their significant innovations: creating a Rastafari argot. The argot, "I-Yound" (I sound), uses *I* and/or *Y* to replace initial morphemes and first syllables in many English words and pursues an alignment between words' sounds and meanings. For instance, a Rastafari might say "I-nana" instead of "banana" to acknowledge a godly relationship between human and plant. I-Yound is the power an enlightened Rastafari can exercise through sounds and words. The argot is also called "Dread Talk," "I-talk," and "Word, Sound, and Power" by the Rastafari.[28]

Symbolic performance of counternorms, such as invoking threatening and vituperative language, was a part of a Rastafari theory of Word, Sound, and Power.[29] The religion scholar Leonard Barrett, who studied Kingston Rastafari during the 1960s, reported, "One of the cult's characteristics is vile language. . . . Some are masters of the art of profanity, especially the Jamaican variety. . . . [For them] words are neither good nor bad but made by thinking."[30] One of the recurrent causes of incarceration or court fines for the Rastafari was foul language.

Another significant aspect of this ascetic orientation was celibacy, which influenced Rastafari gender dynamics for at least a generation. Women were shunned by many of the second-generation radicals, thus diminishing the profile of Rastafari women bearing the faith. For a good while, Rastafari meant male. While there is a greater framework in which the Black Jamaican patriarchy operates, Rastafari men used scripture to justify male dominance and female subordination (see chapter 10). The shift, however, was not a fait accompli. As explained earlier, women were prominent among the first-generation Rastafari, notwithstanding the patriarchy. The male-centered hegemony would begin to erode by the 1980s.

Migration to Ethiopia Discourse Begins to Take Shape

Formal discussion about migration to Ethiopia began around 1950. The EWF's representative in Addis Ababa submitted a petition to Emperor

Selassie in May 1950. The EWF headquarters in New York City notified the secretary of EWF Local 31 in Kingston, in early July 1950, that Emperor Selassie had granted land, in Shashemene, Ethiopia, to the EWF for its members.[31] In Jamaica, the *Daily Gleaner* announced the grant, noting that the land gift was an acknowledgment of the EWF's support of Ethiopia "throughout the many trying years of its existence" and that the Emperor welcomed Black people "desirous of migrating to that country [Ethiopia]." It went on to say that the people who were most needed and ought to apply were "carpenters, painters, plumbers, electricians, upholsterers, farmers and cabinet makers."[32] Who should and should not migrate to Ethiopia would become a contentious issue.

Without a definition of what constituted a true Ethiopian beyond "dark skin" or "Black," it is unsurprising that so many Jamaicans considered themselves a worthy candidate to relocate to Ethiopia. The Rastafari and many Garveyites embraced and promoted the racial identification "Ethiopian." Many of them believed that identifying as Ethiopian was sufficient to qualify; scripture and the Emperor's sympathy for them were sufficient qualifications.

The governor of Jamaica learned that the New York City EWF International president and Pentecostal minister Bishop Robert Clarence Lawson was about to visit Jamaica to discuss the land grant. Lawson had submitted a plan for the emigration of Jamaicans to Ethiopia to the colonial secretary in Jamaica. Lawson took it upon himself, as a part of a larger international tour, to visit Jamaica and convene a "mass meeting" to discuss the land concession.[33]

Lawson met with Jamaica EWF locals and government officials in November 1950 to "discuss the land concessions granted by the Ethiopian Government to Jamaicans who desire to migrate to Ethiopia."[34] Previously, Lawson met with Emperor Selassie, who had awarded him the Star of Ethiopia, an award acknowledging his service to Ethiopia. Lawson declared that the Emperor had set aside roughly five hundred acres for the EWF.[35] Lawson conferenced with acting colonial secretary John O'Regan.[36] (Of interest, O'Regan made no mention of the Back-to-Africa movement or the Rastafari in his memoir, *From Empire to Commonwealth*, which chronicled his colonial civil service career in Jamaica.)[37]

Lawson was unsympathetic to the Rastafari and their conception of migration as repatriation. His view on migration was in line with that of

Jamaican elites who supported migration: people of "ability" should be the only ones the government should consider in its migration policy. He worked to distance the international EWF from the Rastafari: "We could never subscribe to the blasphemous belief that the people hold that Haile Selassie is a God. I have met the man. He is a very devout Christian and would be horrified if he knew that anyone held such a belief."[38] In one meeting, Lawson said he would "get a statement from the Emperor to say that he did not claim himself to be God but that he was a worshipper of God," which "caused ebullitions in the audience."[39] The idea of getting the Emperor to repudiate the Rastafari as a means to disprove their beliefs gained popularity among elites.

The news and discussions of the Emperor's land grant stoked Rastafari anticipation of repatriation and drew the attention of a cross-section of Jamaican society. However, the Rastafari presence in the public eye was also growing for another reason: many Jamaicans were conflating the Rastafari with criminal activity linked to Jamaica's ghettos.

Rastafari, the Ghetto, Crime

Kingston teemed with slums by the 1930s. In parts of West Kingston, such as Facey's Brickyard in Smith Village, people lived on the city dump yard. The colonial government made little provision for social welfare; therefore, tenement dwellings, squatting, and pauperism became serious public problems by the 1940s. A survey of life in Kingston during 1938 mused, "to the casual observer passing along Spanish Town Road, if he were unacquainted with the conditions of life among the poorer classes in Jamaica, it would be a shock of surprise to learn that human beings dwelt behind those derelict iron fences."[40] Several Kingston ghettos—Trench Town, Back-O-Wall, Ackee Walk, Dungle (or Dunghill), and Smith Village—became hothouses for Rastafari ethnogenesis.

The rise in Rastafari activity and the increase in their presence worried elites for reasons other than prejudice and fear: tourism. The Rastafari were active well beyond Kingston, St. Catherine, and St. Thomas. They were active in Montego Bay in Westmoreland Parish, for example, a primary tourist enclave. In Montego Bay, the Rastafari lived among a matrix of vagrants, panhandlers, and petty thieves. Because the Rastafari lived among undesirables, they exacerbated their undesirability.

The identity script of the Rastafari as criminal, idler, and addict gained credence, if false credence, to no small extent because of where the Rastafari lived in the cities.

While some of the Rastafari were busy developing a fearsome identity during early 1950, all of them received unwelcomed assistance from undesirable outsiders: men lacking the moral and faith conviction of the Rastafari began affecting Rastafari mannerisms, such as wearing beards and dreadlocks. Some engaged in grave criminal activity.

On June 11, 1951, the front page of the *Daily Gleaner* blasted, "Rastaman Charged with Palisadoes Murder."[41] Alston Jolly, a.k.a. "Whoppy King," brutally assaulted a teenage couple, stabbing and clubbing the boy to death and raping the girl. Whoppy was described as bearded, as a resident of the Dunghill, and as a "Dreadlocks."[42] The surviving victim identified Whoppy among a lineup of "bearded men," presumably Rastafari. Popular memory portrays Whoppy wearing dreadlocks, which he trimmed after the murder to elude capture.[43] The Palisadoes murder became a cause célèbre because of the callous brutality of the crime and the tender age of the victims and because it affirmed any belief that the Rastafari were a threat to Jamaica's security. The Palisadoes murder precipitated a ferocious crackdown on the Rastafari: literally overnight, their status as threat ballooned. Authorities announced efforts to crack down on the Rastafari, crime, and squatters, especially against those living in the Wareika and Dungle communities of Kingston.

The People's National Party (PNP) resisted the Jamaican Labour Party's (JLP's) immediate move to oust the squatters and increase police patrols. The PNP urged the government to respond cautiously to the Palisadoes murder to mitigate against harming the tourist industry by raising concern abroad that Jamaica was unsafe. The JLP in turn branded the PNP as supportive of criminals (and of the Rastafari).[44] PNP leader Norman Manley responded with a feeble defense: restraint was required until the crime had been thoroughly analyzed, indicating that the PNP supported a punitive response to criminal activity.[45]

The journalist and impresario Vere Johns painted a picture of Kingston in which squatting, crime, and the Rastafari were out of control: "For years, portions of the west end of the City have been crowded with a horde of undesirables and unemployables and each year these have become more daring in their molesting and robbing of unsuspecting citizens."[46] Johns wanted the police to take drastic action and "clean out the thieving murdering rats who are preying on all and sundry."[47] He spewed his severest contempt on the Rastafari: "The worst evil of all are the members of that bearded cult who style themselves the Rastafarites and claim some kinship with Abyssinia. In reality this group has *no* religious significance, do not know where Ethiopia is, and merely adopted their untidy habit of letting their hair and beard grow through laziness and filthiness and a desire to appear more terrifying."[48]

Long before the PNP-JLP "tribal" politics of the 1970s, in which politicians organized communities into voting blocks defended by armed goons, Johns accused the PNP of political chicanery: "It is an unchallengeable fact that some of these vagabonds have been organized into groups by sub-leaders of the People's National Party and are used in trade disputes and political campaigns to create disorder and intimidate employers and workers with the full knowledge (and, I dare say permission) of the Party's executives."[49] Johns worked a story line: "[A] prominent member of the PNP and Trade Union Congress has been in charge of these bearded supporters for at least four years and even sometimes grows his own beard to demonstrate his oneness with them. That individual once told me that he was afraid of them because it was so difficult to control them and it wouldn't take much for them get out of hand."[50] Such inflammatory seeds were planted into the public discourse, adding to the image of Rastafari as threat. This is one example of why many Rastafari would reject Jamaican party politics: the association ruined their collective identity. There are other reasons, as we shall see.

The travel writer Patrick Fermor's travelogue *The Traveller's Tree* demonstrates how casual but insensitive observations about the Rastafari could be turned against them to further stigmatize them and to engender hysteria.[51] Fermor, a worldly Irish former soldier, developed the habit of walking into and through people's lives as a part of his obsession with traveling and writing about his travels. In 1947, Fermor left Southampton, England, for Central America, the goal being to tour the Antilles over a period of six months. During his visit to Jamaica, Fermor happened upon the Rastafari while searching for Kumina practitioners in Trench Town. He wrote a vivid but patronizing account of the Rastafari he met in Kingston. The *Daily Gleaner* columnist Peter Simple used Fermor to caricature the Rastafari. Fermor wrote,

The Rastafari live in a patch of waste land by the railway in the western slums of Kingston known as the Dunghill. . . . From flagpoles above their hovels flutter the red, yellow and green tricolour: flags of Abyssinia; and notice-boards bear messages in clumsily formed letters, which say "Long live Abyssinia" or "We are Ethiopians." It was plain to see that the Negroes lounging among the trees and huts regarded (my) white intrusion with extreme dislike. They looked terrible; a lot of people with expressions of really frightening depravity: All were dressed in the most sordid rags (and all equipped with curling black beards). . . . After a show of hostility the author was permitted to enter one of the huts. . . . The hut was about two yards square and constructed entirely of copies of The Daily Gleaner tied together. A photograph of the Negus [Emperor Selassie], nursing a bat-eared lap-dog with enormous eyes, was stuck to the paper wall.[52]

With retrospect, we can see that in the cultural productions of Fermor's Rastafari interlocutors—flags, notice boards, and photographs of Emperor Selassie—they were rectifying their miseducation. They were both claiming and creating Black history and culture from their own standpoint. In trying to discredit Rastafari adulation of Ethiopia, Fermor recorded this conversation: "But, I said, 'none of the slaves that came to the West Indies were from Ethiopia, which was inhabited by a different, a Semitic race.' He [a Rastafari] waved this aside. 'That's all lies,' he answered, 'that's what the history books say, but the history books are all written by white folks to make a fool of the black men.'"[53] While charges of a slanderous intent were produced by Simple, Fermor, Johns, and others, among the Rastafari emerged organic intellectuals, such as Sam Spence, Sam Brown, and Mortimer Planno, who would take on and rebut the slanderers and also educate Rastafari and outsiders alike (Planno is sometimes called by the surname "Planner"; Mortimer was well-known by the vernacular surname Planno, which I use).[54]

Sam Spence, president of Brotherhood Solidarity of United Ethiopians (BSUE), eloquently argued against the misrecognition and consequent mistreatment of the Rastafari as menaces, explaining factors affecting the Rastafari but beyond their control. Spence noted that for the Rastafari, the "majority [are] humble, passive, intelligent even if

Figure 6.1. Rastafari street meeting: the United Afro-West Indian Federation, West Kingston, 1953; photographed by the anthropologist George Simpson (note that none of the participants wear dreadlocks). (National Anthropological Archives, Smithsonian Institution)

Figure 6.2. A Rastafari youth group meeting, West Kingston, 1953; photographed by the anthropologist George Simpson. (National Anthropological Archives, Smithsonian Institution)

uneducated according to western standards."[55] With regard to abuse for their beliefs, they have "suffered, and are suffering still, all manner of afflictions, persecution, victimisation, scorn and abuse. Most of all they suffer from the lack of opportunity to earn and develop higher social standards of living, as there are very few people, who will employ them, rightly or wrongly, for obvious reasons."[56] Spence acknowledged the damaging effect that criminals and loafers created for the Rastafari. Among the Rastafari, Spence said, "evil men have worked their way in cunningly, by growing a beard and adopting the form and speech of the earnest ones. . . . As soon as these are found out by the true [Rastafari] Cultists, they are chased away."[57]

Rastafari like Spence were growing knowledgeable about Africa's history and current affairs, especially those of interest to the Rastafari. They were organizing and sharing their knowledge among themselves and outsiders (figures 6.1 and 6.2). They relished learning about Black anticolonial resistance movements. As African anticolonial resistance movements began to gain international attention during the 1950s, the Rastafari homed in on the activities of the Mau Mau movement in Kenya.

Mau Mau: An Anti-White and Anticolonial Secret Society Finds Solidarity in Jamaica

The stirrings in Kenya of a people called "Mau Mau," people "sworn to liquidate Kenya's British rulers," was reported in Jamaica as early as September 1952.[58] The Mau Mau Rebellion in Kenya began in earnest in October 1952 with the murder of a European woman and the assassination of a native chief who was a loyal ally of the British. The murders signaled to the British that the Mau Mau had declared war, leading them to declare a state of emergency. "Mau Mau" was the name given to the rebels among the Kikuyu and other people of central and southern Kenya, who resisted and fought the British settlers and army. One interpretation of the name "Mau Mau" is that it means "the hidden ones."

Newspapers were a source of Jamaicans' introduction to the Mau Mau and their war against the British colonial government and against White settlers. Mau Mau activities made for front-page news. The Mau

Mau had a wider effect in that they were "lauded throughout the developing world as representing the struggle of freedom for oppressed peoples everywhere."[59]

The Rastafari scholar Barry Chevannes discredited claims that the Mau Mau rebels inspired the Rastafari to grow locks.[60] General China, a Mau Mau leader, for example, was described as displaying locks: "General China now wears a policeman's blue jersey—instead of his terrorist's white shirt and pants. And his spiky hair has been shorn to a prison cut" (see figures 6.3 and 6.4).[61] General China and other Mau Mau wore locks, though they did not think of their hair in this way.

The up-and-coming Rastafari groups like Youth Black Faith and I-Gelic House shared resemblances with the Mau Mau, some intentional, others coincidental. Both cultivated an antimodern sensibility; both rejected much of British and European ways; and both enshrouded themselves in mysticism. The Mau Mau were described as a "back-fire from the machine of modernization. . . . All things European—clothes, implements, domestic utensils—are taboo to their members and they are sworn to resist every European influence."[62] The same could be said about growing numbers of Rastafari in the Kingston area. Jomo Kenyatta, the Pan-Africanist and anticolonialist, at one point looked the part of a biblical patriarch and shepherd (leader), "sporting a long beard and large staff."[63]

Second-generation Rastafari like Ras Sam Brown, Mortimer Planno, and Brother Bongo were infatuated with the Mau Mau, seeing in them a vibe kindred with their own. Indeed, some Rastafari believed that the Mau Mau were doing the work of Emperor Selassie by revolting against the White settlers to drive them out of Africa.[64] On the other hand, many elites denounced the Mau Mau as vicious extremists, being reminded of their own so-called extremists, the Rastafari.

Key elements of Mau Mau practice, as characterized by sympathizers and detractors, involved acting as fearsome warriors bound to each other through secretive and purportedly chilling rites. Colonizers marked them as frightening, though they also marked themselves as such. The younger and militant members of the Nyabinghi Rastafari would style themselves as fearsome warriors, behave in secretive ways, practice unsettling rites like the Nyabinghi dance, and demonstrate

Figure 6.3. Mau Mau leader General China with spikey locks, ca. 1954. (Magnum Photos, Inc.)

Figure 6.4. Jomo Kenyatta with Mau Mau rebel leader "Field Marshal" Mwariama, 1963. (Getty Images)

provocative but nonviolent resistance against colonial authorities. (The Nyabinghi dance symbolized death to White and Black oppressors. For example, the rhythmic prancing movements called "trample the dragon" symbolize crushing emissaries of evil.) While the Mau Mau fought life-and-death battles with the British, the Nyabinghi Rastafari waged a symbolic war against colonial Jamaican society, although more than a few paid for their resistance with licks, kicks, trimmings, and sometimes their lives.

The connection between the Mau Mau and Jamaica is more than speculative, and it extended beyond news reportage. Dudley Thompson, a Jamaican barrister, traveled to Kenya, where he defended Jomo Kenyatta, imprisoned for alleged leadership of the Mau Mau.[65] Peter Evans, an Irishman, barrister, and purported communist, and others delivered lectures on the Mau Mau to the Jamaican public. Sponsored by the AWIWL, Evans presented a sympathetic account of the Mau Mau as Africans resisting colonialism and exploitative practices such as the British White Highlands policy, which reserved choice mountainous terrain for White settlers.[66]

If You Are Rastafari, Where Is Home?

Between 1955 and 1962, 158,630 Jamaicans migrated to and settled in Britain because they desired work and other opportunities. Recall that during the 1940s, Black Jamaicans wanting to migrate to Liberia complained about their inability to create a fulfilling life in Jamaica. Prior to 1951, less than one thousand Caribbean nationals of all English-speaking islands entered Britain each year.[67] Initially, there was significant hostility toward Black Jamaican immigrants. Yet while some Black Jamaicans were trying to get to Britain, others were trying to get to Africa. One second-generation Rastafari, Brother Alexander, told me that at the time his slogan was, "Africa yes, England no!"

As the party in power, the JLP offered advice to the Rastafari that opposed the rising tide of Back-to-Africa momentum washing on Jamaica: Rasta people, acquire gainful employment, stop malingering, and if you are not Rastafari, do not consider becoming one; it would be a waste of your life:

It is no use the Rastafari insisting that they are Ethiopians and that their home is in Africa. In the first place this is not true. Their home is in Jamaica. . . . There is no reason whatever why we should send them to Africa nor is it ever likely. . . . They should seek to become useful members of the community instead of continuing to be a lawless and idle group which serves no purpose. . . . The way to get to Ethiopia is to work for the necessary money. . . . But there is yet time for Rastafari men to put aside this Ethiopia business and become useful citizens of Jamaica.[68]

Rastafari relocation to Africa invoked competing notions of home and, in Jamaica's colonial context, competing notions of national and racial identity. The Rastafari bellowed that they were Africans in exile, anxious to go "home" to Africa. Many Jamaicans yelled back that Jamaica was home and that the Back-to-Africa movement (as it was called) should come to their senses and be proud to be Jamaican. The Rastafari lambasted the idea that Jamaican nationality should be central to the self-concept of African-descended people. Elites jeered that identifying foremost as African (or Black) was silly. Morris Cargill, a lawyer, politician, and writer, writing under the pseudonym Thomas Wright, exemplified this view: "I should have thought that it would be enough for any person to consider himself, with pride and thankfulness, as Jamaican. It is part of the prevalent sense of inferiority that we should wish to think of ourselves otherwise, and that we should have become so race-conscious. Or is the word Ras-conscious?"[69] The second-generation Rastafari intellectual and organizer Ras Sam Brown might have agreed with the second part of Wright's sarcastic observation: "We have been taught to bow at the shrines of Anglo-Saxon and other European heroes, but never been given a hint of the renown of ourselves [Black Jamaicans], so that the general complex of the West Indian Negro is one of inferiority."[70]

Identity was the heart of the migration-turned-repatriation matter. Although the term had earlier roots, "repatriation" became the term of choice in Rastafari discourse by the early 1950s. "Repatriation" signified moral and theological concerns lacking in the term "migration"; it signified a right of return sanctioned by divine authority. Repatriation became an issue of Rastafari identity and rights. More than a few

Rastafari refused to be quiet on matters so fundamental to their identity, and they raised their voices during the 1950s. Identity and faith entwined in political activity. The BSUE, for example, epitomized how the Rastafari were pressing for their rights. Sam Spence described the organization as focused since 1953 on repatriation to Ethiopia, on recognition as Black nationals of Ethiopia, and on communicating these desires to Chief Minister Bustamante, the colonial secretary, and other "British officials."[71]

By claiming recognition as Rastafari and as Ethiopians—Africa-descended peoples desirous of relocating to Africa—the Rastafari became embroiled in arguments about home, about history, about national identity, about race, about class, and about whose ideas should take precedence in a colony and world buffeted by swelling anticolonialism and independence.

But let us not lose sight of the billowing specter of Rastafari as menace. The desire to exorcise the Jamaican body politic of the Rastafari "cult" continued as a prevailing current.

Efforts to Destroy the Rastafari Coexist with the Continued Growth of the Rastafari

People continued dwelling at Pinnacle after the first raid and maintained it during Howell's absences. The writer J. Martin described Pinnacle in the post-1941-raid era as an operation run by Leonard Howell and his "gang of men." They "instituted a quasi-government inflicting hard punishments to those who fell victim to the law there."[72] He estimated that Pinnacle harbored around two thousand residents during the early 1950s, a substantial increase beyond the estimates of the early 1940s.[73] Yet the Pinnacleites impressed Martin with their display of community, how it was them versus Babylon: "One fact why they cannot be passed unnoticed is the unity of the people of Pinnacle. . . . When 'Babylon' (so they call the police) enters the district to enquire into any matter, the practice of 'in unity lies strength' is noticeable."[74]

While Martin displays a stingy admiration for Rastafari camaraderie, he treats them as a weight around the neck of a "people struggling toward nationhood," a drag on Jamaican nationalism and independence. The Rastafari, Martin concludes, are people "bred in ignorance, false beliefs and of faith in lost causes [and] present a fertile field of labour for Christian missionaries, social workers, and people of goodwill."[75] In Martin's view, the Rastafari must be "fixed." Many people concurred. One immediate fix for the Rastafari problem would be to mount another effort to dismantle Pinnacle.

Police conducted a second major raid on Pinnacle on Saturday, May 22, 1954. Deputy Commissioner of Police L. P. R. Browning led what was reported as the "biggest raid in the local police history on Pinnacle, . . . [seizing] over eight tons of ganja [cannabis] valuing several thousand pounds and [taking] into custody 140 Ras Tafarians."[76] A subsequent raid ensued on May 24. The second "raiding party" rammed its way into Pinnacle, this time announcing its confiscation of two more ganja fields, claiming to have confiscated seven thousand living plants and two thousand "freshly-cut plants."[77]

Since the 1970s, the Rastafari have been, in the minds of many people, synonymous with "ganja." Rastafari had been using cannabis from their beginning, as attested in the innumerable reports of "Beards" arrested for possession of cannabis during the 1930s. By the late 1940s, many but not all Rastafari were using cannabis as a sacrament to commune with oneself, other people, and the natural and supernatural world. In the words of the first-generation Rastafari Bongo Claudie, "Rasta uses herbs feh a constructive purpose in order to gain wisdom, knowledge, and overstanding."[78] Yet we cannot ignore how cannabis also offered some users—Rastafari and others—a respite from the travails of an unrelenting scuffle to make a living. Pinnacle produced cannabis on a grand scale, for resident consumption and for sale. While many Rastafari expressed a positive view of cannabis, elites and authorities held to an opposing view. For them, it was a major cause of deviance and social ills. Jamaican authorities and elites fell prey to fanciful claims that tried to link Pinnacle, the Rastafari, and what they believed were the homicidal effects of consuming ganja.[79] If one believed that ganja incited violent pathology and believed that the Rastafari were "temperamental, violent, and out of step with their fellow Jamaicans," then one could justify oppression of the Rastafari because they were volatile.[80]

Most of the charges against the Pinnacleites involved growing ganja and possession of ganja, both violations of Jamaica's Dangerous Drugs Act (enacted in 1948). Many of the arrestees were women, and many of them received sentences equivalent to the men. Loretta McDonald received the same sentence as her male companion, Elisha Robinson. Both were sentenced to a year of hard labor for possessing 110 pounds of ganja, although Robinson reported that McDonald had nothing to do with the ganja.[81] The same was true for Rupert Prince and Adassa Stewart. Both received one-year hard labor, even though Prince took responsibility for possessing the ganja. Harriet Russell and Sara McKay received one-year hard labor, while Eliza Walker and Amy Powell received nine months' hard labor. Even elderly Pinnacleites were punished. The magistrate sentenced "old man" Robert Stephens, supposedly over eighty years, to a sentence of a year's hard labor. The sentencing message: we will punish you harshly for being Rastafari.

A significant consequence of the second major Pinnacle raid was dispersion of Rastafari into Kingston, Spanish Town, and other surrounding areas. The raid, however, exacerbated a pattern that can be traced to the 1941 Pinnacle raid, when Rastafari who left Pinnacle created mini-Pinnacles in Kingston and beyond in the form of yards and camps, developing the context for general stability and growth: an increase in Rastafari presence and numbers.[82]

The camps and yards were living and gathering places that provided space for the elaboration of Rastafari ideology and the development of communitas. This pattern manifested a reticulate form that connected different Rastafari groups while providing degrees of independence to innovate. Brother Wato King, for instance, left Ferry (between Pinnacle and western Kingston) and made a yard at Ninth Street in Trench Town during the early 1950s. Wato King's yard housed a tabernacle (site of worship), hosted drumming sessions, and fed people. Douglas Mack, a second-generation Rastafari who traveled with the mission to Africa in 1960, recalled details about the development of camps and yards in the greater Kingston area. Brother Lover, for example, was a revered Rastafari, a Pinnacleite who left Pinnacle and founded a camp near Long Mountain and Wareika Hill.[83] Rastafari affiliated with Brother Lover's camp include two well-known musicians and contributors to the development of Rastafari music, Count Ossie and Brother Job. Both were master drummers, the latter teaching the former.[84]

The camps, among other purposes, served as sites where one could acquire the knowledge attendant to becoming Rastafari and thus were vital to Rastafari ethnogenesis. Ras Brenton, born in 1940, recalled that during his teenage years, he would pass multiple Rastafari encampments in western Kingston when running errands for his mother. Although fearful, during his idle time, he would walk past the encampments, motivated by a contrary curiosity as to whether the tales about the Rastafari were true. Did they live like animals? Did they practice rituals supportive of evil? Did they steal children? Later, Ras Brenton's path into Rastafari would involve visiting some of the same encampments he spied on, learning details of doctrine by listening to the reasoning sessions among the men of the various camps. The camps were vectors facilitative of growth, diversity, and durability. It was one thing to ravage a large encampment like Pinnacle. However, it would have required pogrom-like intensity to annihilate the Rastafari camp by camp. Therefore, Rastafari social organization evolved in ways conducive to Rastafari survival and regeneration. A reticulate and acephalous pattern of development became supportive of Rastafari resilience in an environment where power asymmetry and centralization could be a severe disadvantage, given the colonial government's experience with confronting centralized or less powerful adversaries.

With the company of a police superintendent, on March 19, 1958, a citizen set ablaze "50-odd" huts at the Pinnacle site.[85] Pinnacle was declared finished. Nevertheless, the destruction of Pinnacle did not diminish the growth or public presence of the Rastafari. Some Pinnacleites remained in the vicinity of Pinnacle.

Prelude to Inviting Emperor Selassie to Jamaica

Concurrent with the 1954 disruption of Pinnacle was a rise in public interest in Emperor Selassie and Rastafari-relevant concerns such as repatriation, demonstrated in Rastafari and Black Nationalist activity, media coverage, and political debates. J. N. Hibbert wrote a letter to the *Daily Gleaner* editor, published on Emperor Selassie's birthdate, asking "Ethiopians" to celebrate the Emperor: "Let's show the world our national respect and love for the Conquering Lion of Judah."[86] Rising public interest was partially an effect of the enlarged visibility and the defiance of the Rastafari. The idea that Ethiopia was "willing to accept immigrants from the British West Indies to settle in that country" gained currency among the public.[87] Politicians were beginning to acknowledge the repatriation fervor.

Spence's communication with colonial officials led him to conclude, "on the question of immigration to Ethiopia, I have been informed and am convinced that there are possibilities for successful settlement of our immigrants in that country [Ethiopia]." Britain was not about to pay for migration, but Spence believed that it did "not intend to place any obstacles in the paths of those intending to migrate to Ethiopia."[88] Spence urged politicians, bureaucrats, and Back-to-Africa groups to work together to pressure the Colonial Office.

Liberia's head of state, President William Tubman, visited Jamaica during November 1954. Tubman was moving toward alignment with national liberation movements in Africa. Jamaica feted Tubman with a twenty-one-gun salute and thousands of spectators along his tour route. He hit it off well with the then-governor of Jamaica, Hugh Foot, and with Jamaica's chief minister, Alexander Bustamante. Governor Foot allowed the United African Council, a collection of Jamaican "African organizations," to address Tubman. Among them were leaders from the UNIA, the African Study Circle, and the Afro-Brotherhood. Tubman said that Jamaican made a "'lasting, favourable impression' on his mind."[89] His visit intensified the repatriation enthusiasm.

Emperor Selassie I traveled extensively during 1954, spanning Europe and North America. More than a decade before the Emperor's visit to Jamaica, pundits speculated that crowds would rush to see him: "Undoubtedly his visit would be an unforgettable event and in order to prevent extraordinary overcrowding in the metropolis, arrangements could be made for him to visit Montego Bay, Mandeville, Denbigh and Port Antonio." Both the PNP and the JLP argued a version of the view that a visit from the Emperor would raise Jamaica's international status and inspire "coloured people's minds."[90]

Thrust into public discourse, fantasies of Emperor Selassie visiting Jamaica made for fascinating drama. There were the Rastafari who were interested in having their God visit. There were the Black Nationalists who wanted a revered African King to visit. There were politicians, civic leaders, and businessfolk who believed a visit by the Emperor would increase Jamaica's global stature and boost the pride of its citizens. There were people who wanted the Emperor to visit to demonstrate as ludicrous the notion of any real connection between Black Jamaicans, Ethiopia, and the Emperor. And there were folk who saw the invitation issue as a PNP ploy to gain voters. Gaining momentum, like a huge boulder tumbling down a mountain, was an up-and-coming Africa and Black consciousness filtering out beyond the Rastafari and Garveyites. The social climate was shifting: an environment conducive to valorizing Blackness and Blackness itself were under construction.

The idea of inviting Emperor Selassie I to Jamaica became a test of public opinion on the matter. The JLP and its defenders accused the PNP, especially its first vice president, N. N. Nethersole, of pandering to the Rastafari: "it seems to us a most treasonable tendency for the People's National Party to seek to expand in Jamaica the doctrines held by a zany group by which they preach loyalty to Haile Selassie and practise affronts to authority in their own country," complained an editorialist. He argued that the Jamaican public "will no doubt know what judgment to place on a [political and PNP] movement which seeks to elevate local Ras Tafarism into a state-encouraged lunacy."[91]

Nonetheless, Nethersole, a Brown man opining on Rastafari and Black Jamaican affairs, pressed the governor to invite Emperor Selassie to Jamaica. He contended that Jamaicans would derive the "greatest pleasure welcoming—such an outstanding person of their own kin."[92]

On the contrary, the columnist Thomas Wright pleaded for Nethersole to "invite His Imperial Majesty Haile Selassie of Ethiopia to visit Jamaica . . . when he visits the United States [in 1954]." In contrast to Nethersole's racial and political calculation, Wright berated the Rastafari as ignorant about Africa, contending that Ethiopians are unrelated to the "African descendants of Jamaica." Wright's reasoning, which would in coming years gain supporters, was, "It is possible that the Emperor would be considerably shocked to meet those of us [Jamaicans] who describe ourselves as followers of Ras Tafari."[93] An embarrassed Emperor might reject any ascribed divinity and thus force Rastafari to see their faulty theology. Wright perhaps misconstrued Nethersole's motivation: he and the PNP grasped the burgeoning political salience of Black identity and Black nationalism.

As Jamaicans learned more about the Rastafari, Africa, and Black nationalism, the caricature of the Rastafari as simple-minded people came into question. Another vector of information about the Rastafari emerged during this period: scholarship. The anthropologist George Simpson's research is the first published scholarship focused solely on the Rastafari.[94] The *Daily Gleaner* covered Simpson's first article: it discredited a "good many current beliefs about the essentially criminal characteristics of the movement. . . . In the mind of the better classes there is a somewhat blurred picture of Ras Tafarians, in which beards, crime, and ganja are the only recognizable objects. . . . Simpson found that 'not all Ras Tafari groups favour beard-wearing,' . . . yet some beggars, thieves and ganja-users profess to believe in Ras Tafarism."[95] We recognize now that Simpson's explanation for the development of the Rastafari was both a product of the thinking of his time and an incomplete theory. Simpson did not set out to study the Rastafari but bumped into and took an interest in them while studying Revival and Kumina groups in West Kingston. He presented a compensation theory, that the Rastafari were the materialization of an "adjustive activity which enables its members to live with poverty, squalor, and the disdain of the better off."[96] Said differently, being Rastafari was a means to cope with unbridled inequality. Simpson's theory was an advance in thinking about the Rastafari because it ruled out lunacy, instead portraying them as pragmatists seeking a solution to the vexing conditions of poverty and marginality. He cloaked his analysis in the rhetoric of scientific objectivity, and in doing so, he offered a credible, if oversimplified, argument for the motivation and behavior of the Rastafari. There was much that Simpson neglected at the time, such as the Rastafari marriage of Black consciousness, Pan-Africanism, and religion, which offered positive attractions like love and Blackness, while theories like Simpson's emphasized what was lacking.

Mayme Richardson, EWF International Organizer, Visits Jamaica

EWF local 31 invited Mayme Richardson, a Black American soprano singer, to Jamaica (figure 6.5).[97] Described as a "dramatic soprano," she performed at Kingston's major venues, the Ward Theater and Coke Memorial Hall.[98] Richardson was an international organizer for the EWF. Her visit was to celebrate the third anniversary of the reunion of

(c) 1955 The Gleaner Co. (Media) Ltd.

Figure 6.5. Photograph of Mayme Richardson published in the
Daily Gleaner (1955), under the caption, "Ethiopian World
Federation organizer comes." (Courtesy of The Gleaner Co.
[Media] Ltd.)

Ethiopia and Eritrea.[99] Glowing media reports emphasized Richardson's
international touring and lecturing and her "command performance"
in Ethiopia for Emperor Selassie. Local 31 planned the events with
education in mind, as well (Local 1 was also involved). For example,
Richardson's itinerary included showing films made in Ethiopia, and
there would be opportunities for the public to participate in her tour.
Perhaps most important to the EWF was inviting Richardson to discuss Emperor Selassie's land grant.[100] Richardson's visit set ablaze the
simmering but increasing interest in repatriation, the Emperor, and
Ethiopia.

In 1958, the Rastafari Charles Edwards (b. 1915), also known as Prince Emmanuel, organized a monthlong and island-wide convention of Rastafari in Kingston, emphasizing repatriation, to the severe consternation of elite and nonelite Jamaicans alike. People recoiled from the huge number of Rastafari adherents who assembled in Kingston, their nightlong drumming and chanting sessions, and their sporadic expressions of symbolic violence toward non-Rastafari in their vicinity. Prince Emmanuel's organizing occurred during a period of heightened agitation. It was also the moment of Prince Emmanuel's creation of what became another major Rastafari grouping, or "House" or "Mansion," of Rastafari: the Ethiopian Africa Black International Congress (EABIC). The EABIC, led by Prince Emmanuel, implemented strict discipline and rigid adherence to protocol, such as a wearing their dreadlocks wrapped turban fashion, privileging men above women, requiring women to separate themselves from men during menstruation, and strictly adhering to Sabbath rules such as fasting and no work on Saturday. Prince Emmanuel erected an ideology of a holy trinity that consisted of Marcus Garvey as prophet (who urged redemption of Africa), himself as the highest priest, and Emperor Selassie as the ultimate ruler. In later years, Prince Emmanuel was rumored to consider himself divine, an incarnation of Christ. The EABIC, later and better known as the Bobo Ashanti, continued several early Rastafari notions such as an emphasis on Black supremacy and the moral superiority of Black people. The Rastafari were growing very complex.

Crackdown and Outreach: The Coronation Market Riot and the Moral Re-Armament Movement

On May 7, 1959, a riot erupted at Coronation Market in downtown Kingston, with violence spilling over into the surrounding communities. Sidney Maitland, described as a bearded man, was blamed for triggering the unrest.[101] The riot was relevant to Rastafari ethnogenesis because it illustrated a buildup of tension between the Rastafari and fellow Jamaicans that had been developing since at least the Palisadoes murder.

A police officer accosted Maitland, but he resisted. During the struggle with Maitland, another officer pulled his revolver, provoking onlookers.[102] Once Maitland was subdued and taken away, residents protested his treatment. Market employees stopped work; some of the folk in the market began throwing stones and bottles at the officers who had arrived at the scene. A crowd developed, and a police car was set afire. The Rastafari now obviously had non-Rastafari sympathizers, an important development in Rastafari ethnogenesis. Members of the crowd attacked the fire brigade that responded to the fire. The police pursued "rioters" into nearby squatter "tatus" (huts) in the Rastafari strongholds of Kingston Pen and Back-O-Wall. Rioters turned back police with volleys of stones. The police retaliated with tear-gas "bombs," burning out as many as fifty-odd "huts."[103] Police arrested more than eighty people, eight of them women. Although evidence suggests that "beards" participated in the disturbance, authorities framed it as a Rastafari rebellion, a "massive rampage" by the "Rastafari cult."[104]

While there was a crackdown on the Rastafari in Kingston, some Rastafari in Montego Bay were reaching out to North America and beyond. Dr. Frank Buchman, an American and a Lutheran who was a leading influence in creating the Moral Re-Armament movement, invited a group of Rastafari from Montego Bay, along with Jamaican government officials, to visit the United States in August 1959. The invitation gives example to a shift in Rastafarian group dynamics and in public attitudes.[105] Some Rastafari were open to cooperation with their professed adversary—the colonial government—and the invitation illustrates the growth in the Rastafari's international connections as they reached out to groups whose beliefs and motivations were in sync with theirs. Brother Aubrey Brown, along with five other brothers and women (probably Rastafari), attended the Moral Re-Armament Conference at Mackinac Island, Michigan. They were guests of the St. James custos (chief parish magistrate), F. Kerr-Jarrett (see figure 6.6).[106]

The Moral Re-Armament Conference was regular feature of the Moral Re-Armament movement (MRA). Dating to late-1930s America and the precipice of World War II, Dr. Frank Buchman catalyzed the movement. Buchman determined that the world had become war-prone and enamored of arms in a context of a dearth of morality. Weapons, Buchman believed, could not solve the world's conflicts, but moral regeneration could. He reasoned that enlightened morality should be the basis of human action and should infuse the pursuit of prosperity. Although the MRA originated with Christian, right-wing conservative,

Figure 6.6. The custos of St. James Parish, F. Kerr-Jarret (*right*); the mayor of Montego Bay, Jamaica, W. Vernon (*left*); and a group of Montego Bay Rastafari pose for the camera at the Montego Bay Town Hall, 1959. They are celebrating the return of these Rastafari to Jamaica from a Moral Re-Armament conference at Mackinac Island, in Michigan. These Rastafari were the guests of the custos at the conference. The organizer of the Rastafari group, Brother Aubrey Brown, is standing to the right of the custos.
(*The Star*; courtesy of The Gleaner Co. [Media] Ltd.)

and business organizations and was critical of US president Franklin Roosevelt's New Deal policies, it was not a fringe movement. It developed into an international movement inclusive of diverse faiths and people. MRA ideology spun on its notion of Four Absolutes: absolute honesty, absolute purity, absolute unselfishness, and absolute love, all of which were in accord with 1950s Rastafari ideology of love and selflessness. The Four Absolutes were evocative of Robert Athlyi Rogers's vision of Ethiopian redemption and Leonard Howell's notion of L.O.V.E. (long, overflowing, virtuous, and everlasting).

Aubrey Brown acquired the attention and respect of many elites in the Montego Bay area. Inspired by a vision to take leadership in redeeming the Rastafari, Brown focused on setting an example of hard work and enterprise. Brown helped found a thriving furniture and mattress business that serviced hotels and other "large establishments," providing employment to Rasta and non-Rasta alike.[107]

Upon return to Jamaica, Brown delivered a report on the Absolutes and on the conference to a gathering of Rastafari and sympathizers. During the gathering, the assembled sang "Peace and Love," a Rastafari chant, while shouting, "love again Brotherman." Officials touted the trip as a "history-making occasion in that it was the first time that the cultists were allowed to use the Town Hall for any of their activities." A cable sent to thank Buchman noted how the "Montego Bay Mayor with [the] Custos officially welcomed Rastafaris with 300 brethren [into the] town hall accompanied [by] drums and banners."[108]

Widening the Breach While Seeking to Repair It: Reverend Claudius Henry and the African Reform Church

During the late 1950s, Claudius Henry and his Africa Reform Church, Church of Christ, became a significant vector for Rastafari ethnogenesis by ramping up repatriation enthusiasm and by attracting adversarial attention. Yet, in doing so, they reinforced notions that the Rastafari were menaces and crackpots.

Henry spent thirteen years in the United States. He received his preacher's license in 1950 and was ordained a Baptist minister in Cleveland, Ohio, 1953. In December 1957, Henry returned to Jamaica. He said that God had instructed him to return to Jamaica, to direct Black people and poor people in going back to Africa. Henry's congregation originated in Clarendon Parish around 1958 and then relocated to 78 Rosalie Avenue in Kingston, the home of Edna Fisher. Fisher, one of Reverend Henry's ardent devotees, met Henry in 1958, and after hearing him preach, she invited him to erect a church on her land in 1959.

Fisher recalled how Reverend Henry presented himself to her as a "prophet anointed by God. He explained that Emperor Selassie was the returned Messiah, 'who come to carry on where Jesus had left off.'"[109] Before gaining public notoriety, Henry had a reputation for experiencing visions, for considering himself divine, and for being a lunatic. Dubbing himself the "Repairer of the Breach" and "Cyrus" the biblical king, Reverend Henry promoted himself a prophet destined to lead a Black Israel to its new Promised Land. Cyrus the Great, of the book of Isaiah, freed Jews from Babylon's bondage. Black Jamaicans were the "Jews" of the contemporary Babylon. Henry introduced himself as an incarnation of Jesus Christ, while simultaneously holding Emperor Selassie divine. His devoted followers believed that Henry was divine, the embodiment of a father-son relationship with God, Emperor Selassie.[110]

Repatriation was at hand, Henry proclaimed, inciting droves of people who wanted to leave Jamaica for Ethiopia to descend on Henry's Rosalie Avenue Africa Reform Church of Christ (ARC). Graffiti scrawled on walls in Kingston and other urban localities expressed the Back-to-Africa mind-set of the time in phrases such as "Freedom" and "Send us back to Ethiopia or else."[111] Henry called attention to that "historical breach that yawned between Europe and Africa." Drawing on the symbolism of the Old Testament Moses, Henry told audiences that his work was to "gather Israel's scattered children for removal to Africa."[112] He intended to mend it by getting himself and other Black Jamaicans to Africa.[113] This, however, was only the first installment of what became Henry's ignominy. Within a year, authorities branded Henry a revolutionary extremist.[114]

Henry determined that on October 5, 1959, Black Jamaicans would depart from their colonial outpost and travel to their Zion in Africa. ARC pamphlets announced, "This will be our first and last Emancipation Jubilee Celebration in Jamaica, August 1, 1959. The next one will be in AFRICA, celebrating 'Freedom.'"[115] Months before the October 5 departure date, Henry was busy canvassing the island with his message of impending repatriation. He had not yet announced whether his followers would reach Africa by plane or ship. At the close of a meeting in Hayes Square, Clarendon, "light blue cards, for which donations were given, were issued to those desirous of going back to Africa." Henry explained that "'these cards were the passports of intending travelers,' and would entitle each holder and his family to go back to Africa 'free of all incumberances.'"[116] Henry cast the impending passage as divine ordination channeled through himself; therefore, travelers would not need "official" passports. The blue tickets that he created would suffice to reserve a space on board the liberation vessel.

Henry reportedly twice visited Ethiopia to discuss the "repatriation of Jamaicans," the second time returning to Jamaica only a few days before the announced departure to Ethiopia.[117] In a written statement published in *The Star*, Henry wrote, "I am just back from Ethiopia, having gone there on important business concerning Repatriation and the welfare of the Black people of Jamaica as a whole. This has been my second visit to Ethiopia to discuss these matters on the spot, with responsible Ethiopian Officials. The result of these discussions will be made known to the people of Jamaica in the right manner and in due time."[118] Elites wanted to know how Henry intended to fund repatriation, even how he paid for his alleged travel. Vere Johns opined, "Unless Mr. Henry is a man of considerable means, I cannot see how he will be able to transport Jamaicans to Ethiopia."[119] Defending himself, Henry declared that he had written to Emperor Selassie about the EWF land grant but received no reply. Therefore, he decided to visit Ethiopia: "So, I spend the five hundred pounds and go to Ethiopia go see His Imperial Majesty miself [*sic*]."[120] We can only speculate how or whether this inspired Black prophet could acquire and dispense such a considerable sum on international travel.

People began streaming into 78 Rosalie Avenue on Friday, October 2. They came from the western reaches of the island, the eastern parishes, the center of the island, and places nearby, like Cockburn Pen and Trench Town. The assembled, on October 4, were in an "enthusiastic and gay mood . . . singing to the accompaniment of music—'Leave Babylon and come; if you stay here they will laugh you to scorn, so leave Babylon and come.'"[121] However, in the weeks preceding October 5, Henry had complicated his call to repatriation by stressing a need to "make decisions," or participate in conference, on the day in question. A letter he wrote and published in *The Star* said, "Today the 5th of October 1959, is the deadline, the official date of the freedom of all Black people under Colonial Rule; from now on we must actively prepare to come into our own; meaning to manage our own affairs in a righteous and peaceful manner."[122] The message announced freedom and encouraged self-reliance but did not address transportation to Africa.

Henry did not flinch in the face of criticisms. Observers drew comparisons to the prophetic claims some seventy years earlier of Alexander Bedward, who feted a Black God and promised redemption from colonial oppression. A front-page headline scoffed, "No Passports, No Bookings, but 'Going Back to Africa.'"[123] Many of the arrivals at Henry's ARC had sold their possessions and brought with them what they believed they needed to make the voyage. The yard overflowed with hopeful emigrants, who were soon drenched by a soaking rain that generated a muddy mess. Allegedly, Henry commanded God to end the rain, and it ceased. Nevertheless, no seagoing vessels materialized to take the assembled to Africa. Anticipation transformed into despair: some wanted to know, where "the men ah give out de passport?"[124] Henry tried to keep up their spirits by conducting service from a hidden location via loudspeaker. Vague reformulations of the repatriation message flowed through the crowd. For example, Henry claimed that October 5 was not the day of departure but the "Deadline Day of Decision," which was different from departure. Regardless, whether "Repatriation Day" or "Deadline Day of Decision," Henry's idea materialized into a fiasco as participants aired their grievances and authorities observed the attendant chaos.[125] Fiasco, though, was not an impediment to ethnogenesis. The fiasco generated attention and energy that buoyed Rastafari ambition and elite disquiet.

Many of the would-be repatriates were not able to immediately return home. Some were ashamed because they had boasted of leaving Jamaica to a new home in Africa. Some had no money to return home. Despair and disgust engulfed the assembled like a dense fog: "Me want fe hear how dis ting a go for it can't go so," one woman said.[126] Translation: "Someone better explain to me what is happening because it cannot be what I think is happening—I've been duped." Ultimately, the crowd's response was subdued, far different from what elites had imagined: "BUT NOTHING happened—just nothing. There were a few grumbles but the tones were more of regret than of indignation. A few others wondered out loud whether they should call upon the 'Repairer' for an accounting, but their voices were querulous rather than heated."[127]

It is little wonder that Henry was able to stir up such a colossal reaction among the Back-to-Africa movement. It had been brewing since the late 1940s, transforming into a fast boil by the late 1950s. The flame heating the repatriation pot continued to cause the contents to boil.

How serious Henry was about his repatriation call remains unsettled. It might have been inspired prophecy, or it may have been prophecy woven with scheme. Either way, prophecies do not require evidence or necessitate an itinerary. It is not unusual for prophecy to be postponed (see chapter 9). Henry later revised his ideology to replace Africa with Jamaica. In the new formulation, Jamaica functioned as an outpost of Africa-descended people. Instead of repatriating to Africa, Black Jamaicans should rebuild in Jamaica, which Henry and his followers eventually did by creating a thriving block-making and bread-making enterprise in a rural and communal setting.

My discussions with elder Rastafari who knew Claudius Henry and his later group, the Peacemakers, suggest that they were unconventional Rastafari in their deification of Henry. Many of them deviated from convention by going beardless or dreadlock-less. Indeed, Henry asked his male disciples to shave, "clean up," and forsake ganja consumption before departing to Africa.[128] Henry himself was clean-shaven (see figure 6.7), leading the Dreadlocks Rastafari to question his authenticity. Yet, an elder dreadlocked Rastafari, Brother Yendis, a second-generation Rastafari and organizer of Rastafari, explained to me that for him it did not matter that Henry and his followers were idiosyncratic. What made him argue for their inclusion in the Rastafari Federation, a union of Rastafari organizations created during the 1990s, was the tribulation they endured, the self-reliant commune they created in Green Bottom, Jamaica, and that they were willing to join cause with the Rastafari Federation.[129]

Not long after the Decision Day fiasco, Henry left Jamaica to go to New York without letting on why he traveled there, only that it involved "private business."[130] Henry had not given up on the Back-to-Africa movement or his vision of repatriation. There were rumors that he was seeking support from Liberia, Haiti, and the Soviet Union to support the Back-to-Africa movement. Henry was moving in a drastic direction. He told an interviewer, "We have power in America and when the time

(c) 1953 The Gleaner Co. (Media) Ltd.

Figure 6.7. Reverend Claudius Henry, circa 1953. (Courtesy of
The Gleaner Co. [Media] Ltd.)

ready, when the Gentile dip him hood in blood we getting two ship and
plane and machine gun for if we can't go back to Africa by peace we are
going back by force."[131]

Henry had poked his rod into a wasp's nest and further stirred up an
already agitated colony, Rastafari and non-Rastafari alike. Momentum
was building.

The impact of the Rastafari was rapidly expanding. Even if some of
the impact was imagined, it had tangible effect. For instance, the mu-
nicipal authority KSACL fire brigade banned beard-wearing by personnel.[132] While it reasonable that fire personnel who fight fires should
have minimal exposed facial hair, the policy follows on the Coronation
Market melee and coincides with the ARC fiasco. There was a mounting
fear of creeping Rastafarianism and Rastafari sympathy into widening
swaths of Jamaican society.

* * *

"Going home to Africa" was a Rastafari watchword from the 1940s into the 1960s, tumultuous years of Rastafari cultural innovation, dislocation, agitation, and expansion. The Rastafari flexed their muscle, and while authorities resisted, sometimes violently, they had to engage what they saw as a growing threat. The "threat" would intensify.

7

Of Beards, Insurrection, and Rehabilitation

Social Paranoia and Reverend Claudius Henry's Disruptions

I can't tell what is going to happen in the future—anything can happen anytime. There is a possibility the Ras Tafarians could burn down Kingston tonight.
—a police superintendent musing during Reverend Henry's preliminary court hearing about the state of affairs in Kingston during May 1960

The Cuban Revolution provided substance for fantastic fabrications in Jamaica. In 1959, a thirty-three-year-old Cuban, Fidel Castro, helped lead a successful guerilla campaign that overturned the Cuban government of president and dictator Fulgencio Batista. By early 1960, Premier Castro's government had aligned itself with the Soviet Union. Dickie Jobson's 1982 film *Countryman* shows how Jamaica's politics and its anxieties about its Rastafari people collided with the era of national liberation movements. The film's protagonist, Countryman, a Rastafari fisherman living at Hellshire Beach in St. Catherine's Parish, rescued a wealthy White couple from the United States after their plane crashed near Hellshire. Countryman's kind deed drew him into a conspiracy involving homicide, Obeah, Cuban operatives, a dreadlocked assassin, and corrupt Jamaican police and military officers. Countryman symbolized the peace and love Rastafari ethos, while the film cast politicians and police as sinister Babylon. Countryman, and by implication the Rastafari, redeemed themselves at the end of the film, holding fast to a mystical righteousness that could not be undone by politics, corruption, or evil. Yet many Jamaicans deemed the Rastafari of the 1960s corrupt and evil, involved in conspiracies against Jamaica's government, its churches, its property owners, and even against its children. Rastafari ascribed and achieved identity manifested in marked contrasts—malevolent versus righteous—with consequences sometimes disastrous to limb or life.

The Rastafari evolved into a forcible social movement evident in how they became central to Jamaica's public discourse. They also became the "heart" of a Jamaican crisis.[1] The time marked the manifestation of a virile paranoia about Rastafari subversion that fanned extreme reactions. Politics engulfed the Rastafari while they imprinted their stamp on Jamaica's waning colonial order. They were on their way to becoming actors—minor—in a drama involving superpowers and their satellites.

Paranoia, Misguided Compassion, and Identity

Paranoia is a mental condition whereby one's thoughts are so inflamed by anxiety, fear, or distrust that behavior is delusionary or irrational. Collective paranoia toward the Rastafari, fanned by a series of surprising events during the early 1960s, shaped Rastafari ethnogenesis.

Elites altered how they framed Rastafari identity during the early 1960s. For one, they made the Rastafari into an insurrectionary threat greater than any trumped-up charges of sedition leveled against Howell, Hinds, or Reid. Although the threat stemmed from the activities of a small number of people whom outsiders considered to be Rastafari—many Rastafari questioned whether the central characters were Rastafari—all Rastafari had to contend with the consequences of those actions. The Rastafari acquired an onerous "image problem." The anthropologist John Eideson and colleagues explain that people who have a "spoiled" collective identity have limited ability to "influence the framing and alignment of [their identity] categories" beyond their own communities, tarnished with labels that are "both unwanted and unavoidable."[2] The Rastafari show us how members can both acquire and negotiate unwanted labels and images. Negative portrayals did not impede the Rastafari's positive evaluation of themselves as a special and chosen people. Persecution reinforced individual and collective identity.

"Beards" Beware, and Beware of "the Beards"

After Decision Day, the police stepped up their arrests of "Beards" and people possessing ganja. For example, the police implemented

Figure 7.1. "Operation Rasta." Soldiers and police involved in the hunt for Reverend Claudius Henry's son, Reynold Henry, and his accomplices pose for a photograph, 1959. (Courtesy of The Gleaner Co. [Media] Ltd.)

Operation Beards, under the auspices of the commissioner's Special Raiding Squad.[3] Anticrime campaigns targeted the Rastafari and Reverend Henry, identified by names like "Operation Rasta," "Operation Rosalie" (the name of Henry's street address), and "Operation Henry" (see figure 7.1).[4] The names evoked military maneuvers, and indeed the military participated in some of the operations. However, the police often behaved as if they were soldiers at war. The security campaigns disrupted, dispersed, and sometimes destroyed Rastafari communities and the lives of Rastafari individuals under the pretext of ridding Jamaica of guns, gambling, and ganja. The campaigns, especially the ganja campaigns, swept into a dragnet both Rastafari and non-Rastafari, providing context for shared experience of abuse.

Categorizing male Rastafari as "Beards" retained currency into the early 1960s. The marker, however, ignored a salient point made by Rastafari like the Brotherhood Solidarity of United Ethiopians. The BSUE was keen to note that not all men with beards were Rastafari; some Beards were wolves sporting the garb of sheep. People who wore beards and who committed misdeeds sullied Rastafari identity. For instance, a series of attacks on couples sitting in their parked cars on Washington

Boulevard in Kingston was attributed to Beards; an alleged set of Beards threatened a group of schoolchildren in Clarendon by brandishing machetes and calling for their parents' first-born child; and an alleged clutch of Beards was blamed for plundering an Anglican church in Clarendon.[5] Whether the alleged perpetrators identified as Rastafari was left to one's imagination. The Beards had evolved from nuisance into terror, and this in turn fed into further hysteria. Children ran from bearded men, and a Christian might call out for divine protection in a close encounter with a bearded man. I recall a story told to me by several second-generation male Rastafari. An adult woman, dressed for church, not paying attention while walking, literally bumped into a bearded and dreadlocked Rastafari. Looking into his face, she cried out in terror, "Oh, God!" The Rastafari man, calm, putting an index finger to his lips, said, "Shhh. Don't tell anyone that you saw me."

"Beard" insinuates masculinity, emphasizing the "maleness" of Rastafari identity, even though women Rastafari were active and present in Rastafari public affairs such as protests. The moniker "Beard" reinforced the Rastafari's notions of male preeminence. Nevertheless, by the early 1960s, the beard had become such a centripetal metaphor for Rastafari identity that it could draw women into its sphere. One police officer proclaimed, "I have actually seen the queens in this particular movement with beards."[6] Such outlandish claims notwithstanding, a *Jamaica Times* staff reporter tracked down the woman alleged to be the "only woman in Jamaica who sports a beard."[7] The reporter described twenty-five-year-old Daphne McKenzie as a bearded woman devoted to Rastafari and revered by male Rastafari.

The Rastafari were on their own course, creating Rastafari culture, colliding with nonmembers, incorporating budding intellectual configurations such as Black nationalism, contemporary Pan-Africanism, and Marxism. Reverend Claudius Henry illustrates this course of development while also problematizing it.

Claudius Henry's Disruption, Act 2: Dread of Insurrection and Insurgents

Anytime, anything happens to a black man I feel it too.
—Reverend Henry, in reference to the Africa Reform
Church's interest in Nyasaland and Dr. Hastings Banda[8]

Dr. Hastings Banda was born at the turn of the twentieth century in British Central Africa, later renamed Nyasaland. In 1958, Banda returned to British Nyasaland from the United States and United Kingdom after schooling and work there, taking a political leadership role urging anticolonial resistance against and independence from Britain and Rhodesia. He was arrested and imprisoned in March 1959 for his activism. After his release, Dr. Banda became prime minister of Nyasaland and, later, president of Malawi. Rastafari in Jamaica were following anticolonial activism across the globe, especially in Africa. Reverend Henry gives example to this trend.

Act 1, the Decision Day fiasco, brought national attention to the Rastafari, unseen since Howell and Hinds's trial for sedition and Howell's Pinnacle years. Henry's Act 2 precipitated a national crisis. Both acts molded Rastafari collective identity.

During Reverend Henry's court appearance for the Decision Day fiasco, he divulged some of his life story. He recalled his first "revelation" from God, in 1936, and how, as a result, authorities enjoined him to undergo medical observation. While under medical scrutiny, Henry had another vision in which God urged him to read and fulfill Isaiah 58, in which the Lord gives the prophet Isaiah the charge to reprimand sinners and to pursue justice for the poor and hungry and says that if he followed the instructions of the Lord, he would be anointed the "Repairer of the Breach."

Reverend Henry wedded the Old Testament with modern Black nationalism. As the reincarnated great King Cyrus (of the Old Testament) and the contemporary leader of God's (new) Chosen Army, "Pioneering Israel," Reverend Henry connected himself with the US-based African Nationalist Pioneer Movement and the First Africa Corp.

Discretion must not have concerned Reverend Henry. By late 1959, there was wide-ranging evidence that he was up to something. Jamaicans who read either the *Daily Gleaner* or *The Star* would know that Reverend Henry went to New York in November 1959. They would know Reverend Henry *claimed* that he had visited Russia, Haiti, and Ethiopia. The police knew that upon this return from New York to Jamaica, Reverend Henry met his son Reynold (a.k.a. Ronald) and two

Figure 7.2. Billboard near Reverend Henry's Africa Reform Church identifying his "God's Army Camp," 1960. (Courtesy of The Gleaner Co. [Media] Ltd.)

other men at Palisadoes Airport in Kingston.[9] The commissioner of police, Mr. Browning, whom Reverend Henry publicly taunted, was aware that Henry was drilling his followers at the ARC headquarters. All the while, Reverend Henry delivered speeches over loudspeakers. People nearby heard and recorded what he said.

Reverend Henry held his cards only loosely to his chest. A large sign in front of the ARC headquarters read, "GOD'S ARMY CAMP. We training Defence Men for God's Righteous government of Everlasting Peace on Earth Creation's Second Birth" (emphasis in original; see figure 7.2). Indeed, Henry read about himself and his activities in *The Star*.[10] Did Henry behave this way because he was unalarmed about mortal intervention? Or was there some worldly assurance that imparted confidence to him? Reverend Henry publicly accused Premier Norman Manley of buying his and his followers' votes, which he claimed he had delivered. Perhaps it was no coincidence that during 1958, PNP operatives spread rumors that if elected, they would support repatriation.

Authorities Raid Henry's African Reform Church

At four in the morning, Wednesday, April 6, 1960, roughly one hundred heavily armed police raided Henry's ARC headquarters at 78 Rosalie Avenue, Kingston. Police seized an assortment of evidence suggestive of insurrection. Henry had been under surveillance, a part of "Operation Rosalie," since the Decision Day fiasco in October 1959.[11] On April 7, the police conducted a second raid at the ARC; on May 7, four branches of the ARC in Clarendon Parish in central Jamaica were raided.[12] ARC branches, which had been established across Jamaica, faced subsequent raids, and arrests were executed in the parishes of St. Mary, St. Ann, and St. Thomas. Reverend Henry and fifteen of his associates—thirteen men and two women—were arrested and imprisoned without bail.[13] A primary reason for the authorities' raid of the ARC headquarters was concern that Reverend Henry and his hardcore adherents had planned to assassinate government leaders during mid-April 1960.[14]

Over the course of a month, the police and security forces confiscated a stunning assortment of implements that included ammunition, guns, dynamite, daggers, cutlasses, swords, soldering material, and cemented conch shells. Other material confiscated involved banners, letters, manuals (on drilling), men's and women's uniforms (black shirts and caps, yellow blouses, green skirts, armbands, and badges), and lists and books that named the defendants. Authorities might reasonably conclude that the confiscated material was evidence of preparation for calamity. Many of the implements were, however, crude to the point of questioning whether they were dangerous. How much blood could one shed using wooden rifle replicas or cardboard swords? Nevertheless, what boosted authorities' concern were several letters that suggested that Henry and his ARC followers were ready to spark an armed insurrection in Jamaica with the aid of the Cuban government.

If the early days of the Cuban Revolution barely disturbed Jamaicans, Reverend Henry did. His second act led authorities to reassess the impact of the Cuban Revolution on Jamaica. The Cuban Revolution mattered to a secretive group of authorities—intelligence operatives called the "Special Branch," a department of the Jamaica Constabulary and Ministry of Home Affairs—because of the recent proliferation of left-leaning groups, some of which sought the support of communist or socialist governments. The Special Branch provided reports on subversive activity in Jamaica to the Local Standing Intelligence Committee (LSIC).[15] The LSIC consisted of high-ranking government, military, police, intelligence, civil servant, and academic appointees who assessed the Special Branch reports before sending them to the Colonial Office. The Special Branch worried that Jamaica was being destabilized by local and international communists, Marxists, Black nationalists, Pan-Africanists, and perhaps the Cuban government itself. The Special Branch and LSIC reports (some of which are discussed shortly) display the extent to which authorities were aware of what was happening in Jamaica and how deeply they had infiltrated various left-of-center groups, which included some Rastafari.

The public outcry of a cross-section of Jamaicans about the massacre of indigenous South Africans at Sharpeville, March 21, 1960, gave example to what the Special Branch identified as disturbing trends. A group of faculty and students led a demonstration in Kingston that consisted of hundreds of people, including the People's Freedom Movement (communists), noncommunist leftists, and Rastafari. The Rastafari defender Peter Evans, the Irish "communist barrister," was marked as the "ringleader of the affair." (A key source of information on race, Rastafari, and surveillance in Jamaica is the now declassified intelligence document "Racism in Jamaica," discussed in chapter 8.) The support of indigenous South Africans was not limited to so-called rabble. Some political and government elites were boarding the race-conscious boat. The Legislative Council and the Jamaican government raised money for the South African's victims' families; Jamaica was the first nation to boycott South Africa. Premier Manley, speaking to the House, said, "Jamaica, has a peculiar justification [for sympathy with indigenous South Africans] because a vast majority of the people of our country have an association by blood with the people of Africa."[16]

That so many Jamaicans protested the Sharpeville massacre was interpreted by the Special Branch as evidence of race-consciousness that had spread beyond the Garveyites and Rastafari. Race-consciousness apprehensions were aggravated by the LSIC supposition that the "bulk of the unemployed and under-employed in Jamaica are of African descent and could therefore provide a field for recruitment to racist organizations."[17] For LSIC, "racism" and "racist" were synonyms for Jamaicans acting on their beliefs about Black consciousness, whether Rastafari, Garveyites, Black nationalists, Pan-Africanists, or something else. The LSIC designated Reverend Henry's beliefs as racist, and his ARC was tagged as a racist organization.

Soon after the raid on the ARC, the chief of the Criminal Investigation Division (CID), the "crack ex–Scotland Yard detective" George Mullen, flew to New York to investigate Reverend Henry's international connections, one of several "secret missions abroad" to gather intelligence on the international connections of the ARC and other Rastafari.[18] Accompanied by New York City detectives, Mullen visited a Bronx location described as the headquarters of the First Africa Corps (FAC). The FAC, formed in 1958 and based in the Bronx, considered itself a revolutionary organization and targeted Jamaica as a platform for launching its effort to liberate Africa from colonialism. In New York, Mullen met Reynold, who acknowledged that he was the son of Reverend Henry.

Reynold and Mullen toured the FAC headquarters together. There Mullen observed weapons, evidence of drilling activities, and items like the things the police confiscated from the ARC in Jamaica (e.g., uniforms). Mullen noted the people he saw, including two men whom he later identified as Al Thomas and Howard Rollins (the two were later convicted for several murders they committed in Jamaica). Mullen learned of the FAC's Black-nationalist ideology and its antipathy for colonialism and the suppression of Africans and African-descended people.

Business and political elites were alarmed that Henry's bombast and reputation would cause tourists to avoid Jamaica. "An unnerving if infrequent experience for white men in Jamaica this year," *Time* magazine reported, "is to be hailed on the streets of Kingston by a band of bearded Negroes yelling the slogan: 'Fire, lightning, judgment! White man must go! Blood must flow!'"[19] The story, "The Lion of Judah's Men," highlighted Reverend Henry's and the Rastafari's rhetorical symbolic violence, such as calls for neck chopping, blood flowing, or fire burning. Attorney General Leslie Cundall tried to ban the *Time* issue but was unable to prevent one-thousand-odd subscription copies from reaching the island.[20] Cundall worried that the story would exacerbate the hysteria swirling across Jamaica. Reverend Henry's activities were reported in many newspapers in the United States. The *Time* article portrayed the Rastafari as crazed savages: "They get hopped up on hashish and tom-tom music, and hold writhing, shouting services in their own versions of Coptic (ancient Egyptian) Christian rites." It lambasted Reverend Henry: "Families sold their houses, goats and pigs and thronged to Henry's headquarters, where he met them with a sad announcement: 'The Lord isn't ready yet.'" What was feared by Whites in particular but unspoken in public was the prospect of a Mau Mau–like Rastafari attack on Whites: "Henry began his arms buildup, possibly with the help of Cuba's Fidel Castro. . . . Police feared a massacre of whites. But as the cops came crashing through the hedges at Henry's headquarters, he made an abrupt switch to nonviolence. 'Peace and love, brothers,' Henry shouted to his followers as the cops dragged him off."[21] The notion of a Henry-Castro plot, although unsubstantiated, was treated as if it were true.

Time magazine had nosed out the Rasta rehabilitation effort and made light of it: "At least one attempt has been made to convert the Rastas to more peaceful way. The Moral Re-Armament movement last year flew three Rasta preachers to Moral Re-Armament's Mackinac Island retreat. The Rastas enjoyed the food and service for a few months, became great friends with some Mau Mau terrorists that MRA also imported, and went back home as firmly Ras Tafarian as ever."[22]

Outsiders treated the Rastafari as an undifferentiated entity, although there was always a diversity in their beliefs. This conception of homogeneity became less tenable the more government had to make decisions that involved the Rastafari and the more public commentators had to say something sensible about them, even if the general mood was that they had become a "grave problem" and "men with explosive views."[23] Observers were forced to confront the spectrum of Rastafari beliefs, which varied from ardent activist to saintly recluse. Government authorities such as Minister William Seivright invented three categories to define Rastafari diversity: the insurrectionists (Mau Mau–like, espousing symbolic violence); the "ganja growers and traffickers" (which included the "ordinary criminal element"); and the "Back-to-Africa fanatics with peculiar religious beliefs."[24] The insurrectionists and ganja handlers were marked as the greatest threat and worthy of the harshest punishment. Irrespective of the accuracy of the categories, they provided a means to

Figure 7.3. Protestors standing with placards during Reverend Claudius Henry's trial, 1960. Note the placards communicating symbolic violence and Ethiopianist statements. Also, note the presence of women foot soldiers. The placards were confiscated by police under the pretext of intimidation. (Courtesy of The Gleaner Co. [Media] Ltd.)

justify how to deal with the Rastafari-as-threat.[25] Reverend Henry and the FAC forced elites to articulate a theory of Rastafari identity that in turn justified their claims and actions.

Preliminary Hearing on Treason Felony Charge

The court proceedings to determine whether Henry and fifteen of his associates should stand trial for treason felony began on May 2, 1960 (treason felony is the intention to commit treason, not commission of treason). That day, several hundred Rastafari and sympathizers assembled near the Half-Way Tree Courthouse, where Alexander Bedward was tried. The crowd was raucous, flashing banners, singing Rastafari chants, and threatening bystanders with symbolic violence (figure 7.3). For instance, one banner pronounced, "Fire and Blood, Freedom or

Death; Give Us Our Leader or Be Prepared to Take Twenty Thousand to the Lock Up."[26] Police responded to the rowdy Rastafari by beating them back with batons and choking them with tear-gas bombs. Some of the assembled Rastafari retreated to the nearby Half-Way Tree Cemetery, from which they launched stones at the police.

Barrister Peter Evans, who defended Mau Mau rebels in Kenya, represented Claudius Henry and thirteen of his male associates, while Stanley Fyfe represented the two women, Edna Fisher and Hazel Collins. Of note, Reverend Henry and the thirteen men were clean-shaven; they did not present as Beards, though the courts, press, and others called them Rastafari cultists. Bail was denied to Henry and the coconspirators, including the pregnant Hazel Collins. But detaining Henry and his associates did not prevent a harrowing twist in the performance of Act 2.

Desperadoes in the Red Hills

On June 21, 1960, a small band of men waylaid five British soldiers of the Royal Hampshire regiment in the Red Hills district of St. Andrew's Parish, killing two of them. The ambushed soldiers were searching for the assassin(s) of three Jamaicans described as Rastafari, whose decomposed remains were discovered by security forces in a shallow grave buried shoeless, one atop the other. Jamaican authorities deemed Reynold a primary suspect. Authorities knew that Reynold had returned to Jamaica in June 1960, but they failed to keep close enough tabs on him and his colleagues to prevent the killings. The murders intensified public anxiety about the Rastafari and about national security in Jamaica. The Rastafari and national security became intertwined.

The band of wanted men—five Americans and two Jamaicans— dodging the police and security forces were dubbed by *The Star* as "the Desperadoes" (Americans Reynold Henry, William Jeter, Howard Rollins, Titus Damon, and David Kenyatta; Jamaicans Eldred Morgan and Albert Gabbidon).[27] The Desperadoes eluded the police and military security for several days by commandeering vehicles at gunpoint and holding citizens hostage in exchange for food or a place to rest. The Desperadoes prematurely launched into action because of their encounter with the Royal Hampshire regiment. Police and security forces believed that the Desperadoes had planned to launch their insurrection in August

1960, targeting the General Penitentiary, the Central Police Station, and Headquarters House, the office of the colonial secretary and home to the Jamaica Legislature.[28]

The Desperadoes became desperate because there was dissent within their ranks—disagreement over tactics and suspicion of informants—that resulted in the murder of the three alleged Rastafari. One of the deceased was Reverend Henry's henchman Calvert "Thunder" Beckford (a.k.a. Claude or Calvin; more about Thunder shortly). After a week, the "biggest manhunt ever in the annals of local history ended dramatically on its 7th day . . . at Bamboo, in the hills of St. Catherine."[29]

The First Africa Corps, the African Nationalist Pioneer Movement, and the Africa Reform Church

The FAC funded its operation through robbery in New York. A Jamaican-born New York police officer, Noel Agard, was one of several people indicted in the FAC "fund-raising" scheme. Ammunition and weapons were reported missing from the pier that the officer was assigned to guard.[30] Authorities concluded that the arms were shipped to Jamaica. It is curious that Reynold and company would pursue violent intervention in Jamaica after having been identified by Mullen. But they did. They entered Jamaica under assumed names, at different times.

Jamaican authorities kept quiet about the "arms and ammunition" smuggled into Jamaica from the United States.[31] However, Time magazine published a second article on the unfurling drama in Jamaica: "The Boys from Brooklyn" (the reference to Brooklyn was misleading given that the "Boys" were headquartered in Harlem and the Bronx). The Jamaican government banned Time magazine a second time, this time under the pretext of averting a full-fledged panic. Perhaps. Again, Time sketched an unflattering portrait of Jamaica as a land of mayhem overtaken by unhinged cultists:

Jamaica's whites and government officials were at first only amused last October when a self-anointed Negro holy man, the Rev. Claudius Henry . . . stirred an estimated 20,000 bearded cultists into a back-to-Africa frenzy. No one paid much attention, even when Henry's "Ras

Tafarians" pranced about holding aloft an empty platter they swore would hold Premier Norman Manley's head if he blocked their way. In April, when raiding police found a cache of firearms and cement-packed conch shells (obviously intended as missiles) in a Ras Tafarian church, Jamaican authorities decided that the Rev. Claudius Henry was no joke. He was jailed on a charge of treason. Even with their leader in jail . . . the new goal is to convert Jamaica itself into a Ras Tafarian–run island republic.[32]

The second *Time* article portrayed a New York–based insurrectionary plot that incompetent Jamaican and British law enforcement allowed to unfold in the open and spiral beyond their control. It nourished beliefs that Black governance, especially Rastafarian participation in it, would be detrimental to Jamaica's stability.

Reynold and Reverend Henry were influenced by the African Nationalist Pioneer Movement (ANPM). Carlos Cooks, born in the Dominican Republic, was a zealous Garveyite who created the ANPM soon after Garvey died. Cooks was concerned with keeping Garvey's ideas alive and in developing his own brand of militant, atheistic, and authoritarian Black nationalism. Founded in 1941, the ANPM described itself as "composed of people desirous of bringing about the establishment of a progressive, dignified, cultural, fraternal and racial confraternity amongst the African People of the world."[33]

Cooks was earnest about repatriation. He lobbied President Truman and congressmen to support repatriation to Africa, and he created his own African Colonization Society.[34] An innovator in urging African-descended people to "buy Black" (patronize Black merchants), Cooks promoted Black pride (as in natural hairstyles), and he despised African-descended people who were uninterested in Black nationalism.

Information on the FAC is scarce. Its origins trace to the ANPM and the influence of Garvey's ideas. Under arrest, the Black American citizen Al Junior explained that he was a "member of the first African Pioneer Movement in New York": "[Reynold] Henry was thrown out of the Movement and I left too. . . . [Reynold] told me of the Back to Africa Movement, I joined and attended meetings at his flat."[35] Reynold's temper and interest in armed Black insurrection did not suit ANPM leadership. Expelled from the ANPM, Reynold set out to build his own organization, courting people like Junior and Agard.

Figure 7.4. African Nationalist Pioneer Movement members marching in the annual Marcus Garvey Day Parade, in Harlem, New York, 1963. (Klytus Smith, photographer)

Several things suggest that Reynold and Reverend Henry were influenced by the ANPM. For one, the "Code AFRIC," the ideology of the ANPM, states, "I further pledge that I shall do everything in my power to bring about the liberation of Africa from the tentacles of European colonialism" and "When Africa strikes physically for freedom I shall volunteer as a soldier fighting my people's battle."[36] The Black American Titus Damon told the court, during his trial for treason felony, "I got involved in this outfit as the organization was going to Africa to take over a certain Colony, the name of which I do not know. A fellow named Kenyatta . . . [the Black American David Ambrister] was commander-in-chief in New York. . . . [Reynold] Henry told me we were going to Jamaica to train some Rastafarians to go to Africa."[37] The Black American Eldred Morgan testified that he traveled to Jamaica to "train" Rastafarians in preparation for their journey to Africa to "liberate" Africans from colonialism.[38] Second, one of Reverend Henry's slogans was "pioneering Israel Back to Africa." He had five thousand copies printed of a document that proclaimed, "Standing in the gap with unquestionable truth pioneering Israel Back to Africa."[39] Third, black suits, caps, and boots were recovered as evidence during the raid of the ARC, and photographs show the ANPM similarly dressed (figure 7.4). Fourth, the ANPM drilled its members military-style, and Henryites did so as well, apparently at the instruction of Thunder and the Black Americans.

The relationships among the ANPM, Reynold's FAC, and Reverend Henry and his ARC are incongruous. Cooks was a raving atheist who concluded that belief in God was an impediment to the liberation of Black people from White supremacy: "The bible is a joke book. Every time I want a good laugh, I read the bible."[40] He called Emperor Haile Selassie an "imposter," insulting him with the name "Highly Silly Assie."[41] Would Cooks find Reverend Henry and the Rastafari worth his interest? Probably not. Would Reverend Henry join cause with an acerbic critic of the Emperor? Perhaps Henry did not know this. Conceivably it was Reynold who forged a union of the notions and fantasies of the ANPM, FAC, and ARC. Maybe Reynold took it upon himself, with the assistance of Thunder, to make Reverend Henry and the Henryites into revolutionaries.

Intrigue, Self-Anointed Rebels, and the Desperadoes Trial

The detained Desperadoes identified Reynold as the "commander" responsible for directing their activities in Jamaica. They accused him of ordering the killing of the three "Rastafarians" and Albert Gabbidon of carrying out Reynold's orders. Several of the group were unable to dissuade Reynold from believing that Thunder had plans to kill all of them and plans to poison the Kingston water supply (an idea that Reynold rejected). Because of the killings and the plot to cause destruction, Reynold became the "villain of the piece," the central, evil figure.[42]

The trial attracted intense interest. On the day of the verdict, thousands came out to lay eyes on the Desperadoes. Observers likened the verdict atmosphere to a royal visit: "I see a queen pass up here and two princesses but none of them ever get such a welcome," said an "old timer."[43] All of the Americans and Jamaicans accused of murder were found guilty of at least one murder.

Reverend Henry's trial began on October 5, 1960. His trial did not attract as much attention as that of the Desperadoes. During the first few days of Henry's trial, the courtroom audience consisted mostly of "middle-aged women who bore all the earmarks of being followers of Henry's movement."[44] Although the weapons charges were serious, the letters seized in the raid on ARC headquarters attracted attention because they were central to the charge of felony treason against Reverend Henry.

Thunder: The Other Villain

If Reynold was the "villain of the piece," he had a competitor for the title in Thunder. Reynold, Thunder, and Reverend Henry, in different ways, were self-anointed rebels who were ill prepared to materialize their respective visions. In retrospect, the trials suggest that deception, witlessness, blind loyalty, and miscommunication overshadowed any notion of collusion with a foreign government. Thunder, who had been under police surveillance since August 1959, joined Reynold as the other "bad man" of Act 2.

Several of Henry's codefendants told how Thunder had taken over the ARC a few months before Henry left for New York. They testified that Reverend Henry was displeased with the state of his flock when he returned. Thunder had driven off some adherents because he preached violence and because he threatened them with violence if they did not do his bidding. He was singled out among ARC members for his violent view of repatriation. Defendant Lascelle Stone affirmed that it was Thunder who wanted to "fight [a] jungle war in Africa."[45] Defendant Wilfred Brown said that Thunder oversaw the drilling operation at the ARC. Thunder told them, said Brown, that "they needed nimble bodies if they were to go back to Africa."[46] The ARC members drilled with wooden guns and sticks (called "batons" by police and "staffs" by ARC members). Thunder generated a schism in the ARC between those he enticed to drill in the Red Hills and those who refused.

Incriminating Letters, Speech, and Weapons

Authorities recovered three letters, two suggesting insurrectionary intent by Reverend Henry, ARC, and the FAC. The letters and Act 2 in general are relevant to Rastafari ethnogenesis because they show how Rastafari association with radical leftist politics and militant Black nationalism was a local manifestation of international trends but also implicated, perhaps too broadly, all Rastafari as possessing radical and revolutionary impulses. Nevertheless, radical and revolutionary politics' concern with social justice and righteousness toward the dispossessed jibed with Rastafari sensibilities.

One of the two letters was addressed to Premier Fidel Castro. In part, the Castro letter read, "We are getting ready for an invasion of Jamaica, therefore we need your [Castro] help and personal advice." The letter asked for a meeting with Castro, claiming that Reverend Henry and Reynold had "20,000 people engaged in the formation of a government known as the 'Leper's Government.'" The Castro letter expressed a desire for Jamaica to fall into the "hands of the Cuban Prime Minister before they [the ARC and FAC] return to Africa."[47] The reply address for the Castro letter was a Beekman Avenue location in Bronx, New York, implicating Reynold. The second letter complained about British colonialism and predicted new revolutionary leadership for Jamaica: "Fidel Castro will be the leader of Jamaica in the very near future." This "bluster letter" promised that Reverend Henry (with Reynold's support) would "defend his [Castro's] government with . . . 20,000 people." The ARC and the FAC would be repatriated to Africa, "if not in peace then in war."[48] Reverend Henry admired Castro because he advocated for poor people.[49] Because his work was "spiritual," Reverend Henry claimed that his power surpassed that of Castro and his revolutionary politics. The court and the press gave a third letter little attention.[50] Ultimately, the confiscated letters were not presented to the jury, which was the course Barrister Evans had urged all along.[51]

What, then, inspired Reverend Henry's punishment? The court took seriously a speech that Reverend Henry delivered at a gathering at Rocky Point in St. Thomas Parish.[52] The speech and gathering were interpreted as encouraging violence. At Rocky Point, Reverend Henry and followers posed with wooden and cardboard swords. He was quoted as saying, "Proclaim ye this among the Gentiles; prepare war, wake up the mighty men, let all the men of war draw near. . . . Beat your plowshares into swords and your pruning hooks into spears." On the stand, Reverend Henry downplayed the references to violence, pointing out that he took the language from Joel 3 of the Old Testament. In Joel 3, the Lord promises protection and regeneration for Israel and retribution for abuse of Jerusalem and Judah during their captivity in Babylon. Henry said he was not preparing for war but moving away from it.[53] As a modern and Black incarnation of Israel, the ARC had the Lord to fight for them. Barrister Evans argued that war talk was common in Jamaican politics, as was political violence, but authorities treated neither as treasonous. Reverend Henry's violent talk was exactly that: talk. Nonetheless, the court found Reverend Henry guilty of three counts of felony treason and sentenced him to ten years' hard labor on each count (to run concurrently).

Reverend Henry was released from prison in 1967. Later, he gave the Rastafari scholar Barry Chevannes an ex post facto account of what landed him in prison. The account that Chevannes reported is consistent with news reporting and much of Henry's court testimony. However, what kind of fellow was Reverend Henry?

Reverend Henry: A Complicated and Tragic Figure

Was Reverend Henry as belligerent as reports suggested? Henry's codefendants recalled a man different from press and government reports of him. Several reported never hearing Henry talk about blood or war; they recalled a man who "preached to the people about peace, love, righteousness, justice and equality to all men. Also, about relocating to Africa."[54] For codefendant Lascelles Stone, God's Army Camp was a place where Henry sought to prepare people for their journey to Africa: "Some of the men in the organization were hooligan and would not discipline themselves. The Rev. Henry issues caps and boots to improve them."[55]

Reminiscing in 2013, Sybil Hibbert, a court reporter and journalist, recalled interviewing Reverend Henry in 1960. Hibbert was perhaps the only reporter who interviewed him at length. She recalled two "deluded men," Reverend Henry and Thunder, who held her hostage for several hours, under the threat of armed "bearded men" wearing black uniforms. Hibbert recalled how Thunder wanted to kill her, while Reverend Henry kept him at bay.[56] Hibbert's account reinforces other accounts, such as the acquisition of uniforms and weapons, and the malicious behavior of Thunder. Her account also suggests that Reverend Henry felt, erroneously, that he could control Thunder. Hibbert painted a terrifying portrait of the ARC, led by men mired in distorted and violent conceptions of repatriation and African liberation.

Reverend Henry's followers lacked a grasp of his vision (which was not in sync with Thunder's or the FAC, though he indulged both). Many of Reverend Henry's adherents were untutored. Coconspirator Kenneth Morgan told how he "did hear talk of the 'Leper's Government' and 'God's righteous Government,' but did not know what they mean."[57] What captured the attention of members was Henry's talk of Emperor Selassie's divinity, of Ethiopia, of repatriation, and of prophecy. As co-conspirator Reuben Jackson proposed, Henry was their prophet and Messiah, who, like in the biblical past, would lead the "children of Israel back home."[58] Yet Revered Henry dangled before his people the prospect that Jamaica could also be their "home": "It may not be God's will that we go back to Africa, he may want us to stay right here in Jamaica."[59] We must juxtapose the image of the saintly Reverend Henry with the pugnacious one calling for heads to roll and blood to run if anyone got in his way. He was both and more.

Reverend Henry's version of Rastafari deserves mention. In asking his men to shave, for example, he asked his followers to do things that differed from the dominant Rastafari ethnogenesis trend. Reverend Henry said that he did not care for some Rastafari, especially those unwilling to "reform."[60] Reform meant "clean," literally and figuratively. Literally, Henry wanted the men to shave, trim down their head hair, and dress nicely (hence provision of caps and boots). Metaphorically, reform meant spiritual cleansing by avoiding use of foul language or cannabis. Nonetheless, Reverend Henry was zealous in his belief that Haile Selassie was the returned Messiah, and he harped on the idea of repatriation. In these ways and others, Reverend Henry and his like-minded followers were Rastafari. However, Henry's version of Rastafari was idiosyncratic and "Combsome" (post-first-generation Rastafari who did not grow dreadlocks). He presented himself as a divine prophet, differing from a Nyabinghi Rastafari view of each person as Godly in their own right. Christianity persevered in Henry's vision. However, the Reverend's practice was not unusual for the time. There coexisted many versions of Rastafari, and, for some, Christian trappings loomed large. During late 1990, I recall visits to Prophetess Esther's Church of Israel in Kingston, where she performed rituals such as foot washings alongside invocation of Emperor Selassie as God and King.[61] Barrister Evans concluded that Reverend Henry was an idiosyncratic hybrid: "Henry is a racial and religious fanatic, a man of little judgment and logic, and a very naive character. He has taken the shreds of Garveyism and mixed with this: the idea of Watch Tower and Jehovah Witness and mixed further with a Black man's Zonology, the idea of going back to Africa."[62]

We must consider Reverend Henry's impact on Rastafari ethnogenesis. Chevannes wrote, "In the minds of many people the government had uncovered a vast plot engineered by Henry and his son to take over the country. . . . Forced by these incidents, the society began to take a good look at the Rastafari. . . . A change was indeed taking place. . . . The [Rastafari] movement as a whole forced the middle and upper strata to rethink their conception of the multiracial base of Jamaican nationalism and at long last to accept the African heritage."[63] Henry's two acts caused crackdowns on the Rastafari while creating opportunities for the Rastafari to advance their influence.

Paranoia Meets Rehabilitation

Although Reverend Henry's Act 2 panicked Jamaicans, attitudes among some elites toward the Rastafari were becoming nuanced. There was a burgeoning acknowledgment by a range of citizens, including some arts and voluntary association elites, that police and citizens routinely abused the Rastafari. This line of reasoning supposed that if the Rastafari could be certain that they would not be mistreated, then perhaps they would be open to "rehabilitation." Rehabilitation for these folks meant to improve one's being through constructive activity. This thinking presupposed that the Rastafari needed assistance, education, and employment—rehabilitation—and that government should lead the rehabilitation charge. In exchange for rehabilitation, the Rastafari should relinquish their identity: "no beard, no matted hair, no sensational clothes. . . . No ganja is to be smoked or grown . . . [and] all children must be sent to school."[64] Rastafari identity was interpreted as a symptom of their presumed condition: poverty and illiteracy. Indeed, authorities developed a Rastafari rehabilitation plan.

Government planning to rehabilitate the Rastafari was a secret, though it had a public complement. Some people were beginning to see what they considered a positive change among the Rastafari. For example, Prince Edward, founder of a major Rastafari Mansion (or community), the Ethiopia Africa Black International Congress, was alleged to have taken the advice of the visiting Ethiopian economists who told him and his flock to live peacefully and work hard. Premier Manley signaled that "something positive will be done for the welfare of the members of the Rastafarian movement." The Jamaica Social Welfare Commission sponsored a reading center in support of the Rastafari, collaborating with the Addis Ababa Bookshop, which was run by a communist.[65] Attitudes and practices were shifting, albeit piecemeal.

* * *

The Rastafari developed a race-conscious anticolonial ethos that fed into and was fed by international political events like the Cuban Revolution and burgeoning notions of Black nationalism. The global scene conjoined with Rastafari activities involving protest and armed violence, heightening their status as threat, justifying government crackdowns on them. Within the midst of the violent oppression, suppression, and repression, though, were subtle changes in attitude toward the Rastafari by some elites.

8

The Report on the Rastafari

Its Effects and Concealed Motives

The Report on the Rastafari Movement in Kingston, Jamaica (1960) made a key contribution to revising the unflattering and inaccurate narrative about the origins and identity of the Rastafari. The *Report* was a consequence of Reverend Henry's two acts and of the frightening reputation plastered onto the Rastafari. The *Report* domesticated the Rastafari, bestowing them a lineage, an ideology, and a collective persona of peace mottled with a few troublemakers. Although the *Report* drew on interviews with the Rastafari, it still amounted to ascription: outsiders portraying others.

A press release announced the forthcoming *Report*:

> A meeting was held on the evening of Monday July 4 [1960] between the Principal of the University College of the West Indies and some of the chief members of the Ras Tafari movement. Some of these had written to the Principal asking that the College should initiate a sociological study of the movement, its ideals, aspirations and needs. At the meeting the Principal introduced three members of the UCWI staff who will spend the next two weeks with members of the Ras Tafari movement, undertaking the study which has been requested. . . . The team would be operating only at the request of these leading members of the movement, who promised to support it fully. A report would be produced, which would be available to the public. On the basis of this report, further discussions would be held to determine what the next steps should be.[1]

Scholarship and Rastafari lore propagated the *Report* narrative for decades. Among the first studies of the Rastafari, the *Report* acquired canonical status among Rastafari scholarship. As the scholarship on the Rastafari developed during the 1970s and into the 1980s, the *Report* became a go-to source. Published under the aegis of distinguished Caribbean scholars, it offered a (partial) social and historical perspective—largely unknown up to that point—on the Rastafari and, notably, encouragement to investigate the feasibility of Jamaican migration to Africa. The *Report* reached a wide Jamaican audience, with the assistance of the Jamaican press—*The Star* offered its own summary and analysis, while the *Daily Gleaner* published it verbatim as a serial.

The *Report* influenced Jamaicans' attitudes and behavior. The historian Robert Hill says that he was seventeen when he first saw the *Report* and recalls, "It was like a meteor had crashed into the whole world. Jamaica has never been the same since that August day when I first saw it."[2] It emboldened many Rastafari. Two constables, setting out to arrest a woman, "the Queen of Sheba," for using indecent language, had to retreat when a group of Rastafari and their non-Rastafari sympathizers were summoned to defend her. The police noted that the Rastafari were "claiming that the Premier and Dr. Lewis . . . had said they were to be 'untouchable.'"[3] A columnist opined that it was "quite inevitable that certain of Jamaica's Rastafari brethren would interpret a show of concern for their aspirations by Government as a signal that, not only are they regarded as a people apart from the rest of the community, but that their every action would be viewed with sympathy and deference."[4]

The *Report* provided a medium to support affirmative representations of the Rastafari. Dr. L. C. Leslie, a former mayor of Spanish Town, commended the report and spoke a "good word" for the Rastafari of Linstead, St. Catherine, praising them as "industrious" and disinterested in "subversive activities."[5] The impresario and journalist Vere Johns, a self-described Brown man and elite, noted his respect for a Rastafari man he knew, and he criticized depictions of all Rastafari as rascals and criminals: "As an illustration, I give you Rastafarian Brother Tucker, an attendant at the Majestic Theatre, beard and all. He is a very fine and respected citizen and the assistance he gives me on Friday nights in keeping capacity audiences at their best behavior could not be achieved by twenty policemen. The police once picked him up for questioning and I saw red—they let him go fast."[6] Nevertheless, some elites expressed hostility toward the *Report*. For example, the Jamaican Monsignor Gladstone Wilson, a Roman Catholic priest, esteemed intellectual, and holder of four PhDs, called *The Report* unscientific in its methodology and "unworthy of scholars."[7]

The mollifying narrative that the *Report* spun concealed the ethics of why the *Report* was created in the first place. Robert Hill describes the *Report* as a "massive deception engaged in by all concerned with the *Report*."[8] Assessing a range of documents and interviews, Hill has debunked many *Report* claims, concluding that the Rastafari did not request the research, that Rastafari leader Mortimer Planno was not involved in the production of the *Report*, and that the research for the *Report* was conducted over nine days (not two weeks as claimed). A major motive informing the *Report* was to infiltrate the Rastafari and learn what they were up to and, ultimately, to co-opt the Rastafari and defuse their left-leaning radicals. Hill argues that the "university performed the facilitating role of a typical front organization, part of the necessary disguise to conceal the true purpose of the operation." "Right from the start," Hill contends, "the Report was a covert operation aimed at stemming an imagined insurgency of Rastafari in Jamaica. It was in that sense a classic counterinsurgency operation."[9]

The Jamaican anthropologist Michael Smith, trained in military intelligence during World War II, was worried that Jamaica was in a state of "social breakdown" and "moral panic."[10] He believed that the shift of some Rastafari toward combining Black nationalism and revolutionary Marxism could lead to impending catastrophe. The aim of the *Report* was less about introducing the Rastafari to the public (which it did) and more about both placating and disrupting the Rastafari. During May 1960, Smith briefly served on a "top-secret" committee dubbed the "Rastafari Rehabilitation Committee," run by the minister of home affairs. Their objective: to reform and defang the Rastafari. The Rastafari and the public were duped and in different ways contributed to the deception by treating the *Report* as serious scholarship instigated by the Rastafari themselves, which many people, including myself, earnestly believed.

The geographer Colin Clarke lived in Jamaica during 1961 and 1968 and knew the *Report*'s authors. Clarke, concurring with Hill that the *Report*'s narrative was deceptive, writes that the "Ras Tafari Report was researched and written by Mike Smith, with his coauthors . . . playing minor supporting roles." Smith's role was to "meet, identify, and explore the most dangerous Rastafari (such as [Ras] Boanerges and [Ras] Sam

Brown), to divide the Rastas, . . . to manipulate them by proposing a government-sponsored Mission to Africa, and to co-opt those leaders who were susceptible to emigration or rehabilitation."[11] Of interest, Planno was not identified as a threat despite his commanding influence among the Rastafari and some outsiders.

Clarke concludes that the *Report* initiated conflict among the politically oriented Rastafari groups, fostering infighting that rendered them ineffective. One result was that the "religious" Rastafari like Planno gained ascendancy over the "political" Rastafari like Brown.[12] By the early 1960s there developed among the Rastafari a palpable ethos against political engagement that continued through the end of the twentieth century.[13] Politics came to mean "politricks," a profane realm, a realm of broken promises and of violence that was shunned by many Rastafari.[14] For example, during the early 1960s, Ras Shadrach of the Church of Jah Rastafari, in response to the growing conflict between nonpolitical and political Rastafari, proclaimed, "We would like to make it known to the Government and the public of Jamaica that none of us, the [apolitical] brethren of the Church of Jah Rastafari was involved in such a clash [in reference to a violent confrontation among Rastafari]. . . . Those political bearded men who call themselves churchical brethren are not of us; we . . . do not deal with violence or politics."[15] Ras Shadrach was hinting at Ras Sam Brown and his like-minded peers (more about Ras Sam Brown shortly).

Radical Left, Racism, Rastafari

Jamaicans' move toward independence and their growing race consciousness became entangled with radical politics. Without a doubt, some Rastafari and some radical leftists were forging a common cause. Recall the FAC's revolutionary ambitions and international connections. Then there were the visits of radical leftist Jamaicans to Cuba and the Soviet Union, alongside the emergence of Jamaican political organizations such as the People's Freedom Movement (PFM), the revival of the People's Political Party (PPP), and the creation of the Black Man's Political Party (BMPP). For example, Stanley Grant, an activist, international traveler, and Pan-Africanist, visited Cuba during February 1960. Grant was interested in organizing the Rastafari movement along radical leftist lines and used his public speeches to promote a blend of Pan-Africanism and a critique of imperialism.[16] Jamaican authorities designated Grant a communist. Stanley Beckford founded the Repentance of Reparations Movement, which became the United Negro Christian Movement. Beckford had by the early 1950s organized workers, a repatriation association, and a weekly Pan-Africanist paper, *The Black Man's Cry*.[17] By 1960, he had a reputation as a race man and had won the attention of some Rastafari because he promoted African heritage and African unity. The LSIC determined that by 1960 the United Negro Christian Movement had communist members and that Beckford himself was a communist. Beckford publicly voiced his interest in acquiring support from communist nations like Russia, Romania, Czechoslovakia, China, and Hungary.[18]

Hugh Buchanan migrated from Jamaica to Cuba at the age of sixteen. Living in Cuba had the profound effect of introducing Buchanan to pride in national (Cuban) identity. He was active in the UNIA in Cuba and later introduced Marxism into Jamaica; he was of Jamaica's earliest Marxist thinkers and activists.[19] Buchanan became a trade-union activist in Jamaica, cofounding the Jamaica Workers and Transport Union.[20] Buchanan pursued solidarity with the Rastafari, believing them indispensable to building a broad leftist movement in Jamaica. He ingratiated himself to Reverend Henry, serving as the Reverend's adviser through February 1960, backing away when he recognized that the Reverend had moved to "manufacture weapons."[21]

William Seivright, minister of home affairs, argued that "certain elements of the Rastafarian movement were being used as 'pawns in a bigger game.'"[22] What Seivright meant by "bigger game" was ambiguous. Was the bigger game communism? Revolution? Perhaps both. Seivright and other authorities believed that "there was a new Rastafarian movement afoot."[23] This "new" movement had Marxist and Black-nationalist leanings. Jamaica's insecurity was amplified by a sense among law enforcement that the country could be invaded at any time by foreigners via "nearby cays [or] by ships or planes and brought ashore by a Rastafari fisherman. It was also possible for them to leave the same way," said the commissioner of police.[24] The "bigger game" notion made possible continued cultivation of fear and blame, laid at the feet of the Rastafari.

The police and Special Branch surveilled the Rastafari and leftists in systematic ways.[25] The Special Branch and LSIC manipulated Rastafari and leftists by pitting them against each other, and they manipulated public perception by providing false information. They observed or planted people in meetings, they counted the number of people at meetings and protests, and they calculated the number of Rastafari in Kingston and beyond. The document "Racism in Jamaica" demonstrates how closely authorities surveilled and intervened in the activities of Rastafari and leftists.[26]

Racism, "Racism in Jamaica" pronounces, is not only Black Jamaican enmity toward Whites but also Jamaican antipathy toward "English expatriates, . . . Brown Jamaicans, Jews, Syrians, Chinese, and even other Black Jamaicans who are believed to represent colonial institutions such as government."[27] Racism in Jamaica, in 1961, was Black racism. Black racism meant Rastafari, Black nationalism, and Pan-Africanism. Black racism was critical of Jamaica's racial inequities and desirous of upending them. Defining "racism" this way permitted authorities to designate Black consciousness as a threat in an environment of rising Black consciousness.

The Special Branch asserted that the number of Rastafari in Kingston and beyond had grown and that Reverend Henry was responsible. The implication of the assessment was that alongside the growing number of Rastafari was the growth in racism, a direct consequence of the Rastafari. "Racism in Jamaica" contended that the number of Rastafari in Kingston increased from 700 in January 1959 to 1,400 in October 1959 to 2,000 in March 1960. According to "Racism in Jamaica," the total number of Rastafari in the "country parishes" also grew during the same period, from 1,640 to 2,400 to 3,180. How the figures were calculated is uncertain, though the estimates were "conservative." While Henry claimed 20,000 members and sympathizers, "Racism in Jamaica" insisted that the ARC membership never exceeded 1,000.[28]

With the existence and influence of Rastafari, Black nationalists, and leftists expanding, the LSIC depicted groups like the People's Freedom Movement (PFM) as opportunists taking advantage of "racist" organizations. The PFM was cofounded in 1953 by the Jamaican Marxist Richard Hart (who had been expelled from the PNP a year earlier for being a communist) and by Millard Johnson, the resuscitator of Marcus Garvey's People's Political Party who had turned into a Black nationalist. However, one could argue that leftists like Hart, Buchanan, Grant,

Beckford, and others had moved beyond a purely class-based analysis to consider how race (Blackness) was an inextricable part of exploitation and of resistance.

Leftist, Black, Rastafari: Ras Sam Brown and the Black Man's Political Party

Dubbed by the LSIC as the leader of the "Foreshore Road Locksmen," Sam Brown was described as a "rabble rouser," a "clever, unscrupulous opportunist," and an organic intellectual.[29] Brown, in his early seventies when I met him in early 1998, was still active in Rastafari organizing. I maintained a relationship with him until he died during the summer of 1998. Brown was feisty and cantankerous. I once extended a hand to assist him onto a stage for a Leonard Howell celebration, and he waved off my hand, retorting, "Man, do I look like a cripple?" "No," I said, watching him clamber onto the platform. I began interviewing him about this life, although we completed only two interviews.

Some of what I learned about Brown through the LSIC and Clarke was new, mainly because it involved a slice of time that Brown and I had yet to discuss.[30] Nevertheless, because of these accounts, I recognized what previously for me were outlines. For example, Brown told me about an occasion when he was shot and spent time in hospital. He was evasive when I asked for details, but I wondered if it was an assassination attempt. Or perhaps someone was simply pissed off with him. I never considered Brown a scoundrel, but he could rouse "the rabble" (e.g., the Rastafari and sympathetic Black Jamaicans) with fiery speeches that smoked with biblical and Black-nationalist tropes. What intrigued me was Brown's Marxist-like analysis expressed in Rastafari idiom. One of his favored topics was exploitation—especially how Europe exploited Jamaica and how Jamaicans exploited each other. I was unsurprised to learn of Ras Brown's involvement in Jamaica's flirtation with communism during the 1960s and 1970s. Indeed, several of the second-generation Rastafari I knew in Kingston were sometimes called communists by other Rastafari.

Hugh Buchanan brought Brown into his political orbit, with the intention of Brown leading a new political party. The Garveyite, lawyer, and PPP leader Millard Johnson drew closer to Buchanan, who in turn connected Johnson with Brown: "Both Johnson and Buchanan realized that full support of the Rastafarians [for a leftist–Black nationalist co-alition] would only be forthcoming with the influence of a Rastafarian leader. Through the efforts of Buchanan, this leader now emerged in the person of Samuel Brown."[31]

Garvey's PPP, relaunched by Johnson in April 1961, held consider-able Rastafari interest because its platform promoted Pan-Africanism and spoke to racial and class inequities experienced by Black Jamaicans. Johnson's views and pronouncements agitated his critics, who pro-claimed that he promoted race hatred with observations such as that the Black man "eats the least, wears the least, owns the least, prays the most, works the most, suffers the most, and dies the most."[32] The phrasing was extravagant but truthful. Such race talk appealed to the Rastafari, and the PPP courted Rastafari votes, for example, passing a resolution urging the government to send a second mission to Africa.

Both Buchanan and Brown were discharged from the PPP, probably at Johnson's request. One explanation for their dismissal was their es-pousal of "Black supremacy" (a Rastafari concept; see chapter 2). The PPP was struggling to counter charges of race hatred, while Brown espoused militant Black nationalism and Black supremacy. Getting rid of Brown and Buchanan also distanced the PPP from the communists and Marxists, although Johnson sported a leftist pedigree tracing to his union organizing days. Brown soon announced his own candidacy with the Black Man's Political Party, supported by Buchanan, thus re-inforcing Johnson's view that the two conspired to steal PPP votes. Buchanan created the BMPP constitution and provided campaign support.

The BMPP was inaugurated in February 1961 and was attended by a number of "security subjects," meaning leftists under government surveillance.[33] A fledgling Jamaican Labour Party (JLP) politico and eventual prime minister who was not a leftist, Edward Seaga, attended the inauguration. What Brown did differently from the dominant Rastafari trend was to urge the Rastafari to assume political power and openly align the BMPP with communism (see figure 8.1). Brown's association with Johnson, however, caused the BMPP to become an appendage of Johnson's PPP. Come election day, Brown received a pitiable eighty-one votes.

Figure 8.1. Ras Sam Brown delivering a campaign speech, Kingston Jamaica, 1962. Notice the placard messages. (Courtesy of The Gleaner Co. [Media] Ltd.)

Brown had a complex conception of Jamaican politics. He regarded government as indispensable to exercising self-determination and power: "A political victory for us [Rastafari, Black Jamaicans] is a necessity. . . . Repatriation cannot be achieved by any means other than denouncing the present government set up and by declaring a government that comprises the masses."[34] Many of the Rastafari who did not shy away from politics shared a similar view. Rastafari needed power as much as prayer. Brown argued that the Rastafari should first gain recognition as a legitimate identity and faith and thus their "reward" in Jamaica before repatriating to Africa.[35]

For Rastafari of varied theological (or "churchical," in Rastafari vernacular) stripes, Brown and similar others were political opportunists using Rastafari for personal gain: "Those political opportunists who see the Rastafarian Brethren's name as a road for them to come to the people. We shall suffer no more for them. We will abide in the Church of Jah Rastafari."[36]

Mission to Africa

One thing that nearly all Rastafari accepted was the idea of repatriation, although they did not agree on what it meant. The Mission to Africa, however, led many Rastafari to a new and pragmatic conception of repatriation: they should not wait for divine intervention. They would need to plan and prepare in order to resettle in Africa. But this did not happen right away.

The somber, optimistic, and dreamy notions of repatriation that saturated reggae music of the 1970s does not fully communicate the fervor and intensity that propelled Jamaicans during the 1950s and 1960s. Repatriation seemed both imminent and feasible. Premier Manley announced in August 1960 that he had in principle accepted the idea of repatriation and that he was willing to meet with "accredited" Rastafari leaders such as now well-known names like Prince Edward and Solomon Wolfe.[37] The government had entered into a dialogue with the Back-to-Africa movements, even though critics believed that after Reverend Henry's second act, it was "doubtful that any African nation would welcome the Ras Tafari cult members . . . after the recent exhibition of lunacy."[38]

Chanting "We want to go home a we yard" ("home" being Africa), "hundreds of Ras Tafarians and many more hundreds of other people" gathered at a public meeting chaired by Brown and convened to select representatives to meet with Premier Manley and other government officials about migration to Africa.[39] (The Manley government preferred the term "migration" over "repatriation," because they believed "migration" encompassed the various Back-to-Africa movements, while "repatriation" suggested a Rastafari concern.) The roughly twenty Rastafari representatives chose four men to enter into talks with the colonial government about migration to Africa.

Participants for the Mission to Africa (MtA) were selected by the government in December 1960. At the time, three Rastafari were included: Sam Brown, Mortimer Planno, and George Williams (of the United Rases Organization). Planning meetings for the trip began in January 1961. Both Brown and Williams withdrew from the mission.[40] This forced the government to find replacements, leading to the selection of Filmore Alvaranga and Douglas Mack, who represented the Rastafari of eastern and central Kingston.[41] The Mission to Africa departed Jamaica on April 4, 1961.[42]

Several thousand Jamaicans attended a reception for the MtA representatives upon their return (figures 8.2 and 8.3). The enthusiastic reaction that Planno experienced upon return compared to the other MtA delegates indicated the respect he had won from a cross-section of Jamaicans. Planno presented a judicious account of the trip, cautious of promoting false hope in such a tumultuous climate and careful not to preempt the forthcoming MtA report. He told the crowd that there was "plenty of milk in Ethiopia," invoking biblical symbolism of bounty, pointing out that Ethiopians had "66 million heads of cattle." Yet he contributed to a misguided notion of Ethiopia as a place of abundance: "'Ethiopia was a place where no one could [be] hungry,' he said, to the accompaniment of great applause." During the early 1970s, famine would ravish Ethiopia. Planno recounted how Emperor

Figure 8.2. The Rastafari participants in the first Mission to Africa received a festive reception upon return to Jamaica from Africa, 1961. (Courtesy of The Gleaner Co. [Media] Ltd.)

Figure 8.3. "Africa for Africans . . . and not for Europeans" became a popular refrain during the early 1960 and beyond. These Rastafari were attending the welcome for the three Rastafari participants in the Mission to Africa, 1961. (Courtesy of The Gleaner Co. [Media] Ltd.)

Selassie told Dr. Leslie that "Jamaica should take care to send the right people" to Ethiopia. He warned that Jamaican migrants would have to submit to the priorities and customs of Ethiopians, not behave as if they were in Jamaica: "You will have to live in unity and conduct yourselves properly and cut out badmanship because the Ethiopians love their country and the Emperor so much that bad men are hanged in the public square," said Planno.[43] The Rastafari celebrated the idea of the land of milk and honey while dodging the logistics of actually relocating to Africa.

The "Majority Report" was the official statement on the MtA, but the three Rastafari disagreed with the non-Rastafari account of the MtA.[44] Nonetheless, mission delegates agreed that African nations, except Sierra Leone, were amenable to the immigration of African-descended people of the Diaspora to their countries, and they wanted the world to know. Mission delegate Z. Scarlett Munroe of the Afro-West Indian Welfare League (AWIWL) peddled the accomplishments of the MtA as evidence of the Jamaican government's backing of the migration of its African-descended citizens to Africa. Scarlett sent copies of the Majority Report to US President John Kennedy and copied US Secretary of State for African Affairs G. Mennen Williams. The AWIWL sent a memo to the queen of England and the British government on the same matter.[45] They sought to convince Western Hemisphere governments that supporting migration of African-descended people to Africa was something worthwhile and feasible. Their correspondence did not elicit any serious reply from the upper echelons of government in the United States or Britain.

The first MtA produced no immediate results toward the Rastafari getting to Africa.

What motivated Premier Manley to treat repatriation and the Rastafari as subjects worth examination? As suggested, one possibility was to placate the Rastafari and another to disrupt their growing influence. A third possibility was that Manley knew that solemn and sincere Rastafari like Altamonte Reid were invested in their faith and identity; he believed that they deserved a hearing. A fourth possibility was posed by critics who saw Manley's consideration of repatriation as a "vote catching gesture . . . at the taxpayers' expense."[46] The criticism was plausible because he needed support for a referendum on the West Indies Federation—a union of Caribbean nations into a single state—while the JLP, PPP, and the Left wanted to prevent a federation. Manley was probably motivated by all of these scenarios.

The Second Mission to Africa

The PNP government appointed a commission, headed by Commissioner of Lands R. Foreman, to study the reports of the MtA and to develop a strategy. Planners hatched a second mission to Africa, slated to depart Jamaica in January 1962 and return in March 1962. The foci of the second mission, sometimes referred to as the "Technical Mission to Africa," were the logistics of immigration to Africa, trade relations with host countries, and cultural exchange with host countries.[47] The Technical Mission visited Ghana, Nigeria, and Ethiopia, having decided that these were the best prospects for accepting Jamaican immigrants. In Ghana and Nigeria, the Technical Mission focused on bilateral trade and cultural exchange. It put on an exhibition of "Jamaican manufacture, handicraft, and art, and pictures of Jamaican life" to introduce the Africans to Jamaicans.[48]

Ultimately, Ghana and Nigeria expressed disinterest in accepting large numbers of Jamaican immigrants. Both were busy decolonizing and charting their development paths. They had no need for agricultural or low-skilled laborers because they had a surfeit of both. Ethiopia was in a different position because it was not seeking its way after European colonization. The Emperor was "willing to take migrants from Jamaica without stipulation as to quantity, on the only conditions that those who come should be willing to work hard to build Ethiopia, to assimilate into Ethiopia, and be loyal to the crown," as Ethiopian World Federation leaders pointed out.[49] The Technical Mission also failed to launch government-supported repatriation into motion.

In April 1962, the JLP defeated the PNP by winning 283,351 votes of the 569,781 cast. The PPP fared poorly, winning fewer than 4,900 votes. The *Jamaica Times* barked that the "PPP's racial programme has been decisively rejected." It admonished Brown: "The debacle of the 81 votes for the lone Rasta candidate should serve notice to the cultists that they are not the influential group they believe they are."[50]

Jamaica gained its sovereignty and independence from Britain on August 6, 1962.

A Third Mission to Africa

The JLP did not immediately abandon the PNP-initiated repatriation probes, however. The JLP leadership announced a third "mission" for October 1962, to explore immigration to Tanganyika. Minister of Housing D. Clement Tavares traveled to Tanganyika in October 1962 to "discuss with the Tanganyika government the possibility of Jamaicans migrating to the country."[51]

During 1962, Tavares advocated for Jamaican migration to Africa, focusing on Uganda, Tanganyika, and Ethiopia. Tavares had political ambitions to lead the JLP; perhaps his ambition drove his African pursuits. During this period of growing interest in Africa, Jamaican elites visited Africa to support African independence celebrations, and African elites visited Jamaica to partake in Jamaica's independence celebrations. These interactions were framed as cultural exchanges, as cooperation overtures, or as a common bond engendered by the enslavement of Africans in the New World. The interactions signaled the mood of times: Jamaica's effort to join forces with newly emergent Black African polities. Such efforts were in sync with Rastafari interest in linking with these African polities.

The third mission to Africa also afforded an opportunity to celebrate Uganda's independence and to meet with government officials. On October 4, Tavares and Tanganyika's prime minister, minister of housing, and minister of home affairs conferenced. Tavares was "assured by the Prime Minister, that Tanganyika would be prepared to receive Jamaicans and to provide land for them." Tavares met with Dr. Julius Nyerere, president designate of the recently independent Tanganyika, who confirmed that "land would be provided for Jamaicans and that they would be welcome."[52] The government of Tanganyika determined to follow up its promise in writing. How the venture stalled is unclear. However, a community of Diaspora and indigenous Rastafari developed in Tanzania (formerly Tanganyika), apparently unconnected to the third mission.[53]

A third mission to Africa did not lead to formal government assistance in repatriating the Rastafari to Africa.

Paradoxical Patterns: Backlash, Compassion, Concord

Three patterns coalesced for the Rastafari during the early to mid-1960s: backlash, compassion, and concord. In a fragmentary fashion, sentiments of consideration and concord toward the Rastafari surfaced, only to brush up against the persistent sentiments of fear and abhorrence. Animosity and ridicule continued. As an illustration of passive hostility and mockery, Bim and Bam's play "John Ras I" played to "standing room only crowds."[54] The play lampooned the Rastafari, though it hinted at a worrisome trend for elites: a few middle-class folk were becoming interested in Rastafari. In the play, John Ras I is a prosperous man with a trophy wife who is persuaded by another woman to become Rastafari.

The advances of the Rastafari generated backlash, for example, in the negative reaction of some Jamaicans to both the MtA and the *Report*. Partly, the backlash emanated from elites who concluded that the Rastafari were unable to appreciate an independent Jamaica. A citizen opined, echoing a prevalent view of elites, that "Rastafarians in their present state are unfit to be taken into the New Jamaica. They belong to the dark age. In their present state they have no contribution to make to the building of a New Jamaica."[55]

Compassion for the Rastafari sprouted here and there. Class-conscious elites like contributors to the *Jamaica Times* were questioning notions of Rastafari as essentially inferior beings, though the concern was inspired by faulty reasoning. The range of people becoming Rastafari was broadening to include more people of working- and middle-class status.[56] Vere Johns considered himself an equal-opportunity critic and defended the Rastafari against what he saw as overt discrimination against them: "This time I am critical of the stance police adopted toward members of the Rastafarian cult. . . . Each [citizen] is entitled to equal treatment with any other citizen and his rights must be respected. The police seem to work on the principle that every 'beard' is a Rasta and every Rasta is a lawbreaker. How stupid!"[57] We shall see that Johns had reason to change his tune for the Rastafari: he was benefiting from Rastafari talent in Count Ossie's band and that of other Rastafari music makers. (During the early '60s, some Rastafari would not describe themselves as musicians but as "players of harps" or some other phrase.)

The *Jamaica Times* columnist Ken Nelson made a case in favor of the Rastafari. He described the men as "these conscious African sons." He acknowledged positively their identity and beliefs and provided them an opportunity to speak to the public. A band of Wareika Hill Rastafari told Nelson, "We do not come to these shores of our own free will. . . . We arrived here in chains. Therefore, it is not our problem how the return fares shall be paid. We must be repatriated. We are not migrants going to a new land as they have published in the paper. We are Africans returning home. Furthermore, we have no money. We are very poor. It is the responsibility of Government to send us home. . . . We are peaceful people. We live and practice the doctrine of peace and love." Nelson and his Wareika Rastafari interlocutors broadcast their message to all Jamaicans, challenging them to assess their prejudices: "You can go back to the people of Kingston and tell them how you found us. Tell that we are not wild and dangerous illiterate men lurking in the bushes. Tell them that they are welcome to come up and talk to us. No harm will come to them. You have seen for yourself that the stories in some of the papers about us in the past were pure propaganda." Nelson bolstered the appeal with his own assessment: "Not only were the Rastas of Wareika Hill sane and intelligent men; they were kind. But more so they showed a better understanding of life and the Jamaica society than even some of our citizens who are inclined to condemn them."[58] Nelson advised tolerance of the Rastafari.

The nascent signs of concord include Rastafari-initiated efforts. To illustrate, a group of Rastafari, led by Ras Arthur Joseph of the Church of Jah Rastafari, attended a Church of Christ service in St. Andrew, with the aim of demonstrating their tolerance for non-Rastafari faiths, while introducing their own faith to the congregation. Joseph explained to the church members that Rastafari stood for "peace and love" and that they rejected "race hatred"—their flock included Chinese and Indian people.[59] At the conclusion of meeting, the group's "leader," Ras Shadrach, invited Church of Christ members to attend one of its ceremonies. Church of Christ members welcomed the gesture of the Rastafari, though some were unconvinced that the Rastafari were a legitimate faith community. These displays of concord, though, were overshadowed by continuing conflict and violence.

Crucifixion and Concord: The Coral Gardens Perturbation

During a February 1963 public lecture on race relations at the University of the West Indies, twenty Rastafari interrupted the meeting to question the lecturer, the trade unionist and purported communist Frank Hill, to ask about where the Rastafari sat in relation to racial and class integration in Jamaican society. Apparently, Hill was aware of the nascent scholarly explanations for Rastafari behavior and identity. Rhetorically, he asked, "What we ought to ask our-selves is what is wrong with our society that causes a group—and an important group—to act as they do. Because what started as a religious sect of our population has now been spreading—and will continue to spread—into what I would call secular-Rastafarianism. And that has led to what I would call 'negritude' or the acceptance of black as good in itself."[60] Hill considered the Rastafari a consequence of an exploitative political-economic system that began with enslaved African labor and that ceaselessly produced disposable people, a system the Rastafari contested. He argued that the Rastafari were undergoing secularization and numerical growth alongside, if not caused by, growing Jamaican interest in Black pride.[61] Hill's perspective allowed for the view that it was not that the Rastafari were "maladjusted" but that the "Rastafarian was considered by society to be maladjusted."[62] He properly noted that one of the Rastafari's extraordinary contributions to Jamaica was that of valorizing Blackness. The irreverent Rastafari who interrupted Hill protested that the Jamaicans (elites) who could address their demands for recognition and repatriation did not treat them seriously. "If we have to take oath like the Mau Mau, you will understand that we are serious [about repatriation]. We not making joke," exclaimed Mortimer Planno, one of the twenty.[63] Being Mau Mau meant willingness to sacrifice oneself for the collective.

Rastafari discourse like Planno's bombast fed into ideas that Jamaica had developed its own Mau Mau–like resistance, natives ready to wreak havoc on Jamaican society. Such symbolic violence could in return justify physical violence.

Police were called to the scene of arson and murder on Thursday, April 11, 1963, to find a burned-out gas station and eight people dead—three Rastafari, two police officers, and three citizens—allegedly at the hands of bearded men. There now exist many reconstructions of the affair.[64] The Coral Gardens Incident, also known as the "Holy Thursday Massacre," was treated as an insurrection when really it was a local dispute gone haywire.[65] The violent incident transformed into a national issue that endangered the security and livelihood of countless Rastafari.

Rudolph Franklin, a bearded man whose Rastafari identity was contested by locals, had been singled out for abuse by a local landowner and the police because he squatted on a piece of land connected to Rosehall Estate, a plantation house and property in St. James Parish. Whether Franklin identified himself as Rastafari is unclear, but some people who knew him saw his interest in Black consciousness and his expression of kindness as defining a Rastafari philosophy.

An employee of the gas station told an estate overseer that Franklin was using the land without permission, which led to several confrontations, the final one among Franklin, the overseer, another estate employee, and three police officers. Franklin was shot several times and gravely wounded, allegedly by the overseer. Franklin's wound required prolonged hospitalization; upon release, he was jailed for possession of ganja. One account has it that Franklin was mortally wounded and faced a slow, ignominious death.[66] Franklin formed a grudge that he intended to resolve even if it meant taking life. The murders at the gas station were connected to Franklin's grudge. Franklin and two of his four accomplices, men who took up Franklin's cause, were killed during the "manhunt" that ensued after the burning of the gas station and murder of civilians.

The Rastafari regard the Coral Gardens Incident as the basis of a massacre, a ruthless cruelty inflicted on their community for something they had no control over. In their parlance, it was a mass crucifixion.[67] As a result of the event, anyone deemed a "Beard" or "Dreadlocks" or a sympathizer was liable to be confronted and viciously punished. Outsider response was a crucifixion in the sense of the Rastafari interpretation of scripture: modern-day Roman soldiers and vigilante civilians rounding up and punishing the children of the Black Messiah, a struggle between good and evil. The anthropologist Deborah Thomas recounts a story of a new mother forced to stand all day in blazing sun with her six-week-old baby because police could not find her dreadlocked man.[68] The woman, also a Dreadlocks, had her locks forcibly combed out (which can be excruciatingly painful) as retribution for being a Rastafari. Coral Gardens catalyzed a renewed crackdown on the Rastafari, one in which their livelihood and lives were immaterial to the potential threat that a cross-section of Jamaican citizens believed that they posed to the nation.

The vicious reactions to the murders committed by the Coral Gardens five were informed by notions that the Rastafari were berserk. An editorialist opined, "We must, too, be alarmed at the growing tension which has been built up due to the abuse, vilification, and violent attacks by these people [Rastafari] on law abiding citizens of the country. The incident at Montego Bay is certainly not the first nor the only one of its kind. We still remember what happened not long ago in the Red Hills [Reverend Henry's second act]."[69]

The Coral Gardens Trial

The Coral Gardens trial began on July 16, 1963. Three men dubbed as Rastafari, Franklin's associates, were charged with murder by "common design" in connection with the death of five people in the Coral Gardens area (Franklin and two other accused were dead). "Common design" implied a conspiratorial plan.

The court emphasized that the Rastafari doctrine was not on trial; three accused murderers were. The disclaimer was a tacit acknowledgment of Jamaica's post–Claudius Henry volatility and of explicit prejudice against the Rastafari. Indicating that the Rastafari doctrine was not on trial suggests that court officials recognized that public excoriation was ineffective. The justice noted that some witnesses, such as Elkana Gardner, "would appear to be biased against Rastafarians." Gardner, employed as a cane cutter on the Rosehall property, said that the Rastafari were thieves, "disgusting people," whom he would gladly see dead.[70] Gardner's beliefs motivated him to play callous vigilante, pursuing and capturing Rastafari of his own volition after the killings.

Like major Rastafari trials such as those of Howell and Reverend Henry, the Coral Gardens trial was a vector instructing about Rastafari practices. The trial justice noted that stories about the Coral Gardens massacre were "greatly bandied about from one end of the country to the other" by newspapers and now by radio.[71]

The court and the press continued the practice of giving the Rastafari a national platform for their beliefs and, now, for what was treated as their plight. Albertha England, a prosecution witness and female relative of one of the accused murderers, Clifton Larman, confessed on the stand that she was born Rastafari, that Emperor Selassie "is the great I, in other words the great Almighty that forms the base of [her] religion," that the Rastafari "doctrine" spread from one Rastafari to another, that her "home" was in Ethiopia, and that the time would come when she would repatriate there.[72] England said that she communicated with the Emperor and that the Emperor communicated with her in the form of visions.

Or consider the report of George Plummer, the gas-station attendant who was present at the station the morning of the murders:

> Franklin ordered him to open the door and he refused. He ran into a bathroom and they [assailants] shouted that they would kill him if he did not open. . . . The men broke down the door and window. . . . Franklin demanded to know what he was doing there. Plummer said that he answered, "Love." Franklin asked him who was love and before he could reply, Waldron [a Franklin accomplice] said "kill him." He pleaded with them "don't kill me. I am Brotherman." Franklin said who was brotherman and a witness said he answered Halie Selassie. Franklin asked him, where was his beard, and he told him that he could not wear it on the job. At this stage Larman [another Franklin accomplice] said "man free. He is a Rasta."[73]

Being a Rastafari could get one killed; it could also protect one in circumstances involving Rastafari sympathizers. The accused murderer Rudolph Franklin illustrated Rastafari love as sincere; he refused to harm another Rastafari even though the man did not bear a beard or dreadlocks. An alleged bad man could act in good faith.

Two of the original five bearded men were sentenced to death by hanging; one of the accused was released upon appeal. Tolerance was disrupted but not obliterated by the Coral Gardens massacre.

The missions to Africa heightened Rastafari organizing for recognition, repatriation, and justice. Although the Organization for African Unity met for the first time in May 1963, during the tumult of the

Coral Gardens Incident, it contributed to the hope among the Rastafari for unity among continental Africans and the Diaspora of African-descended people. Emperor Selassie took leadership of the Organization for African Unity, increasing the luster of his currency among the Rastafari. Their God was now the cornerstone of a uniting Africa that intended to bury colonialism and strengthen its member nations.

* * *

Politics pulled the Rastafari in conflicting directions during the 1960s. Politicians and authorities sought to undermine and to placate the Rastafari; a minority of Rastafari embraced radical leftist politics, while a majority rejected politics and censured those Rastafari who participated. In conjunction with the political tussles, the nascent show of compassion for the Rastafari labored beneath the burden of persisting oppression, suppression, and repression. Yet, even with these complex and opposing tensions, the star of the Rastafari would continue to rise.

Growing Influence Brings Growing Pains

Unification and Fragmentation Tussle

In 1961, it seemed that the Rastafari were about to realize their dream of repatriation to Africa, and with Jamaican government support. By 1963, repatriation and government support seemed like a pipe dream. The Coral Gardens affair in 1963 momentarily diminished the Rastafari's progress to a preexisting status of oppression, suppression, repression, and stigmatization. However, by 1968, Rastafari ethnogenesis was spiraling beyond the confines of the established modes of oppression, suppression, repression, and stigmatization to the point where the Rastafari began to call them discrimination or violations of human rights. But the bigotry did not disappear; anti-Rastafari sentiment continued into the 1970s, especially among conservative-leaning folk: "The Rastafarian, the criminal, the communist, the followers of the Black Power movement have a like objective—the overthrow of the present system of government, the present rulers and their offices, therefore, the overthrow of all order and decency. In this they are all one—a menace to democracy, to society, to the Jamaican way of life. They must be stamped out, exterminated, or God Help Jamaica, our native land."[1] Nevertheless, by the 1970s, for reasons local and international, the field had shifted in favor of the Rastafari. The post-1968 era generated growing pains, one reason being the growing numbers and the growing popularity of Rastafari. Along with growing pains came fragmentation and efforts to unify.

A perturbation can bring into view things that have been developing over time but not readily discernable in their complexity or in their break with the present. Rising numbers of Jamaicans had been paying attention to the Rastafari and their beliefs irrespective of the detractors. Emperor Selassie's visit to Jamaica revealed this for all to see. On April 21, 1966, Emperor Haile Selassie's plane landed at Palisadoes Airport in Kingston, Jamaica.[2] The Emperor was greeted by multitudes of

Figure 9.1. A dreadlocked Rastafari man with a dreadlocked boy at Palisa-does Airport who caught a glimpse of Emperor Selassie, 1966. (Original caption: "A bearded brother and his boy have seen the Emperor"; courtesy of The Gleaner Co. [Media] Ltd.)

Figure 9.2. Emperor Selassie plants a gold coin in the hand of a Rastafari, Kingston, Jamaica, 1966. (Courtesy of The Gleaner Co. [Media] Ltd.)

Jamaicans, Rastafari and non-Rastafari, many of them swarming with reckless zeal onto the tarmac to greet the Emperor, while other assemblages squeezed together along the road the Emperor traveled from the airport to his reception at the National Stadium (figures 9.1 and 9.2). The Emperor's visit created the opening for a new status for Rastafari. Emperor Selassie did not denounce the Rastafari as many elites had expected. He greeted a delegation of Rastafari and gifted each of them a gold coin and was rumored to have encouraged the Rastafari to organize and centralize for their future development. Many non-Rastafari reevaluated their view of the Rastafari after the Emperor's visit, and some themselves became Rastafari, expanding the numbers of the community. The boost to the standing of the Rastafari became enmeshed with Jamaica's Black Power and Black consciousness movement in Jamaica.

The Walter Rodney Rebellion

If the visit of Emperor Selassie to Jamaica revealed the number of Jamaicans willing to sacralize him, then the uprising resulting from banning the historian Walter Rodney from returning to Jamaica demonstrated the grip of Black Power and Blackness on Jamaican consciousness.

The Walter Rodney rebellion crystallized how Jamaica and the Rastafari were shifting during the late 1960s. (The rebellion is also called the "Rodney Riots" or "Rodney Affair"; I call it a rebellion given the reverberation of the uprising.) College students were at the forefront of a youthful rebellion clamoring for change during the late 1960s into the 1970s. Overall, youth discontent reflected a decline in young people's respect for traditional authority and its values. In Jamaica, elites interpreted the discontent of college students as spanning two poles. Liberal-oriented folk imagined youth disillusioned with democracy and modernity but open to reform. Conservative-oriented folk imagined youth enamored of revolutionary Marxism, communism, and Maoism, desirous of toppling capitalism and democracy. The Guyanese and Marxist historian Walter Rodney's intellectual interests and political inclinations fit the conservative view of youth discontent and thus set up Rodney to become a threat to Jamaica's established order.

Born in Georgetown, Guyana, Rodney studied history at the University College of the West Indies (UCWI) Mona Campus as an undergraduate.

He earned the intellectual respect of Mona faculty and in time won a graduate scholarship to London University, where he excelled in his study of African history. Upon acquisition of his PhD, Rodney traveled to East Africa and taught briefly at the University of Dar es Salaam. In January 1968, Rodney accepted an appointment as a lecturer on African history when the vice chancellor of UCWI Mona, Philip Sherlock, hired Rodney to develop UCWI's interest in African history.[3]

In Rodney's philosophy of democratizing knowledge and public participation in the service of decolonization, he reasoned that academic knowledge should be accessible beyond university confines. The Rastafari, wage workers, the unemployed, students, and other Jamaicans became Rodney's students and colleagues in sessions that convened where people were—sports clubs, churches, schoolrooms, gullies, and "rubbish dumps"—where they discussed Africa, Black Power, and revolutionary politics.[4] These sessions "grounded" participants, to use Rodney's phrase in his *Groundings with My Brothers*, in the workings of history, race, class, and politics.[5] The Rastafari themselves had begun digging into African history during the early 1950s, as attested to by Rastafari intellectuals like Sam Brown, Sam Spence, and Mortimer Planno.

Rodney's impact on the thinking of some Rastafari was palpable. I met Rastafari who grounded with Rodney, and I noticed the historical and Marxist influence of Rodney in their discourse. It was not unusual for them to explain the economic conditions of Jamaica using notions of imperialism, colonialism, or capitalist development. Their view of Africa and Ethiopia leaned toward pragmatism rather than romanticism, erected on evidence as much as idealism. While Rodney endeared himself to some of the political Rastafari and intellectually curious rude boys (rebellious and sometimes violent young men of lesser means), he was not uniformly embraced by either community, with some being put off by his intellectual Marxist jargon, others by his secular Black nationalism.[6]

Rodney left Jamaica for Montreal, Canada, to attend the Congress on Black Writers. Upon Rodney's return to Jamaica on October 15, 1968, he was refused admittance into Jamaica. Prime Minister Hugh Shearer of the Jamaican Labour Party was no fan of Black nationalism or student agitation and spun his decision on Rodney as a matter of the national security of the fledgling independent nation. The Shearer government's decision to outlaw Rodney's return to Jamaica, and hence to deny him his university appointment and access to his family, sparked an uprising. During the morning of October 16, demonstration turned into riotous rebellion. Later that day, Rodney's wife, Patricia Rodney, addressed protestors, saying about the protest, "It shows that my husband has support for what he has been trying to do. All he has been doing is to help the black man to be a man."[7]

The demonstrators' numbers grew into the hundreds, with the unmistakable participation of the Rastafari, youthful Black Jamaican men who were not college students, and opportunists, all shouting "Black Power." The chants and the processional advance of the protestors metamorphosed into looting and destruction, a significant amount of it directed toward symbols of elite power: the Ministry of Home Affairs, the Ward Theater, the Chamber of Commerce, Marzouca's department store, and motor cars at the Supreme Court building. A band of youth commandeered several city buses, crashed as least one, and burned out scores more; protestors brandished iron pipes and hurled stones at police. Acting with impunity, the police were urged on by Shearer's dictum to show no mercy to hooligans. Within seventy-two hours of the eruption, relative calm returned in the wake of staggering material destruction.

Rodney catalyzed what was already simmering in late 1960s Jamaica. The Rastafari were primed to take advantage of their rising recognition and new relationships. The unemployed, marginally employed, and criminal opportunists (the lumpenproletariat, or the unorganized and apolitical underclass in Marxist language) were primed by their ability to cause mayhem for elites and nonelites alike; the heady theories of leftist intellectuals like Rodney had assigned them the status of change agents. Such groups and ideas were intersecting by the late 1960s.[8]

Student activists were a new challenge for the JLP. The rebuke evident in the student protestors' demands and strategies scalded Shearer: "I want to record my disappointment at the conduct of those students who claimed to be interested in the distribution of wealth and living standards in the society and who claim that they would like that imbalance corrected. . . . These students have only been able to repeat old cliches . . . [and] copy the vulgar conduct [direct action] that they learned from others abroad. . . . They are still today discussing the lousy theory of Karl Marx which were enunciated in 1848, which is some 120 years ago."[9] The students disappointed Shearer because they displayed solidarity with the Rastafari, the unemployed, the disaffected middle class, and UCWI Mona leftist faculty. The students in the eyes of the JLP had become part of an ominous coalition. Rodney was a flashpoint, though, not the fundamental problem of 1968 Jamaica.

The Shearer administration smeared Rodney as a national security threat. They fingered him, students, and hooligans in a "Castro-type revolution" conspiracy, with Rodney as the chief. This was one of the primary reasons Shearer offered for preventing Rodney's reentry into Jamaica: "Jamaican students themselves ought to be aware that they have been duped into supporting a destructive anti-Jamaican cause. . . . It leaves open to question the loyalty of any Jamaican who knowingly supports anything which harms his country."[10] The foreigners whom Shearer referenced were UCWI Mona student government leaders from other Caribbean islands and England. In banning Rodney, Shearer asserted that he had saved Jamaica from national calamity. He disrupted the Rodney cabal by surprise before its "plot" had reached its "maximum potential" for destruction.[11] Yet Shearer was prevaricating and drawing on faulty Special Branch intelligence. The Special Branch intelligence was all over the place; someone who uttered an otherwise harmless mention of revolution, Black Power, or communism could become a security "interest."

There was reason for the JLP to be concerned about the social climate in Jamaica. During Shearer's ministership, a loose coalition of Rastafari, students, lumpenproletariat, union laborers, leftists, and alienated middle-class folk—inspired by Black Power, the US civil rights movement, and revolutionary movements like those in Cuba, Latin America, and Africa—had coalesced. The Special Branch noted this: "[Rodney] is potentially dangerous since he might succeed in bringing together various disaffected elements in Jamaica."[12] This was Shearer's primary concern, but he did not mention it in his public hyperbole about Rodney.

Shearer believed Jamaica was a "volcano" ready to erupt. He was right on that score. The Rodney rebellion showcased the emergent coalition in a form that was fearsome to him and the establishment, as Rodney noted: "The Black Brothers in Kingston, Jamaica moved against the Government of Jamaica. That is the point that must come home. Let us stop calling it student riots. What happened in Jamaica is that the black people of the city of Kingston have seized upon this opportunity to begin their indictment against the Government of Jamaica."[13]

The Special Branch traced Rodney's subversive status to his student years at UCWI Mona, when in 1961 he was selected as a delegate to the 1962 International Union of Students Congress held in Leningrad. And he twice visited Cuba during 1962. Shearer presented Rodney as a student with "extreme communist views." Upon Rodney's return to Jamaica in 1968, Shearer said, "He lost little time in engaging in subversive activities. . . . He quickly announced his intention of organising revolutionary groups for what he termed . . . 'the struggle ahead,' and then closely associated himself with groups of people who claimed to be part of the Rastafarian Movement and also with Claudius Henry." Speaking especially to elites, Shearer stressed how Rodney advocated that White and Brown Jamaicans should have their assets confiscated and redistributed equitably. Shearer sought to terrify them into supporting his actions: "In recent months Rodney stepped up the pace of his activities and was actively engaged in organising groups of semi-literates and unemployed for avowed revolutionary purposes. He constantly reiterated the necessity for the use of violence in attaining his ends. The procurement of firearms and training in their use was recently a major topic of discussion."[14]

Shearer cast the education sessions of Rodney's people as the organization of marginalized dissenters beyond what they themselves were capable of: "No wonder that a Rastafarian at one of Dr. Rodney's campus meetings publicly declared, and here I quote: 'We have the brawn, you have the brains, all we need are the guns.'"[15] These words were uttered by Ras Negus at a meeting at the UCWI Mona Students Union. The political scientist Rupert Lewis makes clear in his seminal article on Rodney that Ras Negus's "words bore no relationship to political action and reflected social anger and desperation."[16] Nevertheless, the Shearer government used the quote to portray Rodney as training grassroots terrorists. Another source of evidence used against Rodney was a confiscated student-produced pamphlet called *Tactics Tactics Tactics Tactics*, which charted strategies for a student takeover of the Mona campus.[17] Shearer attributed *Tactics'* ideas to Rodney's influence.

Without doubt, Shearer mispresented Rodney's academic and organizing work. Still, Rodney expressed a revolutionary view of political change that accepted violence, though it was not central to his activity in Jamaica. This meant that Rodney's words could always be used against him, to cast him as a threat to established order.[18]

Rastafari beliefs were finding concrete support. Their valorization of Blackness was confirmed by the Black Power movement that emerged in Jamaica: "In our epoch, the Rastafari have represented the leading force of this expression of black consciousness. They have rejected this philistine white West Indian society. They have sought their cultural and spiritual roots in Ethiopia and Africa."[19] The Rodney rebellion disclosed new relational possibilities for the Rastafari, exemplified by the loose coalition of misfits who contemplated the possibility of surmounting class, racial, and age divisions, which promised the possibility of unity.

An alliance of Rastafari, students, UCWI professors, and community members collaborated to produce a newspaper titled *Abeng*, led by the then graduate student and later historian and professor Robert Hill. The title referenced the Jamaican Maroons' hollow cow horn that they blew like a trumpet to communicate with each other during periods of resistance against the British colonizers bent on subduing the Maroons. (The Maroons were African-descended Jamaicans who lived in remote areas of Jamaica's interior and who had created and successfully defended their free communities under the British enslavement regime.) First published in February 1969, *Abeng* sought to assist Jamaicans in developing a critical perspective on themselves and their society. Contributors discussed issues of race, class, and liberation in Jamaica and abroad. In Rodney-like fashion, the publication sought to communicate with all Jamaicans irrespective of their station in life. The publication was short-lived, hampered by infighting about the content. For example, some Rastafari contributors wanted to highlight Emperor Selassie's divinity, whereas some of the Marxist or socialist contributors believed that religion impeded Jamaicans' revolutionary potential or they disagreed that the Emperor was divine. The bottom line is that the coalition that disturbed Shearer so much was far more fragile than his braggadocio asserted.

During 1968, it became clear that growing numbers of people were joining cause with the Rastafari, with some becoming Rastafari. Rastafari adherents from the middle class became noteworthy by the late 1960s, given that the Rastafari represented things that the middle-class ethos had loathed: Blackness, Africa, cannabis, poverty, and uncombed hair. And the middle and upper classes represented what the Rastafari loathed: Eurocentrism, colonialism, and acceptance of bald inequities.

New Vectors, Growth, Emergent Accommodation

Count Ossie and his musicians contributed to Jamaica's accommodation to the Rastafari. They were the vanguard in moving Rastafari music and culture into the Jamaican popular music scene without compromising the Rastafari message. Count Ossie, the front man for the group that became the Mystic Revelation of Rastafari, along with his Rastafari colleagues such as Cedric Brooks, contributed to the development of indigenous Rastafari music (see chapter 6). Ossie's group were steadfast advocates of Rastafari, and their emphasis on peace, love, and community and openness to engaging non-Rastafari created openings for them to communicate with outsiders in the realms of music production. For example, Ossie's group performed onstage during the late 1950s with Marguerita Mahfood, a popular dancer and vocalist of Lebanese ancestry. By chance, she heard the Ossie drummers and was smitten by the rhythms. She wanted to include them in her dance act.[20] Because of Mahfood, the Ossie drummers secured the opportunity to play at two of Jamaica's premier halls, the Ward and Carib Theaters, on a Christmas Day, despite the initial resistance of the music promoter and Rastafari basher Vere Johns (the journalist of note cited in previous chapters). The Christmas Day performance of Mahfood backed by the Ossie drummers was a hit with the audience. The journalist Hélène Lee recaps the long-term impact of this serendipitous encounter: "It was a woman, and a half-white woman at that, who forced Rasta music into Jamaican pop and eventually around the world. Without her, it might have stayed hidden in the ghetto and withered. There might never have been a music called reggae."[21] Suddenly, after the performance, Johns, also a talent producer, skirted around his Rastafari prejudices, eager to promote the group. The Ossie drummers created a path for other Rastafari performers to demonstrate their talent to mainstream Jamaican audiences.

The Mystic Revelation became Rastafari ambassadors beyond their music. They were not above engaging with churches or mainstream Jamaicans. They, for instance, created a community development center to "attack the problems of inadequate housing, lack of educational facilities and cultural impoverishment which . . . not only existed in that community but was presently existing islandwide."[22] Ossie and the Mystic Revelation promoted education, reading, and access to medical services, practices shunned by many fundamentalist Rastafari of the time.

Rastafari and the Arts

Another sign of the collective Rastafari shift from pariah to cultural force before reggae became fashionable materialized in the arts.[23] The impact of the Rastafari on Jamaicans was bolstered through the arts, in the broad sense of the term: painting, drawing, sculpture, textiles, poetry, drama, and music. Art became a new vector in Rastafari ethnogenesis.

Rastafari art is as old as the Rastafari faith itself. From its origins, its content, symbols, themes, and styles focused on concerns central to the new faith and people: Emperor Selassie and Ethiopia. Recall that in 1937, Leonard Howell flew a red, gold, and green flag ornamented with a lion over his King's mission; the fences were painted red, gold, and green; early Rastafari took to wearing patches of cloth or strings showing red, gold, and green, identifying them as bearers of the faith.

Elite Jamaica embraced talented artists trained in Eurocentric art aesthetics. Artists operating outside this hegemony were lumped into "primitive" and "naïve" art. Such artists were inspired to create art, but without formal training. The terms reveal how elites understood the art and artists as inferior to the established arts. A sympathetic columnist, for example, observed arrogantly, "Ras Dizzy is not really a 'primitive', for he does not paint like one: he has somehow miraculously retained the vision and the way of painting of a child and he must surely have a child-like mind to go with it."[24]

Born Albert Livingstone in 1932, Ras Dizzy became a famous Rastafari artist. He was known for his bold, colorful, straightforward paintings, as well as his poetry; the constraints of convention failed to restrain him. A nomad who told fanciful stories such as boxing the famous Cassius Clay (later known as Muhammed Ali), Ras Dizzy discovered fame during the late 1960s as an artist who marched to his own rhythm. His visions, imagination, and experience appeared in his art; for example, his claim to have rode with the film star John Wayne is expressed in his colorful self-portrait as a masked Lone Ranger (a masked heroic character of the western film genre who crusaded against villainy). In 1979, David Boxer, the former director of the National Gallery in Kingston and an art scholar and collector, included Ras Dizzy's art in the seminal Jamaican exhibit *The Intuitive Eye*. Ras Dizzy later exhibited in the United States and England.

Rastafari art forms and artists gained prominence by the late 1960s. Their art had vaulted Jamaica's fences and walls, departed its tabernacles, and been washed from its garments and other media that conveyed their creative work. It found a chastened welcome, though, in the homes and galleries of middle- and upper-class Jamaicans. Wolfgang Bender's impressive *Rastafarian Art* (2005) chronicles a range of the art and artists, educating people about Rastafari creativity while documenting the art and artists whose contributions might have vanished without a trace.

Outsiders in Jamaica and beyond began to show keen interest in Rastafari art. Rastafari like Everald Brown were presenting their work to non-Rastafari in venues such as the Creative Arts Centre at UCWI. The viewers saw oil paintings such as *Nyabinghi Hour*, a depiction of a Nyabinghi ceremony cast in enthralling hues of green, yellow, red, orange, and blue.[25] If the viewers had no conception of a Nyabinghi ceremony before the exhibit, Brown provided a vivid illustration of key elements like the eternal fire and the players of musical instruments.

Born into a Pentecostal household in 1917, in Clarendon Parish, Everald Brown, a carpenter, became Rastafari after experiencing a vision of Emperor Selassie.[26] Nature, spirits, and his Rastafari faith inspired his art. Veerle Poupeye, an art historian and curator, notes how Brown's early art adorned the walls of the church he created.[27] Brown was a prolific artist whose creations caught the eye of Jamaican art consumers. Winning the Silver Musgrave Medal in 1973, Brown's work was featured in exhibitions in the United States, Cuba, and Central America. The expansion of Black-pride sensibilities ushered along admiration of things indigenous to Black Jamaica, like the Rastafari and their art.

By the mid-1970s, Rastafari artists were winning awards in Jamaica. Albert Artwell, born in 1942 in St. James Parish, exemplifies the Rastafari visual artists. After having a vision during the late 1960s that impelled him to become Rastafari, Artwell's adoration for the Bible inspired his creativity. Beginning his artistic odyssey by writing Bible verses in decorative handwriting, Artwell moved on to paint biblical scenes.

Deloris Anglin is usually the lone woman artist mentioned in the context of Rastafari intuitive artists. Unlike the male Rastafari artists, no references to her faith or path to artistry is usually mentioned. Common in Anglin's paintings are religious themes and scenes of Black people interacting. Women feature prominently in her scenes, which sometimes feature women only. For example, in her multicolored *Tree of Life*, Anglin depicts nine women rejoicing in the presence of a bounty-laden tree of fruit, berries, and other food.

Ras Daniel Heartman (Heart Man) engraved a deep artistic imprint on Jamaica, though his contributions are less known than one would expect. Heartman's drawings of Rastafari children and men have traversed the world. Because Heartman never copyrighted his art, people may recognize his work, such as the stern face of a Rastafari child called "Rasta Baby," but have no idea that Heartman is the creator. Drawing, dancing, writing, and performing were Heartman's talents. Lloyd Roberts was Heartman's birth name. Around 1959, at the age of seventeen, Heartman affiliated himself with the Rastafari Mansion Church Triumphant of Jah Rastafari. With this Mansion, Heartman benefited from the guidance of noted Rastafari leaders such as Ras Dizzy and the brothers Ras Shadrach, Ras Meshach, and Ras Abednego. In 1966, Heartman was among the Rastafari men who received a gold coin from Emperor Selassie during his visit to Jamaica. The first Rastafari man to perform as a movie actor was probably Heartman, playing the companion to the central character, Ivan, in the 1972 movie *The Harder They Come*. The film introduced viewers outside of Jamaica to reggae music and to the Rastafari.

Jamaica's cultural movement to recognize intuitive art and artists as creations worthy of audiences and praise took advantage of the new ways of thinking ushered in by Black Power, Pan-African, and left-wing movements and by Rastafari who put their art onstage for Jamaica and the world to see and praise. Art aided in the dispersal of Rastafari culture and identity.

Politicians, Rastafari, and Cultural Resource Mobilization

Cultural resources, in forms such as ideas, language, and symbols, can be mobilized in ways that cause economic, political, and cultural consequences.[28] Religious imagery can appeal across class and race, speaking to people's moral concerns; it can express what people feel, what they hope for. Recurrent themes in Jamaica's biblical repertoire—unrestricted to the Rastafari—are redemption, wickedness, deliverance, overcoming, and apocalypse. The People's National Party in particular utilized Rastafari symbols and language to rally voters, thus creating a vector through political activity. Politicians spread Rastafari symbols and language.

Between 1967 and 1976, the JLP and the PNP used biblical and religious imagery, and the cultural resources developed by the Rastafari, in their election campaigns. The JLP, for instance, began many of its campaign meetings with the hymn "Onward Christian Soldiers," which evokes martial imagery implying a political fight for morality and against evil. The Harvard-trained anthropologist and politician Edward Seaga, of Lebanese, European, and Indian parentage, represented western Kingston, one of the city's poorest wards. He conducted fieldwork among peasants in St. Catherine's Parish and lived among Kingston's urban poor. He used these experiences to build social capital that he plied into political capital.

Seaga grasped the power of religious symbols to mobilize Jamaicans, becoming a Revival "consecrated Shepherd," which some Jamaicans interpreted to mean that he had supernatural power.[29] Seaga was not above using these beliefs to his advantage; such beliefs diminished the class and racial distance between him and his ardent supporters. He projected an image of himself as a "roots man" and insinuated himself as Jamaica's Jesus Christ through recourse to slogans such as "closer than a brother," which evokes the Christian hymn "Closer than a brother, my Jesus is to me," and through his manipulation of religious imagery such as Christ at the Garden of Gethsemane, saying in public, on bended knees, "would this cup pass from my lip," hugging an imaginary cup.[30]

Michael Manley, who was the son of Norman Manley, the leader of the PNP after 1967, and the prime minister of Jamaica beginning in 1972, was also effective in mobilizing biblical and religious cultural resources toward political ends. A lawyer and advocate for Jamaicans like his father, Norman, Michael became an ardent defender of rank-and-file Jamaicans. An example of Manley's ability to use cultural resources for political gain was his "Rod of Correction." In October 1969, Manley visited Shashemene, Ethiopia, as a part of a tour of five African nations (Prime Minister Shearer of the JLP had visited the site a couple of weeks earlier).[31] A youthful Jamaican senator, P. J. Patterson, and Michael Manley claimed to have met with Emperor Selassie and received from him a cane, which Manley dubbed the "Rod of Correction." Manley used the rod to symbolize discipline, divine authority, and an end to Jamaica's political corruption, economic malaise, and neglect of its dispossessed. In Manley's hands, the rod had the power to "correct" the JLP. At the end of his 1972 campaign speeches, Manley would methodically uncover and remove the rod from a box, raise it, and shake it. Audiences would go wild, crying, "Let us touch it."[32]

Manley's use of Rastafari symbolism was effective and encouraged some Rastafari to participate in Jamaican electoral politics. Indeed, one could argue that Manley's ploy won him the 1972 election. The insertion of Rastafari identity and culture into politics worked as a vector injecting Rastafari beliefs and language into mainstream Jamaican life. Manley won a second term in 1976, still drawing on appeals to Rastafari symbolism as well as leading a deep foray into creating a socialist Jamaican society. The challenges of creating a socialist Jamaica were so great that it caused significant distress—shortages in currency and goods, US intervention—and Manley lost a third bid for prime minister in 1980 to Edward Seaga and the JLP.

The rise of the JLP signaled a turn from the heady times of the late 1960s and 1970s to an austere conservativism that privileged market capitalism and individualism. The swing also signaled a coming change in the upsurge of a new and increasingly digitized form of dancehall music that displaced reggae as Jamaica's popular music of choice. Dancehall was unconcerned with love, peace, and unity; it touted violence, sex, and selfishness. The dancehall displacement of reggae meant that the most potent vector for the Rastafari was losing its reach. This did not indicate a decline in Rastafari presence or numbers, but it portended change. The Rastafari as a cultural and religious icon found unlikely competition: dons (as in crime bosses) and the "badman" (violent thug): "By the 1980s the Rastafarian role model of the 1960s was to be tragically replaced by political gun-men, drug dons, and criminals."[33] Nevertheless, let us briefly explore reggae music as a vector.

A Far-Reaching Vector: Reggae, Jamaica's Popular Music

Perhaps the most far-reaching vector for transmitting Rastafari culture was music and the media used to perform and communicate it. Once the conditions existed for extensively spreading Rastafari beliefs, so too did the possibility for another qualitative shift in Rastafari ethnogenesis. The new conditions consisted of both new technologies and social change. Jamaican music, no longer confined to a placed-based setting, became increasingly portable by the mid-1960s, both the sources of the music and the means to play it. While the transistor radio made the radio portable and LP records became more accessible, an important advance in general was the audio cassette and player (the eight-track came first). The cassette tape became available to the consumer public during the mid-1960s. It was a significant advance because it allowed one to play *and* to record music. Portable tape players entered the market, increasing the mobility of tape-recorded music. These forms became affordable with mass production.

During this period, new musical forms were emerging in Jamaica: ska, rock steady, and reggae. Ska, an up-tempo music like calypso and mento but with infusions of rhythm-and-blues and jazz, traces to the late 1950s. The Skatalites, a legendary ska band, formed in 1963. Ska provided a platform for the development of another musical style, the short-lived but influential "rock steady." Rock steady presented a rhythm slower than ska and offered a matrix for reggae. The "Israelites," a rock steady–reggae hit created by Desmond Decker and the Aces in 1968, foreshadowed the coalescence of Rastafari-inspired Jamaican popular music that expressed Jamaica's rising engagement with the Rastafari and with Black consciousness.

Jamaicans had established another vector, the "sound system," which came to describe a disc jockey (deejay) who assembled a heap of speakers and related sound equipment to blast the music that he (typically male) played on record turntables. The sound system man played dance halls and yards, though some made mobile music their business, turning trucks and vans into sound systems that moved from one community to another.

Jamaican sound system operators and popular musicians, recognizing that their audiences liked heavy drum and bass beats, began to experiment with these sounds. Manifesting a beat slower than rock steady, reggae emphasized the bass and drum and the first and third beats. One of the earliest reggae artists was Toots Maytal, who titled a song "Do the Reggae" (1968). Though Toots was not a self-described Rastafari at the time, his concentration on drum, bass, and beat was consonant with Rastafari music's use of the funde, repeater, and bass drums. Rastafari began to use the reggae musical repertoire to broadcast their own lyrics and rhythmic sensibilities.

The point is that reggae music, sound systems, dance halls, and theaters became means to disseminate Rastafari sensibilities in an environment that was increasingly sensitive to the issues that Rastafari musicians critiqued: poverty, crime, violence, political corruption, government incompetence, racial injustice, colonialism, and the despoliation of nature. Reggae began and continued as protest music. Yet it did more than protest and critique. It glorified Emperor Selassie, love, unity, and Black consciousness (as well as romantic concerns). The vectors allowed for transmission of Rastafari ideas and music among Jamaicans first and, by the early 1970s, audiences in the United States and the United Kingdom.

"Rasta message reach the world," Rasta Ivey would tell me again and again, referring to the global reach of reggae. It drew attention to the Rastafari. It provided them with a megaphone. Reggae educated and inspired. The music dramatized Jamaica's African heritage and illustrated the ongoing abuses of African-descended people.

Reggae promoted Rastafari, but it also secularized and commercialized them. It stereotyped the Rastafari, for example, in the way album covers portrayed mostly men wearing dreadlocks, using cannabis, employing the speech of Rastafari, and displaying the symbols of the Ethiopian flag and images of Emperor Selassie. Rastafari musicians and other reggae performers made possible the crafting of durable images of the Rastafari as peaceful, loving, righteous, uninterested in material trappings, and critical of exploitation, especially the abuse of Black and poor people. In stereotyping the Rastafari for commercial appeal, this promotion also exacerbated the emphasis on male Rastafari at the expense of female Rastafari. With some notable exceptions, such as the I-Threes, the female backing band of Bob Marley and the Wailers, or Sister Carol, Rastafari-inspired reggae came off as a man's game. The images were not in perfect sync with reality, but images are a representation of reality, not reality itself.

The commercialization of reggae made possible Rastafari as a fad and fashion; it enabled the expansion of people who affected Rastafari mannerisms without committing to the tenets of the faith—pseudo-Rastafarians, in the view of the communications professor Stephen King.[34] Musicians, irrespective of their position on Rastafari, became stand-ins for the ardent and faithful. The existence of pseudo-Rastafari was not new, as we have seen. But reggae encouraged an explosion.

The barriers to knowing about Rastafari or becoming Rastafari were lowered, if not erased, by vectors like reggae music. One now had access to Rastafari without setting a foot into a Rastafari camp or sitting at the feet of an elder. Increasingly, one would be free to style oneself Rastafari, if only for a while. Opportunities for becoming and being Rastafari in Jamaica or abroad had multiplied.

The *Daily Gleaner* changed its Rastafari tune after the Rodney rebellion and the rise of reggae music. It crossed over from disparagement and criticism of the Rastafari to accommodate them. Changes in personnel at the *Daily Gleaner* and swings in the national discourse, which could no longer avoid topics such as race, class-based inequalities, and alternatives to capitalism, allowed for seeing the Rastafari in a different light. The *Daily Gleaner* began to interview Rastafari and reggae artists and report their accounts in their own words without the coating of disparagement. It utilized Rastafari as columnists, such as Arthur Kitchen and Stephen McDonald. The rise of reggae music strengthened the influence of the Rastafari and further contributed toward the shift in people's attitude toward them.

The Concert: A Significant Vector Amplifying Rastafari Images and Messages

Reggae music concerts, especially large and momentous concerts, show the expanding reach and influence of the Rastafari in Jamaica and abroad. Exemplars of this effect included the Rastafari Robert "Bob" Marley's 1976 Smile Jamaica Concert, his 1978 One Love Peace Concert, and his 1980 Zimbabwe concert. These vectors and attractors contributed to forging Rastafari identity in new contexts. (Records, of course, were major vectors, but here I focus on concerts that project Rastafari ideology and that actualize Rastafari.)

Born in St. Ann's Parish to a Black mother and White father and raised in the Trench Town section of Kingston, Bob Marley grew up hardscrabble in impoverished and turmoil-stricken parts of Kingston. Fascinated with music, Marley gravitated toward the musical forms of his time, beginning by singing and playing rhythm-and-blues-inspired music and ska. Living in the midst of so many Rastafari himself, he grew aware of the message and lifestyle of the Rastafari, and guided by revered older Rastafari gurus like Mortimer Planno, he embraced Rastafari. Marley's musical companions Winston "Peter Tosh" McIntosh and Neville "Bunny" Livingston were on similar identity trajectories. Their identity transformations (into Rastafari) and Kingston's poverty, crime, and politically motivated violence molded their Rastafari-inspired reggae. The Wailers, spearheaded by Marley, Tosh, and Bunny, disbanded over disagreements about their musical direction and their relationship with the producer and owner of Island Records, Chris Blackwell. Tosh and Bunny determined to pursue musical careers on their own. The Wailers became Bob Marley and the Wailers.

Marley tossed in his lot with the Prophet Gad's Twelve Tribes of Israel. Prophet Gad, born Vernon Carrington, in 1968 founded the Twelve Tribes of Israel, one of the four major Rastafari communities. The Twelve Tribes began as a coupling of an Ethiopian World Federation chapter and a Rastafari community of the Ethiopian Orthodox Church.[35] Several practices distinguish the Twelve Tribes among the Rastafari of Jamaica. They give an explicit role to Christ in their cosmology, though there is not unanimity on whether Emperor Selassie is the second advent of Christ or whether the Emperor was a vessel of Christ rather than the Christ returned.[36] Other distinctions include that they recognize executive female leadership; they are the most successful among the Rastafari in settling members in Ethiopia; they welcome non-Black people among their ranks; and they embrace reggae music as a part of their social organization, arranging performances and promoting their own musicians. These distinctions at times produced tension between the Twelve Tribes and other Rastafari communities such as the Nyabinghi Order or the Bobo Ashanti (Ethiopia Africa Black

International Congress). Bob Marley was baptized into the Ethiopian Orthodox Church in Jamaica just before his death.

BOB MARLEY: EXEMPLAR OF RISING RASTAFARI SWAY

On December 5, 1976, Bob Marley and the Wailers played the Smile Jamaica Concert in Jamaica. Two days previous, two carloads of gunmen smashed into Marley's Hope Road studio and home on December 3, shooting several of his associates. Bob and Rita Marley were among the wounded. A hesitant but resolute Bob Marley played the Smile Jamaica Concert two days later, without the benefit of his full band.[37] He put on a moving performance.

The Smile Jamaica Concert began as the idea of a PNP operative who believed that the violence in Kingston and surrounding areas (much of it politically motivated) had become so devastating that intervention was necessary. The operatives' idea found support in Marley's desire to put on a large and free concert for Jamaicans. Hope of unity rested with Rastafari and their message; government and politicians were incapable of brokering any accord. Roger Steffens, a reggae music historian and founder of the path-breaking Los Angeles reggae radio program *Reggae Beat*, observes that the "Smile Jamaica concert was meant to give people a positive sign that Rastafari was a way to unite them for a better life."[38]

Marley's determination to perform despite the gunshot wounds and the ostensible assassination attempt on his life summoned an image of the mystical and righteous Rastafari. Playing songs about political violence, covert operations, love, and unity, the Smile Jamaica Concert amplified the growing perception that the Rastafari embodied some-thing special—a remedy for corruption, violence, exploitation, racial injustice, poverty, enmity, and so on. Marley performed his song "Rat Race," which with simplicity brilliantly distilled Jamaica's crises and the Rastafari promise:

> When the cat's away
> The mice will play
> Political violence fill ya city, yeah!
> Don't involve rasta in your say say
> I'm sayin'
> Rasta don't work for no CIA[39]

L.O.V.E. MEETS POLITICS

In April 1978, Bob Marley and the Wailers played the One Love Peace Concert in Kingston. "One Love," a Rastafari phrase, means unity. The One Love Peace Concert revisited the themes and urgencies that characterized the Smile Jamaica Concert. For one, the trends of 1976 persisted. The influence of the Rastafari on Jamaica's popular culture continued to wax. Both the political rivalry between the PNP and JLP and the lethal violence persisted, especially in Kingston. The number of gun charges such as firearm possession and "shooting with intent" surged from 304 in 1975 to 791 in 1976 to an astounding 1,960 in 1977, the year before the One Love Peace Concert.[40] In 1977, 409 civilians were murdered, compared to 367 in in 1976 and 226 in 1975.[41] Again, Marley played the uniter, demonstrating Rastafari L.O.V.E. (long, overflowing, virtuous, and eternal) that traced to their beginnings and to Leonard Howell in particular.

Two "area leaders," "Claudie" Massop and "Bucky" Marshall, militia marshals and organizers for the PNP and JLP, respectively, hatched the idea for a concert that would inspire unity (area leaders may be called "gun men," "bad man," or "dons" if they act as violent enforcers in their respective communities).[42] Massop and Marshall spearheaded violence ordered by party leaders toward the opposing party's constituents. The men recognized their role as pawns in party machinations and sought to extricate themselves from the political webs that entangled them. One step toward changing their relationship with politicians was pursuing "peace," showing their capacity to lead, and thus demonstrating the inadequacies of Jamaican politics.[43] Massop and Marshall believed that they needed Bob Marley—the Rastafari—for their plan to succeed. They grasped well how Marley and the Rastafari were becoming symbols of unity, peace, and love in Jamaica and abroad. The effect of the area leaders promoting unity in conjunction with the Rastafari and the Rastafari message is another signal element of this phase of Rastafari ethnogenesis. The combination indicated what was unimaginable to many Jamaicans: violent men seeking unity and peace and the Rastafari no longer persona non grata but Jamaica's potential salvation.

The One Love Peace Concert, convened April 22, 1978, was planned by organizers to acknowledge and commemorate Emperor Selassie's visit to Jamaica on April 21, 1966. Rastafari participation in the planning allowed them to advance their ideas of love and unity. The sacred crossed into the profane, with the Rastafari (at least those who were at ease with coordinating with Babylon) easing themselves and being eased into a cauldron of market calculations. For example, one could pay to sit in the "togetherness section" for $J2, the "love section" for $J5, or for $J10, the "peace section" of the One Love Peace Concert. The degree of expressed unity was defined by a fee; peace cost more than love. Nevertheless, the concert and its lofty themes fed hope for a turn to moral authority, a readiness of ordinary Jamaicans to do what politicians were unwilling to do: "It is a tribute to the Peace Movement that they [Marley and others] were able to achieve a successful and incident free celebration of such mammoth proportions with the theme of 'One Love.' It is an outstanding achievement that they were able to get Mr. Manley and Mr. Seaga to hold hands aloft in acknowledgment of the crowds' acclamation."[44]

The One Love Peace Concert was unforgettable because Marley (with the assistance of Massop and Marshall) negotiated to have the PNP and JLP party leaders, Michael Manley and Edward Seaga, appear onstage together as a display of unity. What both leaders did not anticipate was Marley forcing them to take a greater step: clasping their hands as a gesture of One Love. Bob said to the politicians, "[Let's] show the people we are gonna make it right, we've got to make it right. The moon is right over my head, and I give my love instead."[45] The crowd erupted into frenzy as Marley hoisted the hands of Manley and Seaga above his head. Neville Garrick, a Jamaican artist, photographer, and comrade of Bob Marley, likened Marley holding aloft Manley's and Seaga's hands to Jesus Christ on the cross sandwiched between two thieves.[46] Given Marley's music and influence, it is unsurprising that in Rastafari cosmology, he has been anointed a prophet. He pursued love and unity, and he became a major instrument dispersing the Rastafari message.

The influence of the Rastafari and the turbulence of Jamaica were on display for the world to see during the One Love Peace Concert (it was video- and audio-recorded). The influence of the Rastafari in their 1970s form showed in the identity of the performing artists and the songs they played—for instance, Culture's "Natty Take Over," Dennis Brown's "Children of Israel," Peter Tosh's "Get Up, Stand Up," Judy Mowatt's "Black Woman," John Dillinger's "The War Is Over," and Jacob Miller's "Peace Treaty." Except for Dillinger, all were Rastafari. In sum, the artists were saying that the Black children of Israel's (Rastafari's) time had come; they were taking their rightful and righteous place in Jamaican society, partially because they had stood up but also because others were acknowledging their capacity for witnessing for love and peace. The peace treaty (truce) between warring political factions was an iridescent example.

While the sense of unity would crumble after the One Love Peace Concert, some people who were close to the violence during the time believe that if not for the peace treaty, far more people, many of them innocent, would have died than the reported count of 381 murders for 1978. The Rastafari deserve credit for the outcome. The sway of the Rastafari continued in no small part because of reggae music and efficient vectors of dance halls, concerts, and recording media broadcasting their messages.

AFRICA UNITE: BOB MARLEY AND ZIMBABWE'S INDEPENDENCE

Bob Marley and the Wailers released the album *Survival* in 1979, a paean to African liberation, Pan-Africanism, and decolonization. *Survival* was the top album in Zimbabwe in April 1980. The colonial government banned the album, but it was reported to be a favorite of the Zimbabwe African National Union freedom fighters. Rastafari and reggae music manifested global impact by now. Both had captured the imagination of Africans interested in decolonization, independence, and Black pride. "Zimbabwe," one of the songs on the *Survival* album, demonstrates Marley's and the Rastafari's concern with the political struggles for decolonization and African sovereignty and the traps contained therein:

> To divide and rule could only tear us apart
> In everyman chest, there beats a heart.
> So soon we'll find out who is the real revolutionaries
> And I don't want my people to be tricked by mercenaries.
> Brother, you're right, you're right . . .
> We'll 'ave to fight (we gon' fight), we gonna fight (we gon' fight)
> . . . fighting for our rights![47]

The new nation of Zimbabwe (formerly Southern Rhodesia under British rule, then later Rhodesia after a revolt by the White minority) invited Bob Marley and the Wailers to play its official independence celebration in 1980. The celebration marked an end to the civil war in Rhodesia and to racial apartheid and European colonialism. Marley was so impassioned about the opportunity to perform at the independence celebration that he paid his own expenses because Zimbabwe was unable to do so. The independence celebration symbolized so much of what was important to the Rastafari of the 1970s: African liberation, Pan-Africanism, decolonization, dismantlement of White supremacy, and Black independence.

Marley was disappointed to learn that Zimbabwe's newly independent citizens and the Zimbabwe African National Union had not been invited to the official independence celebration. It was largely an affair for elites, nationals, and visitors. This led Marley to put on a second performance for the uninvited people. Such instances of inequity in African polities pressed Marley and many Rastafari to come to terms with postcolonial Africa (e.g., the proliferation of autocratic leadership and internecine strife), something absent in the pre-1970s Rastafari conceptions of Africa as a land of milk and honey.

The growing global presence of the Rastafari—as attested to by Marley and reggae music—made more urgent their need to pay attention to managing their own affairs in Jamaica and abroad. My field research and Rastafari organization meeting notes and correspondence show, for example, that by the early 1990s, Jamaican Rastafari were well aware of the necessity to prioritize promoting and defending their collective interests in a Jamaica and world that appropriated their culture while sidelining the foot soldiers who created and embodied that culture.[48] Yet Rastafari organization and organizing—unification—needed to occur in a context where they prized individuality and decentralization.

Unification and Fragmentation

Many critics, including Rastafari themselves, lament how contemporary Rastafari have a surfeit of individualism and an insufficiency of organization. They are divided and unable to unify. From the beginning, the Rastafari manifested tensions relating to intense individuality, forceful personalities, and collective organization. We can couple these tensions with a collective distrust of politics, organization, and "the system."

These tendencies grate against each other but do not completely grind down the collective Rastafari body.

Rastafari organizations are perpetually pitted against fragmentation because of the intense individuality of the Rastafari. The scholar and Rastafari Michael Barnett summarizes the matter: "Being Rasta means individual freedom of expression, with almost unlimited boundaries and few restrictions."[49] Given such radical freedom, organization is always tenuous and fragmentation always looming. Yet the decentralization that facilitates fragmentation has proven adaptive. As genetic and phenotypic diversity in a population enhances the ability of a population to endure harsh change, the individuality and reticulation of the Rastafari have abetted their survival in the face of systematic oppression, suppression, and repression. Organization and fragmentation are endemic to the Rastafari and unlikely to dissipate soon. These tendencies, though, are not unique to the Rastafari of Jamaica. Congregations may break into new sects or political parties into contending factions. Rastafari organizations commonly break apart only to reconstitute with a different configuration of people. Fissiparity may work against maintaining long-lasting organizations, but it does not mean the Rastafari are *unorganized*.

The Rastafari organization and organizing recounted in scholarship or news stories represent a fraction of what actually occurs. For example, Brother Yendis told me that during the 1970s he and a delegation of Rastafari visited several eastern Caribbean islands, St. Vincent being one of them, "sowing the gospel of Ras Tafari." In *Oba's Story: Rastafari, Purification and Power*, the Rastafari man Oba describes his encounter with visiting Jamaican Rastafari and how they encouraged him to promote and organize Rastafari in St. Vincent.[50] In St. Vincent, Barbados, and Guyana, Rastafari have been effective in winning concessions from their governments, such as land grants, subsidies for their organizations, or the decriminalization of cannabis. Perhaps long in coming, the Rastafari now have standing as a recognized religion in Jamaica, and cannabis is decriminalized. These reforms are fruit born of Rastafari labor, especially the political Rastafari and their pragmatic use of non-Rastafari support.

Organizing the Rastafari people beyond the established Mansions became the project of the Rastafari Federation (RF). Formed in 1995, the

Rastafari Federation, an organization of Rastafari organizations, formed out of the deliberation of many Rastafari Mansions over untold years, driven by their interest to unify and coordinate the Rastafari. Their mandate was to organize and centralize the many Rastafari groups to leverage their collective effort toward a joint agenda.[51] The RF recruited new member organizations, scheduled meetings, and organized demonstrations, rallies, celebrations, conventions, and conferences throughout Jamaica. The RF was an explicit intervention to counteract the proliferation of Rastafari acting on their own behalf—fragmentation. Unification and fragmentation tussle.

During the late 1990s, I joined cause with the RF, affording me first-hand experience of Rastafari organization and fragmentation.

The RF conceit was that any Rastafari agenda required an organized Rastafari front. Brother Yendis, a driving force of the RF, was known as a political Rastafari, meaning that he was not averse to engaging politicians or mainstream organizations if they supported Rastafari interests (Ras Sam Brown was also active in the RF). The RF used Euro-American forms of bureaucratic organization like the role hierarchies of president, vice president, secretary, and executive committee, rather than indigenous Rastafari organization built around charismatic leaders committed to their own version of Rastafari doctrine. The RF approach stirred up Rastafari's skepticism of organization, politics, and "the system," inciting anxieties of becoming corrupted by their enemy, Babylon.

During the late 1990s, the RF comprised roughly seventeen Rastafari Mansions from across the island. These organizations were diverse— remnants of Reverend Claudius Henry's community (the International Peacemakers); Nyabinghi Mansions from St. Thomas and Hanover Parishes; Ethiopian World Federation locals; and a Rastafari women's Mansion, Rasses International Sistren. Members paid dues to the RF; as members, they deliberated on goals and priorities such as purchasing a headquarters or working to decriminalize cannabis.

Maintaining a pan-Rastafari organization in Jamaica presented challenges. One was the diversity of participants. More than a few Rastafari were skeptical of empowering a central organization spearheaded by political Rastafari. Another issue, perhaps the most severe, was a dearth of money. Members and their Mansions were underresourced. Dues did not arrive on schedule. Sometimes members were unable to pay for trips to scheduled meetings. Needed equipment like a fax machine or computer could not be purchased. The RF did not own a building but rented from a private owner (albeit at reduced price). Eventually, the landlord decided to sell the building, notwithstanding the significant re-habilitation that the RF made to the formerly dilapidated structure and the tacit agreement that they ultimately would purchase it. Stricken by the pressure of acquiring new headquarters, maintaining membership, and continuing its business, the RF dissolved. It literally faded away, the mural-enshrined building falling silent and empty. Yet the work of the RF was not done. Brother Yendis and other Rastafari, some from the RF and some from new leadership and organizations, materialized into a new umbrella organization.

During the summer of 2007, I attended a planning meeting of a recently formed Rastafari group, at the time called the Rastafari Mil-lennium Council (RMC).[52] The members described themselves as an "interim organization" working to create a central council of Rastafari (with international representation). When the group assembled behind several rectangular tables laid end to end, in a drab, gray concrete room in a drab, gray concrete building in eastern Kingston, I saw faces familiar to me and many fresh faces. Brother Yendis was one of several Rastafari, male and female, who guided the dialogue. The RMC drew my atten-tion to the fluid nature of Rastafari organization. The RMC, I gathered, continued the work of the RF and headed in new directions. For one, it created a council of elders as the "head" of the organization, bringing it into closer alignment with indigenous Rastafari forms of organiza-tion. The RMC developed an explicit international orientation, intend-ing to represent the global Rastafari community. Members identified the need to protect their cultural heritage and intellectual property from commercial profiteers. They also formed a list of demands to present to the Jamaican government, reparations prominent among the demands. Their conception of reparations was sophisticated; it concerned not only slavery but also compensation for specific brutalities and damages, like the destruction of Pinnacle, the Coral Gardens Incident (1963), and the razing of the Rastafari stronghold Back-O-Wall in Kingston (1966). In 2008, Brother Yendis passed on. The RMC continued its work for many years but gradually attenuated. Many of the people involved in the RMC continue to be active in different capacities and organizations. The imagined global, diverse, long-lasting, centralized, and unified Rastafari organization remains an aspiration, and perhaps that is good in and of itself. It is an alluring idea, like repatriation, that impels the Rastafari to continue to mobilize, agitate, and pursue a Rastafari program that transcends the local concerns of Jamaican Rastafari.

* * *

Rastafari ethnogenesis has shown resilience in the face of major challenges. Consider their renewed status as a threat to Jamaican national security and an internal tendency toward fragmentation that scuffles with unity. Still, Rastafari magnetism and reach continued to grow between the 1960s and 1980s, propelled by the visit of Emperor Selassie to Jamaica and new vectors like art and reggae music. Still, growth and events beyond the control of the Rastafari invited new challenges.

10

New Challenges for the Rastafari

Assault on the House of David, Commodification of
Rastafari Culture, and Gender

By the early 1970s, Ethiopia's political economy was eroding; the 1973 oil embargo exacerbated a dismal situation. Perhaps most unsettling, a catastrophic famine struck Ethiopia in 1973. Simultaneously, the military grew restless, with renegades among the lower ranks demonstrating insubordination toward the higher ranks. Incursion followed incursion, each bolder and bolder. In 1974, Emperor Selassie cut short his participation in an Organization of African Unity conference after a dispute with Siad Barre of Somalia (the Organization of African Unity was a federation of African countries). Barre was trying to annex parts of Ethiopia populated by Somalis, which the Emperor rejected. He wanted a unified Ethiopia under his control, yet the nation was cracking apart.

What Happens If God Is Pronounced Dead?
The Shifting Fortune of Emperor Selassie

At the age of eighty-one, Selassie I had not named a successor. Crown Prince Asfaw-Wossen Tafari suffered a debilitating stroke in 1973, and Emperor Selassie did not select his daughter, Princess Tenagne-Work, as heir to the throne. Instead, the crown prince's son, Prince Zera-Yakob, a twenty-year-old Oxford student at the time, was named "acting heir apparent" in 1974.[1]

The overthrow of Emperor Selassie was not a single catalytic event, such as an audacious proclamation by a new regime or a parade of rebels storming the Jubilee Palace. The disjointed and unfolding revolution did not immediately appear as the machinations of a power-thirsty cabal. Framing the revolution as peaceful helps explain some of the Rastafari reactions to initial announcements of the coup: that it could not be a revolution because the Emperor remained in the palace.

Rastafari in Jamaica kept abreast of happenings in Ethiopia. Reports on the rising upheaval in Ethiopia were published in Jamaican newspapers. For instance, an editorialist observed how the "mood of rebellion among her [Ethiopia's] armed forces . . . [and] dissension among sections of the population . . . will most likely mark a major shift in the Ethiopian tradition of unquestioned political authority on the part of Emperor Hailed Selassie."[2]

The Rastafari Movement Association (RMA), a collective of politically savvy Rastafari, saw the invasion of the armed forces into the Jubilee Palace as instigating needed change in Ethiopia and its government. The RMA wrote, "[We] view the present situation in Ethiopia, our beloved country, [as] very interesting for us Ethiopians [i.e., Black people] to watch closely and to learn that our God and King is using the army to bring about radical changes within that country."[3] The RMA believed that it was "good for the army to lock up all of the men who were keeping the masses backward over the years": "We must learn that while we are here in Jamaica, wanting to go home, our brothers and sisters at home are demanding more freedom from their societies."[4] Rastafari like the RMA were confident that the Emperor—the divine superhero—was manipulating all of it. After all, the Emperor was unharmed, and the RMA noted that, for a revolution, up to that point no blood had been shed. They concluded that much of what was reported about Ethiopia was riddled with inaccuracies. The sign that something was remiss appeared around April 1974 in leaflets scattered across Addis Ababa, attributed to "elements of the military."[5]

The critics of the Rastafari were also interested in the unfolding events in Ethiopia, as the RMA recognized: "The Ethiopian situation meanwhile has given vent to the anti-Rastafarian feelings of many Jamaicans who are watching the situation closely and with great interest, hoping the developments will confound the arguments of the brethren."[6]

With hindsight, we know that the years 1973–74 were a tipping point preceding an explosive bifurcation—a qualitative change in Ethiopian governance. The Coordinating Committee of the Armed Forces, Police, and Territorial Army, better known as the "Derg," announced its presence and intention to take control of the Ethiopian government in June 1974. Mengistu Haile Mariam became the leader and face of the Derg and the leader and face of the terror that for nearly twenty years smothered Ethiopians in executions, torture, and political imprisonment. The Derg continued to arrest dignitaries. The dignitaries did not resist, and Emperor Selassie did not defend them. In August 1974, the Derg showed its military wares; tanks, trucks, and marching officers cavalcaded through Addis Ababa. It launched a smear campaign against the Emperor, accusing him of deserting Ethiopia when the Italians invaded in 1935, of pilfering the Ethiopian treasury, of causing the 1973 famine, and of holding lavish parties while Ethiopians lived in poverty or starved. The Emperor fiddled while Ethiopia burned was the picture painted by the Derg.

The Derg took the Emperor into their custody on September 12, 1974. The army marched the Emperor out of the former Jubilee Palace— renamed National Palace, Palace of the People—in plain sight, commandeering him into a Volkswagen Beetle that drove him to the headquarters of the Fourth Army Division, where he was held captive.[7] That same day, the Derg rescinded the constitution and disbanded Parliament. On November 23, 1974, sixty dignitaries and royals were executed.

Mariam terminated the monarchy early in 1975. The three-thousand-year reign of the House of David was toppled by the decree of a dictator. On August 28, 1975, the Derg announced that the Emperor had died the previous day of complications from an operation. The Emperor's physician and the abuna, the head of the Ethiopian Orthodox Church, were not allowed to see his body; the military did not allow an autopsy. Only the Emperor's closest servant claims to have seen the Emperor's corpse. Rumors abounded about what happened to the Emperor's body, but the Emperor's grandnephew Asfa-Wossen Asserate maintains that Mengistu had the Emperor buried under a floor in one of the Emperor's palaces.[8] Ras Kawintseb, an elder Rastafari and musician who repatriated from Trinidad to Ethiopia, identified a signal concern for the Rastafari regarding Emperor Selassie's disappearance: "The Derg *announced* that he had died. This is what we should say."[9] What the elder meant is that the evidence for the Emperor's death is sketchy.

The Divine Emperor Selassie I

In *Emperor Haile Selassie,* the African legal and governance scholar Bereket Selassie describes the factors that generated an image of the

Emperor as divine, an image that he himself helped create.[10] The *Kebra Negast*, an Ethiopian literary epic, chronicles the union of King Solomon and the Queen of Sheba, linking the Ethiopian monarchy to Christ. Emperor Selassie embraced this notion and defined himself as a part of King Solomon's lineage through Solomon's father, King David. King Ras Tafari, upon the death of Empress Zewditu (also known by the title "Queen of Kings," reigning 1916–30), released a proclamation, which read, in part, "Since it is the long-standing custom that when a King, the Shepherd of this people, shall die, a King replaces him, I being upon the seat of David to which I was betrothed, will, by God's charity, watch over you."[11] At age thirty-seven, King Ras Tafari became the Emperor of Ethiopia. By taking on his baptismal name Haile Selassie, the Holy Trinity, he signaled his unassailable godliness.

During the early 1930s, the birthplace of Emperor Selassie, Ejersa Goro, was "renamed Bet-Lehem."[12] King David was born and raised in the biblical Bethlehem. Bethlehem was the birthplace of Jesus Christ. Although it is unclear who made the decision to rename Ejersa Goro, the new name enabled the man who assumed the titles "Elect of God" and "Conquering Lion of the Tribe of Judah" to directly connect himself to Christ, a member of King David's lineage.

Article 4 of the revised constitution of Ethiopia described the Emperor as "inviolable": the "person of the Emperor is sacred." This language could encourage a notion of the Emperor as divine. And the Emperor did not contest this language. Why would he? To do so might lead people to contest the personage enshrined in the constitution and in historical lore. Through collective reasoning and narrative making, the Rastafari developed their own account of the sacrosanct status of the Emperor, without access to documents such as the Constitution of Ethiopia.

Once a community concludes that a savior is at hand or that doom is imminent, reason or counterevidence are unlikely to shake its convictions. If cataclysm or salvation fails to arrive at the appointed time, it may be postponed to a later date. If a Messiah falls short of divinity—say they die—a corpse may be insufficient to convince the faithful of the Messiah's mortality. In *When Prophecy Fails*, the psychologist Leon Festinger and his colleagues were among the first to demonstrate how people seek consistency in their beliefs even when it entails ignoring or recasting counter evidence.[13] Festinger and colleagues joined a group of unidentified flying object (UFO) believers who concluded that the world would end by flood in December 1954. The believers prepared themselves, although they determined that an alien-navigated UFO would rescue them from the catastrophic deluge before it happened. However, the flood never came, and neither did the UFO. The UFO group found a way out of their quandary: they concluded that they did such a good job of preparing for the end that neither the flood nor the UFO was necessary. The nucleus of the UFO group, Mrs. Marian Keech (a pseudonym), did not abandon her belief in alien intervention, and she and her husband continued to communicate with other alien believers and to reach out to entice new adherents, unsuccessfully, in the end.

Among the many views of the Rastafari on the Emperor as a deity, a prevalent one, drawing on Christianity's cultural resources, is that God twice visited Earth in mortal form: as Melchizedec (king and priest) and as Jesus Christ (priest of the Order of Melchizedec). Gnostic texts and Old Testament books such as Hebrews, Genesis, and Psalms link Melchizedec, King David, and Jesus Christ. Some Rastafari have taken these texts together to mean that Melchizedec and Christ are the same, with Christ being a reincarnation of Melchizedec. Revelations 5:5 says, "Weep not: behold, the Lion of the tribe of Judah, the Root of David, hath prevailed to open the book, and to loose the seven seals thereof." The Messiah would return to claim his rightful place as ruler of Earth. Thus, King Ras Tafari became Emperor Selassie I, the third mortal incarnation of God. The Rastafari developed a narrative that they expanded and revised continuously under conditions of persecution and ridicule. Their narrative and outsider reactions to them make Rastafari ethnogenesis possible and durable. Rastafari narratives produce meaningfulness that allows adherents to celebrate Blackness, faith, and being a unique community. The satisfaction derived from embracing the narrative as truth is rewarding enough to prompt adherents to revise the identity narrative in ways that allow them to hold onto their beliefs. The Rastafari are invested in their narrative.

Rastafari Reactions to the Announcement of Emperor Selassie's Death

The announcement that Emperor Selassie was dead—murdered—roused incredulity among both Rastafari and outsiders. For outsiders, it mostly was a matter of how Emperor Selassie's star sank so fast. For the Rastafari, it was a matter of whether God can die. Many Rastafari were quick to ask, "Where is the body if the Emperor is dead?" Perhaps the news was false, or perhaps it was a ploy to test the faithful. Nevertheless, the Rastafari had to confront the news, and they created a resolution. They had precedents.

The announcement of the Empress Menen's death in February 1962 led some Rastafari to defend their conception of ever-living life: "I Ras Shadrach, an inspired son of King Alpha [Emperor Selassie] and Queen Omega [Empress Menen], are the keepers of the tree of life. I know that many could not see the truth for they are spiritually blind. John was in the spirit on the last day and he heard a voice from Zion and this was what it said. 'I am Alpha and Omega the beginning and the end behold I live forever more.'"[14] The evaporation of breath from Empress Menen's body was unimportant to a Rastafari conception of eternal life. One does not worry about death because ever-living life is beyond the ken of most mortals, except for the enlightened Rastafari. Prince Shale Selassie died in April 1962 of liver and gastrointestinal problems along with pneumonia at the age of thirty-one.[15] The rapid succession of death in the royal family brought to the fore the view among some Rastafari that human life is meant to be eternal and that to die is a consequence of one's inability to elevate one's mind and body to a level beyond that of ordinary unenlightened mortals. However, the enlightened Rastafari presumed the Emperor and Empress, Alpha and Omega, respectively, to be masters of such elevation.

Through interviews and conversations with first- and second-generation Rastafari and through review of news stories and interviews of Rastafari conducted by others, I have concluded that the Rastafari addressed the announcement of the death of the Emperor in four ways, some of them overlapping. One was that God cannot die; another was that humans can never fully know the mysteries of God; a third was the claim that the crowning of the Emperor heralded that a new dispensation had begun, and the faithful had to continue to move forward in an environment of unknowns; and a less evident but contested view was to embrace a new narrative of the Emperor as great but not God. Each perspective expressed a means to reconcile dissonance between reports of the Emperor's death and faith in the Emperor as divine.

The death of Emperor Selassie had rattled Rastafari ethnogenesis and collective identity development without derailing it. New narratives were created to address the disruption. A new dynamic condition emerged, one in which self-identified Rastafari live with and create a position on the Emperor's immortality or mortality. Thus, this prospect has fostered further diversity and conflict among the Rastafari. Both collective identity formation and belief in the supernatural are not bound by the truth standards of Western science and logic. The fundamental contributions of identity and belief in the supernatural are the creation of community, the establishment of a way to anchor oneself in the world, the means to bond people together, and the generation of a malleable schema for making sense of the world.

Emperor Selassie's remains were exhumed in February 1992. Roughly twenty-five years after his death, the Emperor was formally buried in Addis Ababa in November 2000, but without a state burial. The family kept attendance at the funeral small. Rita Marley, the widow of Bob Marley, attended. Some Rastafari made the effort to attend the funeral, though without official invitation.

Many Rastafari, however, scoff at the claims that the remains are those of Emperor Selassie. They point out that no autopsy was performed, no forensic report, no DNA testing, no murderer fingered who could provide testimony about what transpired. Emperor Selassie's disappearance is a mystery. In this sense, accepting the death of the Emperor also requires faith without conclusive evidence.

Thus, cynical Rastafari do not find consolation in a funeral held for Emperor Selassie and a casket alleged to contain his remains lowered grudgingly into the earth (the casket would not fit into the grave, and masons had to be summoned to enlarge the pit). Ras Kawintseb sees it this way:

> So [for the Derg and others to] deny all of that [the history of Emperor Selassie's lineage], you would have to bring out the head of the man you just cut off . . . and show it to the nations that it is no longer a living roaring lion. . . . We have killed him. He doesn't exist anymore. . . . Just like they killed Christ. They did it publicly. And they humiliated him and put him [on a cross] to show that he couldn't be such a great God after all. "Look at what we can do to him."[16]

The announcement of the death of Emperor Selassie did not foreclose Rastafari belief in his divinity or, for some Rastafari, his greatness absent divinity. The crucifixion of Christ is perhaps the most substantial force of Christian ethnogenesis. The death of Christ is interpreted as Christ not dying in the common sense of death; the death of Christ signifies Christ becoming immortal. The Rastafari are different in that immortality is not only the province of the Emperor but also available to humans like the enlightened Rastafari. The announced death of Emperor Selassie did not lead to the demise of the Rastafari. Indeed, one can make the case that the influence and impact of the Rastafari continued to increase *after* the death of the Emperor.

The challenges to Rastafari identity did not abate during the 1980s into the 2000s. Indeed, during the postcolonial era, new challenges have arisen, one being control of one's image in a Jamaica structured by neoliberal capitalism.

Creeping Commercialization of Rastafari Identity and Culture

Jamaica had functioned as a tourist enclave for the wealthy since the 1930s, though tourism did not become a realistic source of revenue until the 1950s. By the late 1970s, both political parties and economic elites saw tourism as the foundation of Jamaica's economy. However, a development strategy of promoting sun, beaches, and natural beauty had limits because most Caribbean nations were doing the same thing. Jamaica needed additional enticements.

One lure was to tout reggae music. Reggae was known best for its association with the Rastafari. Thus, to peddle reggae as a tourist attraction meant that by default the Rastafari would also be peddled.[17] This took policy form by 1982 as the Jamaica Tourist Board began to promote vacation packages that included reggae. The selling of reggae and Rastafari began in earnest during the late 1970s. This became an integral part of "Brand Jamaica." As a respondent said in a research interview about tourism, "Bob Marley put us on the map."[18] Marley's song "One Love," for example, was destabilized as a message for Jamaicans to resist violence and division and reinscribed as a generic jingle used to sell tourism and groceries. The Rastafari as a race-conscious religion and social movement were unwelcome realities for the capitalist conception of Rastafari as fun and cool.

The Jamaican Tourist Board and Jamaica Information Service continue to promote reggae and concert packages but are less explicit these days in promoting the Rastafari. They are not currently promoting cannabis, though it was decriminalized in Jamaica in 2015. Nevertheless, the Rastafari and cannabis remain strong attractions for Jamaican tourists. Despite Jamaica's reputation as a cannabis mecca, its emergent cannabis industry must compete against a much larger and well-funded cannabis industry in the United States and in the Netherlands.

Rastafari in Pursuit of Community Development

In a tourist-driven environment of unfiltered neoliberal capitalism, the Rastafari have adapted. For these and other reasons, many Rastafari are less reluctant to engage Babylon. This is not to say that the Rastafari have capitulated. Ethnogenesis involves change, internal and external to groups. We should expect adaptation. One change is that some Rastafari are active in managing their identity, the brand Rastafari, but not so much as a base commodity but rather akin to treasures in a museum. One pays a fee to enjoy the experience, but one can only take away the experience, not the treasure itself. One example of this is the Rastafari Indigenous Village in Montego Bay, Jamaica.

Billed as a living cultural center, the Rastafari Indigenous Village offers visitors an opportunity to learn about Rastafari Livity (righteous life force), culture, and history.[19] The village seeks to carve out a slice of the Jamaican tourist market interested in experiencing Rastafari culture and history. It symbolizes the effort by Jamaican Rastafari to wield control over Rastafari identity and culture. Yet, without careful management, introducing people into one's community and cultural heritage runs the risk of turning both into a commodity. Labeled "community tourism," the village operates on the idea that a Rastafari community can create a source of revenue from visitors who come to learn about their community and culture. The village offers nature tours, lectures (on Rastafari philosophy, culture, and history), Rastafari cuisine, a gift shop, and performances of Rastafari rituals such as drumming or chanting, for a fee. Authorities tout community tourism as sustainable tourism because people do not have to leave their communities to make a living. Yet the village entrepreneurs have developed a strategy that implicates them in the very system that many of their antecedent Rastafari rejected or at least strongly critiqued.

The National Heritage Trust of Jamaica emphasizes national history and national pride. However, the National Trust has been reluctant to add the Rastafari to its catalogue of national treasures. The Rastafari must continue to valorize their culture and identity themselves, as they have done in the past. However, the post-1980s era poses new challenges. Speaking generally, the Rastafari do not face severe systemic oppression comparable to before the 1980s. Many of the vectors and causes that propelled Rastafari ethnogenesis for decades, such as repatriation or reggae music, to offer two examples, over time have become enfeebled. They are no longer sources of significant growth. If we conjoin the shifting vectors with an unbridled capitalism, then we must consider the consequences of Rastafari culture and identity existing as a commodity that eludes the control of the Rastafari themselves.

An Existential Threat: Rastafari Identity and Cultural Appropriation

I have asked both first- and second-generation Rastafari about the popularity of Rastafari culture, such as people who wear dreadlocks but are not Rastafari. Many of these Rastafari saw it as confirmation of their faith that people were adopting their practices, practices reviled by outsiders for decades. Some, however, saw such appropriation as blasphemous and disrespectful. Generally, the older the Rastafari, the more likely they were to see cultural appropriation as vindication of their faith. When I put the question to third- and fourth-generation Rastafari, I usually got a different response. These younger Rastafari tended to point out the many commercial, Jamaican government, and other interests profiting from Rastafari identity and in Jamaica treating it like a national trademark without the Rastafari themselves benefiting. The extensive presence of Rastafari culture among non-Rastafari in Jamaica and beyond looks to me more like blasphemy than blessing.

How is it that the Rastafari were turned into the very things they have resisted and critiqued? This is a pattern of the post-1970s era that has become ever more complex. For example, why would one impersonate a Rastafari or use one's Rastafari identity to obtain sexual or material favors? The prospect of such behavior implies that Rastafari harbor a powerful attraction for people who are not Rastafari.

Commodity Rastafari: Rent-a-Dread

The attorney and journalist Suzann Dodd put her fingers on the pulse of a new development among the Rastafari during the late 1980s. In a tongue-in-cheek column, Dodd described the phenomena of the "Rent-a-Dread" in Jamaica (or in Patois, "Renta"):

> It is not that difficult to tell Renta from a Rasta. Rentas usually wear a sapsy smile, affect an American accent and are always opportuning. The man sitting on the wall in front of a hotel is most likely a Renta. The dreadlocks calling "Hi Baby!" is a Renta. Never confuse a Renta with a Rasta. . . . If he sees you and gives you a smile and starts the chat, he is most likely a Renta. If he turns and glares, he is a Rasta. . . . It has become the norm for female Yuppies to attend Sunsplash [reggae concert] with a dread in tow. . . . So great is this demand that many young men have begun to grow locks to cash in on this opportunity.[20]

Reggae music did more than spread the Rastafari message. In a low-wealth nation dependent on tourism, it provided a milieu for Rastafari to become a commodity. It was beyond the sale of records and concert performances. An unanticipated blending of reggae, cannabis, and Jamaican culture and history fueled a Rastafari mystique that brought people both to Jamaica and to the Rastafari. The Rastafari man as an icon of self-confidence, natural living, righteousness, and organic philosophy appealed especially to foreign women.

Foreign women, mainly but not solely White, see in Jamaican men an opportunity to attend to their desires, to initiate a relationship that they believe they control, to satiate fantasies involving Black men (of less wealth), or to be the center of attention in ways they do not experience at home. Certainly, some foreign women are serious in their pursuit of romance, while others are frivolous fling-seekers. The Jamaican man has other motivations. He may need money to eat or to feed his people;

he too may want romance that he believes he cannot get at home. But let us separate Jamaican men from Rastafari men. The Rastafari man is distinguished from other Jamaican men by his faith, his dreadlocks, and his way of being in the world. Ideologically, a Rastafari man should oppose a relationship based in materialism and unfettered sexuality. Consequently, the Rent-a-Dread has a dilemma that does not trouble non-Rastafari Jamaican men. He is seen as a hustler, gigolo, or traitor to the Rastafari faith. He must defend or disguise his behavior to the Jamaicans who hold such a view. The Rent-a-Dread (a.k.a. Rent-a-Rasta) became a subindustry of tourism in Jamaica.

A Rastafari or a Rastafari impersonator plays the role of cultural liaison and escort, and the foreign woman plays the role of culturally interested financier of the transaction that might turn into a relationship. The ethnographers Deborah Pruitt and Suzanne LaFont have analyzed this phenomenon: "Since the 70s, young men living in the tourism areas who grew their hair in dreadlocks have attracted special attention from foreigners in general and women in particular. Therefore, those men interested in trading with foreigners, whether selling handicrafts, or marijuana, . . . or generally acting as companions to ease the way for foreigners through the largely informal society, have increasingly styled themselves as Rastafarian. They 'locks' their hair, speak in the Rasta dialect, and develop a presentation that expresses the Rastafarian emphasis on simplicity and living in harmony with nature, in effect, constructing a 'staged authenticity.'"[21]

Nonetheless, the Renta phenomena (both Rastafari impersonators and Rastafari)—a commodification of Rastafari culture—exemplifies the popularity and allure of Rastafari identity and culture. It is not a blessing in the way that some Rastafari see reggae as spreading their message. The Rent-a-Dread phenomena is not limited to Jamaica. One can find it in other Caribbean islands where there is a strong Rastafari presence, such as Dominica, or in the United States, where reggae events are popular.

The Rent-a-Dread is a hustle that *promises* more than a straightforward hustle. It promises *satisfaction* to both parties. The promises are complex because they play out in a larger environment where not everyone is okay with men affecting Rastafari identity for their own material and sensual purposes or with foreign women cherry-picking Jamaican men. In essence, the Renta has misrepresented his sales good. He is not tacking true to the sense of righteousness of the Rastafari with his representation; he is seeking personal gain from a collective good to which his claims may be dubious. Even if the man identifies as a genuine Rastafari, he is pursuing materialism and carnal motivations, which are at odds with Rastafari ideology. He is also making things difficult for the other, genuine Rastafari who do not share his motives. Foreigners may assume that the Renta is a likeness of the genuine Rastafari. The Renta, whether naked impersonator or Rastafari at heart, knows that the genuine Rastafari frown on his practice. Yet the practice continues because it promises remuneration and opportunity.

The Renta is only one instance of how complex Rastafari identity has become. In this instance, Rastafari identity complicates the norms and taboos of race and class in ways that the Rastafari never imagined, until it happened. The White woman, for example, now purchases sex from a less wealthy Black man. The Rastafari are being represented in ways at odds with their hard-earned identity as paragons of Blackness, righteousness, and adherence to Emperor Selassie. The Renta phenomenon shows how in a capitalist world, one's collective identity is at risk of becoming a commodity that does not benefit the bearers of the collective identity.

Patrick Cariou v. Richard Prince: *The Sacred Has No Protection from the Profane—Do the Rastafari Have a Right to Protect Their Image?*

To become popular in a capitalist world is to court co-optation. For collective identity, exoticness can translate into co-optation. One of the effects of co-optation on group identity, as suggested by the Renta phenomenon, is that a people who become popular are at risk of losing control over their culture and identity because it becomes a source of material currency in the form of money. Co-optation, as I see it, is cultural appropriation that is inconsistent with, if not antagonistic toward, the appropriated culture and identity; it implies that the co-opted culture and identity is hijacked without the active oversight of the co-opted. The indigenous peoples of the United States and other nations are a prime example. So too are the Rastafari.

Imagine a black-and-white photograph of a real Rastafari man—shirtless, slender, muscular body; heavy dreadlocked beard; his head laden with knee-length dreadlocks. He stands straight, clad in gym shorts and calf-length rubber boots, his deep-set eyes staring pensively at something the viewer cannot see. Lush but blurred tropical brush constitutes the backdrop. It is a striking image that would cause one to pause and closely examine the portrait. The photograph is one of numerous striking portraits of rural Jamaicans, most of them dreadlocked Rastafari, that grace the pages of Patrick Cariou's book of photographs *Yes Rasta* (2000). Cariou, a native of France, lived among these Rastafari to gain their trust and respect, to photograph them in their natural state, as it were. Seven thousand copies of *Yes Rasta* were printed. Cariou sold a few of the photographs to people he knew well, but he did not sell them commercially. (I do not know whether Cariou shared any of his proceeds with his artistic subjects.)

Now, imagine the same portrait, the same man, but the Rastafari man's hand now holds a superimposed electric guitar, his face covered with a ghastly white mask; he sports clunky tennis-shoe-like boots instead of his rubber boots. To his right is a nude, dark-skinned woman wearing locks and what could be white boots. Her dark body is bent forward exposing her buttocks, her left breast jutting outward; her left hand rests naughtily on the left side of her buttocks. Further to the man's right is another imposing dreadlocked Rastafari man with a menacing skeletal grimace. To the same dreadlocked man's far right is a nude woman, breasts pendulous, reaching out with an ashen hand and malformed right foot. To the man's left is another nude woman. This woman, phenotypically White, is frozen into an unnatural pose, weighted down by gargantuan feet. This collage is titled "Specially Round Midnight."

Imagine another collage, "Cheese and Crackers," with the same dreadlocked Rastafari man. In this one, he has distorted hands and feet. He is sandwiched on his right by a woman with her legs spread and vaginal region exposed, her face a lurid caricature of a human face, her right hand deformed. To the left of the Rastafari man is another nude woman, stomach down, in a contorted pose, a deformed foot contorted toward her head. Her breasts hanging, the woman extends an arm that possesses a misshapen hand, with open palm and spread fingers, as if imploring someone for alms. Ben Mauk, a *New Yorker* writer, asked the rhetorical question, which he did not answer, "Who owns this image?"[22]

The two collages are the work of the appropriation artist Richard Prince. Prince is an internationally recognized artist, renowned for appropriating the work of other artists without permission, for his own purposes. Prince takes images that he likes and twists them to reflect his own agenda. In 2005, Prince came across *Yes Rasta* in St. Barts. He must have been impressed by the images because he ripped thirty-five pages out of *Yes Rasta*, attached them to a board, and thus formed one of his first installations.[23] The *Yes Rasta* originals then became the centerpiece of an exhibition called *Canal Zone* that debuted in 2007 in St. Barts and then exhibited in New York City in 2008. *Canal Zone* consisted of thirty-five "adaptations" of *Yes Rasta* images. Adaptation here is questionable if it means revision with express purpose. Prince painted blots over the mouths and faces of Cariou's interlocutors, superimposed grotesque appendages, and inserted crude violence with images of nude women. He sold the Cariou-based images for thousands of dollars, inviting rich celebrities like the football player Tom Brady and the musical performers Jay-Z and Beyonce Knowles to his *Canal Zone* exhibition. Prince commanded more than $10 million for the *Canal Zone* images and another $8 million in swaps for other artworks. He did not seek Cariou's permission to use the images. Neither Cariou nor the subjects of Cariou's photographs benefited from the largesse Prince generated. As of 2010, Cariou had made only $8,000 off *Yes Rasta*, with 5,791 of 7,000 printed books sold.[24]

Cariou discovered Prince's work and sued for copyright infringement. In 2011, the US District Court for the Southern District of New York heard the case, determining that Prince had infringed on Cariou's copyright of the *Yes Rasta* photographs.[25] The court acknowledged that an artist can use the work of others under specific circumstances—teaching, reporting, criticism, scholarship, research, and commentary—that benefit public or commercial interests. For instance, a professor could use the *Yes Rasta* images for a course or a scholarly publication. Or a journalist might write a story that uses the photographs. Copyright law requires permission and a payment of a fraction of any proceeds that exceed a determined amount of use.

One can legally use the work of others if one adequately revises it so that the revision is "transformative" enough to create new meaning that distinguishes it from the original. The district court determined that Prince's superimpositions were insufficiently transformative of the originals: "The Court finds that Cariou's Photos are highly original and creative artistic works and that they constitute 'creative expression for public dissemination' and thus 'fall within the core of the copyright's protective purposes. . . . Consequently, this factor weighs against a finding of fair use.'"[26] The district court instructed Prince and Gagosian Gallery to turn the installation over to Cariou for disposal (as he saw fit). No monetary or damage compensation was awarded. Prince and his partners appealed.

Prince the appropriator needed a defense. He turned to "fair use." The fair use clause of the 1976 copyright law establishes that one may use the work of another, as a secondary use, if certain conditions are met regarding "the nature of the original copyrighted work, the extent of the original work used, whether the secondary use is commercial or noncommercial, and whether the secondary use replaces the market for the original."[27] While the district court found that Prince's creative contribution was "slight," the appellate court concluded that Prince's alterations were transformative even if they were "jarring," "crude," or "provocative," which in the court's estimate made his art transformative. Other indicators of transformative effect were the large size of the installations (one was roughly eight feet in length), compared to the coffee-table-book-sized pages of Yes Rasta. Another was that the artists pursued different markets. Cariou was not profit driven, and thus his market was not in competition with Prince's market, people who would pay hundreds of thousands for his artwork.

Cariou v. Prince raises an important question: Did Prince defile the Rastafari in his artistic appropriation? A related concern is whether artists and commercial interests should have a responsibility to respect the cultural integrity of people they represent in their work. These questions are challenging because in the United States, artists are allowed freedom of creative expression, protected by law. My rendition or use of your culture may violate your cultural mores, but I have a right to do so. This right is unbalanced because well-resourced entities like corporations have the ability to contest uses of what they copyright, whereas underresourced entities like the Rastafari—or indigenous people—struggle to control and defend how outsiders represent them. Contemplate, for example, how Native Americans have been used as coarse logos for sports teams like the Cleveland Indians or the Washington Redskins or how sacred headdresses become Halloween costumes. The Rastafari face a similar challenge, for example, with dreadlocked wigs, stuffed Rastafari toys, or Rastafari likenesses used to appeal to tourists.

Prince's alterations to Cariou's photographs were cosmetic and not transformative. He daubed paint here and there and superimposed guitars and pornographic images on the originals. My impression of Prince's ghoulish art was that he had conjoined the sacred and the profane. The Rastafari man is the natural mystic, surrounded by pornography. Prince said in his district court deposition that he was uninterested in the message of the original works and that he did not "really have a message" of his own. Two of the three appellate court judges decided that the "lozenges" (blots) that Prince emblazoned on the faces of the characters made them look "anonymous" and that the superimposed grotesque appendages and guitars made them look "not quite human." These, for the judges, constituted a transformation of the artwork. "Anonymous" and "not quite human" are the antithesis of the Rastafari identity project, a theology of humanizing Blackness, Africanness, and the stance of Black people toward each other and toward nature. Prince's collages do not say more than, "Look at me and wonder what you see."

Neither the district nor appellate court addressed cultural integrity or cultural representation in their opinions. This is instructive for Jamaica's Rastafari. The appellate court decision is problematic because it has increased the realm of possible invocations of fair use now that the law does not expect a secondary use to make commentary. This, in turn, increases the challenge of the Rastafari to protect their cultural products, heritage, and integrity. The cultural products—art, song, symbols, intellectual property, and whatever else—cannot be guaranteed protection by copyright law from exploitation because one can claim fair use. While this is the case in the United States for certain, it also has implications for Jamaica. Jamaica's Copyright Act of 1993 has not afforded the Rastafari protection of their cultural resources. There remains the possibility that outsiders will derive greater benefit from the original Rastafari products than the Rastafari themselves do. And so far, the Rastafari have not found a way to use the law in their favor. There is a struggle over Rastafari collective identity, between appropriators and appropriated.

Richard Chused, a professor of law and an authority on copyright law, was disturbed by the findings of the appellate court in this case. In an email conversation with me, he wrote, "My proposition is that copyright law does not take into account the impact of potential infringements on parties NOT involved in the litigation. . . . In this case, the dispute was between Cariou, the photographer, and Prince the artist. The Rastafarians were irrelevant for legal purposes. . . . In the Rastafarian case, I'm interested in the potential harm that Prince might have caused them. . . . The harm may exist independently of their knowledge."[28] Chused has elaborated this point in an article: "It is clear that Prince's reconstruction of Cariou's images was highly antithetical to the basic beliefs of the community—the centrality of blackness, the largely male dominated character of the society and the declination to circulate widely in white culture, the refusal to parade oneself among nude, especially female, figures, and the distinctly regal, confident quality of the people portrayed in Cariou's *Yes, Rasta*."[29] Chused believes that to gauge potential harm to the Rastafari, one should know about the "culture of the rural members of the Rasta community relevant to a case like this, their belief structure, the nature of any of their privacy concerns and the causes for them, and any other issues that publication of the images might cause."[30]

The judges did not discuss the people who were the basis of *Yes Rasta*, a faith community that finds abhorrent the images that Prince rendered casually. In a cursory probe, I showed Prince's images of the aforementioned Rastafari man or explained it in detail to several male and female Rastafari, and to a person, they all recoiled in disgust. They concluded that Prince's work is criminal, yet it is legal, upheld by leading courts and jurists. Do subjects like the Rastafari have a right to contest their representation? Perhaps, but this is a struggle that has yet to be waged in Jamaica in a way that casts into relief the obstacles and opportunities. Jamaican copyright law is similarly inclined to favor powerful interests— tourism and government—in matters of cultural integrity and cultural representation. What can the Rastafari do to protect their cultural integrity and cultural representation in a world inclined toward favoring commercial interests?

The Rastafari might learn from the experience of Native Americans in the United States and Canada who are clawing back some authority over their cultural integrity and cultural representation. Native Americans have the status of recognition as sovereign nations, though this recognition is severely circumscribed to federal recognition, reservations, and subject to legal whim, thus leaving many legitimate Native American groups unrecognized. Attaining sovereign status is unlikely for Jamaica's Rastafari. Nevertheless, some Rastafari have taken it upon themselves to pursue indigenous people status in Jamaica. They appeal for recognition as a religion, and now they have that status. Recognition is a sine qua non for protecting cultural integrity and cultural representation in the contemporary capitalist world system.[31] Third- and fourth-generation Rastafari are more comfortable engaging government—Babylon—their spiritual and ideological enemy. They have precedents set in motion by their elders, those Rastafari of the 1960s who pursued Ethiopian nationality and renouncement of Jamaican nationality and who looked to the United Nations and its human-rights declaration. And they have organizations like the Rastafari Millennium Council that are willing to tackle these concerns but remain hampered by a lack of financial resources.

Another new post-1980 challenge for the Rastafari involves Rastafari women reframing gender relations. This challenge differs from the questions posed by the end of the House of David or the commodification of Rastafari because it is a matter generated by the Rastafari themselves rather than external intrusion. Though it is important not to censure Rastafari men or Rastafari gendered notions of culture, it is useful to trace how gender relations are shifting.

The Two Must Become One: Rastafari Women's Shifting Views on Gender

In late 1998, I met and interviewed Sister Emm, a Rastafari woman of slender build with a licorice skin tone, a third-generation devotee who became Rastafari during the mid-1970s. She lived in Kingston in a hardscrabble section of a community called Southside. Warm, generous, and industrious, with a stern visage, Sister Emm had a no-nonsense attitude. She had no patience for witlessness. I would stop and talk with her while she was out marketing crafts and produce. I asked her about male-female (gender) relations among the Rastafari in Jamaica, and it turned out to be something about which she had given deep thought. During our talks, she repeated a version of "Dem man take woman fe something less than dem." She observed how men behaved as if their interests were more important than women's interests simply by virtue of their being male. She radiated confidence in her capacity as a Rastafari woman and as a human being to be independent and to care for people: "From I a trod [i.e., grew up carrying a burden], I did have the power [just] like the man because you see . . . I never know the Father [Emperor Selassie is called "Father" by male and female Rastafari] through no man, but through Himself. . . . Everyone of I n I [we] have a power, as a people, from you born you get that power. 'Cause from I a baby, my [paternal] father say I a ruler because . . . I can take care of everyone." Sister Emm was not an outlier among the Rastafari women in my Jamaican network with regard to her sense of being a self-governing Rastafari woman critical of Rastafari gender ideology. The octogenarian Rasta Ivey told me several times, "Dem man get vex wid me." What she meant was that Rastafari men did not welcome her questioning of male prerogatives. Neither Rasta Ivey nor Sister Emm, women of different generations, tolerated a patriarchy that required subservience. They decried how a movement pursuing Black liberation and redemption would consign its own Black women to a subordinate status. As a first-generation Rastafari, Rasta Ivey witnessed the rise of the patriarchal hegemony that would characterize the Dreadlocks, while Sister Emm was socialized into gendered notions that downplayed any questioning of cultural proscriptions that privileged male interests and delimited female pursuits.

In the book of Genesis, an omniscient narrator describes how God created man and woman:

> But for Adam there was not found an help meet for him [i.e., a worthy helper]. And the Lord God caused a deep sleep to fall upon Adam. . . . He took one of his ribs, and closed up the flesh. . . . And the rib, which the Lord God had taken from man, made he a woman, and brought her unto the man. And Adam said, "This is now bone of my bones, and flesh of my flesh: she shall be called Woman, because she was taken out of Man. Therefore shall a man leave his father and his mother, and shall cleave unto his wife: and they shall be one flesh."[32]

Many Rastafari, especially the older male Rastafari, interpret this narrative literally—that woman was born of man's body, designed to be his helper, to provide him company. This notion, however, is losing currency, while the idea of a man cleaving unto his wife, the two creating a balance permitting them to act as one, is gaining interest among Rastafari women in Jamaica and beyond.

A patriarchal culture in a patriarchal nation, Jamaican Rastafari emphasize the masculinity of Emperor Selassie, the man and the father as the head of the family, and the man as leader in central matters of the faith and its major rituals. Women are subject to the guidance and supervision of men. Second-generation Rastafari like the Dreadlocks saw themselves as imposing a strict gendered interpretation of scripture, an approach that the first generation did not take. (More than a few of these second-generation Rastafari men submitted themselves to celibacy for years, seeing women as a distraction from their pursuit of godliness.) Nevertheless, there have always been Rastafari women and women of other faiths in Jamaica who contest such proscriptions. In addition to Rasta Ivey and Sister Emm, we may recall the Revivalist Annie Harvey, a woman spiritual leader who was self-assured in her capabilities, irrespective of strictures that demanded that women—presumably lurking in the background—do not preach, do not administer the holiest rituals, and do not contest male leaders.

Scholarship has amplified Rastafari conceptions of gender. Most Rastafari researchers have been men, and they have bestowed a preponderance of attention on male Rastafari. Much of what we know about Rastafari women has come from female researchers and Rastafari women themselves.[33]

Rastafari women's position on patriarchy is complex. Some women accept the patriarchal dimensions of the faith, grounding their view in a literal interpretation of scripture, such as the Apostle Paul's rebuke, "Let your women keep silence in the churches. . . . They are commanded to be under obedience as also saith the law. . . . If they will learn anything, let them ask their husbands at home: for it is a shame for women to speak in the church."[34] Rastafari use passages like this to justify a view that women should keep silent during assemblies and seek tutelage from their men. For some women, not all aspects of Rastafari patriarchy are objectionable. Some may subscribe to the notions that men are the head of the family and that males and females have different roles, yet they insist on equality and equity.

Returning to Genesis 2, Rastafari woman are developing the idea of male and female Rastafari constituting a balance that makes them equals. Male and female Rastafari each bring something to the union that can create a balance—not a prescription etched in ideology but emergent in the connections of Rastafari male and female relationships. The Rastafari scholar Shamara Alhassan makes this point: "Rastafari woman's notion of balance . . . denotes the equity and synchronicity between masculine and feminine energies. Both sistren and brethren have equal roles to play in the fight for Black liberation, and it is only through balance between them that this can be achieved."[35]

Since at least the early 1980s, women Rastafari have been expanding their spheres of influence and questioning some of Rastafari's gendered practices. Women Rastafari are organizing their own associations and conferences and are calling out the unilateral standard of the Rastafari man as the embodiment of righteousness and critic of injustice. Rastafari women are pointing out that the achievements of the Rastafari would be naught without their contributions: caring for children, provisioning meetings and rituals, providing organizational support as secretaries and repositories of culture such as Rastafari chants (hymns).

Women's movements have influenced Rastafari women's consciousness about rights, equity, and justice in relation to men. The influence does not mean, however, that Rastafari women's concerns exactly mirror the concerns of some non-Rastafari women. For example, this evolving Rastafari perspective among women does not reject gendered differentiation in roles but insists on treating gendered differences as complementary rather than allowing for exclusion or suppression. Today, Rastafari women pursue a range of opportunities that were unavailable to most of them forty years ago. Rastafari peasant origins continue to shape their views; however, during the past forty years, Jamaica and the Rastafari have changed. Rastafari women are now accomplished artists, authors, teachers, professors, organizers, and entrepreneurs. Those women who became Rastafari after the mid-1970s have developed in an environment where women's subjugation is increasingly challenged as unacceptable, in turn challenging the beliefs of preceding generations. Women Rastafari are gaining prominence in Rastafari affairs. This shift in Rastafari gender dynamics—a "matriarchal shift," as the educator and Rastafari scholar Deena-Marie Beresford calls this repositioning—is a source of new ideas and practices that may exert growing influence on Rastafari ethnogenesis in the twenty-first century.[36] How Rastafari men address the concerns raised by women remains to be seen, though both the RF and the RMC have shown an openness to prominently positioning Rastafari women.

* * *

Social change confronts any collectivity in ways that force it to react, and if it is to survive, it must adapt. Change and adaptation are fundamental aspects of ethnogenesis. What we want to identify is how collectivities respond. Resilient collectivities adapt and create a justification for their response. Emperor Selassie's disappearance did not obstruct Rastafari ethnogenesis in Jamaica; neither has a rampant capitalism that makes possible the commodification of their identity. The Rastafari are on their heels for now, seeking to manage their identity in ways that are beneficial to them. Internally, the growing international concern over eradicating women's oppression has not bypassed the Rastafari. Rastafari women are questioning Rastafari gender practices, both reacting to change and instigating it. The Rastafari of Jamaica remain resilient, with challenges spurring persistence.

Conclusion

So-called mainstream religions have had hundreds of years
to develop, evolve, branch off into sects, and adapt to soci-
etal changes. The propensity of some researchers of Rastafari
to demand an immediate and "systematic theology" . . . from
Rastafari is both misplaced and unfair.
—Monique Bedasse, "Rasta Evolution"

The Rastafari of Jamaica are at a crossroad. I have heard this trope
repeated over the past twenty-five years by academics, pundits, and lay-
people alike. By "crossroad," they mean that the Rastafari are at a critical
point in their development, that there are decisions they must make, and
that any change in the state of the crossroad or any decisions made will
be far-reaching. The Rastafari, however, are not actually at a crossroad.
If they are at a crossroad now, then they have been at one or another
crossroad since 1933. What may happen is what has happened since 1933.
A group or configuration of Rastafari takes an action or is the subject
of an action that has implications for all Jamaican Rastafari, as well as
for many non-Rastafari Jamaicans. Consider, for example, the effect of
Reverend Claudius Henry's decision to challenge Jamaica's government
or the results of a handful of Rastafari in Coral Gardens in April 1963
deciding to pursue revenge against their offenders. Or the Rastafari
could surprise everyone, again, persisting, say, because of women Rastafari gaining prominence. The past has always happened, we are always
in the present, and the future never comes. Thus, it is not possible to
describe the future of the Rastafari. But we can know about Rastafari
ethnogenesis on the basis of the past and the present.

This book has asked, How did the Rastafari grow from a scattering
of people into a diverse community and identity that altered Jamaican's
understanding of race, nationality, and religion? By answering this question, we have gained understanding of how a group forms and evolves

under conditions of duress, what factors were involved, and what happens if the pressure lessens.

While this book is about the Rastafari, it is also about ethnogenesis and collective identity formation. It has advanced five propositions that ought to inform an ethnogenetic account: power asymmetries; nonlinearity; engines of growth (e.g., vectors); nonmembers; and mobilization of resources. These factors and others interact to generate emergence in a way that is far greater than any single factor alone could have done. We see these factors, for example, in exchanges between the colonizers and non-White colonial subjects; unpredictable outcomes and unanticipated disruptions that have substantial consequences; vectors that feed Rastafari growth and resilience; and cultural resources, both repackaged and entirely novel. I have made the case that ethnogenesis entails collective identity formation. The two operate in tandem; a group's evolution shapes its sense of collective identity. Both ethnogenesis and collective identity formation beg for an analysis that is sensitive to complexity and to qualitative detail.

Human behavior in the "real" world does not exhibit the neat boundaries that can be created in an experiment or under controlled and thus *unnatural* conditions. By establishing initial conditions, we can begin to grasp the *range* of factors and the interaction of these factors that help to explain the people we are interested in, whether living or vanished. We must think about and begin to deal with the process of emergence: how something novel is generated out of the interaction of multiple elements or factors.

I have argued that the growth and entrenchment of the Rastafari in Jamaica owes to the pervasive efforts to oppress, suppress, and repress them, in concert with vectors capable of spreading their beliefs. Rastafari ideology and identity encapsulate powerful messages about faith, race, history, and ethical practice (e.g., L.O.V.E.), appealing to people who recognize that they have been miseducated about these very things or who seek to embody these things.

As this book has established, ethnogenesis is a promising approach to collective identity formation. I have shown how the Rastafari draw on cultural resources and movements of the past while remaking them for their own purposes. The Black rebel leader Paul Bogle, the Revival preacher Alexander Bedward, Ethiopianists interested in Ethiopia, the race man Marcus Garvey, and more, created and repurposed cultural substrates of their time and in turn created cultural substrates that offer cultural resources available to those who would use them.

Analysis of ethnogenesis may require evidence that is often over-looked, especially in cases where the people studied have left little evidence of their own or where the evidence is treated as inferior. In this case, I utilized news reports, available government and other official documents, interviews, field notes, and cultural products (e.g., tracts, hymns, songs) to support my argument. Astonishingly, the most abundant and perhaps richest source of evidence—news reports—has barely been tapped. I took advantage of this fact, cautiously using it and other evidence in conjunction with established scholarship.

I have presented a case for a qualitative and historical approach to ethnogenesis and collective identity formation. Such an approach offers promise for improving how we explain collective identity, which in turn can enhance theorizing. There are options for explaining how a collectivity like the Rastafari evolved, acorn to oak. As we saw earlier, one cluster of approaches—cultural selection, transmission, or evolution—emphasizes how information, say, the proclaimed divinity of Emperor Haile Selassie I, is learned and transmitted over time and across space. Such modeling has its value in translating complexity into elegant simplicity. But what do we lose in the process of translation? A lot of detail relevant to outcomes. Imagine this scenario: information moving from brain to brain with greater or less fidelity among early Acheulian toolmakers in East Africa one million years ago or the Rastafari in 1933. We do not have access to the brains of these people. But we have other evidence that requires tedious searching and compiling. This option should not be neglected.

What are the initial conditions that make possible the advent of a faith, a racial and anticolonial collective identity? We must identify the cultural resources such as ideologies, symbols, and the people that our subject of interest draws on and how they utilize the resources. The cultural infra-structure of pre-Rastafari Jamaica consists of many of the themes that characterize the first generation of Rastafari: racial solidarity; a Black savior, anticolonialism; resistance to oppression, suppression, and repression; and the practice of preaching to assembled groups.

There are many factors that influence whether a collectivity will thrive, flounder, wax, or wane. One factor involves the nature of the adherent pipeline. Is there a way for the collectivity to increase its numbers or at least not lose members? The old religions like Christianity and Islam could grow their numbers through conquest or colonization. Of course, this was not an option for the Rastafari. What they had was a message that gained traction among a section of Black Jamaica. Their original engines of growth—word of mouth, street preaching, and the occasional tract—might have increased numbers on their own. They received, however, an unlikely boost: unbridled oppression, suppression, and repression. The Jamaican national newspaper, the *Daily Gleaner*, arrogated to itself the responsibility to tell Jamaica how rotten the new Rastafari pests were. Oppression, suppression, and repression of the Rastafari emboldened their conviction in their own importance. Their collective response was, "They want to stamp us out because we are God's chosen people. We will sacrifice ourselves for what we believe." If the assistance of Jamaican newspapers was not enough, the colonial government's effort to sacrifice two of the fledgling Rastafari's leading lights on the altar of the judicial bench for sedition amplified their nascent message and ideology—cultural resources. Four years after King Ras Tafari's coronation, his name and iconicity reentered Jamaica's national discourse, a consequence of the news coverage of the trial. One group's effort to stamp out another inspired the victims.

Events beyond the control of the Rastafari created context for continued growth and further development of cultural resources. For example, the invasion of Ethiopia inspired Black people of the diaspora, and the Rastafari in particular, to rally in support of Ethiopia. The invasion reignited Ethiopianism, a racial ideology that valorized Blackness. It also motivated the Emperor to create the Ethiopian World Federation, which in turn motivated many Rastafari and Garveyites to create chapters in Jamaica. Although the Garveyites sometimes objected to Rastafari involvement in the chapters, their ideas intermingled, as did people seeking to participate in the chapters and learn about Ethiopia and the Emperor. Why was there such animosity among the Rastafari toward Rome and the popes of the Catholic Church? One might easily misapprehend why pope-bashing is central to Rastafari thinking without the historical context we have traced in this book. Denouncing the papacy was not misguided Black nativism but a critique of the Catholic Church's role in the invasion of Ethiopia and, generally, of its failure to condemn the exploitation of Africa and its people.

The Rastafari capacity to sink roots in Jamaica, to become entrenched, had much to do with the cultural resources they created and cultivated—Black pride and a critique of colonialism and White hegemony—resources that became available to people who were not Rastafari. The Pinnacle compound exemplifies the Rastafari's development of cultural resources, and it also became a source of growth; it was a major vector between the mid-1940s and mid-1950s. The people who lived at Pinnacle cultivated a way of life that translated conceptual ideas such as self-reliance, communal enterprise, and resistance against the colonial government into practice. Charges of ganja selling or praedial larceny aside, one can see the colonial government's motive to destabilize Pinnacle at every opportunity. Why should they allow Pinnacle to poke them in both eyes and perhaps encourage other Jamaicans to follow their example? Yet a contradictory and unforeseen consequence of destroying Pinnacle was that it allowed dislocated Pinnacleites to spread the faith to other parts of the island. Therefore, we can see why and how the Rastafari acquired the mark of menace, a mark that lingered into the 1970s. The label involved more than their public meetings, squatting, and verbal insults of non-Rastafari; they defied authority, challenged established beliefs, and called for racial justice—and they could be theatrical in doing so. Yet being a menace, from a Rastafari standpoint, was about standing for righteousness and their way of life.

Ethnogenesis is not simply about a group's effort to establish and perpetuate itself. Groups must operate in a world that changes in ways that they cannot anticipate; they must adapt. Who would have imagined in 1954 that a mere six years later, the government that sought to stamp out the Rastafari would change its tune to invest in exploring repatriation to Africa (although the government called it "migration" rather than "repatriation")? Or that another six years later, Emperor Selassie would visit Jamaica and turn on its head the elite's anticipation that the Emperor would rebuke the Rastafari? These unforeseen but seismic occurrences elevated the Rastafari, grew their numbers, and elaborated on and legitimized their cultural resources. The Rastafari were becoming a cultural force in Jamaica. Yet the unforeseen continued to loom large, and the consequences were far-reaching. Even as the Rastafari gained clout, Reverend Henry's debacles and the Coral Gardens massacre provided context for continued oppression, suppression, and repression.

The cultural resources developed by the Rastafari served them well, in that many elements of their belief found companionship in the new ideas of the 1960s and '70s. Third Worldism, Marxism, Black Power, contemporary Pan-Africanism, civil rights, and hippie sensibilities could find common cause with Rastafari thinking and with many Rastafari themselves. The Rastafari were proving themselves right on so many scores. People noticed, and some of them threw in their lot with Rastafari: a rising tide, so forcible that the Rastafari could be incorporated into a winning People's National Party campaign.

Rastafari diversity increased apace, witnessed in new formations (Houses and Mansions) like the Bobo Ashanti, Twelve Tribes, Ethiopian Orthodox, and Coptic Zion, not to mention a multitude of less-known Mansions or unaffiliated persons. This diversity in the evolution of Rastafari collective identity is unsurprising. Growth breeds variation. Consider the many variants of Christianity or Islam. The Rastafari were never monolithic, but by the 1970s, this was obvious. Yet a dominant query became, "Why are the Rastafari not organized?" The answer is that they are organized, just not in the centralized form that Westerners consider organized or in a form that allows them to exercise the concerted energy of a centralized authority. It might be useful to think of Rastafari organization as akin to the notion of segmentary lineage: an amalgam of small unities that can scale up into larger units if pressed to do so.

The post-1968 period was one of Rastafari growth.[1] The rising tide gained additional momentum from a powerful new vector in reggae music and reggae concerts, and icons like Bob Marley gave the Rastafari message prophetic and humanistic urgency. Whether recorded or performed live, reggae became a vector for Rastafari ideology, transmitting it across the planet. Along with movement of the music arose Rastafari communities in far-flung places: Tanzania and Guam; Ghana and New Zealand; Venezuela and Japan. In Jamaica, new Rastafari suitors emerged among the rude boys and disaffected middle class, as well as the Black Power, leftist, contemporary Pan-African, and student movements. The Rastafari serve as a beacon for the miseducated.

By opposing violence and political corruption and embracing Blackness, love, and community, the Rastafari offered an alternative ontology. Indeed, the Rastafari outcompeted other ideologies in Jamaica, such as Eurocentrism, unionism, Marxism, and arguably, for a brief while, political parties and Christianity. Functioning as an alternative to established identifications and ideologies is another element that is integral to Rastafari ethnogenesis. While Rastafari-as-alternative was relevant from the beginning, it began to exert greater influence over time as the ideas of the Rastafari converged with events and cultural trends identified earlier.

The popularity, though, came at a cost. Rastafari became commodified in ways that benefit few Rastafari. The appeal and lure of the Rastafari ethos is so compelling that one—a man, that is—can use Rastafari to acquire sex, material goods, or new opportunities. Tourism marketers use Rastafari cultural resources to promote tourism. Other advertisers sell Rastafari ideas of "One Love" or "Natural Mystic." And if that were not enough, one can profane Rastafari identity in pursuit of personal gain under the guise of fair use law (in the United States). Popularity can breed superficiality and commercialism. More than a few of the people who affected Rastafari identity during the 1970 and '80s were not deeply committed to it. Popular media seemed to revel in reporting on people who once identified themselves as Rastafari but would later renounce it for Christianity or something else.

The Rastafari have critiqued and skirted around capitalism but must continually contend with it as both they and capitalism evolve. The Rastafari have adapted. In general, they have moved toward engagement with Babylon. For example, some Rastafari are entertaining commercial ventures such as Rastafari tourism as cultural education and a source of revenue. This would have been unthinkable forty years ago. Many more Rastafari groups today are open to working with government entities on issues such as repatriation, sacralizing cannabis, protecting Rastafari heritage and indigenous knowledge (brand Rastafari), or commercial ventures. This is not to say the Rastafari have capitulated. Ethnogenesis involves change that is both internal and external to groups. We should expect change, but of course, not all are pleased with the forms change may generate.

The strength of Rastafari reggae, a mighty vector, has waned since the 1990s, superseded by variations of Jamaica's dancehall music, much of it driven by vulgar and violent sensibilities that are incompatible with Rastafari reggae. Reggae music continues to prosper, but the Rastafari presence is not as vaunted as what it was between the 1970s and 1990s. The language and rhetoric of the Rastafari persist in the music—Emperor Selassie, Babylon, ganja, critiques of violence and poverty—but the presence of the Rastafari themselves as cultural paragons has attenuated. Reggae as a vector of Rastafari ideology and identity has lost its luster, and thus its impact on Rastafari ethnogenesis is increasingly diffuse. Whether it remains a source of growth in Rastafari numbers as it did for two decades is dubious.

There are other trends to watch. Given the influence of the internet in the lives of nearly everyone, it has become easier to learn about the Rastafari past and present. The internet has become a vector. For instance, not only can one find Rastafari websites created by Rastafari, but Rastafari are using the internet to communicate with each other and to host events. Even so, it is too early to make any strong claims about the potential impact of the internet on twenty-first-century Rastafari ethnogenesis. Another trend to watch is the growing prominence of women Rastafari and their critique of patriarchy and narrow-minded masculinity. The writing, poetry, and art of women Rastafari are infusing new ideas and energy into Rastafari thinking and dialogue, broadening notions of equity and equality that are so central to Rastafari discourse.

* * *

The Rastafari evolved from a scattering of marginalized people who heralded a new Black Messiah, Emperor Haile Selassie I, into a broad but distinct community—a people. They evolved into a people who have altered Jamaicans' sense of race, faith, nationality, and thus, Jamaican collective identity. Because of the Rastafari, Jamaicans of all stripes talk about race rather than behave as if it does not exist; because of the Rastafari, Blackness is treated as an asset rather than a liability; because of the Rastafari, Jamaican notions of faith can entertain a deity that is represented as Black rather than White; because of the Rastafari, many Jamaicans feel kinship with the African continent and its diverse people. In charting the ethnogenesis of the Rastafari, we have spanned their development from the first generation through the fourth generation. A handful of individuals whose public expression of their faith could incite contempt or harsh punishment evolved into a people whose beliefs enthralled the hearts and minds of people the world over. The Rastafari moved from being despised to being admired and emulated, from separatists at one point to unifiers at another.

New groups or reformulated groups that persist past the first generation beg for us to explain how they happened, how they developed, and their experience of being members, as well as their impact on others.

If a new group is suppressed, if it has an appealing ideology, if antagonists do not entirely defang it, if it builds and protects cohesiveness, if it has effective vectors to propagate its message and identity, if its ideas offer the possibility of falling onto fertile cultural and historical terrain, then the conditions exist for the group's persistence for another generation or more. If none of these happen, the group or community may not perish, though it might remain small and fragile. This is a key lesson of Rastafari ethnogenesis. Another lesson is to consider group evolution and identity as coterminous, allowing for connecting aspects of identity with actual events and influences, say, specific instances of suppression, repression, and oppression. A third lesson is that there is value in providing a historical and qualitative account of the complex process of ethnogenesis and collective identity formation. Such an analysis can show us what us-and-them looks like and why, the nature of people's attachment to a given collective identity, or how people variously package the cultural resources that animate their collective identity over time. A fourth lesson, a recurring theme, is to develop an approach that addresses multiple interacting factors such as memories and symbols of the past, pursuit of community, new ideas, and resistance to people who contest the new ideas.

The Rastafari offer an example of how cultural resources are raw fabric for the making of human realities (plural intended), such as how new conventions are established. The Rastafari were rebuked because they contested established notions of race, God, and proper decorum. They created a new reality under severe oppression, adding to Jamaica's existing realities, a reality that later tens of thousands of Jamaicans would embrace. The notion of a Black God, that cannabis should be a sacrament, that one should not comb or trim one's hair, and that the tyranny of colonialism, capitalism, racism, and class oppression masquerading as progress and the natural order were unnatural and disordering came to be understood by many people as "true"—true not in an absolute sense but in the sense that over time people internalized the ideas as "real," and in doing so, they contributed to the creation of new conventions, new realities, and new truths. The Rastafari force us to confront the fact of multiple overlapping realities, while, paradoxically, many of them argue for the absoluteness of the reality they created. This should not perplex us. One can scoff at the notion that Emperor Selassie I is divine, but today tens of thousands of people believe it. A new truth and a new reality—albeit contested—has taken its place, invited or not, among other truths and realities.

ACKNOWLEDGMENTS

So many people assisted me in the writing and publishing of this book, more people than I can recall and some people whom I have never met, including the people who assembled this book. I may be the author, but my achievement rests on the contributions of many people. I want to thank as many of them as I can. Forgive me if I have neglected you. It was not intentional.

Students played an important supporting role in my research. I worked with talented undergraduates at the University of North Carolina–Chapel Hill. Caitlin Passaro assisted with research on Ethiopia, Virginia Hamilton assisted in collecting stories on the Ethiopian World Federation, Ashley McCleod (UNC-Greensboro) entered corrections for chapter 5, and Emily Yelton (whose affiliation I do not recall) entered corrections for chapter 6. Massie Minor (UNC-CH) tracked down some obscure sources for me. This book might be unfinished if not for the work of then-undergraduate extraordinaire Mary Glenn Krause. Mary began working with me the summer before her third year at UNC-CH and continued past her graduation and into her new career as an archaeologist. Mary is an indefatigable researcher; she pored through boxes of microfilm, searched many archives, and managed a considerable volume of images, news stories, and documents. She pursued images and copyright permission and finessed with angelic grace the folk who did not deliver what they promised or who seemed determined not to reply. Mary, thank you for your unflagging support and excellent work. At Temple University's College of Education and Human Development, graduate students Sidra Sheikh, Mariah Davis, and Emmaline Ellis assisted in collecting and organizing news stories for periods of the 1960s, 1970s, and 1980s. I thank Richard Lambert III (UNC-CH) for translating Austrian news articles into English. Bongo B.J. Bryant Jr., seventh grader and my grandson, assisted in typing up my handwritten notes.

The UNC-CH library was a vital source of support. Geneva Holiday, head of Interlibrary Service, and her staff provided remarkable help over the years. They are academic detectives. If there was something I could not find or something I ought to know but did not, I went to Interlibrary Service. Kirill Tolpygo, Slavic and East European Studies librarian, stepped in on more than one occasion to support my research. One result is that UNC-CH's Davis Library now holds some of the colonial records on the Rastafari. I thank Silvia Tomášková for her interest in my research and for connecting me with Kirill. I also benefited from the assistance of talented librarians at the Library of Congress in Washington, DC, the Yale University Library, and the Schomberg Center for Research in Black Culture. Temple University's Charles Library staff copied book chapters and articles and filled interlibrary loan requests. And thanks to the welcoming librarians at the Haverford Township Free Library in Havertown, Pennsylvania.

A UNC-CH University Research Council publishing grant (2016) helped me get a good start on the book. The Institute for Arts and Humanities at UNC-CH provided a faculty fellowship during 2017 that helped to advance the book during its midway point. Thanks to Evelyn Newman-Phillips of Central Connecticut State University and Lisa Poirer of DePaul University for providing an opportunity for me to present my thinking on ethnogenesis and collective identity.

Sheree Rhoden of the Information Systems Department of The Gleaner Company (Media) Limited toiled in searching out print-worthy versions of the many images I requested. It is lamentable that so many of the *Jamaica Times* original images are lost. The anthropologist John Homiak introduced me to the anthropologist George Eaton Simpson's photographs of the Rastafari taken during his 1950s field research in Jamaica. The Smithsonian Institution provided permission to use some of these images.

There are several readers I must thank. Dorothy Holland, my colleague at UNC-CH, was an advocate for this book and for the notion of ethnogenesis. Dorothy passed away in April 2019, but I will never forget the lessons I gathered from her about identity and ethnogenesis. Gregory Anderson read and commented on the full manuscript. Robert Sauté has been my Rock of Gibraltar. Robert meticulously read all the chapters at different stages of development and was generous in sharing his critical and thoughtful assessment for improvement. Both the book and I are better for Robert's contribution. I thank the four anonymous reviewers for New York University Press who provided useful advice and insight. In particular, I thank the reviewer who shared their comments written on the full draft of the manuscript. The comments and observations were perspicacious. Last but not least, I thank Jennifer Hammer, a senior editor at NYU Press. Jennifer demonstrated the patience of a great saint in waiting for me to complete this book. I am so fortunate to have learned so much from Jennifer. Jennifer, thank you for your patience and generosity.

Eleanor Edwards provided excellent counsel on keeping perspective on work and life balance. My daughter Courtney exercised an unfailing ability to encourage me to take a break from work and go on an adventure of one kind or another. And thanks to my mother for supporting all that I do. Thanks to the Most High, for good people and for long, overflowing, virtuous, and everlasting love (L.O.V.E.).

NOTES

INTRODUCTION

1. *Jamaica Times*, 7/12/41.
2. *Daily Gleaner*, 5/25/54.
3. Price 2009.
4. Gopnik 2012.
5. The names of Rastafari people are often preceded by honorifics such as "Rasta," "Brother," "Sister," "Ras," "Prophet," and "Prophetess." "Rasta" expresses endearment and signifies one's identity as Rastafari. "Brother" and "Sister" convey the idea of the Rastafari as a family of faith and identity beholden to love one another. "Ras," meaning "head," connotes royalty and the patriarchal notion of the father as the head of a family and God as the father of humankind. "Prophetess" or "Prophet" denotes the visionary and predictive abilities of a given Rastafari.
6. Price 2018.
7. Waters 1985.
8. Van Dijk 1998.
9. Lee 2003.
10. Paton 2015:160–62.
11. Adas 1979.
12. *Daily Gleaner*, 12/29/38, 8.
13. CSO Minutes, February 26, 1937.
14. Hervik 2011.
15. Hervik 2011:15.
16. A few news pages are so degraded that it is impossible to identify the page number or exact date of publication. In such cases, no date is abbreviated "n.d.," and no page number is abbreviated "n.p."
17. *Public Opinion*, 6/26/37, 3.
18. *Public Opinion*, 11/6/37, 14.
19. Cobham 1986:172.
20. Froude 1888:4.
21. Rosenberg 2007.
22. *Jamaica Times*, 5/28/38, 2.
23. E.g., Becker 1963.
24. Gray 1991:34.
25. Stone 1983; Post 1978:32.
26. Hoenisch 1988:436.

27. Hoenisch 1988:436, 439.
28. Earle et al. 2004:68.
29. Earle et al. 2004:66.
30. Earle et al. 2004:67.
31. E.g., Clarke 2016.
32. *The Star*, 7/3/61, 12.

CHAPTER 1. EXPLAINING RASTAFARI ETHNOGENESIS

1. Given similar initial conditions in different societies, we might find that similar processes produced different outcomes. To identify initial conditions does not imply a post hoc analysis that assumes that because A happened before B, then B is the result of A. Rather, initial conditions require that we identify the complex relationships between A and B and whatever else to explain the evolution of a people.
2. Gruesser 2000.
3. Gruesser 2000.
4. Frey 2009; Lockley 2012:9.
5. Frey 2009:54.
6. Shannon 2012:73.
7. Shannon 2012.
8. Webb (ca. 1919) 2008.
9. R. Rogers (ca. 1924) 2000.
10. Pettersburgh (ca. 1926) 2003.
11. *Daily Gleaner*, 6/6/27, 12.
12. *Daily Gleaner*, 5/17/27, 7.
13. Robert Hill (2001) says that the Harveys returned in 1931; however, the advertisement quoted shortly in the text is dated 1930, so I shall assume that they were in Jamaica in 1930.
14. *Daily Gleaner*, 9/20/30, 5 (original spelling).
15. Hill 2001.
16. *Daily Gleaner*, 2/7/34, 22.
17. West and Martin 2009:1.
18. *Daily Gleaner*, 1/18/30, 12.
19. Moore 1994:925.
20. Melucci 1995.
21. Sidbury and Cañizares-Esguerra 2011:199.
22. Edmonds 2012:71. These figures are rough estimates given the lack of effective censuses that count Rastafari in Jamaica or elsewhere, the lack of recognition of the Rastafari as a population worthy of counting, and the predilection of the Rastafari to avoid official counting.
23. Lewens 2015.
24. Runciman 2009:19.
25. Tsuda 2011.
26. Tsuda 2011:84.

27. Notions of cultural appeal and cultural attraction are more pronounced among cultural evolution theorists (see Buskell 2016:436 on Morin 2015).
28. Eerkens and Lipo 2007.
29. Morin 2015:104.
30. Morin 2015.
31. Brusse 2017:309.
32. Buskell 2016:439.
33. E.g., Cavalli-Sforza 1981.
34. Quoted in Tsuda 2011:104; Runciman 2009.
35. Sturtevant 1971; Sturtevant and Cattelino 2004.
36. Galloway 1995.
37. Haley and Wilcoxon 2005.
38. Bell 2005.
39. Gladney 1990:4–5.
40. Peterson and Brown 1986.
41. E.g., Hu 2013; Weik 2014.
42. Hudson 1999.
43. Gowricharn 2013.
44. Polletta and Jasper 2001.
45. Eidson et al. 2017:341.
46. Major sources for these categories include Ashmore, Deaux, and McLaughlin-Volpe 2004; Fominaya 2010; Holland, Fox, and Daro 2008; Melucci 1995; Polletta and Jaspers 2001; Reed and Pitcher 2015; Rupp and Taylor 1999.
47. Ashmore, Deaux, and McLaughlin-Volpe 2004:92.
48. Garcia 2010. The analogy implies a range of behaviors and expectations—between strict control ("stick to the script") and improvisation ("take the script and run with it"). People create archetypes of identities that frame their and others' expectations and responses; scripts are also ascribed to others.
49. Tilly 2007; Coser (1956) 2011.
50. *Daily Gleaner*, 3/15/34, 20 (emphasis in original).
51. CSO 5073/34, September 1, 1934.
52. CSO 5073/34, February 24, 1937.
53. *Sunday Gleaner*, 10/14/45, 8.
54. *Daily Gleaner*, 8/6/34 ("Ras Tafari Doctrine"), 5.
55. Cassidy 1971:158–59.
56. *Daily Gleaner*, 3/17/34 ("Chief Justice"), 6.

CHAPTER 2. INITIAL CONDITIONS

1. Southard 1931:682–83.
2. Rasta Ivey, personal communication, 1998.
3. Heb. 7:3 (KJV).
4. Blum and Harvey 2012.
5. Brooks 1917; Pierson 1969; Chevannes 1994; Satchel 2004; Watson 2008.

6. Brooks 1917:7.

7. Brooks 1917:8.

8. *Daily Gleaner*, 9/19/1893, 6.

9. *Daily Gleaner*, 9/14/1893, 7.

10. *Daily Gleaner*, 9/14/1893, 7.

11. *Daily Gleaner*, 9/14/1893, 7.

12. *Daily Gleaner*, 9/14/1893, 7.

13. *Daily Gleaner*, 9/28/1893, 8.

14. *Daily Gleaner*, 10/4/1893, 7.

15. *Daily Gleaner*, 10/4/1893, 7.

16. Paton 2015:252.

17. *Daily Gleaner*, 4/30/1895, 6.

18. *Daily Gleaner*, 1/22/1895 ("Bedward Arrested"), 3.

19. *Daily Gleaner*, 1/22/1895 ("Bedward Arrested"), 3.

20. Watson 2008:238.

21. Watson 2008:240. Watson cites "The Trial of Bedward," *Gall's Daily Newsletter*, April 30, 1895.

22. Sergeant Nelson was not asked to testify during Bedward's preliminary examination.

23. *Daily Gleaner*, 1/22/1895 ("Interview"), 6. The interview took place before the arrest and was published on the same date as announcement of the arrest.

24. *Daily Gleaner*, 1/22/1895 ("Interview"), 6.

25. *Daily Gleaner*, 5/2/1895, 7.

26. *Daily Gleaner*, 5/2/1895, 7.

27. *Daily Gleaner*, 5/21/1921, 1.

28. *Daily Gleaner*, 5/5/21, 6.

29. Price 2003:47.

30. *Daily Gleaner*, 5/5/21, 6.

31. *Daily Gleaner*, 5/21/21, 1.

32. *Daily Gleaner*, 5/21/21, 1.

33. *Daily Gleaner*, 5/21/21, 1.

34. Lyall-Grant et al. 1916:3.

35. Shepperson 1952.

36. Shepperson and Price 1958:26.

37. Booth (ca. 1897) 2007.

38. Rotberg 2005.

39. Rotberg 2005:37.

40. Linden and Linden 1971:644–45.

41. Lyall Grant et al. 1916:3, 6.

42. On versions of Ethiopianism, see Price 2003, 2014.

43. Linden and Linden 1971:632.

44. Lyall Grant et al. 1916:6.

45. Garvey 1923:952.

46. Webb (ca. 1919) 2008:13.
47. The *New York Times* reported on a Webb address under the headline, "Says a Black King Will Rule the World" (9/15/24, 11).
48. Advertisement in the *Negro World*, 10/3/25, 10.
49. R. Rogers (ca. 1924) 2000:36.
50. Pettersburgh (ca. 1926) 2003:5.
51. R. Rogers (ca. 1924) 2000.
52. Lee 2003:50; Hill 2001:18; *Daily Gleaner* 1/13/20, 3. Garrison was listed as a passenger on the United Fruit Company's steamer *Tivives*. I was unable to find a return date to Jamaica for Garrison.
53. *Daily Gleaner*, 12/18/25, 18.
54. *Daily Gleaner*, 12/24/25, 17. "Hamatic" is the name of the church, different from "Hamitic," which describes a racial category. However, "Hamatic" was probably intended to mean the same thing as "Hamitic."
55. *Daily Gleaner*, 12/24/25, 17.
56. *Daily Gleaner*, 3/19/26, 11; 3/30/26, 18.
57. *Daily Gleaner*, 6/6/27, 12.
58. Christianity was officially recognized in Ethiopia in 330 CE.
59. Yesehaq 1989:viii.
60. J. Rogers (ca. 1936) 1982.
61. *Daily Gleaner*, 10/10/30, 5.
62. *Daily Gleaner*, 10/10/30, 5.
63. *Daily Gleaner*, 10/10/30, 5.
64. *Daily Gleaner*, 10/10/30, 5.
65. *Daily Gleaner*, 8/18/30, 16.
66. *Daily Gleaner*, 10/29/30, 21.
67. *Daily Gleaner*, 11/4/30, 18.
68. The trope of the seventy-two nations is deployed in a range of Rastafari discourses, such as their hymns or musical recordings. The celebrated drummer Ras Michael Negus, for example, sings of how seventy-two "different nations bow before Jah presence, for he is the King of Kings, Lord of Lords, Conquering Lion of Judah." The nations were interpreted as showing obeisance for Earth's rightful ruler, the Lion of the Tribe of Judah, the one spoken of in Revelations (5:5) as opening the seals on the great book of life.
69. *Daily Gleaner*, 11/3/30, 16.
70. *Daily Gleaner*, 11/3/30, 16.
71. *Daily Gleaner*, 11/2/32, 2.
72. *Daily Gleaner*, 11/15/32, 1.

CHAPTER 3. VECTORS, COLLISIONS, CONTENTION

1. There is much more to the story. The evolution of Christianity is a story of ethnogenesis, shaped by states, suppression, conquest and colonization, communities of practice, and so on.

2. Lee 2003.
3. *Daily Gleaner*, 11/18/32, 9.
4. Hill 2001.
5. *Daily Gleaner*, 3/15/34, 20. Howell went on to say that he was in Africa during the time of the coronation and that he had traveled across Africa. This claim remains unverified.
6. Bishton 1986:110.
7. Webb (ca. 1919) 2008:5.
8. *Daily Gleaner*, 4/22/31, 26.
9. Tafari 2000:5.
10. Tafari 2000:5.
11. Walker said that Howell claimed to be an ambassador to Ethiopia and that he identified himself as the "same Jesus Christ that was crucified" (Bishton 1986:111).
12. Lee 2003:59; Hill 2001.
13. Hill 2001:27.
14. Dorman 2013:151.
15. Hill 2001:27; Dorman 2013:149.
16. Dorman 2013:142.
17. Dorman 2013:143.
18. Dorman 2013:143, 144.
19. While providing court testimony on March 15, 1934, Howell made reference to a "revivalist [who] was holding a meeting at Seaforth when he reached there on the night in question." Was this Annie Harvey? Nevertheless, this gives example to the overlap of Revival and Rastafari early on. Howell may have intended to catch remnants of the Revival crowd or to be invited to talk after the Revival meeting (he mentioned being invited to talk). *Daily Gleaner*, 3/15/34, 20.
20. Hill 2001:27.
21. *Daily Gleaner*, 8/10/33, 6; *Daily Gleaner*, 3/31/34, 21; *Daily Gleaner*, 3/3/34, 6; *Daily Gleaner*, 2/7/34, 22.
22. *Daily Gleaner*, 8/10/33, 7.
23. *Daily Gleaner*, 8/10/33, 7.
24. Deut 18:11 (KJV).
25. Deut 18:18 (KJV).
26. *Daily Gleaner*, 8/10/33. 7.
27. *Daily Gleaner*, 2/7/34, 22.
28. *Daily Gleaner*, 3/2/34, 6.
29. *Daily Gleaner*, 3/31/34, 21.
30. In 2020, a £10 fine would be roughly equivalent to US$921; £25 bail would be roughly equivalent to US$2,300. MeasuringWorth.com n.d.
31. Hill 2001:27.
32. E.g., *Daily Gleaner*, 7/4/33, 23; 11/13/33, 19.
33. CSO 5073/34; Lee 2003:64.
34. *Daily Gleaner*, 3/15/34, 20.

35. *Daily Gleaner*, 12/27/33, 13.

36. *Daily Gleaner*, 10/5/34, 4; *Jamaica Times*, 10/18/34, 14–15.

37. *Daily Gleaner*, 10/5/34, 1.

38. *Daily Gleaner*, 12/27/33, 13.

39. *Daily Gleaner*, 3/14/34, 21.

40. *Daily Gleaner*, 3/14/34, 21 (original emphasis).

41. *Daily Gleaner*, 3/14/34, 21.

42. *Daily Gleaner*, 2/1/34, 16.

43. *Daily Gleaner*, 3/15/34, 20.

44. *Daily Gleaner*, 3/15/34, 20.

45. *Daily Gleaner*, 3/15/34, 20.

46. *Daily Gleaner*, 1/5/34, 9.

47. Lee 2003:71.

48. *Daily Gleaner*, 1/5/34, 9.

49. *Daily Gleaner*, 1/5/34, 9.

50. *Daily Gleaner*, 1/5/34, 9. The writer paraphrased the magistrate's admonishment.

51. *Daily Gleaner*, 1/5/34, 9. I was unable to determine if Hinds actually served any time for the conviction.

52. *Daily Gleaner*, 12/27/33. 13.

53. Lee 2003:70.

54. Coser (1956) 2011.

CHAPTER 4. RASTAFARI ON TRIAL, 1934

Epigraph: Quoted in Elkins 1977:1.

1. *Daily Gleaner*, 3/15/34, 20.

2. *Daily Gleaner*, 3/15/34, 20 (original emphasis).

3. *Daily Gleaner*, 3/15/34, 20.

4. *Daily Gleaner*, 3/10/34, 12. Theophilus Jackson's case had been dropped by early March 1934, though there were no explanations why.

5. The law went on to say that such meeting or assembly must be disbanded within thirty minutes of notice or participants would face arrest for felony charge, liable for up to four years' imprisonment. The act was revised several times, perhaps as late as 1973.

6. *Daily Gleaner*, 1/22/31, 8.

7. *Daily Gleaner*, 3/14/34, 21.

8. *Daily Gleaner*, 3/14/34, 21.

9. *Daily Gleaner*, 3/14/34, 21.

10. *Daily Gleaner*, 3/14/34, 21.

11. *Daily Gleaner*, 3/14/34, 21.

12. *Daily Gleaner*, 3/16/34, 16.

13. *Daily Gleaner*, 3/15/34, 20.

14. *Daily Gleaner*, 3/16/34, 16.

15. Hill 2001:42.

16. *Daily Gleaner*, 3/15/34, 20.
17. *Daily Gleaner*, 3/15/34, 20 (original emphasis).
18. *Daily Gleaner*, 1/23/1895, 7.
19. *Daily Gleaner*, 3/15/1934, 20.
20. *Daily Gleaner*, 3/16/34, 16.
21. *Daily Gleaner*, 3/15/34, 20.
22. The anthropologists Carole Yawney and John Homiak have emphasized this point (2001:259).
23. *Daily Gleaner*, 3/15/34, 20.
24. *Daily Gleaner*, 3/15/34, 20.
25. Southard 1931:682.
26. Blum and Harvey 2012.
27. The Native Baptists gave Christ the status of prophet rather than God almighty.
28. *Daily Gleaner*, 3/15/34, 20.
29. Post 1978:246–47.
30. Maynes, Pierce, and Laslett 2008.
31. *Daily Gleaner*, 3/15/34, 20.
32. *Daily Gleaner*, 3/15/34, 20.
33. *Daily Gleaner*, 3/17/34 ("Howell Given 2-Year Term"), 6.
34. In my usage, "Dreadlocks" functions as a proper noun. It refers to a specific subset of the Rastafari, the "Dreadlocks" or "Dreadlocks Rastafari," as well as to the coiffure (dreadlocks) that also names the specific subset of Rastafari.
35. *Daily Gleaner*, 3/17/34 ("Howell Given 2-Year Term"), 6.
36. *Daily Gleaner*, 3/17/34 ("Howell Given 2-Year Term"), 6.
37. Bogues 2003:16, 19.
38. *Daily Gleaner*, 3/17/34 ("Howell Given 2-Year Term"), 6.
39. *Daily Gleaner*, 3/17/34 ("Howell Given 2-Year Term"), 6.
40. Jer 8:21.
41. *Daily Gleaner*, 3/17/34 ("Howell Given 2-Year Term"), 6.
42. *Daily Gleaner*, 3/16/34, 16.
43. *Daily Gleaner*, 3/17/34 ("Howell Given 2-Year Term"), 6.
44. *Daily Gleaner*, 3/17/34 ("Howell Given 2-Year Term"), 6.

CHAPTER 5. CONFLICT AND RETREAT

1. *Daily Gleaner*, 7/9/34, 12 (emphasis added).
2. Interviewed by the Rastafari scholar Barry Chevannes (1998b:98).
3. *Daily Gleaner*, 8/6/34 ("Ras Tafari Doctrine"), 5; cf. *Jamaica Times*, 1/19/35, 2.
4. Chevannes 1998a:77.
5. Blagrove 2002.
6. Whitehouse et al. 2017.
7. CSO 5073/34, September 5, 1934.
8. Rachel Patterson to His Excellency, September 3, 1934, CSO 5073/34.
9. Delrosa Francis to "His Excellency," September 1, 1934, CSO 5073/34.

10. "Paramour" here means "beloved" rather than "illicit lover."

11. Delrosa Francis to "His Excellency," September 1, 1934, CSO 5073/34.

12. Rachel Patterson to "His Excellency," September 3, 1934, CSO 5073/34.

13. James Findley to "His Excellency," September 1, 1934, CSO 5073/34.

14. Augustus Gordon and Amelia Gordon to His Excellency, September 3, 1934, CSO 5073/34.

15. The people charged were Gertrude Nathan, Denail Price, Delrosa Francis, Francella McNish, James Findley, Rachel Patterson, and Augustus and Amelia Gordon.

16. Correspondences among CSO staff do not indicate any concern with the accused people's counterclaims.

17. Rachel Patterson to "His Excellency, the Officer Administering the Government in, and over the Island of Jamaica and Its Dependencies," September 3, 1934, CSO 5073/34.

18. Acting Colonial Secretary to Price, Nathan, Gordon, and Findley, September 14, 1934, CSO 5073/34.

19. Note written by an unidentifiable official, September 10, 1934, CSO 5073/34.

20. Maragh (ca. 1935) 2001:7.

21. Maragh (ca. 1935) 2001:5.

22. Maragh (ca. 1935) 2001:5.

23. Spencer 1998:385.

24. *Jamaica Times*, 5/28/38, n.p.

25. Philos 1935b, 9. Translated into English from the German.

26. United Aid for Ethiopia 1936:1–2.

27. Philos 1935a:80.

28. *Jamaica Times*, 12/7/35, 22.

29. *Jamaica Times*, 12/7/35, 23.

30. *Jamaica Times*, 12/7/35, 23.

31. H. Selassie 1936.

32. *Jamaica Times*, 7/27/35, 1.

33. *Jamaica Times*, 8/17/35, 1, 4; 12/21/35, 1.

34. *Jamaica Times*, 12/21/35, 1.

35. *Jamaica Times*, 7/20/35, 27.

36. *Jamaica Times*, 8/3/35, 24.

37. Philos 1935a:81.

38. Scott 1972:132.

39. United Aid for Ethiopia 1936:2.

40. Scott 1972; Bonacci 2013.

41. *Daily Gleaner*, 9/15/38, 13.

42. *Daily Gleaner*, 9/15/38, 13.

43. Bonacci 2013:78–79; for a thorough historical account of the EWF, see Bonacci 2013.

44. Bonacci 2013.

45. Personal communication, 1998.

46. Price 2009:128.
47. *Daily Gleaner*, 1/18/37, 28.
48. *Daily Gleaner*, 1/18/37, 28.
49. Whitehouse et al. 2017:1.
50. *Daily Gleaner*, 1/18/37, 28.
51. *Daily Gleaner*, 1/18/37, 28.
52. *Daily Gleaner*, 1/18/37, 28.
53. *Daily Gleaner*, 1/18/37, 28.
54. *Daily Gleaner*, 1/18/37, 28 (original emphasis).
55. *Daily Gleaner*, 1/18/37, 28.
56. *Daily Gleaner*, 1/18/37, 28.
57. Minutes, handwritten note, signature indecipherable, February 26, 1937, CSO 5073/34.
58. Thomas 2017.
59. KSACL to Governor Denham, January 1937, CSO 5073/34.
60. Altamont Reid et al. to Governor Denham, January 1937, CSO 5073/34.
61. Altamont Reid et al. to Governor Denham, January 1937, CSO 5073/34.
62. *Daily Gleaner*, 3/22/38, n.p.
63. *Daily Gleaner*, 3/9/39, 18.
64. *Daily Gleaner*, 5/3/39, 18.
65. *Daily Gleaner*, 12/29/38, 8.
66. *Daily Gleaner*, 3/9/39, 18.
67. *Daily Gleaner*, 5/3/39, 18.
68. *Daily Gleaner*, 12/29/38, 8.
69. *Daily Gleaner*, 3/9/39, 18.
70. Price 2009:71.
71. *Daily Gleaner*, 5/3/39, 18.
72. *Daily Gleaner*, 3/9/39, 18.
73. *Daily Gleaner*, 3/9/39, 18.
74. *Daily Gleaner*, 3/9/39, 18.
75. *Daily Gleaner*, 5/3/39, 18.
76. *Daily Gleaner*, 2/9/40, 1.
77. *Daily Gleaner*, 4/3/39, 24; 12/27/39, 17.
78. The "rules of the Ethiopian Salvation Society" were certified by Jamaica's acting attorney general, February 18, 1939, CSO 5073/34.
79. "The Living and Trading Scheme," Jamaica National Archives, 1B/5/79.
80. Price 2013.
81. *Daily Gleaner*, 11/23/40, 26.
82. *Sunday Gleaner*, 12/22/40, n.p.
83. *Sunday Gleaner*, 12/22/40, n.p.
84. *Sunday Gleaner*, 12/22/40, n.p., cited in CSO 5073/34.
85. *Sunday Gleaner*, 12/22/40, n.p.; cf. Attorney General to Colonial Secretary, December 23, 1940, CSO 5073/34.

86. McNeill sent a telegraph to Jamaica's colonial secretary, December 23, 1940, CSO 5073/34. The *Sunday Gleaner* story that McNeill referenced in the telegraph is "Plight of Ras Tafarians at Camp Pinnacle in St. Catherine" (12/22/40).

87. Telegraph, McNeill to the Colonial Secretary, December 23, 1940, CSO 5073/34.

88. Attorney General to the Colonial Secretary, December 23, 1940, CSO 5073/34.

89. Clerk of Parochial Board, St. Catherine, to Assistant Director Medical Services, Island Medical Office, Kingston, April 30, 1941, CSO 5073/34.

90. Report from Medical Officer of Health, St. Catherine, February 5, 1941, CSO 5073/34.

91. Assistant Director of Medical Services to Colonial Secretary, January 16, 1941, CSO 5073/34.

92. Report from Clerk of the Parochial Board St. Catherine to Assistant Director Medical Services, Kingston, February 7, 1941, CSO 5073/34.

93. Assistant Director of Medical Services to Colonial Secretary, January 16, 1941, CSO 5073/34.

94. Letter to Acting Colonial Secretary, January 17, 1941, CSO 5073/34.

95. Report from Corporal R. Samuels to Inspector in charge of St. Catherine, June 12, 1941, CSO 5073/34.

96. Samuels to Inspector.

97. *Daily Gleaner*, 7/9/41, 1.

98. *Jamaica Times*, 7/12/41, 1.

99. *Daily Gleaner*, 7/31/41, 16; 8/25/41, 16.

100. *Daily Gleaner*, 7/15/41, 14.

101. James Nelson to Sergeant Major of Spanish Town Police, June 14, 1941, CSO 5073/34.

102. Commissioner of Police to Colonial Secretary (confidential), June 18, 1941, CSO 5073/34.

103. Sergeant Major Malabre to Inspector in charge of St. Catherine, June 17, 1941, CSO 5073/34.

104. Malabre to Inspector.

105. Unidentifiable official to Acting Colonial Secretary, July 2, 1941, CSO 5073/34; *Jamaica Times*, 7/12/41, 1.

106. *Daily Gleaner*, 7/31/41, 16.

107. Commissioner of Police to Colonial Secretary, July 17, 1941, CSO 5073/34.

108. The press overstated the number of officers and firearms and extended the beginning of the raid to July 13, 1941 (which is the date that I used in *Becoming Rasta*, 2009). For example, see *Daily Gleaner*, 7/15/41, 1, 14.

109. Commissioner of Police to Colonial Secretary, July 17, 1941, CSO 5073/34.

110. *Daily Gleaner*, 7/26/41, 8.

CHAPTER 6. THE MENACE BECOMES DREADFUL

1. Andrews 2017.

2. *Daily Gleaner*, 3/28/47, 19.

3. *Daily Gleaner*, 9/8/47, 5.

4. *Daily Gleaner*, 7/21/48, 1.

5. *Daily Gleaner*, 7/21/48, 1.

6. *Daily Gleaner*, 7/21/48, 1.

7. See *Baltimore African American*, 8/28/48, 1.

8. *Daily Gleaner*, 12/15/49, 1.

9. Leading Rastafari scholars such as Alston Barrington Chevannes (1994) and John Homiak (1985) give privileged status to founding innovators Youth Black Faith and Higes Knots. Their conclusions are persuasive. We must entertain, however, the possibility that there were other innovators beyond the two groups.

10. Eidson et al. 2017:342.

11. Homiak 1985:183–85.

12. Homiak 1998.

13. Homiak 1998:139.

14. Cassidy 1971:184, 252.

15. Homiak 1998:151–52.

16. Homiak 1998:151.

17. Homiak 1998.

18. Bilby and Leib 1986.

19. Bilby and Leib 1986; Nagashima 1984.

20. Reckord 1977, 1998; Burke 1977; Nagashima 1984. Burru practitioners played drums while enslaved people worked, accompanying their work routine in a fashion similar to how work songs function to synchronize movement, increase productivity, and dissipate tedium.

21. Reckord 1977:8, 1998.

22. Nagashima 1984.

23. Nagashima 1984; Reckord 1977.

24. Nagashima 1984:89; Reckord 1998:240.

25. Homiak 1998:158.

26. Homiak 1998:157.

27. Homiak 1998:157.

28. See Pollard 2000.

29. Price 2009:71–72.

30. Barrett 1968:159.

31. Bonacci 2013:80. Bonacci's *Exodus! Heirs and Pioneers, Rastafari Return to Ethiopia* (2015) is a definitive account of Rastafari settlement of Shashemene.

32. *Daily Gleaner*, 7/31/50, 1.

33. *Daily Gleaner*, 10/23/50, 5.

34. *Daily Gleaner*, 10/23/50, 5.

35. *Daily Gleaner*, 11/13/50, 11; the article incorrectly stated five thousand acres.

36. *Daily Gleaner*, 11/15/50, 12.

37. O'Regan 1994.

38. *Daily Gleaner*, 11/13/50, 13.

39. *Daily Gleaner*, 11/13/50, 13.
40. Stolberg 1990:42.
41. *Daily Gleaner*, 6/14/51 ("'Rasta' Man Charged"), 1.
42. *Daily Gleaner*, 6/14/51, 1 ("'Rasta' Man Charged"); *Jamaica Observer*, 5/13/2012, n.p.
43. *Jamaica Observer*, 5/13/2012, n.p.
44. *Daily Gleaner*, 6/14/51 ("P.N.P. Cited"), 5.
45. *Daily Gleaner*, 6/14/51 ("P.N.P. Cited"), 5.
46. *Daily Gleaner*, 6/14/51 ("Menace"), 6.
47. *Daily Gleaner*, 6/14/51 ("Menace"), 6.
48. *Daily Gleaner*, 6/14/51 ("Menace"), 6 (original emphasis).
49. *Daily Gleaner*, 6/25/51, 6.
50. *Daily Gleaner*, 6/14/51 ("Menace"), 6.
51. Fermor (1950) 2011.
52. *Daily Gleaner*, 6/15/51, 8.
53. *Daily Gleaner*, 6/15/51, 8.
54. *The Earth Most Strangest Man: The Rastafarian* (2006), by Mortimer Planno, is among the few preserved thoughts and writings of the Rastafari intellectuals who were active during the 1950s and early 1960s.
55. *Daily Gleaner*, 4/21/54, 8.
56. *Daily Gleaner*, 4/21/54, 8.
57. *Daily Gleaner*, 4/21/54, 8.
58. *Daily Gleaner*, 9/8/52, 1.
59. Osborne 2015:1.
60. Chevannes 1998; contra Smith, Augier, and Nettleford 1960.
61. *Daily Gleaner*, 3/11/54, 6.
62. *Daily Gleaner*, 10/22/52, 6; 11/17/52, 9.
63. *Daily Gleaner*, 12/15/52, 8.
64. Simpson 1955b:169.
65. *Daily Gleaner*, 10/5/55, 7.
66. Evans 1956.
67. Foner 1985:709.
68. *Daily Gleaner*, 10/5/55, 7.
69. *Daily Gleaner*, 5/5/54, 8.
70. *Daily Gleaner*, 7/9/54, 10.
71. *Daily Gleaner*, 3/26/54 8.
72. Martin 1952–53:51.
73. Martin 1952–53:51.
74. Martin 1952–53:51.
75. Martin 1952–53:51.
76. *Daily Gleaner*, 5/25/54, 1.
77. *Daily Gleaner*, 5/25/54, 1.
78. Homiak 1985:275.

79. Lepinske 1955.
80. Lepinske 1955:23.
81. *Daily Gleaner*, 6/17/54, 5.
82. Mack 1999:61.
83. Mack 1999:62.
84. Mack 1999:62.
85. *Daily Gleaner*, 4/18/58, 11.
86. *Daily Gleaner*, 7/23/54, 10.
87. *Daily Gleaner*, 9/21/54, 8.
88. *Daily Gleaner*, 6/25/55, 6.
89. *Daily Gleaner*, 11/20/54, 1.
90. *Daily Gleaner*, 3/23/54, 1.
91. *Daily Gleaner*, 3/30/54, 8.
92. *Daily Gleaner*, 3/23/54, 1.
93. *Daily Gleaner*, 3/27/54, 8.
94. Simpson 1955a, 1955b.
95. *Daily Gleaner*, 6/30/55, 8.
96. *Daily Gleaner*, 6/30/55, 8.
97. Bonacci 2013:82.
98. *Daily Gleaner*, 9/22/55, 17.
99. *Daily Gleaner*, 9/1/55, 7; 9/22/55, 17.
100. Bonacci 2013; Price 2009.
101. *Daily Gleaner*, 5/8/59, 1, 16.
102. *The Star*, 5/7/59 ("Riot"), 1.
103. *The Star*, 5/7/59 ("Huts"), 1.
104. *The Star*, 5/7/59 ("Riot"), 1.
105. Roger Mais's *Brother Man* was published in 1954. It was perhaps the first sympathetic and insightful—although fictional—account of the Rastafari. The main character, Brother Man, promotes peace and love despite the mistreatment he witnesses and experiences.
106. *Daily Gleaner*, 8/25/58, 14.
107. *The Star*, 6/29/62, 20.
108. *Daily Gleaner*, 8/25/59, 14.
109. *The Star*, 10/22/60, 1.
110. Chevannes 1976:265–67.
111. *The Star*, 9/23/59, 1.
112. *The Star*, 5/11/59, 1.
113. *Sunday Gleaner*, 10/11/59, 10.
114. I described Henry, his followers, and foreign affiliates as "disruption in two acts" in how the repatriation call and subsequent appeal to violence kept Rastafari ethnogenesis on the pariah track. See Price 2009:74–76 for details not included here.
115. Chevannes 1976:275 (emphasis in original).

116. *Sunday Gleaner*, 10/11/59, 10.

117. Chevannes (1976:266) believed that there was no verification for the trip to Ethiopia. Yet at least two different sources, at different times, provide details about the trip. For example, Henry was quoted as saying, "Everyday policeman come here. Even when I come back from Ethiopia them meet me at the Airport and wanlook at mi passport to see if I did really go anywhere." *The Star*, 10/5/59, 1; see also *The Star*, 9/23/59, 1; *Daily Gleaner*, 11/9/59, 2.

118. *The Star*, 10/5/59, 5.

119. *The Star*, 10/17/59 ("Vere John Says"), 6.

120. *The Star*, 10/17/59 ("Book Lock Up"), 7.

121. *The Star*, 10/5/59, 1.

122. *The Star*, 10/5/59, 5.

123. *Daily Gleaner*, 10/6/59, 1.

124. *Daily Gleaner*, 10/6/59, 1.

125. *Daily Gleaner*, 10/6/59, 1.

126. *Daily Gleaner*, 10/7/59, 1.

127. *Sunday Gleaner*, 10/11/59, 10 (emphasis in original).

128. *Daily Gleaner*, 10/7/59, 1.

129. "Rastafari Federation" is a pseudonym. It refers to the same organization referenced in my book *Becoming Rasta: The Origins of Rastafari Identity in Jamaica* (2009). By continuing to use the pseudonym, I intend to maintain continuity between *Becoming Rasta* and this book.

130. *Daily Gleaner*, 11/9/59, 2; *Daily Gleaner*, 11/25/59, 9; *The Star*, 11/6/59, 1.

131. *The Star*, 10/17/59 ("Book Lock Up"), 7.

132. *Daily Gleaner*, 10/8/59, 1.

CHAPTER 7. OF BEARDS, INSURRECTION, AND REHABILITATION
Epigraph: *The Star*, 5/11/60, 12.

1. Clarke 2016:5.

2. Eidson et al. 2017:347.

3. *The Star*, 4/28/60, 1.

4. *The Star*, 6/6/60, 3.

5. *The Star*, 5/2/60, 1; *The Star*, 5/4/60 ("Children Threatened"), 1.

6. *The Star*, 5/4/60 ("Israel"), n.p.; *Jamaica Times*, 9/27/58, 2.

7. *Jamaica Times*, 9/27/58, 2.

8. *The Star*, 10/26/60, 12.

9. *The Star*, 5/4/60 ("Israel"), n.p.

10. *The Star*, 12/11/59, 1; *Daily Gleaner*, 5/4/60, 1.

11. *The Star*, 4/6/60, 1.

12. *The Star*, 5/10/60, 3.

13. I call them "associates" because of their connection to the so-called plot and to distinguish them from rank-and-file members.

14. Clarke 2016:11.

15. Clarke 2016:8.
16. *Daily Gleaner*, 3/24/60, 3.
17. LSIC 1961:1.
18. *The Star*, 4/11/60, 1; *Jamaica Times*, 7/16/60, 1.
19. *Time* 1960b, 17.
20. *The Star*, 4/30/60, 1; *Daily Gleaner*, 5/2/60, 1.
21. *Time* 1960b, 17.
22. *Time* 1960b, 17.
23. *Jamaica Times*, 6/25/60 ("Grave Problem"), 6.
24. *Jamaica Times* 7/2/60 ("Complacency"), 1. Of note, similar categories were employed by M. G. Smith, Roy Augier, and Rex Nettleford, the authors of *The Report on the Rastafari Movement in Kingston, Jamaica* (1960).
25. *Jamaica Times*, 7/2/60 ("Complacency"), 9.
26. *Daily Gleaner*, 5/3/60, 1.
27. Roy Malachai, a twenty-six-year-old factory worker and former US Army soldier, was among the first of the Americans arrested. Other Americans included David Ambrister and Lawrence Richberg.
28. *The Star*, 6/25/60, 1
29. *The Star*, 6/27/60, 1.
30. *Daily Gleaner*, 7/27/60, 1; *The Star*, 7/27/60, 12.
31. *The Star*, 7/1/60, 1; 7/2/60, 1.
32. *Time* 1960a, 29.
33. Cooks 1959:30.
34. Harris et al.1992:xv.
35. *The Star*, 9/23/60, 16.
36. Cooks in Harris et al. 1992:7.
37. *The Star*, 9/23/60, 16.
38. *The Star*, 9/26/60, 1.
39. *The Star*, 10/10/60, 12. "Standing in the gap" is probably a reference to one of Reverend Henry's favored metaphors, the "breach." One breach involved the miseducation propagated by all of Jamaica's mainstream churches, such as treating Sunday as the Sabbath instead of Saturday. Reverend Henry deemed himself the repairer of the breach. Another breach involved getting Black Jamaicans from Jamaica to Africa, where he believed they belonged.
40. Cooks in Harris et al. 1992:11.
41. Cooks in Harris et al. 1992:92.
42. *The Star*, 9/29/60 ("Henry Villain"), 1.
43. *The Star*, 9/29/60 ("Thousands Shouted"), 12.
44. *The Star*, 10/5/60, 12.
45. *The Star*, 10/21/60, 7.
46. *The Star*, 10/18/60 ("Accused"), 1
47. *The Star*, 10/12/60, 1.
48. *The Star*, 10/12/60, 1.

49. While on trial, Revered Henry confessed to signing the bluster letter but claimed that he did not sign the Castro letter because he did not like the language.

50. Thunder was central to the drafting of both letters, although his specific contribution is disputed. Thunder had read a letter proposing church improvements to members during a church meeting. Several of Henry's codefendants who signed the letters at Thunder's request thought they were signing the church improvement letter. Thunder apparently switched letters on them.

51. *The Star*, 10/13/60, 2. Justice Herbert Duffus concluded that the letters were immaterial to the case because the "letters were personal and dealt with 'another colony' [not Jamaica] which had no connection at all with the trial now in progress."

52. *The Star*, 10/28/60 ("Counsel"), 1.

53. *The Star*, 10/25/60 ("Henry Testifies"), 12.

54. *The Star*, 10/18/60 ("Defense Opens"), 12.

55. *The Star*, 10/21/60, 7.

56. *Hibbert*, 12/10/2013, n.p.

57. *The Star*, 10/18/60, 12.

58. *The Star*, 10/21/60, 1.

59. *The Star*, 10/24/60, 1.

60. *The Star*, 10/25/60 ("Some Rastas"), 11.

61. Price 2009:148.

62. *The Star*, 10/28/60 ("Henry's Leaflet"), 1.

63. Chevannes 1976:279.

64. *The Star*, 6/28/60, 6.

65. *Jamaica Times*, 7/23/60, 1.

CHAPTER 8. THE REPORT ON THE RASTAFARI

1. *Daily Gleaner*, 7/6/60, 1. The University College of the West Indies released news of the upcoming study.

2. Hill 2013b.

3. *The Star*, 8/26/60, 1.

4. *The Star*, 9/3/60, 6.

5. *The Star*, 8/19/60, 6.

6. *The Star*, 8/27/60, 1.

7. *Jamaica Times*, 10/22/60, 1.

8. Hill 2013a.

9. Hill 2013a.

10. Hill 2013a.

11. Clarke 2016:12, 13.

12. Clarke 2016:19–20.

13. Price 2001.

14. There have always been Rastafari who are politically engaged, even in the context of "politricks."

15. *The Star*, 3/21/62, 7.
16. LSIC 1961:18.
17. LSIC 1961:40.
18. LSIC 1961:16.
19. Bolland 1995:139.
20. Palmer 2014:243; Clarke 2016:178.
21. LSIC 1961:4.
22. *Sunday Gleaner*, 6/26/60, 1.
23. *Sunday Gleaner*, 6/26/60, 1.
24. *Sunday Gleaner*, 6/26/60, 1.
25. The Special Branch operated at least from the late 1950s into 1962.
26. 1961.
27. LSIC 1961:1.
28. LSIC 1961:5.
29. LSIC 1961:23; Clarke 2016:7; Price 2009:163.
30. Clarke 2016.
31. LSIC 1961:23.
32. *Jamaica Times*, 7/29/61, 9. S. George Minott quoting Johnson.
33. LSIC 1961:24.
34. *The Star*, 2/13/61, 1.
35. Clarke 2016:132.
36. *The Star*, 2/17/61, 11.
37. *Jamaica Times*, 8/6/60, 1
38. *Jamaica Times*, 7/2/60 ("By the Way"), 10.
39. *Jamaica Times*, 8/13/60, 5.
40. Brown offered several reasons for withdrawing from the mission: it did not adequately represent the Rastafari; it was not deemed an official mission; and the government did not expect it to succeed because it did not believe African governments would accept unskilled labor. *The Star*, 3/3/61, 12. Brown was also involved in formal political activity at the time, though he did not offer this as a reason for withdrawal. The reason for the withdrawal of the United Rases Organization representative is unclear.
41. *The Star*, 3/10/61, 2.
42. See Price 2009 for the details of the MtA's visit to Nigeria, Ghana, Sierra Leone, Sudan, and Ethiopia.
43. *The Star*, 6/5/61, 1.
44. Price 2009:78–85.
45. *The Star*, 10/27/61, 16.
46. *Jamaica Times*, 8/27/60, 6
47. *Jamaica Now* 1962:2.
48. *Jamaica Times*, 3/24/62, 13.
49. *Jamaica Times*, 5/5/62, 2; see also *The Star*, 4/12/62, 6.
50. *Jamaica Times*, 4/14/62, 1.

51. *Jamaica Times*, 9/8/62, 1.

52. *Daily Gleaner*, 11/12/62, 1.

53. Monique Bedasse chronicles the settlement of Rastafari in Tanzania in her book *Jah Kingdom* (2017), though she does not discuss the Jamaican mission to Tanzania.

54. *The Star*, 11/7/61, 4; also 10/20/61, 4.

55. *The Star*, 5/19/62, 7.

56. *Jamaica Times*, 3/25/61, 8.

57. *The Star*, 9/9/61, 7.

58. *Jamaica Times*, 10/27/62, 10.

59. *The Star*, 2/10/62, 5.

60. *Daily Gleaner*, 2/11/63, 2.

61. *Daily Gleaner*, 2/11/63, 2.

62. *Daily Gleaner*, 8/13/63, 4.

63. *Daily Gleaner*, 2/11/63, 2.

64. Price 2009:85–86; Thomas 2011:173–201.

65. Thomas 2011:188.

66. Thomas 2011:181–83.

67. Price 2009; Thomas 2011:199.

68. Thomas 2011:199.

69. *Daily Gleaner*, 4/29/63, 1.

70. *Daily Gleaner*, 8/24/63, 4.

71. *Daily Gleaner*, 8/22/63, 8.

72. *Daily Gleaner*, 7/17/63, 4.

73. *Daily Gleaner*, 7/17/63, 4.

CHAPTER 9. GROWING INFLUENCE BRINGS GROWING PAINS

1. *Daily Gleaner*, 1/13/70, 8.

2. For a detailed account, see Price 2009:88–92.

3. *Daily Gleaner*, 10/17/68, 27.

4. Rodney (ca. 1969) 1996:64.

5. Rodney (ca. 1969) 1996.

6. King 2002:81.

7. *Daily Gleaner*, 10/17/68, 7.

8. Price 2004; Thomas 2017.

9. *Daily Gleaner*, 11/25/68, 22.

10. *Daily Gleaner*, 10/17/68, 7.

11. *Daily Gleaner*, 10/18/68, 1.

12. West 2005:19.

13. Rodney (ca. 1969) 1996:66.

14. *Daily Gleaner*, 10/18/68, 1.

15. *Daily Gleaner*, 10/18/68, 13.

16. R. Lewis 1994:29.

17. *Daily Gleaner*, 10/18/68, 13.
18. Cf. Rodney (ca. 1969) 1996:29.
19. Rodney (ca. 1969) 1996:61.
20. Lee 2003:252.
21. Lee 2003:252.
22. *Sunday Gleaner*, 8/18/74, 34.
23. Edmonds 2012; Bender 2005.
24. *Daily Gleaner*, 8/14/75, 18.
25. Bender 2005:98.
26. *Sunday Gleaner*, 2/22/70, 10.
27. Poupeye 2007:79.
28. Price 2009:20.
29. Waters 1985:64.
30. Waters 1985:144, 194.
31. *Daily Gleaner*, 10/12/69, 53.
32. Waters 1985:112.
33. R. Lewis 1994:33.
34. King 2002:91.
35. Barnett 2005.
36. Bedasse 2010.
37. Bob Marley was backed by members of the Jamaican reggae band Third World. At the time, Third World had also won international recognition for their music.
38. Steffens 2017:219.
39. Bob Marley and the Wailers 1976.
40. K. Williams 2011:286.
41. *Warren's Blog* 2021.
42. K. Williams 2011:286.
43. Subsequent area leaders gained greater leverage with politicians and community residents using proceeds from drug and arms trafficking to fund their own ventures. See Price 2004.
44. *Daily Gleaner*, 4/27/78, 6.
45. J. Lewis 1980.
46. Steffens 2017:291.
47. Bob Marley and the Wailers 1979.
48. Based in the author's field notes and documents in the author's possession, e.g., the "Summary Resolution," Rastafari International Theocracy Assembly, July 18–25, 1983, Kingston, Jamaica; "Communique from Wadadli Rastafari Working Committee Gathering at Blackout Cultural Park," Diamond, Antigua, February 26–28, 1999.
49. Barnett 2002:55.
50. Colman 2005:59.

51. The religion and Rastafari scholar Ennis Edmonds has made the point that the Rastafari have used organization as a means to present a united front and to engage with the wider society (2020:53).
52. The formal name of the RMC is the Ethio-Africa Diaspora Union Millennium Council.

CHAPTER 10. NEW CHALLENGES FOR THE RASTAFARI

1. Asserate 2015:273.
2. *Daily Gleaner*, 3/15/74, 12.
3. *Rasta Voice* 1974, n.p. The print is faded.
4. *Daily Gleaner*, 8/27/74, 2.
5. Asserate 2015:291.
6. *Daily Gleaner*, 8/27/74, 2.
7. Asserate 2015: 300.
8. Asserate 2015:308.
9. Böll, Ogato, and Dobslaw 2019 (emphasis added).
10. B. Selassie 2014.
11. B. Selassie 2014:53.
12. B. Selassie 2014:57.
13. Festinger, Riecken, and Schachter 1956.
14. *The Star*, 4/3/62, 7.
15. *The Star*, 4/24/62, 8.
16. Böll, Ogato, and Dobslaw 2019.
17. The religion scholar Darren Middleton uses the phrase "branding Rastafari" to describe how Rastafari identity has been commercialized in Jamaica and beyond (2015:224).
18. Sacks 2012:32.
19. Rastafari Indigenous Village 2021. Deborah Thomas discusses the Village in her book *Exceptional Violence* (2011).
20. *Daily Gleaner*, 1/20/88, 6.
21. Pruitt and Lafont 1995:431.
22. Mauk 2014.
23. Cariou v. Prince, F. Supp. 2d 337, 344 (S.D.N.Y. 2011).
24. Cariou v. Prince, 714 F.3d 694 (2d Cir. 2013).
25. Cariou v. Prince, 784 F. Supp. 2d 337 (S.D.N.Y. 2011).
26. *Cariou*, 784 F. Supp at 352.
27. Sheppard, Mullin, Richter & Hampton, LLP 2013.
28. Personal communication, 2018 (emphasis in original).
29. Chused 2019:n.p.
30. Personal communication, 2018.
31. Middleton 2006.
32. Gen 2:20–24 (KJV).

33. E.g., Yawney 1994; Tafari-Ama 1998; Blake-Hannah 2012; Christensen 2014; Alhassan 2020; Beresford 2020.
34. 1 Cor 14:34–35 (KJV).
35. Alhassan 2020:19.
36. Beresford 2020:30.

CONCLUSION

1. Few censuses in any nation count their Rastafari population on a consistent basis.

REFERENCES

Adas, Michael. 1979. *Prophets of Rebellion: Millenarian Protest Movements against the European Colonial Order*. Chapel Hill: University of North Carolina Press.

Alhassan, Shamara. 2020. "'This Movement Is Not about the Man Alone': Toward a Rastafari Woman's Studies." *Ideaz* 15:8–26.

Anderson, Benedict R. (1983) 2006. *Imagined Communities: Reflections on the Origin and Spread of Nationalism*. New York: Verso.

Andrews, Kenneth. 2017. "How Protest Works." *New York Times*, October 21. www.nytimes.com.

Ashmore, Richard, Kay Deaux, and Tracy McLaughlin-Volpe. 2004. "An Organizing Framework for Collective Identity: Articulation and Significance of Multidimensionality." *Psychological Bulletin* 130 (1): 80–114.

Asserate, Asfa-Wossen. 2015. *King of Kings: The Triumph and Tragedy of Emperor Haile Selassie I of Ethiopia*. London: Haus.

Baltimore African American. 1948. "200 Jamaicans Migrate to Liberia." August 28.

Barnett, Michael A. 2002. "Rastafari Dialectism: The Epistemological Individualism and Connectivism of Rastafari." *Caribbean Quarterly* 48 (4): 54–61.

———. 2005. "The Many Faces of Rasta: Doctrinal Diversity within the Rastafari Movement." *Caribbean Quarterly* 51 (2): 67–78.

Barrett, Leonard. 1968. *The Rastafarians: A Study in Messianic Cultism in Jamaica*. San Juan: Institute of Caribbean Studies at The University of Puerto Rico, Río Piedras Campus.

Becker, Howard Saul. 1963. *Outsiders: Studies in the Sociology of Deviance*. New York: Free Press.

Bedasse, Monique. 2010. "Rasta Evolution: The Theology of the Twelve Tribes of Israel." *Journal of Black Studies* 40 (5): 960–73.

———. 2017. *Jah Kingdom: Rastafarians, Tanzania, and Pan-Africanism in the Age of Decolonization*. Chapel Hill: University of North Carolina Press.

Bell, Alison. 2005. "White Ethnogenesis and Gradual Capitalism: Perspectives from Colonial Archaeological Sites in the Chesapeake." *American Anthropologist* 107 (3): 446–60.

Bender, Wolfgang. 2005. *Rastafarian Art*. Kingston, Jamaica: Ian Randle.

Beresford, Deena-Marie. 2020. "Charting the Matriarchal Shift in the Rastafari Movement." *Ideas* 15:27–34.

Bilby, Kenneth, and Elliott Leib. 1986. "Kumina, the Howellite Church and the Emergence of Rastafarian Traditional Music in Jamaica." *Jamaica Journal* 19 (3): 22–28.

Bishton, Derek. 1986. *Black Heart Man: A Journey into Rasta*. London: Chatto and Windus.

Blagrove, Ishmahil, Jr., dir. 2002. *Roaring Lion: The Rise of Rastafari*. London: Rice N Peas Films. YouTube. www.youtube.com/watch?v=hakAKzMGJTM.

Blake-Hannah, Barbara Makeda. 2012. *Rastafari: The New Creation*. Kingston, Jamaica: Jamaica Media Productions.

Blum, Edward, and Paul Harvey. 2012. *Colors of Christ: The Son of God and the Saga of Race in America*. Chapel Hill: University of North Carolina Press.

Bogues, Anthony. 2003. *Black Heretics, Black Prophets: Radical Political Intellectuals*. New York: Routledge.

Böll, Verena, Ambaye Ogato, and Robert Dobslaw. 2019. "Emperor Haile Selassie I. His Burial and the Rastafarians in Shashamane, Ethiopia. A Two-Part Documentary Haile Selassie Film Project (2016–2019)." Max Planck Institute for Social Anthropology. www.eth.mpg.de.

Bolland, O. Nigel. 1995. *On the March: Labour Rebellions in the British Caribbean, 1934–39*. Kingston, Jamaica: Ian Randle.

Bonacci, Giulia. 2013. "The Ethiopian World Federation: A Pan-African Organisation among the Rastafari in Jamaica." *Caribbean Quarterly* 59 (2): 73–95.

———. 2015. *Exodus! Heirs and Pioneers, Rastafari Return to Ethiopia*. Kingston, Jamaica: University of the West Indies Press.

Booth, Joseph. (ca. 1897) 2007. *Africa for the African*. Edited by Laura Perry. Malawi: Kachere Series.

Brooks, Alexander A. 1917. *The History of Bedwardism, or the Jamaican Native Baptist Free Church, Union Camp, August Town, St. Andrew, JA., B.W.I. Kingston, Jamaica*. Kingston, Jamaica: Gleaner.

Brusse, Carl. 2017. "Making Do without Selection—Review Essay of 'Cultural Evolution: Conceptual Challenges' by Tim Lewens." *Biological Philosophy* 32:307–19.

Burke, Shirley. 1977. "Interview with Cedric Brooks." *Jamaica Journal* 11 (1–2): 14–16.

Buskell, Andrew. 2016. "Cultural Longevity: Morin on Cultural Lineages." *Biological Philosophy* 31:435–46.

Cariou, Patrick. 2000. *Yes Rasta*. New York: Powerhouse Books.

Cassidy, Frederic G. 1971. *Jamaica Talk: Three Hundred Years of the English Language in Jamaica*. London: Macmillan Education.

Cavalli-Sforza, Luigi Luca. 1981. *Cultural Transmission and Evolution: A Quantitative Approach*. Princeton, NJ: Princeton University Press.

Chevannes, Alston Barrington. 1976. "The Repairer of the Breach: Reverend Claudius Henry and Jamaican Society." In *Ethnicity in the Americas*, edited by Frances Henry, 263–89. The Hague: Mouton.

———. 1994. *Rastafari: Roots and Ideology*. Syracuse, NY: Syracuse University Press.

———. 1998a. "The Origins of the Dreadlocks." In *Rastafari and Other African-Caribbean Worldviews*, edited by Barry Chevannes, 77–96. New Brunswick, NJ: Rutgers University Press.

———. 1998b. "The Phallus and the Outcast: The Symbolism of the Dreadlocks in Jamaica." In *Rastafari and Other African-Caribbean Worldviews*, edited by Barry Chevannes, 97–126. New Brunswick, NJ: Rutgers University Press.

Christensen, Jeanne. 2014. *Rastafari Reasoning and the Rasta Woman: Gender Constructions in the Shaping of Rastafari Livity*. Lanham, MD: Lexington Books.

Chused, Richard. 2019. "Brief Thoughts on Fair Use and Third-Party Harm: Another Reappraisal of Patrick Cariou v. Richard Prince." *UCLA Law Review* 67. www.uclalawreview.org.

Clarke, Colin G. 2016. *Race, Class, and the Politics of Decolonization: Jamaica Journals, 1961 and 1968*. London: Palgrave Macmillan.

Cobham, Rhonda. 1986. "Herbert George de Lisser (1878–1944)." In *Fifty Caribbean Writers: Bio-Bibliographical Critical Sourcebook*, edited by Daryl Cumber Dance, 166–77. New York: Greenwood.

Colman, George. 2005. *Oba's Story: Rastafari, Purification, and Power*. Trenton, NJ: Africa World.

Colonial Secretary Office (CSO). 5073/34. National Archives, Spanish Town, Jamaica.

Cooks, Carlos. 1959. *The Black Challenge*. New York.

Coser, Lewis. (1956) 2011. *The Functions of Social Conflict*. Abington, UK: Routledge.

Daily Gleaner. 1893. "The Healing Spring of Mona." September 14.

———. 1893. "The Healing Spring of Mona." September 19.

———. 1893. "Mona Water Fraud." September 28.

———. 1893. "Proceedings at August Town." October 4.

———. 1895. "Bedward Arrested." January 22.

———. 1895. "Interview with Bedward." January 22.

———. 1895. "Arrest of Bedward." January 23.

———. 1895. "Bedward's Trial: Scenes in Court." April 30.

———. 1895. "Bedward's Trial: The Verdict." May 2.

———. 1910. "The Medical Law." August 5.

———. 1920. "Passenger Lists." January 13.

———. 1921. "Bedward Tried Yesterday and Sent to Lunatic Asylum." May 5.

———. 1921. "Alexander Bedward Is Now an Inmate of the Lunatic Asylum." May 21.

———. 1925. "Activities of the Churches." December 18.

———. 1925. "The African Church." December 24.

———. 1926. "The Hamatic Church." March 19.

———. 1926. "General Notes." March 30.

———. 1927. "The 'Holy Piby.'" May 17.

———. 1927. "A New Religion." June 6.

———. 1930. "A Warning!" January 18.

———. 1930. "Duke of Gloucester to Ethiopia." August 18.

———. 1930. "Healer." September 20.

———. 1930. "How Rastafari Won to Throne in Abyssinia." October 10.

———. 1930. "Duke of Gloucester's Visit to Abyssinia." October 29.

———. 1930. "Presented New Sceptre to Emperor." November 3.

———. 1930. "Lavish Pageantry at Coronation of Abyssinian King." November 4.

———. 1931. "Waison Found Guilty, Bound Over for Two Years." January 22.

———. 1931. "King of All Negroes and Second Greatest Man in the World." April 22.

———. 1932. "New Chief Justice & C. O. of Local Forces Here Next Thursday." November 2.

———. 1932. "Sixola's Passengers." November 14.

———. 1932. "Our New Chief Justice Gets Warm Welcome." November 15.

———. 1932. "Sixola in Yesterday from New York with Mails and Passengers." November 18.

———. 1933. "Parochial Boards of the Island Elect New Leaders." July 4.

———. 1933. "Appeals from Lower Courts Dealt With." August 10.

———. 1933. "Annual Conference of the St. Thomas Branches Associated of the Agricultural Society." November 13.

———. 1934. "Alleged Sedition in St. Thomas Parish." January 5.

———. 1934. "Committed to Stand Trial for Sedition." February 1.

———. 1934. "'String Beans' Wanted to Clear Man Now Before R. M. Court." February 7.

———. 1934. "Alleged Revivalist and Healer before Court on 2 Charges." March 2.

———. 1934. "Sedition and Murder Cases for St. Thomas Circuit on Monday." March 10.

———. 1934. "Leonard Howell Being Tried for Sedition in St. Thomas." March 14.

———. 1934. "Leonard Howell, on Trial Says Ras Tafari Is Messiah Returned to Earth." March 15.

———. 1934. "'Ras Tafari' Disciple Found Guilty of Sedition." March 16.

———. 1934. "Chief Justice Denounces Leonard Howell as a Fraud." March 17.

———. 1934. "Howell Given 2-Year Term for Sedition." March 17.

———. 1934. "Man and Wife Are Convicted on Charge of Working Obeah." March 31.

———. 1934. "Deluded Creatures." July 9.

———. 1934. "Fooling the Masses." August 6.

———. 1934. "Ras Tafari Doctrine That Is Being Pushed in Eastern Districts." August 6.

———. 1934. "Jamaican Who Went to Abyssinia." October 5.

———. 1935. "Mussolini Strikes in East Africa." October 3.

———. 1937. "Cult Leader's Story ("as Told to Evon")." January 18.

———. 1938. "Lord Olivier and 'Scandal' of West Indian Labour Conditions." March 22.

———. 1938. "Ex Fighters Give Address to Governor at Morant Bay." September 15.

———. 1938. "Accused of Sedition." December 29.

———. 1939. "Jury Unable to Agree on Sedition Verdict." March 9.

———. 1939. "Ethiopian Salvation Society." April 3.

———. 1939. "Altamont Reid Gets 4 Months for Sedition." May 3.

———. 1939. "Port Morant Notes." December 27.

———. 1940. "Governor Puts Ban on 'Rastafari' Meeting." February 9.

———. 1940. "The Ras Tafarites Retreat to Mountain Fastnesses of St. Catherine, John Carradine." November 23.

———. 1941. "Robbed, Tried, Found Guilty, Flogged by Ras Tafarians." July 9.

———. 1941. "Police Raid 'Pinnacle,' Rastafarian Den, Sieze Seventy, but Miss Chief." July 15.

———. 1941. "Cult Leader Held by Police in His Home." July 26.

———. 1941. "Cult Followers Sent to Prison." July 31.

———. 1941. "'Ras Tafarian' Head Convicted at Spanish Town." August 25.

———. 1947. "Notice." March 28.

———. 1947. "Back-to-Africa Move Represented to Sec. of State for Colonies." September 8.

———. 1948. "House Asks Govt. to Assist 'Back-to-Africa' Move." July 21.

———. 1949. "'Liberian Govt Is Doing Everything' for West Indians." December 15.

———. 1950. "Local Organisation Gets Land Concessions in Ethiopia." July 31.

———. 1950. "Settlers-for-Ethiopia Talks Next Month." October 23.

———. 1950. "Ethiopia Needs Craftsmen, Engineers, Doctors: 'No Abortive Back-to-African Movement.'" November 13.

———. 1950. "Talk of Emigration to Ethiopia." November 15.

———. 1951. "The Menace in Our Midst." June 14.

———. 1951. "P.N.P. Cited for Its Opposition in House to Palisadoes Police Move." June 14.

———. 1951. "'Rasta' Man Charged with Palisadoes Murder." June 14.

———. 1951. "It Seems to Me, Peter Simple." June 15.

———. 1951. "It Seems to Me, Peter Simple." June 25.

———. 1952. "Legislature Summoned over Terror Campaign." September 8.

———. 1952. "Kenya Terrorism." October 22.

———. 1952. "Mau Mau Spreads to Coastal Area." November 17.

———. 1952. "Is Jomo Kenyatta a Patriot." December 15.

———. 1954. "General China: 'Reprieve a Step to Peace.'" March 11.

———. 1954. "Invite Selassie Call to Governor." March 23.

———. 1954. "Haile Selassie's Visit." March 26.

———. 1954. "Get It Straight, Thomas Wright." March 27.

———. 1954. "Invite Selassie." March 30.

———. 1954. "Ethiopians in Jamaica." April 21.

———. 1954. "Get It Straight, Thomas Wright." May 5.

———. 1954. "Police Raid Pinnacle Again." May 25.

———. 1954. "Pinnacle Case: Woman, 70, among 32 More Sentenced." June 17.

———. 1954. "Negro Renown." July 9.

———. 1954. "Haile Selassie I." July 23.

———. 1954. "Emigration to Ethiopia." September 21.

———. 1954. "Thousands Cheer Tubman." November 20.

———. 1955. "Migration Problems." June 25.

———. 1955. "The Ras Tafari Movement." June 30.

———. 1955. "US Singer Coming for Ethiopian Body Celebrations." September 1.

———. 1955. "EWF Organizer Comes." September 22.

———. 1955. "Barrister Tells Teachers, 'Africa Needs Social Engineers.'" October 5.

———. 1958. "Pinnacle Shacks Set Afire." April 18.

———. 1959. "Police, Fire Fighters Stoned." May 8.

———. 1959. "Mayor, Custos, Welcome Returning 'Rastas.'" August 25.

———. 1959. "No Passports, No Bookings, but 'Going Back to Africa.'" October 6.

———. 1959. "'Back-to-Africa' Rastas Stranded." October 7.

———. 1959. "Beards—On Doctor's Orders Only." October 8.

———. 1959. "African Reform Church Pastor Flies to NY." November 9.

———. 1959. "Church Leader Back from New York." November 25.

———. 1960. "House Passes Sympathy Resolution." March 24.

———. 1960. "May 2 'Time' Magazine Banned." May 2.

———. 1960. "Treason Felony Probe On." May 3.

———. 1960. "Henry Treason Felony Inquiry." May 4.

———. 1960. "UC Team to Study Rasta Movement." July 6.

———. 1960. "New York Robberies Linked to Plot." July 27.

———. 1962. "Nyerere Confirms Welcome for Jamaicans." November 12.

———. 1963. "Frank Hill Warns Them . . . Rastafarians Query National Standing." February 11.

———. 1963. "Letters to the Editor: No Cause for Alarm." April 29.

———. 1963. "Accused Aunt Testifies at Coral Gardens Murder Trail." July 17.

———. 1963. "Coral Gardens Murder Trial: Neither Bowen nor Larmon Was in Any Confused State at Time of Alleged Incident—Psychiatrist." August 13.

———. 1963. "Judge Reviews Evidence of Six Witnesses." August 22.

———. 1963. "Jury Cautioned about Bowen's Statement." August 24.

———. 1968. "Campus Row Brings Out Vandals." October 17.

———. 1968. "PM Tells House Govt. Acted to Save Nation." October 18.

———. 1968. "Text of Shearer's Speech (con'd)." November 25.

———. 1969. "Manley Sees Rastas in Ethiopia." October 12.

———. 1970. "God Help Jamaica." January 13.

———. 1974. "Ethiopia." March 15.

———. 1974. "Rastas: No Need to Panic." August 27.

———. 1975. "'Primitive' Artists' Exhibition." August 14.

———. 1978. "One Love, No Hate." April 27.

———. 1988. "Rent a Dread Anyone?" January 20.

Dorman, Jacob. 2013. *Chosen People: The Rise of American Black Israelite Religions.* New York: Oxford University Press.

Earl, Jennifer, Andrew Martin, John D. McCarthy, and Sarah A. Soule. 2004. "The Use of Newspaper Data in the Study of Collective Action." *Annual Review of Sociology* 30:65–80.

Edmonds, Ennis Barrington. 2012. *Rastafari: A Very Short Introduction.* Oxford: Oxford University Press.

———. 2020. "Shifting Models of Group Formation: Communes, Houses, and Mansions of Rastafari." *Ideaz* 15:35–55.

Eerkens, Jelmer W., and Carl P. Lipo. 2007. "Cultural Transmission Theory and the Archaeological Record: Providing Context to Understanding Variation and Temporal Changes in Material Culture." *Journal of Archaeological Research* 15:239–74.

Eidson, John R., Dereje Feyissa, Veronika Fuest, Markus V. Hoehne, Boris Nieswand, Günther Schlee, and Olaf Zenker. 2017. "From Identification to Framing and Alignment: A New Approach to the Comparative Analysis of Collective Identities." *Current Anthropology* 58 (3): 340–59.

Elkins, W. F. 1977. *Street Preachers, Faith Healers, and Herb Doctors in Jamaica*. New York: Revisionist.

Evans, Peter. 1956. *Law and Disorder: Scenes of Life in Kenya*. London: Secker and Warburg.

Fermor, Patrick Leigh. (1950) 2011. *The Traveller's Tree: A Journey through the Caribbean Islands*. New York: New York Review Books.

Festinger, Leon, Henry W. Riecken, and Stanley Schachter. 1956. *When Prophecy Fails: A Social and Psychological Study of a Modern Group that Predicted the Destruction of the World*. Minneapolis: University of Minnesota Press.

Fominaya, Cristina. 2010. "Collective Identity in Social Movements: Central Concepts and Debates." *Sociology Compass* 4 (6): 393–404.

Foner, Nancy. 1985. "Race and Color: Jamaican Migrants in London and New York City." *International Migration Review* 19 (4): 708–27.

Frey, Sylvia. 2009. "The American Revolution and the Creation of a Global African World." In *From Toussaint to Tupac: The Black International since the Age of Revolution*, edited by Michael O. West, William G. Martin, and Fanon Che Wilkins, 47–71. Chapel Hill: University of North Carolina Press.

Froude, James A. 1888. *The English in the West Indies; or, The Bow of Ulysses*. New York: Scribner.

Galloway, Patricia Kay. 1995. *Choctaw Genesis, 1500–1700*. Lincoln: University of Nebraska Press.

Garcia, J. 2010. "Identity Scripts." In *Encyclopedia of Identity*, edited by Ronald L. Jackson II and Michael A. Hogg, 373–77. Thousand Oaks, CA: Sage.

Garvey, Marcus. 1923. "The Negro's Greatest Enemy." *Current History* 18 (6): 951–57.

Gladney, Dru. 1990. "The Ethnogenesis of the Uighur." *Central Asian Survey* 9 (1): 1–28.

Gopnik, Adam. 2012. "Inquiring Minds: The Spanish Inquisition Revisited." *New Yorker*, January 16, 70–75.

Gowricharn, Ruben. 2013. "Ethnogenesis: The Case of British Indians in the Caribbean." *Comparative Studies in Society and History* 55 (2): 388–418.

Gray, Obika. 1991. *Radicalism and Social Change in Jamaica, 1960–1972*. Knoxville: University of Tennessee Press.

Gruesser, John. 2000. *Black on Black: Twentieth-Century African American Writing about Africa*. Lexington: University Press of Kentucky.

Haley, Brian, and Larry Wilcoxon. 2005. "How Spaniards Became Chumash and Other Tales of Ethnogenesis." *American Anthropologist* 107 (3):432–45.

Harris, Robert, Carlos A. Cooks, Grandassa Harris, and Nyota Harris. 1992. *Carlos Cooks and Black Nationalism from Garvey to Malcolm*. Dover, MA: Majority.

Hervik, Peter. 2011. *The Annoying Difference: The Emergence of Danish Neonationalism, Neoracism, and Populism in the Post-1989 World*. New York: Berghahn Books.

Hill, Robert. 2001. *Dread History: Leonard P. Howell and Millenarian Visions in the Early Rastafari Religion*. Chicago: Frontline Distribution International.

———. 2013a. "Our Man in Mona: A Conversation between Robert A. Hill and Annie Paul." Interview by Annie Paul. *Active Voice*. https://anniepaul.net.

———. 2013b. "The Rastafari Report: An Academic Betrayal?" Interview by Annie Paul. *Active Voice*, September 27. https://anniepaul.net.

Hoenish, Michael. 1988. "Symbolic Politics: Perceptions of the Early Rastafari Movement." *Massachusetts Review* 29 (3): 432–49.

Holland, Dorothy, Gretchen Fox, and Vinci Daro. 2008. "Social Movements and Collective Identity: A Decentered, Dialogic View." *Anthropological Quarterly* 81(1): 95–126.

Homiak, John. 1985. "The 'Ancients of Days' Seated Black: Eldership, Oral Tradition, and Ritual in Rastafari Culture." PhD diss., Brandeis University.

———. 1998. "Dub History: Soundings on Rastafari Livity and Language." In *Rastafari and Other African-Caribbean Worldviews*, edited by Barry Chevannes, 127–81. New Brunswick, NJ: Rutgers University Press.

Hu, Di. 2013. "Approaches to the Archaeology of Ethnogenesis: Past and Emergent Perspectives." *Journal of Archaeological Research* 21:371–402.

Hudson, Mark. 1999. *Ruins of Identity: Ethnogenesis in the Japanese Islands*. Honolulu: University of Hawaii Press.

Jamaica National Archives 1B/5/79. Spanish Town, Jamaica.

Jamaica Now. 1962. 4 (7): 2.

Jamaica Observer. 2012. "A Brutal Murder, a Savage Rape." May 13.

———. 2013. "Jamaica's First Treason/Felony Trial Featuring the Reverend Claudius Henry." December 10.

Jamaica Times. 1934. "Disillusionment." October 18.

———. 1935. "Pepper Pot." January 19.

———. 1935. "What Would It Mean If British East Africans Assist Abyssinia." July 20.

———. 1935. "Traveller Who Lived In Abyssinia Tells of Ethiopia and Its People." July 27.

———. 1935. "U.N.I.A. Wish to Help Abyssinia." August 3.

———. 1935. "What an Italo-Abyssinian War Would Mean." August 17.

———. 1935. "Secret Society to Destroy Whites." December 7.

———. 1935. "Emperor of Ethiopia Calmly and Resolutely Mans Machine Gun As Bomb Exploded Near Him." December 21.

———. 1938. "Pepper Pot." May 28.

———. 1941. "Victims Tell of Ras Tafarians' Reign of Terror." July 12.

———. 1958. "Bearded Rastafarian Woman." September 27.

———. 1960. "Grave Problem." June 25.

———. 1960. "By the Way." July 2.

———. 1960. "Complacency Lasted Too Long." July 2.

———. 1960. "Kenyatta Still Wanted." July 16.

———. 1960. "Some Rastas Are Changing." July 23.

———. 1960. "Handling the Rastas." July 30.

———. 1960. "'Willing to See a Deputation.'" August 6.

———. 1960. "Rastas Hold Big Meeting." August 13.

———. 1960. "Callous, Country Bumpkins, Ras Tafarians & the Premier." August 27.

———. 1960. "Monsignor Hits Again at the Rasta Report." October 22.

———. 1961. "Some Rastas Are from Good Families." March 25.

———. 1961. "The PPP and Charges of Race Hatred." July 29.

———. 1962. "Jamaica's Mission to Africa." March 24.

———. 1962. "Jamaica Brings Back JLP." April 14.

———. 1962. "Ethiopia Seen Ready to Take Migrants." May 5.

———. 1962. "Tavares' African Mission." September 8.

———. 1962. "'Going Back to Africa Our Only Hope.'" October 27.

Jobson, Dickie, dir. (1982) 2015. *Countryman*. New York: Palm Pictures. YouTube. www.youtube.com/watch?v=LiIo1c6CoOk.

King, Stephen A. 2002. *Reggae, Rastafari, and the Rhetoric of Social Control*. Jackson: University Press of Mississippi.

Lee, Hélène. 2003. *The First Rasta: Leonard Howell and the Rise of Rastafarianism*. Chicago: Lawrence Hill Books.

Lepinske, Harry. 1955. *Jamaican Ganja: A Report on the Marijuana Problem*. New York: Exposition.

Lewens, Tim. 2015. *Cultural Evolution: Conceptual Challenges*. New York: Oxford University Press.

Lewis, James P., dir. 1980. *Heartland Reggae*. Canada Offshore, Media Aides, Tuff Gong Pictures. Video documentary.

Lewis, Rupert. 1994. "Walter Rodney: 1968 Revisited." *Social & Economic Studies* 43 (3): 7–56.

Linden, Jane, and Ian Linden. 1971. "John Chilembwe and the New Jerusalem." *Journal of African History* 12 (4): 629–51.

Lockley, Tim. 2012. "David Margrett: A Black Missionary in the Revolutionary Atlantic." *Journal of American Studies* 46 (3): 1–17.

LSIC (Local Standing Intelligence Committee). 1961. "Racism in Jamaica." Kingston, Jamaica, July.

Lyall-Grant, R. W. (Chairman), A. M. D. Turnbull, J. C. Casson, A. G. B. Glossop, and Claude Metcalfe. 1916. *Report of the Commission Appointed by His Excellency the Governor to Inquire into Various Matters and Questions Concerned with the Native Rising within the Nyasaland Protectorate*. Zomba, Nyasaland Protectorate: Government Printers, April 28.

Mack, Douglas. 1999. *From Babylon to Rastafari: Origin and History of the Rastafarian Movement*. Chicago: Research Associates, School Times Publications.

Mais, Roger. (1954) 1974. *Brother Man*. London: Heinemann.

Maragh, G. G. (Leonard P. Howell). (ca. 1935) 2001. *The Promised Key*. Brooklyn, NY: A&B.

Marley, Bob, and the Wailers. 1976. *Rastaman Vibration*. Island–Tuff Gong Music. LP.

———. 1978. *One Love Peace Concert*. LP.

———. 1979. *Survival*. Tuff Gong Studio. LP.

Martin, J. 1952–53. "What of Pinnacle?" *The Ambassador* 51.

Mauk, Ben. 2014. "Who Owns This Image?" *New Yorker*, February 12.

Maynes, Mary Jo, Jennifer L. Pierce, and Barbara Laslett. 2008. *Telling Stories: The Use of Personal Narratives in the Social Sciences and History*. Ithaca, NY: Cornell University Press.

MeasuringWorth.com. n.d. "Computing 'Real Value' over Time with a Conversion between U.K. Pounds and U.S. Dollars, 1791 to Present." Accessed August 10, 2021. www.measuringworth.com.

Melucci, Alberto. 1995. "The Process of Collective Identity." In *Social Movements and Culture*, edited by Hank Johnston and Bert Klandermans, 41–63. Minneapolis: University of Minnesota Press.

Middleton, Darren. 2006. "As It Is in Zion: Seeking the Rastafari in Ghana, West Africa." *Black Theology* 4 (2): 151–72.

———. 2015. *Rastafari and the Arts*. London: Taylor and Francis.

Moore, John. 1994. "Putting Anthropology Back Together Again: The Ethnogenetic Critique of Cladistic Theory." *American Anthropologist* 96 (4): 925–48.

Morin, Olivier. 2015. *How Traditions Live and Die*. New York: Oxford University Press.

Nagashima, Yoshiko. 1984. *Rastafarian Music in Contemporary Jamaica: A Study of Socioreligious Music of the Rastafarian Movement in Jamaica*. Tokyo: Institute for the Study of Languages and Cultures of Asia and Africa.

Negro World. 1925. "Negro Universal King Coming to Rule the World." October 3.

New York Daily News. 1927. "Comet Tail to Wag World End." November 16.

New York Times. 1924. "Says a Black King Will Rule World." September 15.

Oakland Tribune. 1960. "Cult Stirs in Jamaica." June 23.

O'Regan, John. 1994. *From Empire to Commonwealth: Reflections on a Career in Britain's Overseas Service*. New York: St. Martin's.

Osborne, Myles. 2015. Introduction to *The Life and Times of General China: Mau Mau and the End of Empire in Kenya*, edited by Myles Osborne, 1–39. Princeton, NJ: Markus Wiener.

Palmer, Colin A. 2014. *Freedom's Children: The 1938 Labor Rebellion and the Birth of Modern Jamaica*. Chapel Hill: University of North Carolina Press.

Paton, Diana. 2015. *The Cultural Politics of Obeah: Religion, Colonialism and Modernity in the Caribbean World*. Cambridge: Cambridge University Press.

Peterson, Jacqueline, and Jennifer S. H. Brown. 1986. *The New Peoples: Being and Becoming Métis in North America*. Lincoln: University of Nebraska Press.

Pettersburgh, Fitz. (ca. 1926) 2003. *The Royal Parchment Scroll of Black Supremacy*. Chicago: Frontline Books.

Philos, Federico. 1935a. "The Black Peril." *Magazine Digest* 11 (5): 80–83.

————. 1935b. "Die Verschwörung der Neger." *Neues Wiener Tagblatt*, August 24.

Pierson, Roscoe. 1969. "Alexander Bedward and the Jamaica Native Baptist Free Church." *Lexington Theological Quarterly* 4 (3): 65–76.

Planno, Mortimer. 2006. *The Earth Most Strangest Man: The Rastafarian*. New York: Research Institute for the Study of Man.

Pollard, Velma. 2000. *Dread Talk: The Language of Rastafari*. Barbados: Canoe.

Polletta, Francesca, and James M. Jasper. 2001. "Collective Identity and Social Movements." *Annual Review of Sociology* 27:283–305.

Post, Ken. 1978. *Arise Ye Starvelings: The Jamaican Labour Rebellion of 1938 and Its Aftermath*. The Hague: Nijhoff.

Poupeye, Veerle. 2007. "Intuitive Art as Canon." *Small Axe* 11 (3): 73–82.

Price, Charles. 2001. "Political and Radical Aspects of the Rastafarian Movement in Jamaica." *Nature, Society, and Thought* 13(2):155–180.

————. 2003. "'Cleave to the Black': Expressions of Ethiopianism in Jamaica." *NWIG: New West Indian Guide / Nieuwe West-Indische Gids* 77 (1–2): 31–64.

————. 2004. "What the Zeeks Uprising Reveals: Development Issues, Moral Economy, and the Urban Lumpenproletariat in Jamaica." *Urban Anthropology* 33 (1): 73–113.

————. 2009. *Becoming Rasta: Origins of Rastafari Identity in Jamaica*. New York: New York University Press.

————. 2013. "'History-in-Person': The Cultural Production of Populism among Kentucky Small-Scale Family Farmers." *Social Identities* 19 (2): 158–72.

————. 2014. "The Cultural Production of a Black Messiah: Ethiopianism and the Rastafari." *Journal of Africana Religions* 2 (3): 418–33.

————. 2018. "Outlining a Strategy for Studying Race, Identity, and Acts of Political Significance: Black Racial Identity Theory and the Rastafari of Jamaica." In *Political Sentiments and Social Movements: The Person in Politics and Culture*, edited by Claudia Strauss and Jack Friedman, 237–64. London: Palgrave Macmillan.

Pruitt, Deborah, and Suzanne LaFont. 1995. "For Love and Money: Romance Tourism in Jamaica." *Annals of Tourism Research* 22 (2): 422–40.

Public Opinion. 1937a. "As I See My Country." June 26.

————. 1937b. "Mr. Lescene and the 'The Gleaner.'" November 6.

Rastafari Indigenous Village. 2021. Home page. February 2. https://rastavillage.com.

Rasta Voice. 1974. Kingston, Jamaica.

Reckord, Verena. 1977. "Rastafarian Music—An Introductory Study." *Jamaica Journal* 11 (1–2): 3–13.

————. 1998. "From Burru Drums to Reggae Riddims: The Evolution of Rasta Music." In *Chanting Down Babylon: The Rastafari Reader*, edited by Nathaniel Samuel Murrell, William Spencer, and Adrian Anthony McFarlane, 231–52. Philadelphia: Temple University Press.

Reed, Jean-Pierre, and Sarah Pitcher. 2015. "Religion and Revolutionary We-Ness: Religious Discourse, Speech Acts, and Collective Identity in Prerevolutionary Nicaragua." *Journal for the Scientific Study of Religion* 54 (3): 477–500.

Rodney, Walter. (ca. 1969) 1996. *The Groundings with My Brothers*. Chicago: Research Associates School Times.

Rogers, J. A. (ca. 1936) 1982. *The Real Facts about Ethiopia*. Baltimore: Black Classics.

Rogers, Robert. (ca. 1924) 2000. *The Holy Piby: The Blackman's Bible*. Chicago: Research Associates School Time.

Rosenberg, Leah. 2007. *Nationalism and the Formation of Caribbean Literature*. New York: Palgrave Macmillan.

Rotberg, Robert. 2005. "John Chilembwe: Brief Life of an Anticolonial Rebel: 1871?–1915." *Harvard Magazine*, March–April, 36–37.

Runciman, Walter G. 2009. *The Theory of Cultural and Social Selection*. Cambridge: Cambridge University Press.

Rupp, Leila, and Verta Taylor. 1999. "Feminist Identity in an International Movement: A Collective Identity Approach to 20th-Century Feminism." *Signs* 24:363–86.

Sacks, Adam. 2012. *Travel and Tourism as a Driver of Economic Development in Jamaica*. Oxford, UK: Oxford Economics.

Satchell, Veront. 2004. "Early Stirrings of Black Nationalism in Colonial Jamaica: Alexander Bedward of the Jamaica Native Baptist Free Church 1889–1921." *Journal of Caribbean History* 38 (1): 75–105.

Scott, William. 1972. "Malaku E. Bayen: Ethiopian Emissary to Black America, 1936–1941." *Ethiopian Observer* 15 (2): 132–38.

Selassie, Bereket H. 2014. *Emperor Haile Selassie*. Athens: Ohio University Press.

Selassie, Haile, I. 1936. "Appeal to the League of Nations." Geneva, Switzerland, June 30.

Shannon, David. 2012. "George Liele: Apostle of Liberation and Faith." In *George Liele's Life and Legacy: An Unsung Hero*, edited by David Shannon, 71–83. Macon, GA: Mercer University Press.

Sheppard, Mullin, Richter & Hampton, LLP. 2013. "Yes Rasta! Appropriate Appropriation: Second Circuit Holds That Commentary on Original Work Unnecessary for Fair Use Defense, Only Transformative Quality Required." *Mondaq Business Briefing*, May 7.

Shepperson, George. 1952. "Education Sponsors Freedom: The Story of African Native John Chilembwe." *Negro History Bulletin* 15 (4): 69–72.

Shepperson, George, and Thomas Price. 1958. *Independent African: John Chilembwe and the Origins, Setting, and Significance of the Nyasaland Native Rising of 1915*. Edinburgh: Edinburgh University Press.

Sidbury, James, and Jorge Cañizares-Esguerra. 2011. "Mapping Ethnogenesis in the Early Modern Atlantic." *William and Mary Quarterly* 68 (2): 181–208.

Simpson, George. 1955a. "Political Cultism in West Kingston, Jamaica." *Social and Economic Studies* 4 (2): 133–49.

———. 1955b. The Ras Tafari Movement in Jamaica: A Study of Race and Class Conflict." *Social Forces* 34 (2): 167–71.

Smith, M. G., Roy Augier, and Rex M. Nettleford. 1960. *The Report on the Rastafari Movement in Kingston, Jamaica*. Mona, Jamaica: Institute of Social and Economic Research.

Southard, Addison. 1931. "Modern Ethiopia: Haile Selassie the First, Formerly Ras Tafari, Succeeds to the World's Oldest Continuously Sovereign Throne." *National Geographic*, June, 679–746.

Spencer, William. 1998. "The First Chant: Leonard Howell's *The Promised Key*." In *Chanting Down Babylon: The Rastafari Reader*, edited by Nathaniel Samuel Murrell, William Spencer, and Adrian Anthony McFarlane, 361–89. Philadelphia: Temple University Press.

Star, The. 1959. "Huts Levelled." May 7.

———. 1959. "Riot at Coronation Market." May 7.

———. 1959. "10,000 Said Ready to Go Back to Africa, Deadline Oct. 5, 1959." May 11.

———. 1959. "Rastas Prepare for Ethiopia." September 23.

———. 1959. "'Deadline Day of Decision.'" October 5.

———. 1959. "'The Book Lock Up,' Says the Healer of the Breach." October 17.

———. 1959. "Vere John Says . . ." October 17.

———. 1959. "Rev. C. V. Henry, R.B. Goes on Another Back-to-Africa Trip." November 6.

———. 1959. "Rev. Henry Summoned." December 11.

———. 1960. "Rev. Henry Held in Armed Raid." April 6.

———. 1960. "Mullen on Secret Mission." April 11.

———. 1960. "'Operation Beards' On." April 28.

———. 1960. "Cops Remove 'Time' from Newsstand." April 30.

———. 1960. "Lover's Lane Menace." May 2.

———. 1960. "Children Threatened by Rastas." May 4.

———. 1960. "'Israel, Play with Manley Head If . .'" May 4.

———. 1960. "'Operation Rastas' On." May 10.

———. 1960. "'They Could Burn Down City.'" May 11.

———. 1960. "100 Cops Move against Rastas." June 6.

———. 1960. "Neville Walcott Nabbed." June 25.

———. 1960. "Manhunt Ends: 4 Captured in Room." June 27.

———. 1960. "Dealing with Rastas." June 28.

———. 1960. "Police, Customs Tighten Up Waterfront." July 1.

———. 1960. "A Long Way from Harlem." July 2.

———. 1960. "Local CID Help in Agard Case." July 27.

———. 1960. "Good Word for Rastafarians." August 19.

———. 1960. "Cops Flee from Rastas." August 26.

———. 1960. "Vere John Says." August 27.

———. 1960. "The Law." September 3.

———. 1960. "Rollins Wasn't Shackled to Bed." September 23.

———. 1960. "'Henry Gave Orders to Shoot.'" September 26.

———. 1960. "'Henry Villain of the Piece.'" September 29.

———. 1960. "Thousands Shouted." September 29.

———. 1960. "Insurrection Charge Argued." October 5.

———. 1960. "Oct. 5 D Day for Africa Trek." October 10.

———. 1960. "'Hope to See Jamaica in Castro's Hands.'" October 12.

———. 1960. "Went for Ganja: Found Weapons." October 13.

———. 1960. "Accused: 'I Made a Weapon Myself.'" October 18.

———. 1960. "Defense Opens in Treason Case." October 18.

———. 1960. "The Signal from the Box." October 21.

———. 1960. "She Had No Knowledge of Weapons." October 22.

———. 1960. "Henry Opens Defence." October 24.

———. 1960. "Henry Testifies on War, Peace." October 25.

———. 1960. "Some Rastas 'Undesirable' Says Henry." October 25.

———. 1960. "Evans Asks Court 'to Be Generous.'" October 26.

———. 1960. "Counsel: 'By Their Own Mouths.'" October 28.

———. 1960. "'Henry's Leaflet Traitorous.'" October 28.

———. 1961. "Rastas Seek Political Victory." February 13.

———. 1961. "Church of Jah Rastafari." February 17.

———. 1961. "How They Rave." March 3.

———. 1961. "2 Changes in Africa Mission." March 10.

———. 1961. "'Badmanship' Not Wanted in Ethiopia—Planner." June 5.

———. 1961. "R. Henry's Arms—'Fridge on Block." July 3.

———. 1961. "Vere John Says." September 9.

———. 1961. "'John Ras I' New in Stage Shows." October 20.

———. 1961. "Pleas for U.S. Aid in Back-to-Africa." October 27.

———. 1961. "John Ras I for Country Parts." November 7.

———. 1962. "13 Rastas Attend Church Service at Constant Spring." February 10.

———. 1962. "Jah Rastafari Church Not in It." March 21.

———. 1962. "Selassie Wife Is Queen Omega." April 3.

———. 1962. "African Mission." April 12.

———. 1962. "Selassie's Son Dies." April 24.

———. 1962. "Curb Rastas Now." May 19.

———. 1962. "Leads MoBay Rastas to Prosperity." June 29.

Stark, Rodney. 1996. *The Rise of Christianity: A Sociologist Reconsiders History*. Princeton, NJ: Princeton University Press.

Steffens, Roger. 2017. *So Much Things to Say: The Oral History of Bob Marley*. New York: Norton.

Stolberg, Claus. 1990. *Jamaica 1938: The Living Conditions of the Urban and Rural Poor*. Kingston, Jamaica: University of the West Indies Press.

Stone, Carl. 1983. *Democracy and Clientelism in Jamaica*. Piscataway, NJ: Transaction.

Sturtevant, William. 1971. "Creek into Seminole." In *North American Indians in Historical Perspective*, ed. Eleanor Leacock and Nancy Lurie, 92–128. New York: Random House.

Sturtevant, William, and Jessica R. Cattelino. 2004. "Florida Seminole and Miccosukee." In *Handbook of North American Indians*, vol. 14, edited by Raymond D. Fogelson, 429–49. Washington, DC: Smithsonian Institution.

Sunday Gleaner. 1940. "Plight of Ras Tafarians at Camp Pinnacle in St. Catherine." December 22.

——. 1945. "Jamaica's Great Ras Tafarite Kingdom Comes to an End." October 14.

——. 1959. "Fizzle of the Week." October 11.

——. 1960. "Troops Flush Bushes with Gunfire." June 26.

——. 1970. "Exciting Art of the Rastafarians." February 22.

——. 1974. "MMR Community Centre." August 18.

Tafari, Ras Sekou Sankara. 2000. "Introduction: Come Praise King Ras Tafari for He Is King of the Kings!" In *Dread History: Leonard P. Howell and Millenarian Visions in the Early Rastafari Religion*, edited by Robert Hill, 3–10. Chicago: Frontline Distribution International.

Tafari-Ama, Imani. 1998. "Rastawoman as Rebel: Case Studies in Jamaica." In *Chanting Down Babylon: The Rastafari Reader*, edited by Nathaniel Samuel Murrell, William Spencer, and Adrian Anthony McFarlane, 89–106. Philadelphia: Temple University Press.

Thomas, Deborah. 2011. *Exceptional Violence: Embodied Citizenship in Transnational Jamaica*. Durham, NC: Duke University Press.

——. 2017. "Rastafari, Communism, and Surveillance in Late Colonial Jamaica." *Small Axe* 54:63–84.

Tilly, Charles. 2007. *Contentious Politics*. Boulder, CO: Paradigm.

Time. 1960a. "The Boys from Brooklyn." July 4.

——. 1960b. "The Lion of Judah's Men." Latin American ed. May 2.

Tsuda, Kenta. 2011. "Academicians of Lagado: A Critique of Social and Cultural Evolutionism." *New Left Review* 72:80–109.

United Aid for Ethiopia. 1936. "War in Ethiopia." booklet. New York.

van Dijk, Frank Jan. 1998. *Jahmaica: Rastafari and Jamaican Society, 1930–1990*. Utrecht: Utrecht University Press.

Warren's Blog. 2021. "Jamaica Murder Statistics 1970–2020." February 2. https://commonsenseja.wordpress.com.

Waters, Anita M. 1985. *Race, Class, and Political Symbols: Rastafari and Reggae in Jamaican Politics*. New Brunswick, NJ: Transaction Books.

Watson, Roxanne. 2008. "The Native Baptist Church's Political Role in Jamaica: Alexander Bedward's Trial for Sedition." *Journal of Caribbean History* 42 (2): 231–54.

Webb, James. (ca. 1919) 2008. *A Black Man Will Be the Coming Universal King: Proven by Biblical History*. Kobek.com.

Weik, T. M. 2014. "The Archaeology of Ethnogenesis." *Annual Review of Anthropology* 43:291–305.

West, Michael O. 2005. "Walter Rodney and Black Power: Jamaican Intelligence and U.S. Diplomacy." *African Journal of Criminology and Justice Studies* 1 (2): 1–51.

West, Michael O., and William G. Martin. 2009. "Contours of the Black International: From Toussaint to Tupac." In *From Toussaint to Tupac: The Black International Since the Age of Revolution*, edited by Michael O. West, William G. Martin, and Fanon Che Wilkins, 1–44. Chapel Hill: University of North Carolina Press.

Whitehouse, Harvey, Jonathan Jong, Michael Buhrmester, Ángel Gómez, Brock Bastian, Christopher Kavanagh, Martha Newson, Miriam Matthews, Jonathan

Lanman, Ryan McKay, and Sergey Gavrilets. 2017. "The Evolution of Extreme Co-operation via Shared Dysphoric Experiences." *Scientific Reports* 7:1–10.

Williams, Kareen. 2011. "The Evolution of Political Violence in Jamaica 1940–1980." PhD diss., Columbia University.

Yawney, Carole D. 1994. "Moving with the Dawtas of Rastafari: From Myth to Reality." In *Arise Ye Mighty People! Gender, Class and Race in Popular Struggles*, edited by Terisa Turner and Bryan J. Ferguson, 65–74. Trenton, NJ: Africa World.

Yawney, Carole D., and John Homiak. 2001. "Rastafari." In *Encyclopedia of African and African American Religions*, edited by Stephen D. Glazier, 256–66. New York: Routledge.

Yesehaq, Archbishop. 1989. *The Ethiopian Tawahedo Church: An Integrally African Church*. New York: Vantage.

INDEX

ABOUT THE AUTHOR

CHARLES PRICE is Associate Professor in the College of Education and Human Development at Temple University. His research, writing, and related activities focus on identity (racial, personal-individual, collective), life narrative genres, action research, community organizing, people-centered community development, and social movements, with a geographic concentration on the United States and Jamaica. He is the author of *Becoming Rasta: The Origins of Rastafari Identity in Jamaica* and coauthor of *Community Collaborations: Promoting Community Organizing* and the author of various journal articles and book chapters.